# CONVERSATIONAL CHINESE

# CONVERSATIONAL CHINESE

## WITH GRAMMATICAL NOTES

*PREPARED BY*

TÊNG SSŬ-YÜ

*ASSISTED BY*

CHAO CHING-HUI · HSÜ EN-HSI · JUNE WORK · CHIN WÊN-HAN
T'AN PIN-PIN · HO CHU-HSÜAN · WU YUNG-HSÜN

THE UNIVERSITY OF CHICAGO PRESS
CHICAGO AND LONDON

The Romanization Conversion Table on pages x and xi are taken from *People's Republic of China: Administrative Atlas* (Washington, D.C.: Central Intelligence Agency, 1975, pp. 46-47).

International Standard Book Number: 0–226–79345–1
Library of Congress Catalog Card Number: 47–30857
THE UNIVERSITY OF CHICAGO PRESS, CHICAGO 60637
The University of Chicago Press, Ltd., London


*Published 1947. Midway Reprint 1980. Printed in the United States of America*

# PREFACE

This is a really progressive textbook of elementary Chinese. The lessons are written in idiomatic Kuo-yü, the standard Mandarin spoken in Peiping. The conversations cover various subjects which are all highly useful. The vocabulary is carefully selected and fully illustrated. Grammar is explained in simple and clear terms. The exercises provided at the end of each lesson are very useful. In short, this work by Professor S. Y. Teng is an exceptionally well-balanced book which should be recommended to students of the Chinese language.

Lien-shêng Yang

## ACKNOWLEDGMENTS

The author owes deep gratitude to Dr. Tze-hsiang Ouyang, who worked very hard for the Army Specialized Training Program, and who drafted most of these lessons. His name was to have appeared on the title page of this book as co-author, but he has firmly refused to permit this, because his primary interest is in educational philosophy, not in the compiling of textbooks. The author is indebted to his other colleagues whose names appear on the title page. Each of them gave valuable assistance either in drafting certain of the original lessons, in making corrections and suggestions, or in other ways. He is deeply grateful to Miss June Work, who typed the manuscript for publication, made numerous suggestions concerning grammatical explanations, and did the final proofreading during the author's absence from the University. Without her patience and vigilance, this work could never have been brought to its present shape.

Sincerest thanks are due to Professor Y. R. Chao, a leading philologist of China, who, from the very beginning of the Army Specialized Training Program, has given advice, materials, and help in every possible form. He was particularly kind in carefully checking the list of descriptions of sounds in the section on romanization. This list has also been checked by Professor Otto F. Bond, who has been teaching French for almost a generation, and whose experienced and unbiased opinions on the presentation of the system have been very helpful.

The manuscript has been thoroughly checked by several experts on the Chinese language, and numerous suggestions have been made. Professor Herrlee G. Creel has carefully gone over every line. To Professor Creel the author owes the greatest debt, beyond any repayment, for encouragement in all his work at the University of Chicago. Dr. Lien-shêng Yang, who has taught Chinese at Harvard and Yale Universities and written articles on Chinese grammar, has also carefully gone over the whole manuscript.

The beautiful Chinese characters in the exercise sentences, notes, and index were kindly written by Mr. Shih Chai-chu as a friendly favor which is greatly appreciated, and the model calligraphy on the title page was executed by Professor Leon Chang, to whom the author is deeply thankful. Finally, the author is very grateful to all of his students in military and civilian classes and especially to his wife, for many practical suggestions and much inspiration.

Although so many scholars have participated in this book, the plan, the selection of material, and the grammatical notes are chiefly the work of the present writer, with the able help of those mentioned above. If there is anything worth while in this textbook, it is the contribution of these helpers; the author alone, however, should be held responsible for any shortcomings.

S. Y. Têng

Chung Kuo Yüan
Mills College

CONVERSATIONAL CHINESE

TABLE OF CONTENTS

TABLE OF CONTENTS

# Romanization Conversion Tables

## Wade-Giles to Pinyin

| Wade-Giles | Pinyin |
|---|---|
| a | a |
| ai | ai |
| an | an |
| ang | ang |
| ao | ao |
| cha | zha |
| ch'a | cha |
| chai | zhai |
| ch'ai | chai |
| chan | zhan |
| ch'an | chan |
| chang | zhang |
| ch'ang | chang |
| chao | zhao |
| ch'ao | chao |
| che | zhe |
| ch'e | che |
| chen | zhen |
| ch'en | chen |
| cheng | zheng |
| ch'eng | cheng |
| chi | ji |
| ch'i | qi |
| chia | jia |
| ch'ia | qia |
| chiang | jiang |
| ch'iang | qiang |
| chiao | jiao |
| ch'iao | qiao |
| chieh | jie |
| ch'ieh | qie |
| chien | jian |
| ch'ien | qian |
| chih | zhi |
| ch'ih | chi |
| chin | jin |
| ch'in | qin |
| ching | jing |
| ch'ing | qing |
| chiu | jiu |
| ch'iu | qiu |
| chiung | jiong |
| ch'iung | qiong |
| cho | zhuo |
| ch'o | chuo |
| chou | zhou |
| ch'ou | chou |
| chu | zhu |
| ch'u | chu |
| chü | ju |
| ch'ü | qu |
| chua | zhua |
| ch'ua | chua |
| chuai | zhuai |
| ch'uai | chuai |
| chuan | zhuan |
| ch'uan | chuan |
| chüan | juan |
| ch'üan | quan |
| chuang | zhuang |
| ch'uang | chuang |
| chüeh | jue |
| ch'üeh | que |
| chui | zhui |
| ch'ui | chui |
| chun | zhun |
| ch'un | chun |
| chün | jun |
| ch'ün | qun |
| chung | zhong |
| ch'ung | chong |
| en | en |
| erh | er |
| fa | fa |
| fan | fan |
| fang | fang |
| fei | fei |
| fen | fen |
| feng | feng |
| fo | fo |
| fou | fou |
| fu | fu |
| ha | ha |
| hai | hai |
| han | han |
| hang | hang |
| hao | hao |
| hei | hei |
| hen | hen |
| heng | heng |
| ho | he |
| hou | hou |
| hsi | xi |
| hsia | xia |
| hsiang | xiang |
| hsiao | xiao |
| hsieh | xie |
| hsien | xian |
| hsin | xin |
| hsing | xing |
| hsiu | xiu |
| hsiung | xiong |
| hsü | xu |
| hsüan | xuan |
| hsüeh | xue |
| hsün | xun |
| hu | hu |
| hua | hua |
| huai | huai |
| huan | huan |
| huang | huang |
| hui | hui |
| hun | hun |
| hung | hong |
| huo | huo |
| i | yi |
| jan | ran |
| jang | rang |
| jao | rao |
| je | re |
| jen | ren |
| jeng | reng |
| jih | ri |
| jo | ruo |
| jou | rou |
| ju | ru |
| juan | ruan |
| jui | rui |
| jun | run |
| jung | rong |
| ka | ga |
| k'a | ka |
| kai | gai |
| k'ai | kai |
| kan | gan |
| k'an | kan |
| kang | gang |
| k'ang | kang |
| kao | gao |
| k'ao | kao |
| kei | gei |
| k'ei | kei |
| ken | gen |
| k'en | ken |
| keng | geng |
| k'eng | keng |
| ko | ge |
| k'o | ke |
| kou | gou |
| k'ou | kou |
| ku | gu |
| k'u | ku |
| kua | gua |
| k'ua | kua |
| kuai | guai |
| k'uai | kuai |
| kuan | guan |
| k'uan | kuan |
| kuang | guang |
| k'uang | kuang |
| kuei | gui |
| k'uei | kui |
| kun | gun |
| k'un | kun |
| kung | gong |
| k'ung | kong |
| kuo | guo |
| k'uo | kuo |
| la | la |
| lai | lai |
| lan | lan |
| lang | lang |
| lao | lao |
| le | le |
| lei | lei |
| leng | leng |
| li | li |
| lia | lia |
| liang | liang |
| liao | liao |
| lieh | lie |
| lien | lian |
| lin | lin |
| ling | ling |
| liu | liu |
| lo | luo |
| lou | lou |
| lu | lu |
| lü | lü |
| luan | luan |
| lüan | lüan |
| lüeh | lüe |
| lun | lun |
| lung | long |
| ma | ma |
| mai | mai |
| man | man |
| mang | mang |
| mao | mao |
| mei | mei |
| men | men |
| meng | meng |
| mi | mi |
| miao | miao |
| mieh | mie |
| mien | mian |
| min | min |
| ming | ming |
| miu | miu |
| mo | mo |
| mou | mou |
| mu | mu |
| na | na |
| nai | nai |
| nan | nan |
| nang | nang |
| nao | nao |
| nei | nei |
| nen | nen |
| neng | neng |
| ni | ni |
| niang | niang |
| niao | niao |
| nieh | nie |
| nien | nian |
| nin | nin |
| ning | ning |
| niu | niu |
| no | nuo |
| nou | nou |
| nu | nu |
| nü | nü |
| nuan | nuan |
| nüeh | nüe |
| nung | nong |
| o | e |
| ou | ou |
| pa | ba |
| p'a | pa |
| pai | bai |
| p'ai | pai |
| pan | ban |
| p'an | pan |
| pang | bang |
| p'ang | pang |
| pao | bao |
| p'ao | pao |
| pei | bei |
| p'ei | pei |
| pen | ben |
| p'en | pen |
| peng | beng |
| p'eng | peng |
| pi | bi |
| p'i | pi |
| piao | biao |
| p'iao | piao |
| pieh | bie |
| p'ieh | pie |
| pien | bian |
| p'ien | pian |
| pin | bin |
| p'in | pin |
| ping | bing |
| p'ing | ping |
| po | bo |
| p'o | po |
| pou | bou |
| p'ou | pou |
| pu | bu |
| p'u | pu |
| sa | sa |
| sai | sai |
| san | san |
| sang | sang |
| sao | sao |
| se | se |
| sen | sen |
| seng | seng |
| sha | sha |
| shai | shai |
| shan | shan |
| shang | shang |
| shao | shao |
| she | she |
| shen | shen |
| sheng | sheng |
| shih | shi |
| shou | shou |
| shu | shu |
| shua | shua |
| shuai | shuai |
| shuan | shuan |
| shuang | shuang |
| shui | shui |
| shun | shun |
| shuo | shuo |
| so | suo |
| sou | sou |
| ssu | si |
| su | su |
| suan | suan |
| sui | sui |
| sun | sun |
| sung | song |
| ta | da |
| t'a | ta |
| tai | dai |
| t'ai | tai |
| tan | dan |
| t'an | tan |
| tang | dang |
| t'ang | tang |
| tao | dao |
| t'ao | tao |
| te | de |
| t'e | te |
| teng | deng |
| t'eng | teng |
| ti | di |
| t'i | ti |
| tiao | diao |
| t'iao | tiao |
| tieh | die |
| t'ieh | tie |
| tien | dian |
| t'ien | tian |
| ting | ding |
| t'ing | ting |
| tiu | diu |
| to | duo |
| t'o | tuo |
| tou | dou |
| t'ou | tou |
| tsa | za |
| ts'a | ca |
| tsai | zai |
| ts'ai | cai |
| tsan | zan |
| ts'an | can |
| tsang | zang |
| ts'ang | cang |
| tsao | zao |
| ts'ao | cao |
| tse | ze |
| ts'e | ce |
| tsei | zei |
| tsen | zen |
| ts'en | cen |
| tseng | zeng |
| ts'eng | ceng |
| tso | zuo |
| ts'o | cuo |
| tsou | zou |
| ts'ou | cou |
| tsu | zu |
| ts'u | cu |
| tsuan | zuan |
| ts'uan | cuan |
| tsui | zui |
| ts'ui | cui |
| tsun | zun |
| ts'un | cun |
| tsung | zong |
| ts'ung | cong |
| tu | du |
| t'u | tu |
| tuan | duan |
| t'uan | tuan |
| tui | dui |
| t'ui | tui |
| tun | dun |
| t'un | tun |
| tung | dong |
| t'ung | tong |
| tzu | zi |
| tz'u | ci |
| wa | wa |
| wai | wai |
| wan | wan |
| wang | wang |
| wei | wei |
| wen | wen |
| weng | weng |
| wo | wo |
| wu | wu |
| ya | ya |
| yai | yai |
| yang | yang |
| yao | yao |
| yeh | ye |
| yen | yan |
| yin | yin |
| ying | ying |
| yu | you |
| yü | yu |
| yüan | yuan |
| yüeh | yue |
| yün | yun |
| yung | yong |

# Pinyin to Wade-Giles

| Pinyin | Wade-Giles |
|---|---|
| a | a |
| ai | ai |
| an | an |
| ang | ang |
| ao | ao |
| ba | pa |
| bai | pai |
| ban | pan |
| bang | pang |
| bao | pao |
| bei | pei |
| ben | pen |
| beng | peng |
| bi | pi |
| bian | pien |
| biao | piao |
| bie | pieh |
| bin | pin |
| bing | ping |
| bo | po |
| bou | pou |
| bu | pu |
| ca | ts'a |
| cai | ts'ai |
| can | ts'an |
| cang | ts'ang |
| cao | ts'ao |
| ce | ts'e |
| cen | ts'en |
| ceng | ts'eng |
| cha | ch'a |
| chai | ch'ai |
| chan | ch'an |
| chang | ch'ang |
| chao | ch'ao |
| che | ch'e |
| chen | ch'en |
| cheng | ch'eng |
| chi | ch'ih |
| chong | ch'ung |
| chou | ch'ou |
| chu | ch'u |
| chua | ch'ua |
| chuai | ch'uai |
| chuan | ch'uan |
| chuang | ch'uang |
| chui | ch'ui |
| chun | ch'un |
| chuo | ch'o |
| ci | tz'u |
| cong | ts'ung |
| cou | ts'ou |
| cu | ts'u |
| cuan | ts'uan |
| cui | ts'ui |
| cun | ts'un |
| cuo | ts'o |
| da | ta |
| dai | tai |
| dan | tan |
| dang | tang |
| dao | tao |
| de | te |
| deng | teng |
| di | ti |
| dian | tien |
| diao | tiao |
| die | tieh |
| ding | ting |
| diu | tiu |
| dong | tung |
| dou | tou |
| du | tu |
| duan | tuan |
| dui | tui |
| dun | tun |
| duo | to |
| e | o |
| en | en |
| er | erh |
| fa | fa |
| fan | fan |
| fang | fang |
| fei | fei |
| fen | fen |
| feng | feng |
| fo | fo |
| fou | fou |
| fu | fu |
| ga | ka |
| gai | kai |
| gan | kan |
| gang | kang |
| gao | kao |
| ge | ko |
| gei | kei |
| gen | ken |
| geng | keng |
| gong | kung |
| gou | kou |
| gu | ku |
| gua | kua |
| guai | kuai |
| guan | kuan |
| guang | kuang |
| gui | kuei |
| gun | kun |
| guo | kuo |
| ha | ha |
| hai | hai |
| han | han |
| hang | hang |
| hao | hao |
| he | ho |
| hei | hei |
| hen | hen |
| heng | heng |
| hong | hung |
| hou | hou |
| hu | hu |
| hua | hua |
| huai | huai |
| huan | huan |
| huang | huang |
| hui | hui |
| hun | hun |
| huo | huo |
| ji | chi |
| jia | chia |
| jian | chien |
| jiang | chiang |
| jiao | chiao |
| jie | chieh |
| jin | chin |
| jing | ching |
| jiong | chiung |
| jiu | chiu |
| ju | chü |
| juan | chüan |
| jue | chüeh |
| jun | chün |
| ka | k'a |
| kai | k'ai |
| kan | k'an |
| kang | k'ang |
| kao | k'ao |
| ke | k'o |
| kei | k'ei |
| ken | k'en |
| keng | k'eng |
| kong | k'ung |
| kou | k'ou |
| ku | k'u |
| kua | k'ua |
| kuai | k'uai |
| kuan | k'uan |
| kuang | k'uang |
| kui | k'uei |
| kun | k'un |
| kuo | k'uo |
| la | la |
| lai | lai |
| lan | lan |
| lang | lang |
| lao | lao |
| le | le |
| lei | lei |
| leng | leng |
| li | li |
| lia | lia |
| lian | lien |
| liang | liang |
| liao | liao |
| lie | lieh |
| lin | lin |
| ling | ling |
| liu | liu |
| long | lung |
| lou | lou |
| lu | lu |
| lü | lü |
| luan | luan |
| lüan | lüan |
| lüe | lüeh |
| lun | lun |
| luo | lo |
| ma | ma |
| mai | mai |
| man | man |
| mang | mang |
| mao | mao |
| mei | mei |
| men | men |
| meng | meng |
| mi | mi |
| mian | mien |
| miao | miao |
| mie | mieh |
| min | min |
| ming | ming |
| miu | miu |
| mo | mo |
| mou | mou |
| mu | mu |
| na | na |
| nai | nai |
| nan | nan |
| nang | nang |
| nao | nao |
| nei | nei |
| nen | nen |
| neng | neng |
| ni | ni |
| nian | nien |
| niang | niang |
| niao | niao |
| nie | nieh |
| nin | nin |
| ning | ning |
| niu | niu |
| nong | nung |
| nou | nou |
| nu | nu |
| nü | nü |
| nuan | nuan |
| nüe | nüeh |
| nuo | no |
| ou | ou |
| pa | p'a |
| pai | p'ai |
| pan | p'an |
| pang | p'ang |
| pao | p'ao |
| pei | p'ei |
| pen | p'en |
| peng | p'eng |
| pi | p'i |
| pian | p'ien |
| piao | p'iao |
| pie | p'ieh |
| pin | p'in |
| ping | p'ing |
| po | p'o |
| pou | p'ou |
| pu | p'u |
| qi | ch'i |
| qia | ch'ia |
| qian | ch'ien |
| qiang | ch'iang |
| qiao | ch'iao |
| qie | ch'ieh |
| qin | ch'in |
| qing | ch'ing |
| qiong | ch'iung |
| qiu | ch'iu |
| qu | ch'ü |
| quan | ch'üan |
| que | ch'üeh |
| qun | ch'ün |
| ran | jan |
| rang | jang |
| rao | jao |
| re | je |
| ren | jen |
| reng | jeng |
| ri | jih |
| rong | jung |
| rou | jou |
| ru | ju |
| ruan | juan |
| rui | jui |
| run | jun |
| ruo | jo |
| sa | sa |
| sai | sai |
| san | san |
| sang | sang |
| sao | sao |
| se | se |
| sen | sen |
| seng | seng |
| sha | sha |
| shai | shai |
| shan | shan |
| shang | shang |
| shao | shao |
| she | she |
| shen | shen |
| sheng | sheng |
| shi | shih |
| shou | shou |
| shu | shu |
| shua | shua |
| shuai | shuai |
| shuan | shuan |
| shuang | shuang |
| shui | shui |
| shun | shun |
| shuo | shuo |
| si | ssu |
| song | sung |
| sou | sou |
| su | su |
| suan | suan |
| sui | sui |
| sun | sun |
| suo | so |
| ta | t'a |
| tai | t'ai |
| tan | t'an |
| tang | t'ang |
| tao | t'ao |
| te | t'e |
| teng | t'eng |
| ti | t'i |
| tian | t'ien |
| tiao | t'iao |
| tie | t'ieh |
| ting | t'ing |
| tong | t'ung |
| tou | t'ou |
| tu | t'u |
| tuan | t'uan |
| tui | t'ui |
| tun | t'un |
| tuo | t'o |
| wa | wa |
| wai | wai |
| wan | wan |
| wang | wang |
| wei | wei |
| wen | wen |
| weng | weng |
| wo | wo |
| wu | wu |
| xi | hsi |
| xia | hsia |
| xian | hsien |
| xiang | hsiang |
| xiao | hsiao |
| xie | hsieh |
| xin | hsin |
| xing | hsing |
| xiong | hsiung |
| xiu | hsiu |
| xu | hsü |
| xuan | hsüan |
| xue | hsüeh |
| xun | hsün |
| ya | ya |
| yai | yai |
| yan | yen |
| yang | yang |
| yao | yao |
| ye | yeh |
| yi | i |
| yin | yin |
| ying | ying |
| yong | yung |
| you | yu |
| yu | yü |
| yuan | yüan |
| yue | yüeh |
| yun | yün |
| za | tsa |
| zai | tsai |
| zan | tsan |
| zang | tsang |
| zao | tsao |
| ze | tse |
| zei | tsei |
| zen | tsen |
| zeng | tseng |
| zha | cha |
| zhai | chai |
| zhan | chan |
| zhang | chang |
| zhao | chao |
| zhe | che |
| zhen | chen |
| zheng | cheng |
| zhi | chih |
| zhong | chung |
| zhou | chou |
| zhu | chu |
| zhua | chua |
| zhuai | chuai |
| zhuan | chuan |
| zhuang | chuang |
| zhui | chui |
| zhun | chun |
| zhuo | cho |
| zi | tzu |
| zong | tsung |
| zou | tsou |
| zu | tsu |
| zuan | tsuan |
| zui | tsui |
| zun | tsun |
| zuo | tso |

# INTRODUCTION

The Chinese language is difficult to learn, but not so difficult as people usually think. With hard work, constant practice, and plenty of patience, anyone who has a good mind and a good ear can learn it in an amazingly short time, as has been demonstrated by a considerable number of Americans.

Chinese is one of the most useful languages, and, in regard both to the number of people who speak it and to the area over which it is in common use, it is perhaps the most widely spoken language in the world. As people coming to the United States need to know English, so Americans who go to China need a knowledge of Chinese to facilitate their contacts with the people there, whether they go to engage in business or industrial enterprises, to act in advisory capacities to the Chinese government, to carry on missionary work, or to be teachers, newspaper correspondents, or members of the diplomatic service. Among those who may never go to China, anthropologists, historians, students of linguistics, and others will find the Chinese language a necessary tool in the study of one of the world's oldest living cultures and the only key to one of the greatest and richest of all literatures.

The written language of China has been the same throughout its long history, and is the same for the entire country. Although there are many dialects, speakers of some of which can hardly understand each other, all Chinese who can read and write can communicate with each other in that way. The most common dialect is that of Peking, the so-called "Mandarin", which is now understood by most educated people. As Parisian is considered the criterion for French, so the Peking dialect is recognized as the standard mode of speech all over China and is the chief basis of the Kuo-yü (national language). Therefore, the pronunciations indicated in these lessons are those of Peking. It will do no harm, however, for the student to listen, when he has the opportunity, to Chinese who speak the national language with southern or other local accents, as is naturally the case with the great majority of Chinese. It is the object of this course to teach correct pronunciation and to enable the student to carry on conversation in the speech of the majority of the Chinese people.

The material included in this text was originally compiled for the Army Specialized Training Program. It has been repeatedly tested and revised in use with three successive classes of soldiers and also with several groups of civilian students. In all classes the results have been highly satisfactory. Practical usefulness was the chief criterion in selection of lesson material. Slang, childish and out-of-date expressions, peculiar usages, and uncommon words have been carefully avoided. Consequently, this text includes only 933 characters and 907 phrases, which may be considered basic vocabulary not only for conversation but also for reading modern Chinese literature in colloquial style. The sentences in this text, being in idiomatic conversational style, will be found useful in various parts of China and in different walks of life. Indications of correct pronunciation, including tones and accents, have been carefully checked by the pronunciation of native Pekingese members of our staff, as well as by the standard dictionaries.

It is desirable for those using the vocabulary of this text to commit it to memory, and to learn to recognize the characters included. Practice in writing characters will help the student to remember and recognize their forms. A foreigner in a district where he does not understand the local dialect will find it a great advantage to be able to read street signs and to make his needs known in writing.

Although the primary emphasis of this text has been placed on conversational Chinese, a student who studies the exercises carefully will learn to read and write at the same time. This text will also serve as a firm stepping-stone for those who intend to continue their study of Chinese by reading modern plays, short stories, poems, and newspapers, or by reading classical Chinese in order to do research in Chinese history and literature.

## The Four Tones

A certain high or low, long or short musical pitch of the voiced part of a syllable in the Chinese language is called the tone of the syllable. Each Chinese syllable has various tones according to its varied meanings. For instance, the syllable <u>yü</u> can have the meanings "mud", "fish", "feather", "gem", and more than a hundred others, each of these meanings being represented by a different written symbol. The spelling "yü" alone does not indicate which of these possible meanings is intended, nor does it show the exact pronunciation of the word in question, unless some indication of the correct tone is added. The tone helps in determining the meaning of a word, and in conversation combinations of syllables having the same meaning serve to avoid ambiguity. The total number of separate syllables in the Chinese national language is said to be about 420 as compared with some 1200 in English, but the use of tones multiplies the limited number of different sounds which are available in Chinese.

Although the number of tones in which each Chinese syllable may be pronounced varies according to historical period and local dialect, there are only four tones in the Peking dialect. Professor Herrlee G. Creel, in his Literary Chinese by the Inductive Method, volume I, page 3, gives a description of the four tones which is worth quoting: "The first tone is a somewhat high, level, slightly prolonged tone, like the manner in which one answers 'yes' when his name is called from a roll. The second is a rising tone; when one is absorbed at his desk, and someone knocks on the door, and while still thinking of something else one quickly answers 'yes' with a rising inflection, this approximates the second tone. The third tone starts moderately high, drops rather low, and then rises slightly at the end. When someone says something which seems doubtful, but to which one slowly says 'ye-es' while still questioning it in his mind, this resembles the third tone. The fourth tone is brief, and comes to a full stop, like the end of a sentence. If someone asks whether one is really sure of what he has said, and one answers, shortly and positively, 'yes!', this is like the fourth tone." Another way of describing the four tones is as follows:

First tone - slight surprise - oh.
Second tone - question - oh?
Third tone - doubt - o-oh?
Fourth tone - emphasis - oh!

The four tones are usually indicated in dictionaries and language textbooks by small raised figures (1, 2, 3, 4) following the characters or romanized syllables. In this text they are marked by symbols (ˉ ˊ ˇ ˋ) placed above the main vowel of each romanized syllable, as follows: mā, má, mǎ, mà.

The following table of the four tones together with their

traditional names and the signs used to indicate them, is based on Professor Y. R. Chao's introduction to the 1943 revision of Mathews' Chinese-English Dictionary (p. xiv).

| No. | Chinese name | English name | Description | Pitch | Example |
|---|---|---|---|---|---|
| 1 | 陰平 yīn-p'íng (shēng) | Upper even (tone) | High level | 55: | mā |
| 2 | 陽平 yáng-p'íng (shēng) | Lower even (tone) | High rising | 35: | má |
| 3 | 上聲 shǎng shēng | Rising tone | Low rising | 214: | mǎ |
| 4 | 去聲 ch'ù shēng | Falling tone | High falling to low | 51: | mà |

Correct tones are indispensable to conversational Chinese. A word pronounced with a wrong accent in English may cause misunderstanding, but incorrect tones in Chinese are much more serious. For instance, "kuèi hsìng?" is a polite expression for "[what is your] honorable name?"; while "kuěi hsìng" means "devil's name". Therefore strict attention should be paid to tone drill, from the very beginning, even though it may seem tiresome.

## Romanization

Representation of sounds of Chinese characters by means of Latin letters is called romanization. Several systems of romanization are in use, but none is perfect. After long deliberation, we have decided to use in this text the system which was devised by Sir Thomas Wade and revised by Herbert A. Giles. Although the Wade-Giles system has its defects, it has been considered standard for many years and has been used in textbooks and dictionaries. Herbert A. Giles' Chinese-English Dictionary (second edition, 1912), which is the largest and best dictionary of its kind yet published, and R. H. Mathews' Chinese-English Dictionary (revised American edition, published for Harvard-Yenching Institute, 1943), which is very useful for the spoken language, are used with some modifications as our standards of romanization.

The sounds of a Chinese syllable can conveniently be analyzed, according to common usage, into an initial and a final. An initial consists of a consonant or a consonant cluster, and a final consists of a vowel, a diphthong, or a vowel or diphthong plus the consonant -n, -ng, or -r (written rh in the Wade-Giles system).

The following is an exhaustive list of all initials and finals. A syllable like pla or suf cannot occur in Chinese, since there is no such initial as pl- and no such final as -uf.

Strictly speaking, no sound in any language is like that of

any other language. In the following descriptions, where it says "as in", the equivalence is close enough for all practical purposes. Where it says "sounds like", the approximation is only rough and the Chinese sound should be heard from the teacher or a phonograph record. Aspirated consonants, which are pronounced with more forceful expulsion of the breath than the corresponding sounds in English, are indicated by the use of the apostrophe (').

The Chinese initials may be classified as follows (although in the list they are arranged alphabetically for convenience of reference):

Labials, or sounds articulated by the lips: f, m, p, p'.

Dentals, or sounds formed with the tip of the tongue against or near the upper front teeth: l, n, t, t'.

Dental sibilants, uttered with a hissing sound: ts, ts', tz, tz', s, ss (or sz).

Palatals, or sounds formed with the front of the tongue near or touching the hard palate: ch, ch', hs, preceding the palatal vowels i, ü.

Retroflexes, or sounds formed with the tip of the tongue raised or turned abruptly backward: ch, ch', sh, j; these sounds never precede the palatal vowels i, ü.

Gutturals, or sounds uttered from the throat: k, k', h.

Following each sound in the table of initials and finals, a Chinese word is given in character and romanization to illustrate its use, and for the convenience of teachers who may wish to demonstrate the correct pronunciation.

### Initials

| | | | | |
|---|---|---|---|---|
| ch | (palatal) sounds like "j" in "jeer" | chiāng | "river" | 江 |
| ch | (retroflex) as in "rich", but with tip of tongue curved back | chāng | "open" | 張 |
| ch' | (palatal) as in "cheer" | ch'iāng | "tone" | 腔 |
| ch' | (retroflex)as in "chew", but with tip of tongue curved back | ch'āng | "prosperous" | 昌 |
| f | as in "fan" | fēn | "to divide" | 分 |
| h | pronounced with back of tongue near soft palate, like "ch" in German "ach" | hěn | "very" | 很 |
| hs | between "s" in "see" and "sh" in "she" | hsiēn | "before" | 先 |
| j | has a sound approximately midway between English "r" in "run" and French "j" in "jeune" | jén | "man" | 人 |

| | | | | |
|---|---|---|---|---|
| k | sounds like "g" in "gun" | kào | "to tell" | 告 |
| k' | as in "key" | k'ào | "to lean" | 靠 |
| l | as in "law" | lǎo | "old" | 老 |
| m | as in "man" | mā | "mama" | 媽 |
| n | as in "note" | nǎo | "brain" | 腦 |
| p | sounds like "b" in "bad" | pǎo | "to protect" | 保 |
| p' | as in "park" | p'ǎo | "to run" | 跑 |
| s | as in "sound" | sān | "three" | 三 |
| sh | sounds like "shr" in "shrub", but dwelling less on the "r" than in English | shān | "mountain" | 山 |
| ss | (or sz) same as s (used only before the final ŭ, which see) | ssŭ | "to die" | 死 |
| t | sounds like "d" in "dear" | tǎ | "to strike" | 打 |
| t' | as in "tear" | t'ǎ | "pagoda" | 塔 |
| ts | sounds like "dz" in "adze" | tsuì | "most" | 最 |
| ts' | as in "that's hot" | ts'uì | "brittle" | 脆 |
| tz | same as ts (used only before ŭ, q.v.) | tzŭ | "son" | 子 |
| tz' | same as ts' " " " " " " | tz'ŭ | "this" | 此 |
| w | as in "wade" | wéi | "to do" | 為 |
| y | as in "Yule" | yén | "to say" | 言 |

Finals

| | | | | |
|---|---|---|---|---|
| a | as in "father" | t'ā | "he" | 他 |
| ai | as in "aisle" | kāi | "ought" | 該 |
| an | as in "can" | pān | "class" | 班 |
| ang | "a" plus "ng" as in German "bang" | pāng | "to help" | 幫 |
| ao | as "ow" in "now" | kāo | "high" | 高 |
| eh | as "e" in "yet" | yèh | "night" | 夜 |
| ei | as in "eight" | pēi | "cup" | 杯 |
| en | as in "send" | yēn | "cigarette" | 烟 |
| ê | unrounded "o" or "u" as in "up", lengthened | kê̄ | "elder brother" | 哥 |
| ên | like "en" in "omen" or "un" in "sun" | fê̄n | "to divide" | 分 |
| êng | as "ung" in "sung" | kê̄ng | "soup" | 羹 |
| êrh | as "err" | ế rh | "child" | 兒 |
| i | as in "machine" | tī | "low" | 低 |
| ia | i plus a | chiā | "to add" | 加 |
| iang | i plus ang | ch'iāng | "gun" | 鎗 |
| iao | i plus ao | chiāo | "to teach" | 教 |
| ieh | i plus eh | chiēh | "street" | 街 |
| ien | i plus en | mièn | "face" | 面 |

| | | | | |
|---|---|---|---|---|
| ih | a vocalized "r" | chīh | "to know" | 知 |
| in | like "in" in "machine" | chīn | "gold" | 金 |
| ing | as in "sing" | míng | "bright" | 明 |
| iu | first and second tones as "ew" in "few" | ch'iū | "autumn" | 秋 |
| | third and fourth tones as "yo" in "yoke" | chiù | "to rescue" | 救 |
| iung | i plus ung | hsiūng | "elder brother" | 兄 |
| o | like "aw" in "saw", but shorter | pō | "wave" | 波 |
| ou | as "ow" in "know" | chōu | "island" | 洲 |
| u | as "oo" in "boot" | tū | "capital" | 都 |
| ua | u plus a | kuā | "melon" | 瓜 |
| uai | u plus ai | kuài | "strange" | 怪 |
| uan | u plus an | huān | "to rejoice" | 歡 |
| uang | u plus ang | huáng | "yellow" | 黃 |
| uei | first and second tones as "wee" | k'uēi | "deficit" | 虧 |
| | third and fourth tones as "way" | k'uèi | "ashamed" | 愧 |
| ui | first and second tones as "wee" | huī | "ashes" | 灰 |
| | third and fourth tones as "way" | huì | "to meet" | 會 |
| un | sounds like "wên" | ch'ūn | "spring" | 春 |
| ung | German "ung", or English "oo" as in "book" plus "ng" | kūng | "work" | 工 |
| uo | sounds like "wo" | kuó | "country" | 國 |
| ü | as German "ü". It may be pronounced by closely rounding the lips as if to say "oo", but trying to say "ee" at the same time. | chǖ | "to dwell" | 居 |
| üan | ü plus an | chüān | "to contribute" | 捐 |
| üeh | ü plus eh | yüēh | "about" | 約 |
| ün | ü plus n | chǖn | "army" | 軍 |
| ŭ | a buzzing vowel formed by prolonging a z-sound with lips relaxed and open. This final occurs only after the initials ts, ts', s. Before ŭ, the orthography of these initials is altered to tz, tz', ss (or sz), in order to remind the reader of the buzzing quality of the final. | ssŭ̄ | "to think" | 思 |

## Practice in Aspirated and Unaspirated Consonants

In Chinese the aspirated consonants p', t', ts', ch' (retrofl.), ch' (pal.), and k' are pronounced with more forceful expulsion of breath than the corresponding consonants in English, while the Chinese p, t, ts, ch, k have no aspiration. The difference can be demonstrated by putting a thin piece of paper before the lips while pronouncing the following words. When the aspirated words are pronounced, the paper should vibrate strongly; but when the unaspirated words are pronounced it should remain practically motionless.

| Unaspirated | | Aspirated | |
|---|---|---|---|
| chāng | "open" | ch'āng | "prosperous" |
| chiāng | "river" | ch'iāng | "tone" |
| kǎo | "manuscript" | k'ǎo | "to examine" |
| pà | "to finish" | p'à | "to fear" |
| pǎo | "to protect" | p'ǎo | "to run" |
| tūng | "east" | t'ūng | "to go through" |
| tsài | "again" | ts'ài | "vegetable food" |

In learning the Wade-Giles system of romanization, particular attention should be paid to the apostrophe which is used as the sign of aspiration. If this is neglected, the pronunciation will be as inaccurate as the spelling which results when an inexperienced typist touches the wrong keys.

## Change of Tone and the Neutral Tone

In actual speech, change of tone occurs under the following conditions:

(1) A third tone immediately followed by another third tone changes to the second tone. For example: "Ní hǎo ma?" - "Are you well?", instead of "Nǐ hǎo ma?"

(2) When three third tone words occur in succession in the same phrase, the first as well as the second may change to the second tone, depending upon the emphasis of the first word. For example: "Wó hén hǎo" - "I am very well"; but "Nǐ mái pǐ" - "<u>You</u> buy a pen".

When characters are pronounced singly, and in slow speech, as that of a Chinese teacher before his class, practically every character is pronounced distinctly with one of the four regular tones. But in normal, ordinary speech, in compound words and connected sentences, many syllables are unstressed and lose their characteristic tones. The pitch of such a syllable is determined, not by its original tone, but by its tone environment, chiefly by the tone of the preceding syllable. An unstressed or atonic syllable is called "ch'īng yīn" (輕音, "light sound") in Chinese, and in English is said to have the neutral tone. According to Professor Y.R. Chao's introduction to the 1943 edition of Mathews' <u>Chinese-English Dictionary</u> (p. xvi), particles, interjections, pronouns following verbs, suffixes such as "lê" 了, "tê" 的, "ma" 嗎, "ni" 呢, "êrh" 兒, "tzŭ" 子, and other "hsū tzŭ" (虛字, "empty words"), which do not carry important concrete meaning in the sentence, usually have the neutral tone. For example: "Hǎo-pu-hao?" - "Are you well or not?"; "Ní yǔ-mei-yu?" - "Do you have or not?"; "kāo-tê" - "high ones"; "tuǎn-tê" - "short ones".

In this text, words which have the neutral tone carry no tone symbol.

The 1942 edition of C.H. Fenn's The Five Thousand Dictionary and the 1943 edition of Mathews' Chinese-English Dictionary indicate atonic words and expressions.

It is advisable that students listen attentively to the pronunciation of their instructors, imitating their inflections exactly, in order to acquire such familiarity with the tones that their use will be naturally correct, and to acquire a sense of rhythmic emphasis.

## The Use of Reference Works and Dictionaries

A novice language student is likely to be predisposed either to accept what is offered without criticism, or to inquire in detail into grammatical construction. Neither of these tendencies should be carried to the extreme. Idiomatic Chinese is better acquired by a natural process of imitation, like that of a child learning to speak, than by grammatical reasoning. The best method is to learn idiomatic sentences as they would be spoken or written by the people of China. The use of such sentences is a special feature of this text.

On the other hand, it is worth while for the student to pay some attention to the grammatical and philological aspects of the subject. For those who desire to learn more than is presented here concerning the general characteristics of the Chinese language, it will be helpful to read the article on this topic in the Encyclopaedia Britannica (14th edition, vol. 5, pp. 567-570), Bernhard Karlgren's Sound and Symbol in Chinese (Oxford University Press, 1923), and "A Characterization of the Chinese National Language" by Denzel Carr, in Bulletin de la Société Polonaise de Linguistique (III, 1932, pp. 38-99).

As for dictionaries, the material in this text has been planned and indexed with a view to eliminating their use in the beginning stages of study. Because the Chinese language is not alphabetic, when the student begins to use a Chinese dictionary he must know something about the construction of the characters, upon which their arrangement in most dictionaries is based. The system of the famous K'ang-hsi Dictionary sets apart 214 key characters or elements of characters, often called radicals in English, and classes every other character under one of these keys, which forms an element of its structure. The key of a character usually gives a hint as to its meaning - for example, many words having to do with liquids, as "lake", "river", "wine", "oil", have the "water" key. The remaining portion of a character may suggest its sound or may indicate its meaning. The keys are arranged in a set order, based on the number of strokes used in writing them: those with one stroke before those with two, and so on. In each class the characters are arranged according to the number of strokes they contain, aside from the key itself. To find an unknown character in the dictionary, a student should first determine its key, then count the number of strokes in the rest of the character, and then look, under the proper key, for the list of characters containing that number of strokes.

When the beginning student reaches a point where the need of a dictionary is felt, Fenn's Five Thousand Dictionary and Mathews' Chinese-English Dictionary, mentioned above, will be found useful and convenient. Chauncey Goodrich's A Pocket Dictionary (Columbia University Press, 1944) is particularly good for pronunciation and tones. These dictionaries are all arranged alphabetically according to romanization, with indexes according to the K'ang-hsi system of keys. Another important tool for students of conversational Chinese is Shau Wing Chan's Concise English-Chinese Dictionary (Stanford University Press, 1946).

In this text, the Chinese characters in the vocabularies and reading material are in printed form; those in the exercises and notes have been written by hand. Thus the student will become familiar with both the printed and the written forms of the characters.

CONVERSATIONAL CHINESE

# PART I GREETINGS AND INTRODUCTIONS

## Lesson 1 Greetings

### 1. Useful Words and Phrases

| English equivalents | Pronunciation | Characters |
|---|---|---|
| I, me | wǒ (1) | 我 |
| you | nǐ (2) | 你 |
| he, she, him, her | t'ā (3) | 他 |
| good, well | hǎo | 好 |
| very | hěn | 很 |
| an interrogative particle | ma (4) | 嗎 |
| thanks, thank you | hsièh-hsieh | 謝謝 |
| How are you? | Ní hǎo ma? | 你好嗎? |
| I am very well. | Wó hén hǎo. | 我很好. |
| How is he (she)? | T'ā hǎo ma? | 他好嗎? |
| He (she) is very well. | T'ā hén hǎo. | 他很好. |
| I am fine, thanks | Wó hǎo, hsièh-hsieh. | 我好, 謝謝. |

### 2. Tone and Pronunciation Drill

| | | | | | | | |
|---|---|---|---|---|---|---|---|
| wō | wó | wǒ | wò | nī | ní | nǐ | nì |
| t'ā | t'á | t'ǎ | t'à | hāo | háo | hǎo | hào |
| hēn | hén | hěn | hèn | mā | má | mǎ | mà |
| hsiēh | hsiéh | hsiěh | hsièh | | | | |

3. Exercises

a. "Fill-in" sentences

[Under the above heading, patterns for sentences will be supplied, with blanks for students to fill in. This drill will not only help the students to acquire facility in the use of all the words they have learned so far, but will also give them a sound fundamental knowledge of Chinese sentence construction, so that they can form sentences alone without serious difficulty. For instance, the sentence pattern "... hến hǎo" can be filled out to make "Wǒ hến hǎo"; "Nǐ hến hǎo"; "T'ā hến hǎo". In doing these exercises, it is better for the student to repeat them orally again and again, until they are firmly fixed in the mind, rather than to write them down.]

| | |
|---|---|
| 1. ... hǎo ma? | How are (is) ... ? |
| 2. ... hến hǎo. | ... am (is) very well. |
| 3. Wǒ hsièh-hsieh ... | I thank ... |
| 4. ... hsièh-hsieh ni. | ... thank(s) you. |
| 5. Nǐ hsièh-hsieh ... | You thank ... |

b. Translate the following into English:

[These exercises may be read aloud and the student asked to translate them orally as quickly as possible. This will give students a chance to train their ear and develop their ability in aural comprehension.]

1. Wó hến hǎo, hsièh-hsieh.

2. Ní hǎo ma?

3. T'ā hến hǎo ma?

4. T'ā hến hǎo, hsièh-hsieh.

c. Translate the following into Chinese:

[These exercises may be assigned as home work, to be written in romanized Chinese. The instructor may also desire to have the students translate them once more, orally, in the classroom, to make sure that they really understand the sentence construction, and to increase their conversational ability.]

1. How are you?
2. I am well.
3. I thank you.
4. How is she?
5. She is very well.
6. Are you very well?

## PART I, LESSON 1

NOTES:

(1) "Wǒ", "nǐ", and "t'ā" are the personal pronouns, first, second, and third persons, respectively. In Chinese, the same forms of pronouns are usually used for the accusative and nominative cases, and for the masculine and feminine genders.

(2) "Nín" 您, a respectful word for "you" used to superiors by people around Peking, is not used in this text because it is not common in the national language.

(3) Recently, different forms of 他 "t'ā" have been introduced: 她 for "she" and 它 for "it". The pronunciation of all forms remains the same, and 他 may still be used for any gender.

(4) "Ma" is a question indicator, a particle indicating a question which can be answered by "yes" or "no". It always stands at the end of a sentence, the order of which is the same as that of an affirmative sentence, but which is made interrogative by the use of this particle, somewhat as "eh?" or "huh?" is sometimes added in English to turn an affirmative sentence into a question. When used in this way, "ma" is atonic.

"Ní hǎo ma?" is used as a phrase of greeting, like "good morning", "good evening", or "hello".

(5) Reduplication of a noun or verb in Chinese usually indicates plural number or emphasis, or both. Thus "hsièh" alone means "to thank", "hsièh-hsieh" means "thanks" or "thank you".

(6) "Hǎo" may be considered to have the meaning of "to be good" or "to be well". "Ní hǎo ma?" means "You are-well, aren't-you?" or "How do you do?" In Chinese, no copula is used before a predicate adjective, unless for particular emphasis.

### Word Order

In general, Chinese word order is similar to the normal word order in English - i. e., subject, verb, object. The adjective precedes the noun it modifies, and the adverb precedes the verb, adjective, or adverb it modifies.

Chinese sentences do not change their word order to indicate the interrogative, which is expressed by an interrogative pronoun, adjective, or adverb, or simply by the addition of the particle "ma" at the end of a declarative sentence.

### The Use of the Hyphen and Underlining

In this text, the hyphen is used to join words which are spoken together without any pause.

To help the beginner in learning to read with proper expression, in the first part of this text the word which receives primary stress in each phrase will be underlined. Other syllables on which the tones are marked should receive secondary stress, while atonic syllables are unstressed. In each phrase there is only one syllable which receives primary stress; generally this is toward the end of the phrase, but of course it never falls on a final particle and usually personal pronouns are lightly stressed.

However, since the use of stress varies with circumstances and with individual speakers, the indications given here are merely suggestions. It is very important that the students carefully mimic the intonations of a good native teacher.

## Lesson 2 Introducing People

### 1. Useful Words and Phrases

| English equivalents | Pronunciation | Characters |
|---|---|---|
| surname, to be named | hsìng | 姓 |
| honorable | kuèi | 貴 |
| humble | pì (1) | 敝 |
| is, are | shìh (2) | 是 |
| this | chè | 這 |
| that | nà | 那 |
| this is | <u>chè</u> shìh | 這是 |
| that is | <u>nà</u> shìh | 那是 |
| what | shén-mo (3) | 甚麼 |
| small, little | hsiǎo | 小 |
| elder sister | chiěh | 姐 |
| Miss | hsiáo-chieh | 小姐 |
| before, formerly | hsiēn | 先 |
| to grow, to be born | shēng | 生 |
| Mr., husband, teacher; you, Sir | hsiēn-shēng (4) | 先生 |
| too, very | t'ài | 太 |
| wife of an official, wife, Madam, Mrs. | t'ài-t'ai | 太太 |
| What is your (honorable) name? | Nǐ kuèi <u>hsìng</u>? | 你貴姓? |
| My (humble) name is Li. | Pì hsìng <u>Lǐ</u>. | 敝姓李. |

| | | |
|---|---|---|
| This is Mr. Li. | Chè shìh Lǐ hsiēn-shêng. | 這是李先生. |
| That is Mrs. Li. | Nà shìh Lǐ t'ài-t'ai. | 那是李太太. |
| What is his name? | T'ā hsìng shến-mo? | 他姓甚麽? |
| His name is Wang. | T'ā hsìng Wáng. | 他姓王. |
| She is Miss Wang. | T'ā shìh Wáng hsiáo-chieh. | 她是王小姐. |
| What is this? | Chè shìh shến-mo? | 這是甚麽? |
| What is that? | Nà shìh shến-mo? | 那是甚麽? |

2. Tone and Pronunciation Drill

[Attention should be paid to the distinction between "hs" and "sh". The former is pronounced as a harsh and long "ss", with the breath strongly expelled through closed teeth, while the latter is a soft sound like the English "sh".]

| | | | | | | | |
|---|---|---|---|---|---|---|---|
| hsīng | hsíng | hsǐng | hsìng | shīh | shíh | shǐh | shìh |
| shê̄ng | shếng | shê̌ng | shềng | chê̄ | chế | chê̌ | chề |
| hsiēn | hsién | hsiěn | hsièn | kuēi | kuéi | kuěi | kuèi |
| shê̄n | shến | shê̌n | shền | nā | ná | nǎ | nà |
| t'āi | t'ái | t'ǎi | t'ài | pī | pí | pǐ | pì |

3. Exercises

a. "Fill-in" sentences

[Students are expected to become thoroughly familiar with these sentence patterns, which are used in introductions. Different names, Chinese and English, should be used in the drill.]

| | |
|---|---|
| 1. Chè shìh ... hsiēn-shêng. | This is Mr. ... |
| 2. Nà shìh ... t'ài-t'ai. | That is Mrs. ... |
| 3. Wǒ hsìng ... | My name is ... |
| 4. ... hsiēn-shêng, ní hǎo ma? | Mr. ... , how do you do? |

b. Translate into English:

1. Wǒ hsìng Wáng.

2. Nǐ kuèi hsìng?

3. Chè shìh Wáng t'ài-t'ai.

4. Nà shìh Lǐ hsiēn-shêng ma?

5. Wáng hsiáo-chieh, ní hǎo ma?

6. Lǐ hsiēn-shêng, wó hén hǎo, hsièh-hsieh.

c. Translate into Chinese:

[This exercise, again, is to be written in romanized Chinese, as homework. Students are expected to learn the Wade-Giles system of romanization thoroughly, and to be able to take dictation in this form, giving indications of tones.]

1. What is your (honorable) name?

2. My (humble) name is Wang.

3. What is this?

4. What is that?

5. Mrs. Li, how are you?

6. I am fine, thank you.

7. Is this Mr. Wang?

8. Is that Mrs. Wang?

NOTES:

(1) "Kuèi" and "pì" are polite expressions used in Chinese in the same way as "your humble servant" was formerly used in English. That is, they do not indicate any great degree of respect or humility, but simply fulfill the traditional requirements of courtesy in refined societies.

Usually when a person's name is asked, "nǐ" and "wǒ" are omitted in both question and answer, "kuèi" and "pì", respectively, taking their places. In referring to someone who is not present, "hsìng" is used without "kuèi".

(2) "Shìh", "to be (am, is, are, was, were)", used between two substantives, has the function of equation, as in "Wǒ shìh Wáng hsiēn-shêng" - "I am Mr. Wang". It is not used before predicate adjectives, unless for special emphasis.

(3) "Shén-mo", "what", is an interrogative expression, used to form a question. Note that the word order is the same as in an affirmative sentence, and not inverted as in English interrogative sentences. For purposes of abbreviation, "shén-mo" is usually written 什麽 ("shíh-mo"; "shíh" means "thing"). "Shén-ma" 甚嗎 can be used interchangeably with "shén-mo".

(4) "Hsiēn-shêng" means literally "[one who was] born before" or

"[one who] grew up earlier", hence an elder, a teacher; the use of the term for "Mr." or "you, Sir" is derived from these meanings. Note that "hsiēn-shêng" in the sense of "Mr." and "t'ài-t'ai" in the sense of "Mrs." always follow the surname.

## On Writing Chinese Characters

In China, calligraphy ("beautiful writing") is one of the fine arts, as much as the painting of pictures, and a fine calligrapher must study and practise as diligently as any other artist. Although of course most Western students cannot hope to become artistic calligraphers, some understanding of the value and beauty of Chinese writing adds interest to the study of the language, whether the student plans to acquire only a purely utilitarian knowledge of a few characters, or whether he hopes to learn to write Chinese letters, read Chinese literature, or use Chinese source materials in study or research.

Even for the beginner, it is important to learn to write the characters correctly, according to principles evolved through experience by countless generations of Chinese calligraphers. Chief among these are the following: The pen should move from left to right and from top to bottom (in general, though sometimes, for certain short strokes, it may move slantingly upward to the right or strongly downward to the left, as is shown in the first character below). The appearance of strokes and of characters should be straight, even, and proportional. The component parts of each character should be in proportion to each other, and the size and spacing of characters on a page should be proportional. The action of writing should not be hesitant or uncertain, but firm and vigorous, and the strokes should appear distinct and vivid. If these principles are observed faithfully in practice, the results should be acceptable.

For each character there is a proper order in which its component strokes should be written, although in certain minor details there is variation in the writing of different individuals. The strokes of the large characters below are numbered to indicate their order. The student should write each character at least four times, and should place the proper number beside each stroke the first time. Each future written assignment should be practised in the same way. The student will thus learn not only to write the characters in the conventional Chinese way, but also to count the number of strokes in each character, an essential in consulting dictionaries and indexes. In the long run this system will prove much more efficient and time-saving than mere hit-or-miss copying.

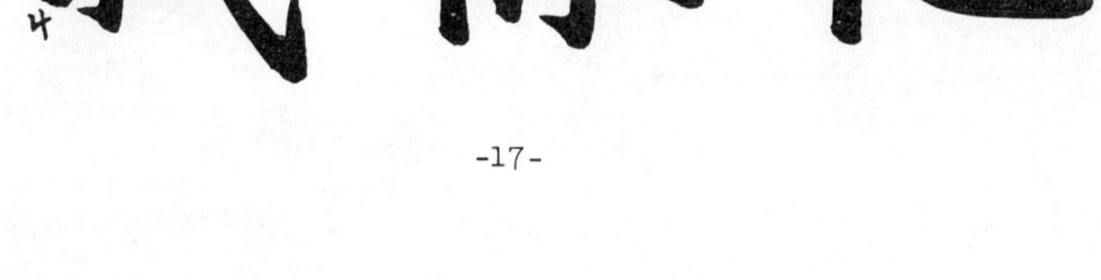

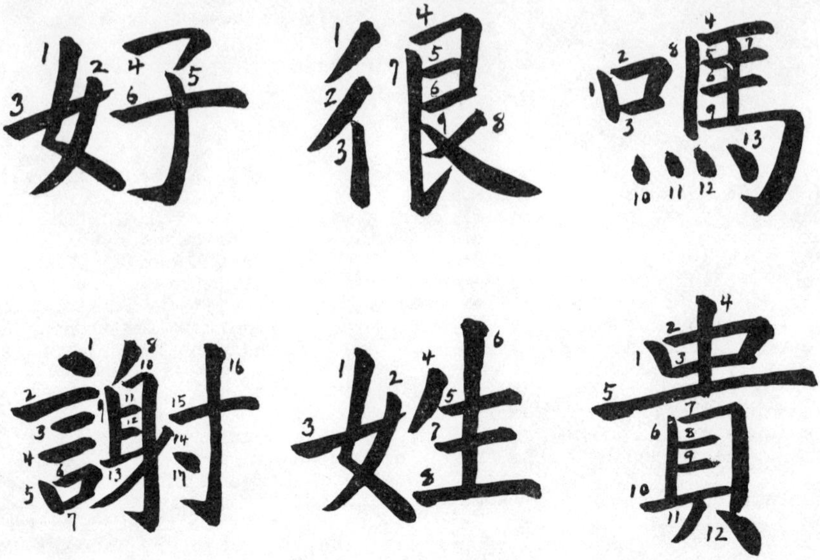

## Lesson 3 Practical Conversation

### 1. Useful Words and Phrases

| English equivalents | Pronunciation | Characters |
|---|---|---|
| who? whom? | shuí? (1) | 誰 |
| sign of possessive (used with any noun or pronoun) | tê (2) | 的 |
| whose? | shuí-tê? | 誰的? |
| my, mine | wǒ-tê | 我的 |
| your, yours | nǐ-tê | 你的 |
| his, her, hers, its | t'ā-tê | 他的 |
| sign of plural (referring to persons) | mên (3) | 們 |
| we, us | wǒ-mên | 我們 |
| you (plural) | nǐ-mên | 你們 |

## PART I, LESSON 3

| | | |
|---|---|---|
| they, them | t'ā-mên | 他們 |
| our, ours | wǒ-mên-tê | 我們的 |
| your, yours (plural) | nǐ-mên-tê | 你們的 |
| their, theirs | t'ā-mên-tê | 他們的 |
| beautiful; America | měi | 美 |
| nation, state | kuó | 國 |
| United States of America | Měi-kuo | 美國 |
| middle, China | chūng | 中 |
| China | Chūng-kuo | 中國 |
| man, person | jén | 人 |
| with, and | kěn (4) | 跟 |
| book | shū | 書 |
| also, too | yěh | 也 |
| all, both | tōu (5) | 都 |
| friend | p'éng-yu | 朋友 |
| a general numerative; one, an individual | kè (6) | 個 |

### 2. Sentences

1. Who is this?
   Chè shìh shuí?
   這是誰？
2. This is my friend.
   Chè shìh wǒ-tê p'éng-yu.
   這是我的朋友.
3. What is your friend's (honorable) name?
   Nǐ-tê p'éng-yu kuèi hsìng?
   你的朋友貴姓？

4. His name is Wang.

T'ā hsìng Wáng.

他姓王.

5. Is Mr. Wang an American?

Wáng hsiēn-shēng shìh Měi-kuo jén ma?

王先生是美國人嗎?

6. He is an American.

T'ā shìh Měi-kuo jén.

他是美國人.

7. Whose book is this?

Chè shìh shuí - tê shū?

這是誰的書?

8. This is my book.

Chè shìh wǒ - tê shū.

這是我的書.

9. Whose is this one?

Chè - kê shìh shuí - tê?

這個是誰的?

10. This one is mine, that one is his.

Chè - kê shìh wǒ - tê, nà - kê shìh t'ā - tê.

這個是我的,那個是他的.

11. He is my good friend; is he also your good friend?

T'ā shìh wǒ - tê hǎo p'éng-yu; yěh shìh nǐ - tê hǎo p'éng-yu ma?

他是我的好朋友,也是你的好朋友嗎?

12. He and I are good friends. We are all good friends.

Wǒ kēn t'ā(7) shìh hǎo p'éng-yu. Wǒ - mên tōu shìh hǎo p'éng-yu.

我跟他是好朋友. 我們都是好朋友.

3. Tone and Pronunciation Drill

| | | | | | | | |
|---|---|---|---|---|---|---|---|
| shū | shú | shǔ | shù | tōu | tóu | tǒu | tòu |
| shuī | shuí | shuǐ | shuì | p'ēng | p'éng | p'ěng | p'èng |
| mēn | mén | měn | mèn | yū | yú | yǔ | yù |
| yēh | yéh | yěh | yèh | kuō | kuó | kuǒ | kuò |

4. Exercises

a. "Fill-in" sentences

1. Chè shìh wǒ-tê ... ... This is my ...

2. T'ā hsìng ... His name is ...

| | |
|---|---|
| 3. Wǒ shìh ... ... jén. | I am ... ... (person). |
| 4. Wǒ-mên tōu shìh ... ... | We are all ... ... |
| 5. Wǒ kēn t'ā shìh ... ... | He and I are ... ... |

b. Translate into English:

1. T'ā shìh wǒ-tê t'ài-t'ai.
2. Chè shìh t'ā-tê shū ma?
3. T'ā shìh shuí?
4. Wǒ-mên tōu shìh Měi-kuo jén.
5. Wǒ-tê p'éng-yu shìh Chūng-kuo jén.
6. Wǒ-mên tōu shìh hǎo p'éng-yu.
7. T'ā-mên tōu hǎo ma?
8. Wǒ-mên tōu hén hǎo, hsièh-hsieh.
9. Chè-kê jén shìh shuí?
10. Nǐ-tê t'ài-t'ai hǎo ma?

c. Translate into Chinese:

1. Is this yours?
2. This man is my friend, that one is my teacher.
3. Who is your teacher?
4. What book is this?
5. He and I are Americans.
6. This is my Chinese friend, Mr. Li.
7. Mr. Smith is my American friend.
8. Our teacher is an American.
9. Your friends are also our friends.

NOTES:

(1) "Shuí" means "who, whom, whoever" (both singular and plural). It is an interrogative pronoun, and when it is used in a question, the interrogative particle "ma" is not used at the end. For example: "Chè shìh shuí?" (literally, "this is who?") - "Who is this?"

(2) 的 , pronounced "tê", is the most important particle of the

Chinese spoken language (and also, pronounced "ti", is an independent word with such meanings as "bull's-eye, clear, evident, accurate"). The commonest use of "tê" is as the sign of the possessive case. In this sense it is usually translated by "'s" or "of", and follows nouns, including proper names, and pronouns, thus forming their possessive case. For instance: "Wáng hsiēn-shêng-tê p'ěng-yu" - "Mr. Wang's friend". Note that the position of "tê" corresponds to that of "'s" in the English phrase "Mr. Wang's friend", never to that of "of" in "friend of Mr. Wang". In Chinese, the possessive always precedes the word or phrase which it governs.

(3) "Mên" is a suffix indicating plural. It is used chiefly with personal pronouns, and occasionally with certain nouns meaning persons, such as "p'ěng-yu-mên" - "friends", "hsiēn-shêng-mên" - "gentlemen". It is not used for plurals in general.

(4) "Kēn" is used colloquially to mean "with" or "and", to connect nouns and pronouns. It is seldom used as a conjunction between clauses.

(5) "Tōu" is used before verbs and adjectives, for emphasis, but after nouns. It may be translated "all" or "entirely".

(6) A numerative (also called measure or classifier) is a word used before a noun after a number to indicate some general characteristics of the noun with which it is used. This usage is somewhat like the English use of "head" in "twenty head of oxen", "rolls" in "three rolls of cloth", or "blocks" in "three blocks of stone". In English the use of a numerative is optional; in Chinese, where it is used at all, it is invariable, except in certain conventional expressions adopted from literary Chinese. It is better to learn the correct numerative with each noun, just as one remembers the proper article with each French noun.

## Calligraphy Practice

The following examples show how the characters in Lessons 2 and 3 should be written, including the order of strokes. The student should practise writing them in accordance with the previous instructions.

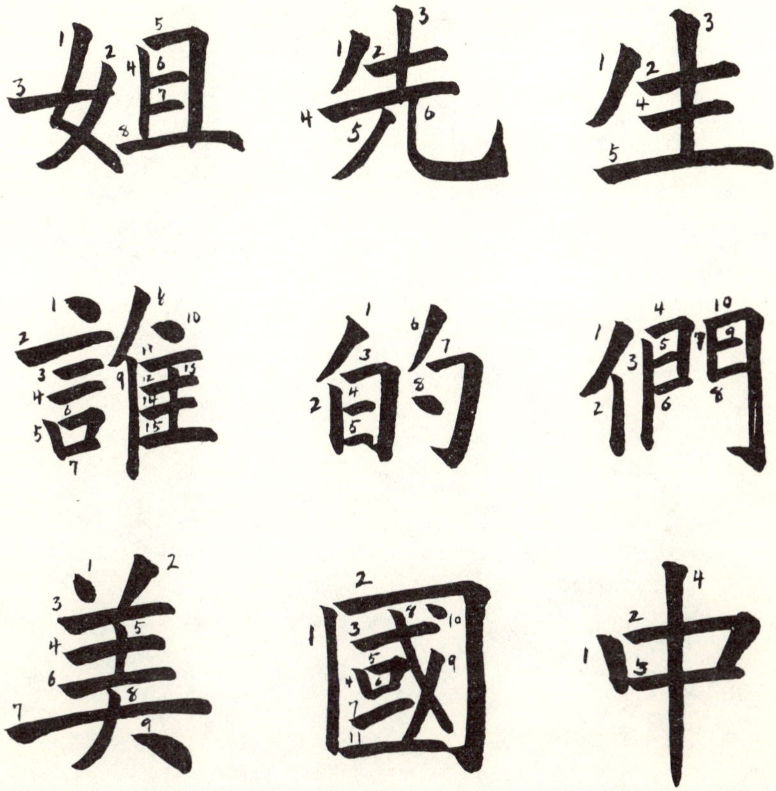


## Lesson 4 Polite Expressions

1. Useful Words and Phrases

| English equivalents | Pronunciation | Characters |
|---|---|---|
| please; to request | ch'ǐng | 請 |
| to sit down | tsò | 坐 |
| Please sit down | Ch'ǐng tsò | 請坐 |
| to ask (a question) | wèn (1) | 問 |
| May I ask .., I beg to ask .. | Ch'ǐng wèn .. | 請問 |

| | | |
|---|---|---|
| to want; sign of future tense | yào | 要 |
| to walk, to go away | tsǒu | 走 |
| a verbal suffix indicating completed action | lê (2) | 了 |
| not, no | pū (3) | 不 |
| not so, not correct | pú <u>shìh</u> | 不是 |
| Is it so? yes or no? | shìh-pu-shih (4) | 是不是 |
| again | tsài | 再 |
| to see, to meet | chièn | 見 |
| see (you) again, goodby | tsài <u>chièn</u> | 再見 |
| to face; opposite | tùi | 對 |
| to rise up | ch'ǐ | 起 |
| excuse me, I beg your pardon, I'm sorry | tùi pu <u>ch'ǐ</u> (5) | 對不起 |
| guest | k'è | 客 |
| air, breath | ch'ì | 氣 |
| Let's not be formal | pú <u>k'è</u>-ch'i (6) | 不客氣 |

2. Sentences

1. May I ask your honorable surname, Sir?
   Ch'ǐng wèn, hsiēn-shêng kuèi <u>hsìng</u>?
   請 問， 先 生 貴 姓?
2. My humble name is Li.
   Pì hsìng <u>Lǐ</u>.
   敝 姓 李.
3. Mr. Li, please sit down.
   Lǐ hsiēn-shêng, ch'ǐng <u>tsò</u>.
   李 先 生， 請 坐.
4. Thank you, let's not be formal.
   <u>Hsièh</u>-hsieh, pú <u>k'è</u>-ch'i.
   謝 謝， 不 客 氣.

5. Are you Miss Li? Are you Miss Li (or not)?

Nǐ shìh Lǐ hsiáo-chieh ma? Nǐ shìh-pu-shih Lǐ hsiáo-chieh?

你是李小姐嗎? 你是不是李小姐?

6. No, my surname is not Li. I am not Miss Li.

Pū, wǒ pú hsìng Lǐ. Wǒ pú shìh Lǐ hsiáo-chieh.

不,我不姓李. 我不是李小姐.

7 Please excuse me. May I ask your honorable name, Miss?

Tuì pu ch'ǐ Ch'ǐng wèn, hsiáo-chieh kuèi hsìng?

對不起. 請問,小姐貴姓?

8. My name is Wang.

Wǒ hsìng Wáng (7).

我姓王.

9. Miss Wang, please sit down.

Wáng hsiáo-chieh, ch'ǐng tsò.

王小姐,請坐.

10. Excuse me, I [shall] not sit down; I am about to go away.

Tuì pu ch'ǐ, wǒ pú tsò; wǒ yào tsǒu lê.

對不起,我不坐,我要走了.

11. Goodby, Miss Wang.

Wáng hsiáo-chieh, tsài chièn.

王小姐,再見.

12. Goodby, Mr. Li.

Lǐ hsiēn-shēng, tsài chièn.

李先生,再見.

3. Tone and Pronunciation Drill

| | | | | | | | |
|---|---|---|---|---|---|---|---|
| ch'īng | ch'íng | ch'ǐng | ch'ìng | tsō | tsó | tsǒ | tsò |
| ch'ī | ch'í | ch'ǐ | ch'ì | tsōu | tsóu | tsǒu | tsòu |
| chī | chí | chǐ | chì | tsāi | tsái | tsǎi | tsài |
| chiēn | chién | chiěn | chièn | k'ē̂ | k'ế | k'ê̌ | k'ề |
| chiēh | chiéh | chiěh | chièh | lē̂ | lế | lê̌ | lề |
| pū | pú | pǔ | pù | wē̂n | wến | wê̌n | wền |
| yāo | yáo | yǎo | yào | wāng | wáng | wǎng | wàng |
| tuī | tuí | tuǐ | tuì | | | | |

4. Exercises

a. "Fill-in" sentences

| | |
|---|---|
| 1. ... hsiēn-shêng, ch'ǐng tsò. | Mr. ... , please be seated. |
| 2. ... kuèi hsìng? | [What is] ...(honorable) surname? |
| 3. ... hsìng ... | ... name [is] ... |
| 4. Ch'ǐng wèn, ... ... ? | May I ask ... ... ? |
| 5. Nǐ shìh ... ... ... ma? | Are you ... ... ... ? |
| 6. Nǐ shìh-pu-shih ... hsiēn-shêng? | Are you Mr. ... (or not)? |

b. Translate into English:

1. Nǐ kuèi hsìng? Pì hsìng Lǐ.
2. Lǐ hsiēn-shêng, ní hǎo ma?
3. Wó hǎo, hsièh-hsieh. Ní hǎo-pu-hao?
4. Ch'ǐng tsò, ch'ǐng tsò. Hsièh-hsieh.
5. Chè shìh wǒ-tê shū, shìh-pu-shih?
6. Pú shìh.
7. Chè shìh t'ā-tê shū ma?
8. Chè pú shìh t'ā-tê shū.
9. Tuì pu ch'ǐ, wǒ yào tsǒu lê.
10. Pú k'ê-ch'i. Tsài chièn, tsài chièn.

c. Translate into Chinese:

[Henceforth the translations into Chinese should be written in characters instead of in romanization. The student who does these exercises carefully should be able, by the time he finishes this book, to write letters and simple essays in Chinese.]

1. How are you?
2. I am well, thank you. How are you?
3. What is your (honorable) name?
4. My name is ... What is your (honorable) name?
5. My name is ... Please be seated.
6. Let us not be so formal.

7. I want to see you.

8. I'll go first.

9. How is your wife?

10. Both she and I are very well.

NOTES:

(1) "Ch'ǐng" - "please; to invite, to request, to ask (someone to do something)" - should not be confused with "wèn" - "to ask a question". It would be incorrect to say "Wèn t'a tsò" in place of "Ch'ǐng t'a tsò" for "Ask him to sit down".

(2) 了 in literary Chinese is pronounced "liǎo", and means "to end, to finish". In spoken Chinese it is usually pronounced "lê". Besides indicating completed action, "lê" has also the functions of adding emphasis or improving euphony. It is one of the most commonly used and most important particles, and its uses will be explained in detail later.

(3) "Pū" is a general negative, which usually precedes the word it modifies. It is pronounced "pū" when standing alone, and, in Peking colloquial, "pú" before fourth tone words, otherwise "pù".

(4) When an adjective or a verb is repeated with a negative word before its second occurrence, the phrase becomes a question, as in "shìh-pu-shih?" - "is it so or not?" When such a phrase is used in a sentence, no question indicator (such as "ma") is needed to show that the sentence is interrogative.

(5) "Tuì pu ch'ǐ", literally "face cannot up", is an expression of apology or regret, implying that the speaker cannot face the person addressed, and is used as English speakers use such expressions as "excuse me", "I'm sorry", or "I beg your pardon".

(6) English has no exact equivalent of "pú k'è-ch'i", which literally means something like "Don't have the air of a guest", and is used as Americans use "Make yourself at home", "You're welcome", "Don't be formal", and similar polite expressions.

(7) There is a tendency among educated Chinese for women to use fewer formal expressions than men do. Thus instead of saying "Pì hsìng Wáng", a woman would say "Wǒ hsìng Wáng".

## On Punctuation

Chinese books have usually not been punctuated; readers were expected to study the texts they read and put in their own punctuation marks after making out the meaning. The modern Chinese system of punctuation, based on that of Western languages, was introduced about a generation ago. On the whole, modern Chinese punctuation is about the same as English, except that quotation marks are usually represented by brackets, personal names are underlined, and place names are frequently indicated by double underlining. When a text is printed in vertical columns instead of horizontal lines, these marks are placed beside the characters, on either the right or the left side. Titles of books are indicated by a wavy line 〰〰 placed under or beside the characters.

In this text, the modern Chinese system of punctuation is followed in part. Question marks, exclamation points, commas, and periods are used about as in English, and quotation marks exactly as in English. Students are advised to follow the same usage in writing exercises.

書 跟 都

朋 友 請

坐 問 要

走 再 對

## Lesson 5 Polite Expressions (continued)

### 1. Useful Words and Phrases

| English equivalents | Pronunciation | Characters |
|---|---|---|
| which? | nǎ (1) | 那 |
| to have; there is, there are | yǔ (2) | 有 |
| no, not (opposite of yǔ 有) | méi | 沒 |
| have not, there is not | méi-yǔ (3) | 沒有 |
| have or not? Is there? | yǔ-mei-yu? | 有沒有? |
| England | Yīng-kuo (4) | 英國 |
| English people | Yīng-kuo jén | 英國人 |
| written language | wén | 文 |
| English language | Yīng-wén (5) | 英文 |
| Chinese language | Chūng-wén | 中文 |
| France, French | Fà-kuo (6) | 法國 |
| to speak, to say | shuō | 說 |
| speech, language | huà | 話 |
| to talk, to speak | shuō-huà (7) | 說話 |
| Chinese spoken language | Chūng-kuo-huà | 中國話 |
| one | ī (8) | 一 |
| a dot, a point | tiěn | 點 |
| a child; a common suffix to substantives | érh (9) | 兒 |
| a little | ì-tiěn-êrh (10) | 一點兒 |
| to understand | tǔng (11) | 懂 |
| not to understand | pù tǔng | 不懂 |

| | | |
|---|---|---|
| do you understand or not? | tŭng-pu-tung(12)? | 懂不懂 |
| to know how to, to be able | huì | 會 |
| cannot | pú huì | 不會 |
| are [you] able to ... or not (do you know how to ..)? | huì-pu-hui? | 會不會 |
| to learn, to study | hsüéh | 學 |
| student | hsüéh-shêng(13) [kè] (14) | 學生 |
| correct, right (see also page 24) | tuì | 對 |
| incorrect; it is not right | pú tuì | 不對 |
| Is it correct or not? Is it so? | tuì-pu-tui? | 對不對 |

2. Sentences

1. May I ask, what is your honorable country?
   Ch'ĭng wèn, kuèi kuó shìh nă kuó?
   請 問, 貴 國 是 那 國?
2. My humble country is America.
   Pì kuó shìh Mĕi-kuo.
   敝 國 是 美 國.
3. My humble country is England.
   Pì kuó shìh Yīng-kuo.
   敝 國 是 英 國.
4. What is your nationality? I am an American.
   Nĭ shìh nă kuó jén? Wŏ shìh Mĕi-kuo jén.
   你 是 那 國 人? 我 是 美 國 人.
5. What is his nationality? He is a Chinese.
   T'ā shìh nă kuó jén? T'ā shìh Chūng-kuo jén.
   他 是 那 國 人? 他 是 中 國 人.
6. He and I are both Chinese.
   Wŏ kēn t'ā tōu shìh Chūng-kuo jén.
   我 跟 他 都 是 中 國 人.
7. May I ask, can you speak Chinese?
   Ch'ĭng wèn, nĭ huì shuō Chūng-kuo-huà ma?
   請 問, 你 會 說 中 國 話 嗎?

8. I can speak Chinese. I can speak a little.

Wǒ hùi shuō Chūng-kuo-huà. Wǒ hùi shuō ì-tiěn-êrh.

我會說中國話. 我會說一點兒.

9. Please speak Chinese.

Ch'íng ni shuō Chūng-kuo-huà.

請你說中國話.

10. Is what I said correct?

Wǒ shuō-tê(15) tùi-pu-tui?

我說的 對不對?

11. What you said is correct. What you said is not very correct.

Nǐ shuō-tê tùi. Nǐ shuō-tê pù hěn tùi.

你說的對. 你說的不很對.

12. Does he understand Chinese? Does he understand Chinese or not?

T'ā tǔng Chūng-kuo huà ma? T'ā tǔng-pu-tung Chūng-kuo-huà?

他懂中國話嗎? 他懂不懂中國話?

13. He does not understand Chinese.

T'ā pù tǔng Chūng-kuo-huà.

他不懂中國話.

14. Are you a student?

Nǐ shìh hsüéh-shêng(16) ma?

你是學生嗎?

15. I am a student.

Wǒ shìh hsüéh-shêng.

我是學生.

16. What are you studying?

Nǐ hsüéh shén-mo?

你學甚麼?

17. I am studying Chinese.

Wǒ hsüéh Chūng-wén.

我學中文.

18. Do you have a Chinese teacher?

Ní yǔ Chūng-wén hsiēn-shêng(17) ma?

你有中文先生嗎?

19. Do you have a Chinese teacher or not?

Ní yǔ Chūng-wén hsiēn-shêng méi-yu?

你有中文先生沒有?

20. I have. I have none.

Wó yǔ. Wǒ méi-yǔ.

我有. 我沒有.

21. Who is your Chinese teacher?

Shuí shìh nǐ - tê Chūng-wến hsiēn-shêng?

誰是你的中文先生?

(Or) Nǐ - tê Chūng-wến hsiēn-shêng shìh shuí? (18)

你的中文先生是誰?

22. Mr. Li is my Chinese teacher.

Lǐ hsiēn-shêng shìh wǒ - tê Chūng-wến hsiēn-shêng.

李先生 是我的中文先生.

23. Can Mr. Li speak English?

Lǐ hsiēn-shêng huì shuō Yīng-wến ma?

李先生會說英文嗎?

24. Mr. Li cannot speak English.

Lǐ hsiēn-shêng pú huì shuō Yīng-wến.

李先生不會說英文.

25. He can speak a little French.

T'ā huì shuō ì - tiěn-êrh Fà - wến.

他會說一點兒法文.

3. Tone and Pronunciation Drill

| | | | | | | | |
|---|---|---|---|---|---|---|---|
| ēֽrh | érh | ěrh | èrh | hsüēh | hsüéh | hsüěh | hsüèh |
| nā | ná | nǎ | nà | huā | huá | huǎ | huà |
| yīng | yíng | yǐng | yìng | huī | huí | huǐ | huì |
| yū | yú | yǔ | yù | tiēn | tién | tiěn | tièn |
| shuō | shuó | shuǒ | shuò | tūng | túng | tǔng | tùng |

4. Exercises

a. "Fill-in" sentences

[In this exercise, if the students' vocabulary is limited, they may use some English words to make up a sentence. As soon as possible, however, they should speak in Chinese entirely. The most important thing is for the students to become familiar with the sentence construction and to learn to think in Chinese. The blanks may be filled in with single words or phrases.]

1. Nǐ huì (verb ... object) ... ma? — Can you ... ... ?

2. Wǒ pú huì ... ... — I cannot ... ...

3. Wǒ shih (country) ... ... jến. — I am a ... (man).

4. Ní tǔng (language) ... ... ma? — Do you understand ... ?

5. Ní tǔng-pu-tung (language) ... ... ? — Do you understand ... ?

6. Ní yǔ ... méi-yǔ? — Do you have ... (or not)?

b. Translate into English:

1. Kuèi kuó shìh năi kuó? Pì kuó shìh Měi-kuo.
2. Wáng hsiēn-shêng pú huì shuō Fà-wến.
3. Wáng hsiēn-shêng tǔng Chūng-kuo-huà.
4. Lǐ t'ài-t'ai pù tǔng Fà-kuo-huà.
5. Ch'ǐng wền, nǐ shìh nă kuó jến?
6. Wǒ shìh Yīng-kuo jến.
7. Ní tǔng Yīng-wến pù tǔng?
8. Wǒ pú huì shuō, wó tǔng ì-tiěn-êrh.
9. T'ā shuō shến-mo huà?
10. Nǐ shìh Fà-kuo jến ma?

c. Translate into Chinese:

1. I am an American. Mr. Li, please speak English.
2. I cannot speak English.
3. He understands Chinese.
4. May I ask, what is his nationality?
5. Miss Wang, do you understand English?
6. Can you or can you not speak Chinese?
7. This is the United States, this is not England.
8. He cannot speak; I can speak a little.
9. My name is Wang, my teacher's name is Li.
10. He can speak English, French, and Chinese.

NOTES:

(1) "Nă" is sometimes pronounced "năi". This pronunciation is a contraction of "nă i" 那一 "which one". Sometimes, especially in Peking, it is pronounced "něi".

(2) When "yǔ" is preceded by a subject, it is translated by "to have"; when it is used impersonally without antecedent in a sentence, it is translated "there is" or "there are".

(3) "Méi-yǔ" denotes completion or past tense. Note that one should never say "pù yǔ" instead of "méi-yǔ".

(4) "Yīng" is an approximate transliteration of the first syllable of "England". This word is seldom used alone.

(5) "Yīng-wén" is the idiomatic Chinese expression for the English language, whether written or spoken, and whether used by English people or Americans. Likewise, the Chinese expression for French, German, etc., can mean either spoken or written language. But "Chūng-kuo-huà" means the Chinese spoken language only, and "Chūng-wén" the Chinese written language, because these are quite different from each other.

(6) "Fà" is the abbreviated form of the approximate transliteration of "France". "Fǎ" 法, used alone, means "method" or "law".

(7) "Shuō-huà" is a verb-noun phrase. "Huà" is the usual object of "shuō". When "shuō" has another object in a sentence, "huà" should be omitted. For example: "Nǐ huì shuō Yīng-wén ma?" - not "Nǐ huì shuō-huà Yīng-wén ma?" for "Do you speak English?" "Shuō", "to speak, to say", is used as a transitive verb; "shuō-huà", which contains its own object, is used as English uses "to speak, to talk", intransitively. There are many other verb-noun phrases like this.

(8) "Ī" is pronounced with the first tone when it is used alone, in the second before fourth-tone words, and in the fourth before other tones.

(9) The original meaning of "érh" is "a child", but it is seldom used alone in conversational Chinese. It is extensively employed in Peking dialect as a suffix to substantives. Used in this way it is pronounced very lightly, as "rh", and is used chiefly for euphonic reasons, or to convert the category of the substantive to a smaller or younger one, like the "let" in "brooklet", or the "lein" in German "Fräulein".

(10) "Ì-tiěn-êrh" is a very common expression in the Chinese spoken language. It means "a little" or "slightly", and it usually precedes the noun it modifies. For example, "I can speak a little Chinese" or "I understand English a little" should be expressed as "Wǒ huì shuō ì-tiěn-êrh Chūng-kuo-huà" or "Wó tǔng ì-tiěn-êrh Yīng-wén", rather than "Wǒ huì shuō Chūng-kuo-huà ì-tiěn-êrh", "Wó tǔng Yīng-wén ì-tiěn-êrh". When "ì-tiěn-êrh" is used at the end of a sentence, it may either be an object of a verb, or it may indicate the comparative degree of an adjective or adverb, with the sense of "a little more".

(11) "Tǔng" - "to understand" seldom takes auxiliaries. The expression "huì tǔng" is used only in certain exceptional circumstances.

(12) "Tǔng-pu-tung" - "understand-not-understand", i.e., "do you understand or not?", exemplifies the method of forming a question already commented upon in Lesson 4, note 4. Repetition of the important verb or adjective (as in "hǎo-pu-hao" - "is it good or not?") in such questions adds emphasis and helps to avoid misunderstanding.

(13) "Hsüéh-shêng" means a student or a pupil in a school. "Shěng" is sometimes used alone by a student to refer to himself in writing

a letter to a teacher. It is also used as a suffix indicating profession.

(14) Beginning with Lesson 8, a numerative is to be introduced after each new noun, so that the student can learn to use the idiomatic numerative with the noun, as a student of French learns the proper article with each new French noun.

(15) Here "tê" may be translated as a relative pronoun meaning "that which" or "what", and "Wǒ shuō-tê" as "that which I said" or "what I said". Or, "tê" can be considered as equivalent to the English suffix "-ing", and "Wǒ shuō-tê" may be translated "my speaking".

(16) The indefinite article, except for specific or emphatic purposes, is omitted in Chinese. In English it is necessary to say "Are you <u>a</u> student?" In Chinese when it is understood that the reference is to only one person, it is unnecessary and unidiomatic to say "í-kê hsüéh-shêng" - "a student" or "one student" in such a sentence as "Nǐ shìh hsüéh-shêng ma?", which means literally "You are student eh?" The answer also is simply "Wǒ shìh hsüéh-shêng" - "I am student".

(17) In this sentence, as explained in the previous note, one would not say "í-kê hsiēn-shêng" - "a teacher" or "one teacher", unless it is desired to specify that it is a question of only one teacher and no more.

(18) The Position of "Shuí"

There is a difference in emphasis between these two sentences. In the first, the emphasis is on "shuí"; the questioner takes for granted the existence of a teacher but wishes to identify him exactly. In the second, the emphasis is on "hsiēn-shêng"; the speaker wishes to learn which one among several possible persons is the teacher in question. Thus the interrogative pronoun is placed at the beginning of the question when the subject is undetermined, and at the end when the subject is determined.

## Lesson 6 Review

### 1. Useful Phrases and Word Combinations

| | | |
|---|---|---|
| 1. I am | Wǒ shìh | 我是 |
| 2. You are | Nǐ shìh | 你是 |
| 3. He is | T'ā shìh | 他是 |
| 4. We are | Wǒ-mên shìh | 我們是 |
| 5. You are | Nǐ-mên shìh | 你們是 |
| 6. They are | T'ā-mên shìh | 他們是 |
| 7. Is it right or not? | Shìh-pu-shih? | 是不是? |
| 8. It is, yes | Shìh | 是 |
| 9. Yes indeed | Shìh-tê | 是的 |
| 10. It is not, no | Pú shìh | 不是 |

| | | |
|---|---|---|
| 11. Quite so, very true | Hěn shìh | 很是 |
| 12. What is it? | Shìh shén-mo? | 是甚麼? |
| 13. I have | Wó yǔ | 我有 |
| 14. You have | Ní yǔ | 你有 |
| 15. He has | T'ā yǔ | 他有 |
| 16. We have | Wǒ-mên yǔ | 我們有 |
| 17. You have | Nǐ-mên yǔ | 你們有 |
| 18. They have | T'ā-mên yǔ | 他們有 |
| 19. Is there (are there) or not? | Yǔ-mei-yu? | 有沒有? |
| 20. [I, they] have, there is | Yǔ | 有 |
| 21. There is (more emphatic) | Yǔ-tê | 有的 |
| 22. There is not, I have not | Méi-yǔ | 沒有 |
| 23. What is there? What [do you] have? | Yǔ shén-mo? | 有甚麼? |
| 24. There is nothing, [I] have nothing | Méi-yǔ shén-mo | 沒有甚麼 |
| 25. What friend(s) have you? | Ní yǔ shén-mo p'éng-yu? | 你有甚麼朋友? |
| 26. I have one good friend | Wó yǔ í-kê hǎo p'éng-yu | 我有一個好朋友 |
| 27. What do you say? | Ní shuō shén-mo? | 你說甚麼? |
| 28. I didn't say anything | Wǒ méi shuō shén-mo | 我沒說甚麼 |
| 29. Who is it? | Shén-mo jén? | 甚麼人? |
| 30. What talk! Bosh! | Shén-mo huà! | 甚麼話! |
| 31. Is it right? Is it so? Does it agree? | Tùi-pu-tui? | 對不對? |
| 32. It is so, it agrees | Tùi, or Tùi-tê | 對　對的 |
| 33. It is not right, it does not agree | Pú tùi | 不對 |

| | | |
|---|---|---|
| 34. Quite so, very true | Hěn tuì | 很對 |
| 35. Not very correct | Pù hěn tuì | 不很對 |
| 36. Very wrong | Hěn pú tuì | 很不對 |
| 37. This is very right | Chè-kê hěn tuì | 這個很對 |
| 38. That is not very correct | Nà-kê pù hěn tuì | 那個不很對 |
| 39. Guest | K'è-jên | 客人 |
| 40. Courteous expression | K'è-ch'i huà | 客氣話 |
| 41. You are too polite | Nǐ t'ài k'è-ch'i lê | 你太客氣了 |
| 42. I am not polite at all | Wǒ í-tiěn-êrh pú k'è-ch'i | 我一點兒不客氣 |
| 43. This person | Chè-kê jén | 這個人 |
| 44. That person | Nà-kê jén | 那個人 |
| 45. Which person? | Nǎi-kê jén? | 那個人? |
| 46. This is very good | Chê-kê hén hǎo | 這個很好 |
| 47. That is not very good | Nà-kê pù hén hǎo | 那個不很好 |
| 48. I am a student | Wǒ shìh hsüéh-shêng | 我是學生 |
| 49. You are a teacher | Nǐ shìh hsiēn-shêng | 你是先生 |
| 50. I am about to go | Wǒ yào tsǒu lê | 我要走了 |
| 51. You needn't go; sit down for a while | Ni pú yào tsǒu; tsò-i-tso (1) | 你不要走,坐一坐. |
| 52. I want to speak Chinese, I don't want to speak French and English | Wǒ yào shuō Chūng-kuo-huà, wǒ pú yào shuō Fà-wén kěn Yīng-wén | 我要說中國話,我不要說法文跟英文 |
| 53. I have no Chinese books | Wǒ méi-yǔ Chūng-kuo shū | 我沒有中國書 |
| 54. Learn well, learn how to | Hsüéh huì | 學會 |

55. Not learn well — Méi hsüéh huì — 沒學會

56. Cannot learn well — Hsüéh pú huì — 學不會

57. I do not know how to do this — Chè-kê wǒ pú huì — 這個我不會

NOTE:

(1) "Tsò-i-tso", literally, "sit a sit", is used to mean "sit for a while". The repetition serves for emphasis and euphony.

2. Translate into English:

1. Wǒ, nǐ, t'ā.
我,你,他.
2. Hěn hǎo.
很 好
3. Wó hěn hǎo, hsièh-hsieh.
我 很 好, 謝 謝.
4. Ní hǎo ma?
你 好 嗎?
5. Ni kuèi hsìng?
你 貴 姓?
6. Pì hsìng Li. Nǐ kuèi hsìng?
敝 姓 李. 你 貴 姓?
7. Pì hsìng Wáng. Lǐ hsiēn-shēng ch'ǐng tsò.
敝 姓 王. 李 先 生 請 坐.
8. Wáng t'ài-t'ai, ch'ǐng tsò.
王 太 太, 請 坐.
9. Hsièh-hsieh.
謝 謝.
10. Lǐ hsiēn-shēng, chè shìh shén - mo? Nà shìh shén - mo?
李 先 生, 這 是 甚 麼? 那 是 甚 麼?
11. Wáng hsiēn-shēng, tuì pu ch'ǐ, wǒ pù tǔng.
王 先 生, 對 不 起, 我 不 懂.
12. Pú k'è-ch'i.
不 客 氣.
13. Lǐ hsiēn-shēng, kuèi kuó shìh nǎ kuó?
李 先 生, 貴 國 是 那 國?
14. Pì kuó shìh Měi-kuo.
敝 國 是 美 國.

15. Lǐ t'ài-t'ai shìh nǎ kuó jén?
李太太是那國人?
16. T'ā shìh Yīng-kuo jén.
他是英國人.
17. Ch'ǐng wèn, nǐ - tê p'éng - yu kuèi hsìng?
請問,你的朋友貴姓?
18. Tuì pu ch'ǐ, chè shìh Wáng hsiáo-chieh.
對不起,這是王小姐.
19. Wáng hsiáo-chieh, ní ch'ǐng tsò.
王小姐,你請坐.
20. Hsièh-hsieh, pú k'è-ch'i.
謝謝,不客氣.
21. Wáng hsiáo-chieh, nǐ huì shuō Yīng-wén ma?
王小姐,你會說英文嗎?
22. Lǐ hsiēn-shêng, tuì pu ch'ǐ, wǒ pú huì shuō Yīng-wén.
李先生,對不起,我不會說英文.
23. Pú k'è-ch'i, wó yěh pú huì shuō Yīng-wén.
不客氣,我也不會說英文.
24. T'ā shìh nǐ - tê Měi-kuo p'éng - yu ma?
他是你的美國朋友嗎?
25. Pū, t'ā shìh Yīng-kuo jén.
不,他是英國人.
26. T'ā huì shuō Yīng-wén, yěh huì shuō Chūng-kuo-huà.
他會說英文,也會說中國話.
27. Ní tǔng - pu - tung Chūng-kuo-huà?
你懂不懂中國話?
28. Wǒ pù tǔng. Tuì pu ch'ǐ.
我不懂.對不起.
29. Shuí huì shuō Yīng-wén?
誰會說英文?
30. Wǒ - mên tōu huì shuō ì - tiěn-êrh.
我們都會說一點兒.
31. Wǒ - mên shìh hsüéh-shêng, t'ā-mên yěh shìh hsüéh-shêng.
我們是學生,他們也是學生.
32. Wǒ kēn nǐ shìh hǎo p'éng - yu.
我跟你是好朋友.
33. Wǒ - mên tōu shìh hǎo p'éng - yu.
我們都是好朋友.

34. <u>Tsài</u> chièn, <u>tsài</u> chièn.
再見，再見。

3. Translate into Chinese:

[The instructor may wish to have the students write out only a part of these sentences, while the rest are demonstrated orally in class.]

1. What is this?
2. Is this yours?
3. What is your (honorable) name?
4. May I ask, what is your (honorable) country?
5. My (humble) country is China.
6. I am [an] American.
7. I can speak Chinese and English.
8. He does not understand Chinese.
9. I understand a little.
10. Can you or can you not speak Chinese?
11. I can speak a little.
12. We are all friends, because* our friends are yours, your friends are ours.
13. Who is your wife?
14. Is their teacher good?
15. He is very good.
16. He is not very good.
17. Do you (or not) understand Chinese?
18. We all understand Chinese and English.
19. Do you say he is not a good man?
20. No, he is very good.
21. You (plural), we, and they are all good students.
22. You and I are Americans.
23. I ask him to sit down.
24. I am also his friend.
25. I can speak French; I cannot speak Chinese.
26. What you say is very good.
27. I have learned English well.
28. I have not learned French well.

*Yīn-wèi, see p. 55.

CONVERSATIONAL CHINESE

## PART II NUMBERS AND DIVISIONS OF TIME

### Lesson 7 Numbers

1. Vocabulary

| | | |
|---|---|---|
| 二 | èrh | Two, second. |
| 兩 | liǎng (1) | Two, both. |
| 三 | sān | Three. |
| 四 | ssǔ | Four. |
| 五 | wǔ | Five. |
| 六 | liù | Six. |
| 七 | ch'ī (2) | Seven. |
| 八 | pā (3) | Eight. |
| 九 | chiǔ | Nine. |
| 十 | shíh | Ten. |
| 百 | pǎi | Hundred. All. |
| 千 | ch'iēn | Thousand. |
| 萬 | wàn | Ten thousand, myriad. |
| 零 | líng | Zero. Remainder. |
| 十一 | shíh-ī | Eleven. |
| 十二 | shíh-èrh | Twelve. |
| 十三 | shíh-sān | Thirteen. |
| 十四 | shíh-ssǔ | Fourteen. |
| 十五 | shíh-wǔ | Fifteen. |
| 二十 | èrh-shíh | Twenty. |
| 二十一 | èrh-shíh-ī | Twenty-one. |
| 二十二 | èrh-shíh-èrh | Twenty-two. |
| 三十 | sān-shíh | Thirty. |
| 一百 | ì-pǎi | A hundred. |
| 一千 | ì-ch'iēn | A thousand. |
| 一萬 | í-wàn | A myriad, ten thousand. |
| 一百萬 | ì-pǎi-wàn | One million. |

| | | |
|---|---|---|
| 一百零一 | ì-păi-líng-ī (4) | A hundred and one. |
| 第 | tì (5) | Number, order, series. |
| 第一 | tì-ī | The first. |
| 第二 | tì-èrh | The second. |
| 第四十五 | tì-ssù-shíh-wǔ | The forty-fifth. |
| 班 | pān (6) | Class. |
| 多 | tō | Many, much, how. |
| 少 | shǎo | Few. |
| 多少 | tō-shǎo | How much, how many. |
| 太多 | t'ài tō | Too much, too many. |
| 太少 | t'ài shǎo | Too little, too few. |

2. Sentences

1. How many people are there in this class?
   Chè - ì pān yǔ tō - shǎo jén?
   這 一 班 有 多 少 人?
2. There are fifty people in this class.
   Chè - ì pān yú wǔ - shíh - kè jén.
   這 一 班 有 五 十 個 人.
3. How many people are there in that class?
   Nà - ì pān yǔ tō - shǎo jén?
   那 一 班 有 多 少 人?
4. There are thirty-eight people in that class.
   Nà - ì pān yǔ sān-shíh - pá - kè jén.
   那 一 班 有 三 十 八 個 人.
5. Who is the first? Who is the second?
   Shuí tì - ī? Shuí tì - èrh?
   誰 第 一? 誰 第 二?
6. He is the first, that student is the second.
   T'ā tì - ī, nà - kê hsüéh-shêng tì - èrh.
   他 第 一, 那 個 學 生 第 二、
7. How many friends have you?
   Ní yǔ tō - shǎo p'éng - yu?
   你 有 多 少 朋 友?

8. I have a hundred friends.

Wó yǔ ì - pǎi - kè p'éng - yu.

我有一百個朋友.

9. Are they all Chinese?

T'ā-mên tōu shìh Chūng-kuo-jén ma?

他們都是中國人嗎?

10. No, there are fifty [who] are Chinese, there are forty [who]

Pū, yú wǔ - shíh - kè shìh Chūng-kuo-jén, yǔ ssǔ-shíh - kè

不,有五十個是中國人,有四十個

are Americans, [and] ten [who] are Englishmen.

shìh Měi-kuo jén, yǔ shíh - kè shìh Yīng-kuo jén.

是美國人,有十個是英國人.

11. Your friends are too many; my friends are too few.

Nǐ - tê p'éng - yu t'ài tō; wǒ - tê p'éng - yu t'ài shǎo.

你的朋友太多,我的朋友太少.

12. His friends are neither many nor few.

T'ā - tê p'éng - yu pù tō yěh pù shǎo. (7)

他的朋友不多也不少.

3. Drill

a. Tone and pronunciation

| | | | | | | | |
|---|---|---|---|---|---|---|---|
| ērh | érh | ěrh | èrh | sān | sán | sǎn | sàn |
| ch'ī | ch'í | ch'ǐ | ch'ì | ssū | ssú | ssǔ | ssù |
| shīh | shíh | shǐh | shìh | chiū | chiú | chiǔ | chiù |
| liāng | liáng | liǎng | liàng | ch'iēn | ch'ién | ch'iěn | ch'ièn |
| yū | yú | yǔ | yù | yǖ | yǘ | yǚ | yǜ |

b. Numerals

í wàn ì ch'iēn ì pǎi ì shíh ī

èrh wàn èrh ch'iēn èrh pǎi èrh shíh èrh

sān wàn sān ch'iēn sān pǎi sān shíh sān

ssǔ wàn ssǔ ch'iēn ssǔ pǎi ssǔ shíh ssǔ

wǔ wàn wǔ ch'iēn wú pǎi wǔ shíh wǔ

liù wàn liù ch'iēn liù pǎi liù shíh liù

ch'í wàn ch'ī ch'iēn ch'ī păi ch'ī shíh ch'ī

pá wàn pā ch'iēn pā păi pā shíh pā

chiŭ wàn chiŭ ch'iēn chiú pái chiŭ shíh chiŭ

4. Exercises

a. "Fill-in" sentences

| | |
|---|---|
| 1. Wó yŭ ... ... | I have ... ... |
| 2. Chè-ì pān shìh (number) ... ... pān. | This class is ... ... class. |
| 3. Ní yŭ ... ... ... ma? | Have you (books, friends, etc.) ... ... ...? |
| 4. Ní yŭ tō-shăo ... ... ? | How many ... ... have you? |
| 5. Wŏ-tê ... ... t'ài tō. | I have too many ... ... |

b. Translate into English:

1. Wáng hsiēn-shêng yŭ sān-kê Mĕi-kuo hsüéh-shêng.
2. Chè ssù-păi jén tōu shìh Chūng-kuo hsüéh-shêng.
3. Nă pān yŭ liù-shíh-kè jén?
4. Nĭ-mên-tê pān yŭ ch'í-kè Yīng-kuo jén.
5. Năi-kê Mĕi-kuo jén huì shuō Chūng-kuo-huà?
6. Tō-pu-to?
7. Pù tō.
8. Wó yŭ ch'í-kè k'è-jên.
9. Ní yŭ tō-shăo?
10. Méi-yú hĕn tō.

c. Translate into Chinese:

1. Does France have forty million people?
2. Which two students can speak French?
3. Which ten Americans understand Chinese?
4. Miss Li has five friends.
5. Are her friends too many?
6. Is this a Chinese class?

7. There are one hundred and two students.

8. We are all Americans.

9. Who is the first in this class?

NOTES:

(1) Both "èrh" and "liăng" mean "two", but they are not used interchangeably. "Èrh" is used chiefly (a) as the regular cardinal number, without numeratives, (b) in the ordinal number "tì-èrh" - "second", (c) as the last digit in numbers larger than ten ("sān-shíh-èrh" - "32"). "Liăng" is used chiefly (a) with nouns preceded by numeratives ("liăng-kê jén" - "two men"), (b) before the larger units of weight, measure, capacity, and time.

(2) and (3) Both "ch'ī" and "pā", like "ī", change to the second tone when pronounced immediately before a word in the fourth tone.

(4) "Líng" is used to express zero in numbers, as "san-păi-líng-ī" - "301". Sometimes "líng" stands for more than one zero, as in "sān-ch'iēn-líng-ī" - "3001"; however, if the figures are read separately, where an American would say "three-0-0-one", a Chinese would say "sān-líng-líng-ī". "Líng" is also used in conjunction with expressions of time, as "liăng-kê yüèh líng sān t'iēn" - "two months and three days".

(5) "Tì", placed before a numeral, forms the corresponding ordinal number. "Tì-ī" may mean "number one", "the first", or "the best".

(6) "Pān" is itself a numerative, as in "ì-pān jén" - "one class of men", "liăng-pān jén" - "two classes of men", "liăng-pān hsüéh-shêng" - "two classes of students". One should not use another numerative with it; to say "í-kê pān" or "liăng-kê pān" would be incorrect.

(7) When "pū" precedes each of two adjectives which are antonyms, as in "pù tō pù shăo" or "pù tō yĕh pù shăo", it indicates the medium between them. More examples will be given later, when we have a larger vocabulary.

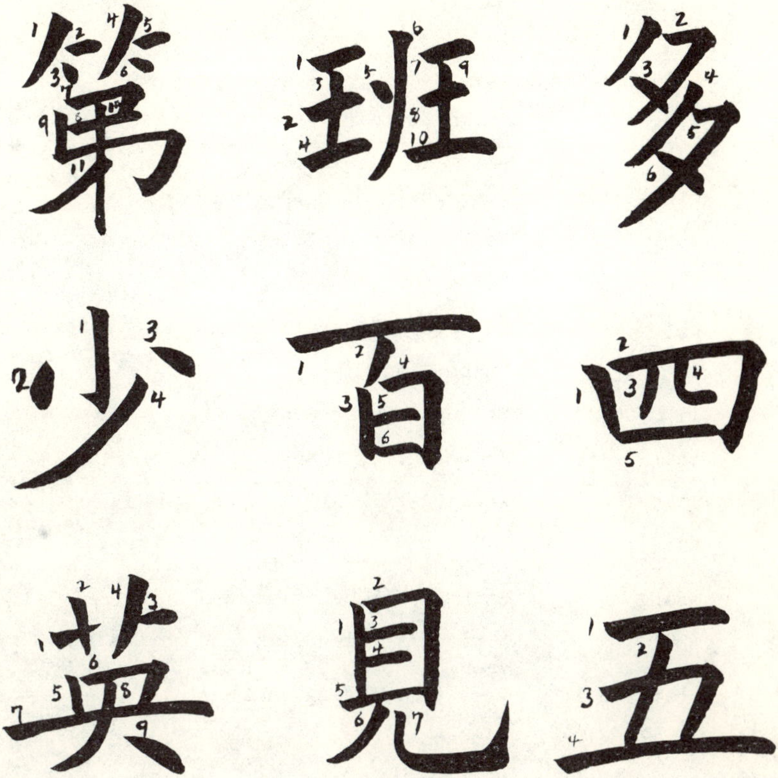


## Lesson 8 Week and Month

1. Vocabulary

| | | |
|---|---|---|
| 年 | nién | Year [ì nién, liăng nién]. |
| 月 | yüèh (1) | Moon, month [í-kê yüèh, liăng-kê yüèh]. |
| 日 | jìh | Sun, day [í jìh, liăng jìh]. |
| 天 | t'iēn (2) | Sky, day [ì t'iēn, liăng t'iēn]. |
| 今 | chīn | The present, now. Recent. [Used as independent word only in literary style*.] A prefix used with words meaning "year" and "day" to signify "this year", "today". |

*Hereafter abbreviated "lit."

| | | |
|---|---|---|
| 今天 | chīn-t'ien | Today. |
| 昨 | tsó | The previous ... Recently [lit.]. |
| 昨天 | tsó-t'ien | Yesterday. |
| 明 | míng | Bright, clear. A prefix used with words meaning "year" and "day" to signify "next year" and "tomorrow". |
| 明天 | míng-t'ien | Tomorrow. |
| 後 | hòu | Behind, after, late. Future. |
| 後天 | hòu-t'ien | Day after tomorrow. |
| 幾 | chǐ | How many? Several, odd (as in "twenty-odd"). |
| 號 | hào | Number, sign, day. |
| 禮 | lǐ | Etiquette, ceremony. |
| 拜 | pài | To worship, to bow, to pay respect to. |
| 禮拜 | lǐ-pài | Week [í-kê lǐ-pài]. |
| 顆 | k'ē̂ | Small round thing. A numerative of stars, pearls, grains of sand, etc. |
| 星 | hsīng | Star [ì-k'ē̂ hsīng or í-kê hsīng]. |
| 期 | ch'í | A period, fixed time. A term of the school year. |
| 星期 | hsīng-ch'í(3) | Week [í-kê hsīng-ch'í]. |
| 禮拜日 | lǐ-pài-jìh | Sunday. |
| 禮拜一 | lǐ-pài-ī | Monday. |
| 禮拜二 | lǐ-pài-èrh | Tuesday. |
| 禮拜三 | lǐ-pài-sān | Wednesday. |
| 禮拜四 | lǐ-pài-ssǜ | Thursday. |
| 禮拜五 | lǐ-pài-wǔ | Friday. |
| 禮拜六 | lǐ-pài-liù | Saturday. |
| 正 | chèng | Correct, orthodox. Just, exactly. |
| 正月 | chēng-yüeh(4) | January. |
| 一月 | í-yüèh (5) | January. |
| 二月 | èrh-yüèh | February. |
| 三月 | sān-yüèh | March. |

四月 ssŭ-yüèh April.

十二月 shíh-èrh-yüèh December.

來 lái To come. Future. About.

去 ch'ù (6) To go to. Past, last.

看 k'àn To see, to read, to consider.

2. Sentences

1. How many months are there in a year?

   Ì nién yú chǐ-kê yüèh?

   一年有幾個月?

2. How many weeks are there in a month?

   Í-kê yüèh yú chǐ-kê lǐ-pài?

   一個月有幾個禮拜?

3. How many days are there in a week?

   Í-kê lǐ-pài yú chǐ t'iēn?

   一個禮拜有幾天?

4. How many days are there in a year?

   Ì nién yŭ tō-shǎo(7) t'iēn?

   一年有多少天?

5. A year has three hundred sixty-five days.

   Ì nién yŭ sān-pǎi liù-shíh-wŭ t'iēn.

   一年有三百六十五天.

6. What day of the week is this?

   Chīn-t'ien shìh lǐ-pài chǐ(8)?

   今天是禮拜幾?

7. Today is Monday.

   Chīn-t'ien shìh lǐ-pài-ī.

   今天是禮拜一.

8. What day is today?

   Chīn-t'ien shìh nǎ-i t'iēn(9)?

   今天是那一天?

9. Today is August fifteenth.

   Chīn-t'ien shìh pá-yüèh shíh-wŭ(10).

   今天是八月十五.

10. Yesterday was August fourteenth.

    Tsó-t'ien shìh pá-yüèh shíh-ssŭ.

    昨天是八月十四.

11. Tomorrow is Tuesday. Day after tomorrow is Wednesday.
Míng-t'ien shìh lǐ-pài-èrh. Hòu-t'ien shìh lǐ-pài-sān.
明天是禮拜二. 後天是禮拜三.

12. Thursday I shall go to see friends.
Lǐ-pài-ssù wǒ yào(11) ch'ü k'àn p'éng-yu.
禮拜四我要去看朋友.

13. On Friday, I shall have some friends coming to see me.
Lǐ-pài-wǔ, wó yǔ p'éng-yu yào lái k'àn wo.
禮拜五, 我有朋友要來看我.

14. January sixth is Saturday.
Chēng-yüeh liù-jìh (or, liù-hào) shìh hsīng-ch'í-liù.
正月六日 (六號) 是星期六.

15. On that day I shall go to China.
Nà-t'iēn wǒ yào ch'ǜ Chūng-kuo.
那天我要去中國.

16. You came just on time. I just want to talk to you.
Nǐ lái-tê chèng hǎo. Wǒ chèng yào kēn nǐ shuō-huà.
你來的正好. 我正要跟你說話.

17. Well then, see you tomorrow. See you again on Wednesday.
Hǎo-lê(12), míng-t'ien chièn. Hsīng-ch'í-sān(13) tsài chièn.
好了. 明天見. 星期三 再見.

3. Tone and Pronunciation Drill

[Particular attention should be paid to the pronunciation of "jih" and "jên", which forms a most important criterion for judgment of the pronunciation of a foreign speaker of Chinese.]

| | | | | | | | |
|---|---|---|---|---|---|---|---|
| chī | chí | chǐ | chì | jīh | jíh | jǐh | jìh |
| ch'ī | ch'í | ch'ǐ | ch'ì | jēn | jén | jěn | jèn |
| ch'ǖ | ch'ǘ | ch'ǚ | ch'ǜ | ssū | ssú | ssǔ | ssù |
| hsīng | hsíng | hsǐng | hsìng | t'iēn | t'ién | t'iěn | t'ièn |
| hāo | háo | hǎo | hào | yüēh | yüéh | yüěh | yüèh |
| hōu | hóu | hǒu | hòu | wū | wú | wǔ | wù |

4. Exercises

a. "Fill-in" sentences

1. Chīn-t'ien shìh ... ... Today is ... ...
2. Tsó-t'ien shìh ... ... Yesterday was ... ...

| | |
|---|---|
| 3. T'ā ... k'àn ni ma? | Is he ... to see you? |
| 4. Nǐ ... k'àn t'a ma? | Are you ... to see him? |
| 5. Wǒ hòu-t'ien ch'ǜ ... | Day after tomorrow I am going ... |
| 6. Í-kê yüèh yǚ ... ... t'iēn. | A month has ... ... days. |
| 7. Lǐ-pài-... shìh ...-yüèh ... | ...day is ... (month) ... (day). |

b. Translate into English:

1. T'ā yú chǐ-kê Měi-kuo p'éng-yu?
2. Lǐ-pài-jìh wǒ ch'ǜ k'àn ni.
3. Míng-t'ien t'ā lái k'àn wo.
4. Nǐ ch'ǜ k'àn Wáng t'ài-t'ai ma?
5. Wó lǐ-pài-sān pù lái.
6. Ní nǎi t'iēn lái?
7. Chè shìh tì-chǐ hào?
8. Chè shìh tì-chiǔ hào.
9. Nǐ yào k'àn shén-mo shū?
10. T'ā-mên méi hsüéh huì Chūng-wén.

c. Translate into Chinese:

1. Who is coming to see me the day after tomorrow?
2. Mr. Wang will come tomorrow.
3. He is not coming today.
4. I asked him; he did not say anything.
5. Where is this group of men going?
6. How many weeks has a month?
7. What he said is exactly correct.
8. The first student is an American.
9. I have studied Chinese for three weeks.
10. He does not understand Chinese, nor does he want to learn it.

NOTES:

(1) Note the idiomatic use of numeratives. It is necessary in

spoken Chinese to say "í-kê yüèh", "liǎng-kê yüèh", "sān-kê yüèh", but a Chinese would never say "í-kê nién", "liǎng-kê nién", "í-kê t'iēn", "liǎng-kê t'iēn", "í-kê jìh", or "liǎng-kê jìh". The omission of "kê" before "nién", "t'iēn", and "jìh" preserves the usage of classical Chinese.

(2) Both "t'iēn" and "jìh" have the meaning "day", but "t'iēn" is commonly used in the spoken language in referring to a number of days and in expressions corresponding to "today" and "tomorrow". "T'iēn" is used as a unit or measure of time, and is never used with a numerative. "Jìh" is the formal word for "day", used in literary style and in documents. In spoken Chinese, "jìh" or "hào" is used to express the day in dates if the number is less than ten: "pá-yüèh wǔ-jìh (or, wǔ-hào)" - "August fifth"; but usually "pá-yüèh shíh-wǔ" - "August fifteenth". "Hào" in place of "jìh" is used especially in dates of the solar calendar as distinguished from the old Chinese lunar calendar.

In Chinese, numbers denoting days of the month do not take the ordinal form (as in English "August fifteen<u>th</u>"), but retain the form of cardinal numbers.

(3) Both "lǐ-pài" and "hsīng-ch'í" mean "week", and they are used in the same way. The former, however, is more common.

(4) It is said that the pronunciation "chēng-yüeh" (instead of "chèng-yüeh") results from an ancient taboo on pronouncing the personal names of emperors. The First Emperor of the Ch'in Dynasty had the syllable "chèng" in his personal name, and the name of the month is said to have been slightly changed to avoid pronouncing this.

(5) "Chēng-yüeh" is usually used in referring to the first month of the lunar calendar, and "í-yüèh" for the first month of the solar year.

(6) It is sometimes difficult to use "lái" and "ch'ü" correctly. Attention should be paid to the fact that "lái" means "to come toward the speaker", and "ch'ǜ", "to go from the speaker". Both "lái" and "ch'ǜ", used alone as the main verb, may indicate either present or future tense, or progressive action.

(7) The Use cf "Tō-shǎo" 多少 and "Chǐ" 幾

When "tō-shǎo" and "chǐ" are used in interrogative sentences, they both generally mean "how many" or "how much". However, "tō-shǎo" may imply an unlimited number, while "chǐ" implies a number less than ten. For example: "Ní yú chǐ-kê p'éng-yu?" implies that the number of friends is less than ten, while "Ní yǔ tō-shǎo p'éng-yu?" implies that the number may be more than ten.

Another difference is that "tō-shǎo" as an interrogative may be used alone or at the end of a sentence without being followed by a numerative. For example:

"Tō-shǎo?" 多少 - "How many?" or "How much?"

"Ní yǔ tō-shǎo?" 你有多少 - "How many (much) have you?"

"Nǐ k'àn lê tō-shǎo?" 你看了多少 - "How many (much) have you read?" or "How many (much) have you seen?"

Besides being used as interrogatives, "tō-shǎo" and "chǐ" are used in affirmative sentences. In such cases, "tō-shǎo" still means "how much, how many", and implies a certain number or amount, while "chǐ" means "several, a few". For example:

"Wǒ méi-yǔ tō-shǎo p'éng-yu" 我沒有多少朋友 - "I do not have many friends".

"Wǒ hsüéh lê chǐ-kê yüèh Chūng-wén" 我學了幾個月中文 - "I studied Chinese for several months".

(8) "Chǐ" in an interrogative sentence also may mean "what?", and does not need any additional question indicator. The position of "chǐ" in an interrogative sentence corresponds to the position of the key word in the expected answer.

"Chǐ" may also indicate a certain number of a series, as of the days of the week or the sons of a family. "Chīn-t'ien shìh lǐ-pài chǐ?" may be considered a simplified form of "Chīn-t'ien shìh chè-kê lǐ-pài-tê tì-chǐ t'iēn?", literally, "Today is number what day of this week?" If one wishes to ask someone's position among his brothers, one may ask: "Nǐ tì-chǐ?" - "You are number what?" The answer may be "Wǒ tì-sān" - "I am number three", i.e., "I am the third [among my brothers or sisters]".

(9) When a Chinese asks "Chīn-t'ien shìh nǎ-i t'iēn?" the expected answer gives the day of the month. When he asks "Chīn-t'ien shìh lǐ-pài chǐ?" the reply should give the day of the week. Students should observe this rule carefully to avoid giving a wrong answer.

(10) In formal written language it is necessary to say "pá-yüèh shíh-wǔ-jìh", but it is more idiomatic and sounds better to omit "jìh" in ordinary colloquial speech.

(11) "Yào" indicates and stresses future tense. It may be omitted in such a sentence as this, and "ch'ǜ" would still have a future meaning because of the context.

(12) "Lê" here has no particular meaning but gives emphasis and euphony, and sounds more polite. If one is in a hurry, he may say simply: "Hǎo, míng-t'ien chièn", with little difference in meaning.

(13) Indications of time, such as "today", "this week", are usually placed at the beginning of the sentence in Chinese, as is illustrated by the sentences in this lesson.

## Lesson 9 The Year and Seasons

1. Vocabulary

前 ch'ién Before, in front. Formerly.

前年 ch'ién-nien Year before last.

去年 ch'ǜ-nien Last year.

今年 chīn-nien This year.

明年 míng-nien Next year.

後年 hòu-nién Year after next.

季 chì Season, quarter of a year, term of a school year.

| | | |
|---|---|---|
| 春 | ch'ūn | Spring. |
| 夏 | hsià | Summer. |
| 秋 | ch'iū | Autumn. |
| 冬 | tūng | Winter. |
| 春天 | ch'ūn-t'ien | Spring, springtime [í-kê ch'ūn-t'ien]. |
| 春季 | ch'ūn-chì (1) | Spring, spring term of a school. |
| 冷 | lěng | Cold. |
| 熱 | jè | Hot. |
| 下 | hsià | Below, under, down. Next. To fall. |
| 天氣 | t'iēn-ch'i | Weather. |
| 因 | yīn | Cause. Because. [Lit.] |
| 爲 | wèi (2) | Because [lit.]. |
| | wéi | To do, to make, to be [lit.]. For, on behalf of. |
| 因爲 | yīn-wèi (3) | Because. |
| 所 | sǒ | Place. That which. A numerative of houses. |
| 以 | ǐ | To use, to consider. According to, with. |
| 所以 | só-ǐ | Therefore, so, accordingly. |
| 華 | huá | Splendor, glory. China. [Lit.] |
| 民 | mín | People, citizens. |
| 中華民國 | Chūng-huá-mín-kuó (4) | The Republic of China. |
| 囘 | huí | A time. To return. |
| 雨 | yǚ | Rain. |
| 雪 | hsüěh | Snow. |
| 常 | ch'áng | Frequently, usually. Common. |

2. Sentences

1. Is the weather fine today?
   Chīn-t'ien t'iēn-ch'i hǎo ma?
   今 天 天 氣 好 嗎?
2. Today the weather is very good.
   Chīn-t'ien t'iēn-ch'i hěn hǎo.
   今 天 天 氣 很 好.

3. Is the weather today hot or cold?
Chīn-t'ien t'iēn-ch'i jè - pu - jê, lěng - pu - lêng?
今天天氣熱不熱，冷不冷？

4. Today the weather is neither cold nor hot.
Chīn-t'ien t'iēn-ch'i pù lěng yěh pú jè(5).
今天天氣不冷也不熱。

5. Are the summers very hot in your honorable country?
Kuèi kuó hsià-t'ien hěn jè ma?
貴國夏天很熱嗎？

6. My humble country is not very hot in the summer; [it is] very cold in winter.
Pì kuó hsià-t'ien pù hěn jè; tūng-t'ien hěn lěng.
敝國夏天不很熱；冬天很冷。

7. Does it often snow in winter?
Tūng-t'ien ch'áng hsià-hsüěh(6) ma?
冬天常下雪嗎？

8. It often snows and rains in winter.
Tūng-t'ien ch'áng hsià-hsüěh, yěh ch'áng hsià-yǚ.
冬天常下雪，也常下雨。

9. Because it snowed yesterday, therefore today is very cold.
Tsó-t'ien yīn-wèi hsià lê(7)hsüěh, só - ǐ chīn-t'ien hěn lěng.
昨天因爲下了雪，所以今天很冷。

10. Are spring and autumn in your honorable country fine?
Kuèi kuó - tê ch'ūn-t'ien kěn ch'iū-t'ien hǎo - pu - hao?
貴國的春天跟秋天好不好？

11. Autumn is very beautiful; in spring it rains often.
Ch'iū-t'ien hěn měi; ch'ūn-t'ien ch'áng hsià - yǚ.
秋天很美，春天常下雨。

12. So, [of] the weather of the four seasons in a year, some is good, some is not very good, is that right?
Só - ǐ ì nién ssǔ chì - tê t'iēn-ch'i, yǔ - tê hǎo(8), yǔ - tê pù hěn hǎo, shìh - pu - shih(9)?
所以一年四季的天氣，有的好，有的不很好，是不是？

13. Yes indeed.
Shìh - tê(10).
是的。

14. Mr. Wang, will you go to China in the fall of this year?
Wáng hsiēn-shēng, nǐ chīn-nien ch'iū-t'ien ch'ù Chūng-kuo ma?
王先生，你今年秋天去中國嗎？

15. I want to go to China in the summer of next year.
Wǒ yào míng-nien hsià-t'ien(11) ch'ù Chūng-kuo.
我要明年夏天　去中國.

16. What day, month, and year is August 15, 1947, in the Republic of China?
Ì - chiǔ-ssǔ-ch'ī(12) nién pá - yüèh shíh - wǔ - jìh(13) shìh Chūng-huá-mín-kuó nǎ - i nién, nǎ - i yüèh, nǎ - i jìh?
一九四七　年八月十五日　是中華民國那一年，那一月，那一日？

17. August 15, 1947, is the fifteenth day of the eighth month of the thirty-sixth year of the Chinese Republic.
Ì - chiǔ-ssǔ-ch'ī nién pá - yüèh shíh - wǔ - jìh shìh Chūng-huá-mín-kuó sān-shíh-liù nién pá - yüèh shíh - wǔ - jìh.
一九四七年八月十五日是中華民國三十六年八月十五日.

18. I went to China at that time; I came back last year.
Wǒ shìh nà t'iēn ch'ù Chūng-kuo tê(14), ch'ù-nien wǒ huí-lai lê.
我是那天去中國的，去年我回來了.

3. Tone and Pronunciation Drill

| | | | | | | | |
|---|---|---|---|---|---|---|---|
| chīn | chín | chǐn | chìn | hsüēh | hsüéh | hsüěh | hsüèh |
| ch'iēn | ch'ién | ch'iěn | ch'ièn | huī | huí | huǐ | huì |
| ch'ūn | ch'ún | ch'ǔn | ch'ùn | jē̂ | jế | jê̌ | jề |
| ch'iū | ch'iú | ch'iǔ | ch'iù | yǖ | yǘ | yǚ | yǜ |
| hsiā | hsiá | hsiǎ | hsià | yū | yú | yǔ | yù |

4. Exercises

a. "Fill-in" sentences

[Note that there is no limit to the number of words which may be used in the blanks in this exercise. Following these patterns, students should try to make as many different sentences as possible, even using an English word occasionally to fill in where the Chinese vocabulary is still inadequate.]

| | | |
|---|---|---|
| 1. | Chīn-t'ien pù ... yěh pù ... | Today is not ... and not ... |
| 2. | Tsó-t'ien ... ... lê. | Yesterday it ... |
| 3. | Yīn-wèi ... só-ǐ ... | Because ... therefore ... |
| 4. | T'ā-mên shuō Měi-kuo-tê t'iēn-ch'i ... ... | They say American weather is ... ... |
| 5. | Yǔ-tê ... ... yǔ-tê ... ... | Some ... ... some ... ... |
| 6. | Ì-chiǔ ... ... nién shìh Chūng-huá-mín-kuó ... ... nién. | The year 19.. is the ... year of the Republic of China. |
| 7. | Ch'ién-nien tūng-t'ien ... ... | The winter before last was ... |
| 8. | T'ā nǎ-i ... lái? | What (year, month, day) ... will he come? |

b. Translate into English:

1. Tūng-t'ien lěng, hsià-t'ien jè, ch'ūn-t'ien, ch'iū-t'ien pù lěng yěh pú jè.
2. Ch'iū-t'ien t'iēn-ch'i hǎo ma?
3. T'ā shuō Měi-kuo-tê t'iēn-ch'i hěn hǎo.
4. Tūng-t'ien hsià-hsüěh; ch'ūn-t'ien hsià-yǔ.
5. T'ā chīn-t'ien lái ma?
6. Ì nién yú chǐ chì? Ná chǐ chì?
7. Ì-chiǔ-wǔ-ì nién shìh mín-kuó nǎ-i nién?
8. Ch'ù-nien hsià-t'ien wǒ hsüéh Fà-wén.
9. Míng-nien Lǐ hsiēn-shêng ch'ù Yīng-kuo.
10. Yǔ-tê hsüéh-shêng shìh Měi-kuo jén, yǔ-tê shìh Chūng-kuo jén.

c. Translate into Chinese:

1. 1949 is the thirty-eighth year of the Chinese Republic.
2. Are you going to China in the fall?
3. It is not very cold in the spring.
4. Which season is very hot?
5. My friend says he is coming this year.
6. Today the weather is not good; I will not go to see her.

7. Because it is snowing, therefore I will not come to see you.

8. Do you often see him?

9. Do you go out* on rainy days?

10. I will come to see you on Sunday.

NOTES:

(1) "Ch'ūn-t'ien", "hsià-t'ien", etc., are more often used in the spoken language; "chì" is used in the written language.

(2) The printed form of 爲 is quite different from its written form 為. In dictionaries it is classified under Key 87 爪.

(3) One of the devices by which the monosyllabic Chinese language is changed to polysyllabic when it is spoken is the joining of two words of similar meaning, for euphony and to avoid misunderstanding. "Yīn-wèi" is a good illustration of this device.

(4) The abbreviated and more common term for the Republic of China is "mín-kuó", "the Republic". Since the republic was established in 1912, the current year of the republic is obtained by subtracting 1911 from the current calendar year. For instance, 1912 was the first year of the republic, 1932 was the twenty-first year of the republic.

(5) Literally, "pù lěng yěh pú jè" means "not cold and not hot", but it is better translated "neither cold nor hot", for the expression "pù ... yěh pù ... " corresponds to the English "neither ... nor ... ".

(6) Literally, "hsià-hsüěh" means "falls snow"; "hsüěh" cannot be used as a verb.

(7) "Lê" here indicates completed action. It is usually used at the end of a sentence, but when there is a subordinate clause, "lê" follows directly after the verb which it modifies.

(8) "Yǔ-tê ... yǔ-tê ... ", literally "there are those who (or, which) ... there are those who ...", means "some ... and some ...". It is used in parallel constructions presenting a contrast. For example: "Yǔ-tê hsüéh-shêng hǎo, yǔ-tê hsüéh-shêng pù hǎo" - "There are students who are good and there are students who are not good", or "Some students are good and some are not good"; "Yǔ-tê tō, yǔ-tê shǎo" - "Some have more, some have less".

(9) "Shìh-pu-shih" - "yes or no?", or "is it so or not?", is almost the same as the French phrase "n'est-ce pas?" at the end of a sentence, turning an affirmative sentence into a question.

(10) "Tê" is used here for emphasis and euphony, without any special meaning. "Shìh-tê" corresponds to the English "yes indeed"; there is no great difference between "shìh" and "shìh-tê" except that the latter sounds a little better and less abrupt.

(11) The Chinese word order usually puts the expression of time first and the subject second if the emphasis is on the time element, or vice versa if the emphasis is on the subject. The indication of time is never placed at the end of the sentence as is commonly done in English. No preposition corresponding to "at",

---

*Ch'ū-ch'ü, see p. 95.

"in", "on" is necessary before expressions of time in Chinese, as is illustrated in a number of sentences in this lesson, including 7, 14, 18.

(12) In Chinese, 1947 is read either as "one thousand, nine hundred, forty-seven year" or as "one nine four seven". Chinese has no expression corresponding to the English "nineteen hundred". Note that in Chinese dates the larger division precedes the smaller, year before month and month before day. In writing addresses, the same principle is followed; the order is: country, province, town, street number.

(13) See Lesson 8, note 10.

(14) "Tê" as a relative pronoun means "the one who, that which". This sentence means literally "I am the one who went to China on that day". This use of "shìh ... tê" is chiefly for emphasis. To make a smooth translation, both words may be disregarded and the sentence rendered simply: "I went to China at that time".

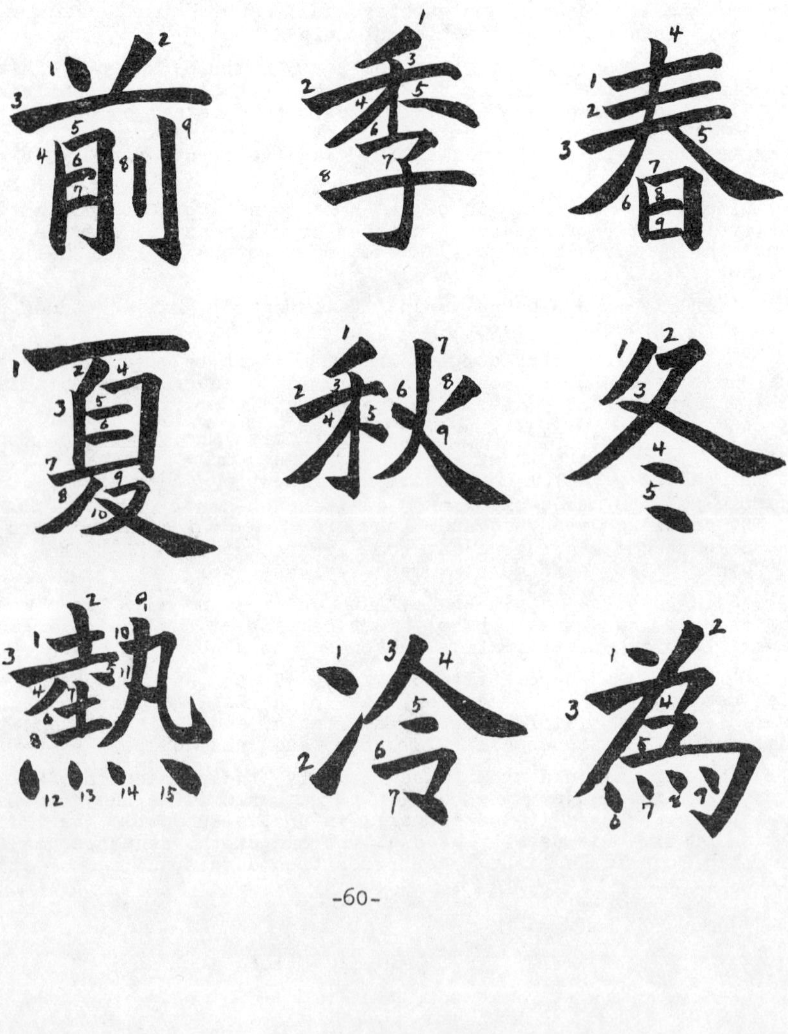

PART II, LESSON 9

## Lesson 10 Time of Day

1. Vocabulary

| | | |
|---|---|---|
| 現 | hsièn | Now, at present. |
| 在 | tsài | To be at. In, at. |
| 現在 | hsièn-tsài | At present. |
| 時 | shíh | Time, hour. |
| 候 | hòu | Period. |
| 時候 | shíh-hou | Time. |
| 鐘 | chūng | Clock, bell [í-kê chūng]. |
| 表 | piǎo | Watch [í-kê piǎo]. |
| 刻 | k'è | A quarter of an hour. |
| 分 | fēn | A minute, a cent. |
| 半 | pàn | Half. |
| 一點鐘 | ì-tiěn-chūng | One hour (literally, one stroke of the clock). |
| 一刻鐘 | í-k'è-chūng | A quarter of an hour. |
| 一分鐘 | ì-fēn-chūng | A minute. |
| 半分鐘 | pàn fēn-chūng | Half a minute. |
| 午 | wǔ | Noon. |
| 上 | shàng | Above. |
| 上午 | shàng-wǔ | Forenoon, a.m., morning. |
| 下午 | hsià-wǔ | Afternoon, p.m. |
| 早 | tsǎo | Early. Morning. |

| | | |
|---|---|---|
| 晚 | wǎn | Late. Evening. |
| 早上 | tsǎo-shang(1) | Early morning, morning [í-kê tsǎo-shang]. |
| 晚上 | wǎn-shang | Night, evening [í-kê wǎn-shang]. |
| 就 | chiù | Then, immediately. |
| 快 | k'uài | Quick, fast, prompt, soon. Sharp (as a knife). |
| 慢 | màn | Slow. Slowly, gradually. |
| 晴 | ch'íng | Clear. |
| 晴天 | ch'íng t'iēn | A fine day. |
| 天晴了 | t'iēn ch'íng lê | [The weather has] cleared off. |
| 差 | ch'à | Difference. To differ, to lack. |
| 差不多 | ch'à-pu-tō | Almost (literally, difference not much). |
| 罷 | pa | A final particle suggesting an affirmative answer or indicating a polite imperative. |
| 要是 | yào-shih (2) | If. |
| 得 | tế | To get, to be able. Ready. A particle sometimes used interchangeably with 的. |

2. Sentences

1. What time is it now?
   Hsièn-tsài shìh shến-mo shíh-hou?
   現在是甚麽時候?
2. What time (by the clock) is it now?
   Hsièn-tsài shìh chí tiěn-chūng?
   現在是幾點鐘?
3. It is a quarter past one now.
   Hsièn-tsài shìh ì tiěn í k'ề.
   現在是一點一刻.
4. It is half past two now.
   Hsièn-tsài shìh liáng tiěn pàn.
   現在是兩點半.
5. It is a quarter to four now.
   Hsièn-tsài shìh ch'à í k'ề ssǜ tiěn.
   現在是差一刻四點.
6. Now it is ten-thirty a.m.
   Hsièn-tsài shìh shàng-wǔ shíh tiěn pàn.
   現在是上午十點半.

7. Now it is five minutes after four p.m.

Hsièn-tsài shìh hsià-wǔ ssǔ tiěn líng wǔ fěn.

現在是下午四點零五分.

8. What time is it by your watch? (Literally, Your watch is what hour?)

Nǐ-tê piǎo chí tiěn lê(3)?

你的表幾點了?

9. Is your watch right?

Nǐ-tê piǎo tùi ma?

你的表對嗎?

10. My watch is a little slow. My watch is a little fast.

Wǒ-tê piǎo màn ì-tiěn-êrh. Wǒ-tê piǎo k'uài ì-tiěn-êrh.

我的表慢一點兒. 我的表快一點兒.

11. My watch is neither fast nor slow, just right.

Wǒ-tê piǎo pú k'uài yěh pú màn, chèng tùi.

我的表不快也不慢, 正對.

12. Is that clock right?

Nà-kê chūng tùi-pu-tui?

那個鐘對不對?

13. That clock is approximately right.

Nà-kê chūng ch'à-pu-tō(4).

那個鐘差不多.

14. Is what I said right or not?

Wǒ shuō-tê tùi-pu-tui?

我說得對不對?

15. What you said is not very correct.

Nǐ shuō-tê pù hěn tùi.

你說得不很對.

16. Are you going to see friends at 3:30 tomorrow afternoon?

Nǐ míng-t'ien hsià-wǔ sān tiěn pàn ch'ù k'àn p'éng-yu ma?

你明天下午三點半去看朋友嗎?

17. It rained at eleven o'clock this morning; now it has cleared off.

Chīn-t'ien shàng-wǔ shíh-ī tiěn hsià-yǔ; hsièn-tsài t'iēn ch'íng lê(5).

今天上午十一點下雨; 現在天晴了.

18. If it is a fine day, I shall go to see friends; if it rains,

Yào-shih t'iēn ch'íng wǒ ch'ù k'àn p'éng-yu; hsià-yǔ

要是天晴, 我去看朋友, 下雨

then I will not go.
wǒ chiù pú ch'ǜ(6).
我就不去。

19. Please speak a little more slowly.
Ch'íng ni shuō màn ì - tiěn-êrh.
請你說慢一點兒。

20. Please walk a little faster.
Ch'íng ni tsǒu k'uài ì - tiěn-êrh.
請你走快一點兒。

21. It's late (literally, not early), let's hurry.
Shíh-hou pù tsǎo lê, wǒ - mên k'uài tsǒu pa(7).
時候不早了，我們快走罷。

22. Because it rained this morning, I came late.
Yīn-wèi chīn-t'ien tsǎo-shang hsià - yǔ, wǒ lái wǎn lê.
因爲今天早上下雨，我來晚了。

23. Your coming is neither early nor late, just on time.
Nǐ lái - tê pù tsǎo yěh pù wǎn, chěng shìh shíh-hou.
你來的不早也不晚，正是時候。

24. I'm sorry; now it is almost twelve o'clock, I am going at once.
Tuì pu ch'ǐ, hsièn-tsài ch'à - pu - tō shíh-èrh tiěn lê, wǒ chiù yào tsǒu lê.
對不起，現在差不多十二點了，我就要走了。

25. See you tomorrow evening.
Míng-t'ien wǎn-shang tsài chièn pa.
明天晚上再見罷。

26. Go slowly, go slowly.
Màn tsǒu, màn tsǒu(8)!
慢走，慢走！

3. Tone and Pronunciation Drill

| | | | | | | | |
|---|---|---|---|---|---|---|---|
| hsiēn | hsién | hsiěn | hsièn | tiēn | tién | tiěn | tièn |
| hsiēh | hsiéh | hsiěh | hsièh | t'iēn | t'ién | t'iěn | t'ièn |
| shēng | shéng | shěng | shèng | tsāi | tsái | tsǎi | tsài |
| shīh | shíh | shǐh | shìh | ts'āi | ts'ái | ts'ǎi | ts'ài |
| ch'ā | ch'á | ch'ǎ | ch'à | tsāo | tsáo | tsǎo | tsào |

chā chá chǎ chà tsōu tsóu tsǒu tsòu

4. Exercises

a. "Fill-in" sentences

| | |
|---|---|
| 1. Hsièn-tsài shìh ... ... ... ? | ... ... is it now? |
| 2. Hsièn-tsài shìh ... ... ... | Now it is ... ... |
| 3. Hsièn-tsài shìh ch'à-pu-tō ... ... ... | Now it is almost (expression ... of time) ... |
| 4. Wǒ-tê piǎo ... ... | My watch is (fast, slow, etc.) ... |
| 5. T'ā ... ... ... ... lái? | (When) ... ... is he coming? |
| 6. Wǒ ... ... ... ch'ǜ k'àn ... ... | I am going to see ... ... at ... ... |
| 7. Ch'íng ni shuō ... ... | Please speak ... ... |
| 8. Ch'íng ni ... ... ... | Please (walk ... slowly ... etc.) |

b. Translate into English:

1. Hsièn-tsài wǒ pú ch'ǜ.
2. T'ā-mên tsǎo-shang lái ma?
3. Nǐ shuō-tê pú tuì.
4. Wǒ shuō-tê t'ài màn, wǒ-tê hsiēn-shêng shuō-tê t'ài k'uài.
5. Nǐ yǔ shíh-hou ch'ǜ k'àn p'ěng-yu ma?
6. Nǐ-tê piǎo tùi-pu-tui?
7. T'ā tsǎo lái lê.
8. Wǎn-shang nǐ pú ch'ǜ k'àn t'a ma?
9. Yào-shih chīn-t'ien wǎn-shang pú hsià-yǚ, wǒ ch'ǜ k'àn t'a.
10. Wǒ-tê piǎo ch'à pàn fēn-chūng pā tiěn.

c. Translate into Chinese:

1. He doesn't know how to read (k'àn) English.
2. It is late now; do you want to go?
3. He has to go at a quarter to seven.

4. It is a little cold at night.

5. They say the afternoons are too hot.

6. It snowed at half past seven in the morning.

7. He will come soon.

8. I study Chinese in the morning; I study French in the afternoon.

9. Please speak a little slowly.

10. Please speak slowly.

NOTES:

(1) "Shàng-wǔ" and "tsǎo-shang" may be used interchangeably, but, strictly speaking, "tsǎo-shang" means "early morning", while "shàng-wǔ" means simply "morning" or "forenoon".

(2) A synonym for "yào-shih" is "jò-shìh" 若是. The former is more generally used in colloquial speech, the latter is more literary.

(3) "Lê" here indicates completion; the meaning is "how much time has passed at this moment?"

(4) "Ch'à-pu-tō", "almost", is a very common idiom which can be used alone. In this sentence the full expression would be "Nà-kê chūng ch'à-pu-tō tuì" - "That clock is almost correct", but in idiomatic speech "tuì" is understood and omitted.

(5) The impersonal "it" in such English expressions as "it is nine o'clock" or "it is raining" does not exist in Chinese. The Chinese uses "t'iēn", "hsièn-tsài", "shíh-hou", etc., as subject in such sentences, or omits the subject entirely and says simply "hsià-yǔ lê", as illustrated in this sentence and the following.

(6) The subordinate clause in Chinese usually precedes the main clause. A Chinese would hardly say: "Wǒ ch'ù k'àn p'ếng-yu, yào-shih t'iēn ch'íng".

(7) See the note on the use of "pa" attached to this lesson.

(8) "Màn tsǒu, màn tsǒu" is a polite expression used in parting with a friend; it corresponds to English expressions at parting when one asks a friend not to hurry, to take care of himself, etc.

## On the Particle "Pa" 罷 or 吧

Some of the important particles of the Chinese language will be discussed one by one in notes following the lessons. The first of these is 罷, which is commonly abbreviated 吧. It has the following uses:

1. The original meaning of 罷 is "to stop, to finish". It is used to indicate a decisive or impatient conclusion.

"Chiù-shih pa" 就是吧 - "Let it be so", literally, "Then it is right, finished".

"Hǎo pa" 好吧 - "all right".

"Pà-liǎo, wǒ-mên tsǒu pa" 罷了,我們走吧 - "All right, let us go". (Note that 了 is pronounced "liǎo" in this use. See Lesson 4, note 2.)

"Pà-liǎo, míng-t'ien tsài shuō pa" 罷了,明天再說吧 - "All right, let's talk again tomorrow".

"Pà-liǎo, pà-liǎo, pú yào tsài shuō lê" 罷了,罷了,不要再說了 - "Well, well, it is not necessary to say any more".

2. It may express a polite imperative.

"Tsò-hsia pa" 坐下吧 - "[Won't you] sit down?"

"Nǐ shuō pa" 你說吧 - "[Won't] you speak?"

"Nǐ lái pa" 你來吧 - "You [had better] come".

"Nǐ ch'ü pa" 你去吧 - "You may go" or "You had better go".

Without "pa", these expressions would be more strongly imperative.

3. It may indicate a suggestion. In this use "pa" may often be translated "let's".

"Shíh-hou pù tsǎo lê; wǒ-mên tsǒu pa" 時候不早了,我們走吧 - "It is late; let's go".

"Wǒ-mên kěn t'ā ch'ü pa" 我們跟他去吧 - "Let's go with him".

4. It may express doubt or uncertainty.

"T'ā pù lái pa" 他不來吧 - "He may not come".

"T'ā yào tsǒu pa" 他要走吧 - "He may wish to go away".

"T'ā shìh í-kê hǎo jên pa" 他是一個好人吧 - "He may be a good man" or "I think he is a good man".

"Chè pú shìh nǐ-tê pa" 這不是你的吧 - "This is not yours, is it?"

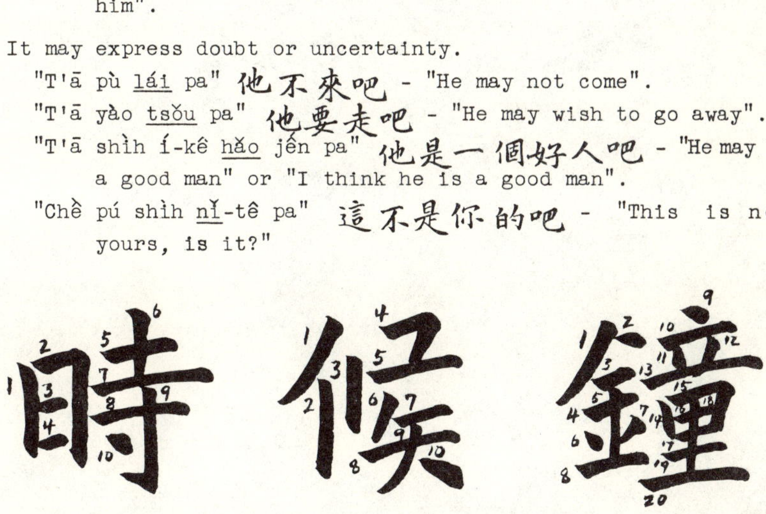

## Lesson 11 Weights and Measures

1. Vocabulary

| | | |
|---|---|---|
| 碼 | mǎ | Yard. |
| 尺 | ch'ǐh | Foot (measure), ruler. |
| 寸 | ts'ùn | Inch. |
| 分 | fēn | The smallest linear unit, one one-hundredth of a ch'ǐh. A minute, a cent, to divide. |
| 尺寸 | ch'íh-ts'un(1) | Measurement of length. |
| 畝 | mǔ or mǒu | "Chinese acre", approximately one sixth of an English acre. |

| | | |
|---|---|---|
| 里 | lǐ | "Chinese mile", approximately one third of an English mile. |
| 噸 | tùn | Ton. |
| 斤 | chīn | Catty, 16 Chinese ounces or one and one third pounds. |
| 磅 | p'àng | Pound. Twelve ounces or three quarters of a chīn. |
| 兩 | liǎng | Ounce, tael. See also page 42. |
| 公 | kūng | Public, official. Just, fair. |
| 公分 | kūng-fēn (2) | Centimeter. |
| 公尺 | kūng-ch'ǐh | Meter. |
| 公里 | kūng-lǐ | Kilometer. |
| 公斤 | kūng-chīn | Kilogram. |
| 標 | piāo | A mark, a signal [lit.]. |
| 準 | chǔn | Exact. |
| 標準 | piāo-chǔn | Standard. A mark. |
| 重 | chùng | Heavy. |
| 輕 | ch'īng | Light. |
| 高 | kāo | High, tall. |
| 矮 | ǎi | Short of stature, (physically) low. |
| 長 | ch'áng | Long. |
| 短 | tuǎn | Short (not used of stature), brief, deficient. |
| 寬 | k'uān | Broad. |
| 窄 | chǎi | Narrow. |
| 大 | tà | Great, large. |
| 量 | liáng | To measure. |
| | liàng | A measure, capacity. |
| 合 | hé | To be equivalent to, to agree. |
| 條 | t'iáo | Branch, twig. Numerative of long or slender objects. |
| 路 | lù | Road [ì-t'iáo lù]. |
| 地 | tì | Land. |

2. Sentences

1. How many inches make one foot?
Ì ch'ǐh yú chǐ ts'ùn(3)?
一尺有幾寸?

2. Twelve inches make one foot. Ten inches make one Chinese foot.
Ì ch'ǐh yǔ shíh-èrh ts'ùn. Chūng-kuo ch'ǐh yǔ shíh ts'ùn.
一尺有十二寸. 中國尺有十寸.

3. How many feet make one yard?
Ì mǎ yú chí ch'ǐh?
一碼有幾尺?

4. Three feet make one yard, [which] is equivalent to two feet seven inches in Chinese measure.
Ì mǎ yǔ sān ch'ǐh, hé Chūng-kuo ch'ǐh èrh ch'ǐh ch'í ts'ùn.
一碼有三尺, 合中國尺二尺七寸.

5. How many acres of land have you? I have two acres of land.
Ní yǔ chí mǔ tì? Wó yǔ liáng mǔ tì.
你有幾畝地? 我有兩畝地.

6. This road is wide; that road is narrow.
Chè-t'iáo lù k'uān; nà-t'iáo lù chǎi.
這條路寬; 那條路窄.

7. Please measure it.
Ch'íng ni liáng-i-liang.
請你量一量.

8. This road is ten meters [and] five centimeters wide, [and] two kilometers long.
Chè-t'iáo lù yǔ shíh kūng-ch'ǐh wǔ kūng-fēn k'uān, liǎng kūng-lǐ ch'áng.
這條路有十公尺五公分寬, 兩公里長.

9. The measurement is not right. The length is not right.
Ch'íh-ts'un pú tùi. Ch'áng-tuǎn pú tùi.
尺寸不對. 長短不對.

10. The size, height, and weight are all incorrect.
Tà-hsiǎo, kāo-ǎi, kēn ch'īng-chùng tōu pú tùi.
大小, 高矮, 跟輕重都不對.

11. This is a standard ruler; it is correct.
Chè shìh piāo-chún ch'ǐh; tùi-tê.
這是標準尺，對的.

12. How tall [and] how heavy are you?
Nǐ tō kāo tō chùng(4)?
你多高多重?

13. I am six feet tall, a hundred forty-five pounds in weight.
Wǒ liù ch'ǐh kāo, ì-pǎi ssù-shíh-wǔ pàng chùng.
我六尺高，一百四十五磅重.

14. How long is this? Not very long.
Chè yǔ tō ch'áng? Méi-yǔ tō ch'áng.
這有多長? 沒有多長.

15. I am tall, you are short.
Wǒ kāo, ní ǎi.
我高，你矮.

16. I am big, you are small.
Wǒ tà, ní hsiǎo.
我大，你小.

17. This weighs three tons and eighty pounds.
Chè-kê yǔ sān tùn pā-shíh pàng chùng.
這個有三噸八十磅重.

18. How much do you want?
Nǐ yào tō-shǎo?
你要多少?

19. I want one and a half catties.
Wǒ yào ì chīn pàn.
我要一斤半.

20. Sixteen ounces make one catty.
Ì chīn yǔ shíh-liù liǎng.
一斤有十六兩.

21. Two catties make one kilogram.
Ì kūng-chīn yú liǎng chīn.
一公斤有兩斤.

3. Tone and Pronunciation Drill

| | | | | | | | |
|---|---|---|---|---|---|---|---|
| ch'īh | ch'íh | ch'ǐh | ch'ìh | lī | lí | lǐ | lì |
| chīn | chín | chǐn | chìn | liāng | liáng | liǎng | liàng |
| chūng | chúng | chǔng | chùng | pāng | páng | pǎng | pàng |
| chāi | chái | chǎi | chài | ts'ūn | ts'ún | ts'ǔn | ts'ùn |

4. Exercises

a. "Fill-in" sentences

| | |
|---|---|
| 1. Ì ... yŭ ... ... | One (foot, etc.) ... has (inches, etc.) ... ... |
| 2. Ní(yŭ)tō ... ? | How ... are you? |
| 3. Chè-... lù ... | This road is ... |
| 4. Nĭ yào ... ... ? | ... ... do you want? |
| 5. Wŏ ... , nĭ ... | I am (tall, etc.) ..., you are ... |
| 6. Chè-kê ... nà-kê ... | This one is (long, etc.) ..., that one is (short, etc.) ... |
| 7. Chè yŭ tō ... ... ? | How ... is this? |

b. Translate into English:

1. T'ā-tê t'ài-t'ai hěn kāo, t'ā hén ăi.
2. Ch'íng ni liáng-i-liang chè-t'iáo lù.
3. Chè-kê chūng hěn chùng.
4. Wó tsăo-shang tsŏu lê liăng kūng-lĭ.
5. Ch'íh-ts'un chèng hăo.
6. Ní yŭ èrh-păi pàng chùng ma?
7. Wŏ yào ì-tiĕn-êrh.
8. Ì kūng-lí yŭ tō-shăo kūng-ch'ĭh?
9. Nà shìh piāo-chŭn chūng.
10. T'ā liáng-tê ch'ĭh-ts'un pú tuì.

c. Translate into Chinese:

1. That is a standard clock.
2. It is two feet, four inches, and five fĕn long.
3. One yard is equivalent to two feet seven inches in Chinese measure.
4. I have four acres of land.
5. How many ounces make a catty?
6. The road is very broad.

7. Let us measure the width of the road.

8. The husband is very tall, the wife is very short.

9. I want one half.

NOTES:

(1) Abstract concepts of quantity are more difficult to express in Chinese than concrete objects. Usually the combination of two words of opposite meaning forms an abstract noun of quantity. Thus the combination "ch'íh-ts'un" means "measurement", "ch'īng-chùng" - "weight", "kāo-ǎi" - "height", "tà-hsiǎo" - "size", etc.

(2) Terms of the metric system are prefixed by "kūng", indicating that the system is "public" or international.

(3) One Chinese foot is about fourteen English inches, or one third of a meter.

(4) Sometimes people say "Ní yǔ tō kāo?", to which the answer may be "Wó yǔ liù ch'ǐh kāo."

On Forming Questions in Chinese

The syntax of Chinese questions is simple. A golden rule is "ask as you would be answered"; the question should be put in the normal word order of an affirmative sentence, but usually with a question indicator such as "ma" or "mo" at the end. The various methods of indicating a question may be summarized as follows:

1. By the use of "ma" or "mo" at the end of a statement (cf. Lesson 1, note 4). Examples:

a. "Ní hǎo lê ma?" 你好了嗎 - "Are you well now?" or "Have you recovered?"

b. "Chīn-t'ien pú shìh hsīng-ch'í mo?" 今天不是星期嗎 - "Is today not Sunday?"

2. By the use of interrogative pronouns and adjectives such as "shuí" 誰 "who?", "shén-mo" 甚麽 "what?", "nǎ" 那 "which?", and "chǐ" 幾 or "tō-shǎo" 多少 "how much, how many?" Examples:

a. "T'ā shìh shuí?" 他是誰? - "Who is he?"

b. "Chè shìh shuí-tê shū?" 這是誰的書? - "Whose book is this?"

c. "Chè shìh shén-mo?" 這是甚麽? - "What is this?"

d. "Nǎ-i kè?" 那一個? - "Which one?"

e. "Ní chǐ shíh lái-tê?" 你幾時來的? - "When did you come?"

f. "Nǐ lái lê tō-shǎo t'iēn lê?" 你來了多少天了? - "How many days [ago] did you come?"

g. "Tō kāo?" 多高? - "How tall?" or "How high?"

3. By the use of the affirmative-negative construction, as in "Yŭ-mei-yu?" 有没有? - "Have [you] or not?"; "Hăo-pu-hao?" 好不好? - "[Is it] good or not?" Examples:

a. "Ní yŭ-mei-yu shū?" 你有没有書? - "Have you a book?" or "Have you books?"

b. "Ní yŭ shū méi-yŭ?" 你有書没有? - "Have you a book?" or "Have you books?"

c. "Nĭ shìh-pu-shih hsüéh-shêng?" 你是不是學生? or:

d. "Nĭ shìh hsüéh-shêng pú shìh?" 你是學生不是? - "Are you a student?" (Note that in these sentences the predicate noun or adjective may come either before or after the negative expression without changing the meaning.)

e. "Ní hăo-pu-hao?" 你好不好? - "Are you well or not?" - "How are you?"

f. "Chè-kê tuì-pu-tui?" 這個對不對? - "Is this right or not?"

Special attention should be paid to the following points:

1. When an interrogative pronoun or adjective or the affirmative-negative construction is used, no question indicator such as "ma" is needed at the end of a sentence. It would be incorrect to say "Nĭ shìh nă-kê jén ma?", for "nă" sufficiently indicates a question.

2. It is courteous to begin a question with the words "Ch'ĭng wèn", "May I ask". For example:

"Ch'ĭng wèn, hsièn-tsài hsià-yŭ pu hsià-yŭ?" 請問現在下雨不下雨? - "May I ask, is it raining now?"

"Ch'ĭng wèn, hsièn-tsài chí tiĕn lê?" 請問現在幾點了? "May I ask, what time is it now?"

Since it is much more polite to begin a question in this way, the student should acquire the habit of using "Ch'ĭng wèn" from the beginning.

3. "Kuèi hsìng?" or "Nĭ kuèi hsìng?" and "Kuèi kuó?" or "Nĭ kuèi kuó?" may be considered as idiomatic abbreviations of "Nĭ kuèi hsìng shìh shén-mo?" - "What is your honorable surname?" and "Nĭ kuèi kuó shìh nă-i kuó?" - "What is your honorable country?" "Kuèi" is not an interrogative word.

There are a few other methods of forming questions in Chinese, which will be introduced in later pages.

碼 畝 里

噸 磅 尺

重 高 矮

寬 窄 量

## Lesson 12 Special Drill in Tones and Pronunciation

[A good foundation for correct pronunciation should be laid at the beginning stage of learning a language. If records of Chinese pronunciation are available for these lessons, the students should listen to them frequently. They should also take dictation as frequently as possible, in order to develop their ability in aural comprehension. If there are Mandarin-speaking Chinese on the campus, the novice language students are advised to talk with them in Chinese; even though the conversation is necessarily limited to a small vocabulary, it will be very helpful in developing both speaking ability and understanding. This lesson consists of material for special drill on words with which students usually have difficulties of tone and pronunciation. The instructor should of course correct the students' pronunciation and grammatical construction from time to time.]

1. Vocabulary

| | | |
|---|---|---|
| 同 | t'úng | With, and. Same. |
| 新 | hsīn | New, recent. |
| 喜 | hsǐ | Pleased with. Joy. |
| 事 | shìh | Affair, matter, business. |
| 件 | chièn | Article. A numerative of clothing, affairs, etc. |
| 喜事 | hsǐ-shìh | Joyful event, wedding [í-chièn hsǐ-shìh]. |
| 追 | chuī | To pursue. |
| 吹 | ch'uī | To blow, to puff. |
| 飽 | pǎo | Satiated. To eat enough. |
| 跑 | p'ǎo | To run, to go away. |
| 蠢 | ch'ǔn | Stupid, foolish. |
| 告 | kào | To tell, to report, to sue. |
| 靠 | k'ào | To depend upon, to lean upon. |
| 古 | kǔ | Ancient, old. |
| 苦 | k'ǔ | Bitter. In bad circumstances. |
| 水 | shuǐ | Water. |
| 沙 | shā | Sand [ì-k'ê̄ shā]. |
| 蝦 | hsiā | Shrimp [í-kê hsiā]. |
| 舌 | shé | Tongue. |
| 雙 | shuāng | Pair. A numerative for things in pairs. |

| | | |
|---|---|---|
| 鞋 | hsiéh | Shoe [ì-shuāng hsiéh]. |
| 包 | pāo | A parcel, a package. |
| 枝 | chīh | Branch. A numerative of flowers, pens, cigarettes, etc. |
| 煙 | yēn | Cigarette, tobacco [ì-chīh yēn, a cigarette, ì-pāo yēn, a package of cigarettes or a package of tobacco]. |
| 鹽 | yén | Salt [ì-pāo yén]. |
| 湯 | t'āng | Soup, gravy. |
| 糖 | t'áng | Sugar [ì-pāo t'áng]. |
| 買 | mǎi | To buy. |
| 賣 | mài | To sell. |
| 打 | tǎ | To strike. to make. |
| 答 | tá | To answer. |
| 隻 | chīh | Single. A numerative for animals and for singles of things usually found in pairs. |
| 眼 | yěn | Eye, hole. |
| 眼睛 | yěn-ching | Eye [ì-chīh yěn-ching, ì-shuāng yěn-ching]. |
| 鏡 | chìng | Mirror. |
| 副 | fù | Set, pair. Numerative for things in sets or pairs, as spectacles, gloves. |
| 眼鏡 | yěn-chìng | Eye-glasses [í-fù yěn-chìng]. |
| 認 | jèn | To recognize. |
| 識 | shìh | To know. |
| 認識 | jèn-shih | To know, to be acquainted with. |

2. Four-tone Phrases

[Note that in the following phrases the first word is in the first tone, the second in the second, and so on. In this way, the tone drill, by means of meaningful sentences, will be more interesting than before. Clear pronunciation and conception of the four tones should be stressed.]

| | | |
|---|---|---|
| 1. T'ā hěn hǎo k'àn. | 2. T'ā t'úng (1) wǒ ch'ǜ. | 3. Chūng-kuó hěn tà. |
| She is very pretty. | He goes with me. | China is very large. |
| 他 很 好 看 | 他 同 我 去 | 中 國 很 大 |

4. Hsīn nién hsǐ-shìh.
The New Year's joyful event.
新年喜事

5. Chīn nién hěn jè.
It is very hot this year.
今年很熱

NOTE:

(1) The Distinction between "T'úng" and "Kĕ̄n" 跟:

Used as a conjunction, "t'úng" means the same as "kĕ̄n", but "t'úng" is more commonly used in south China, "kĕ̄n" in the north.

3. Unaspirated and Aspirated Consonants

[Attention should be paid to the distinction between aspirated and unaspirated consonants. This is very important, for a mistake in this respect can completely change the meaning of a sentence.]

| | | | |
|---|---|---|---|
| chuī | ch'uī | Wǒ chuī-i-chui.<br>I pursue a while. | Wǒ ch'uī-i-ch'ui.<br>I blow a while. |
| pǎo | p'ǎo | Wó pǎo lê.<br>I am satisfied. | Wó p'ǎo lê.<br>I ran away. |
| chǔn | ch'ǔn | T'ā shuō-tê chǔn.<br>What he said is exact. | T'ā shuō-tê ch'ǔn.<br>What he said is stupid. |
| kào | k'ào | Wǒ kào t'a.<br>I sue him. | Wǒ k'ào t'a.<br>I depend upon him. |
| kǔ | k'ǔ | hén kǔ<br>very ancient | hén k'ǔ<br>very bitter |

4. Drill on "sh" and "hs"

[Chinese "sh" is pronounced like English "sh" in "she", but with the tip of the tongue curled back. The pronunciation of "hs" is described on page 15. For purposes of review, a few examples are given below.]

| shā | hsiā | shǎo | hsiǎo | shé | hsiéh |
|---|---|---|---|---|---|
| sand | shrimp | few | small | tongue | shoe |

5. Drill on the Retroflex "j"

[The pronunciation of "j" has been described on page 5. Students should learn to pronounce the following sentences distinctly.]

1. Chīn jìh hěn jè.
Today is very hot.

2. Chè-kê jén wǒ jèn-shih.
I know this man.

3. Nà-kê jén wǒ pú jèn-shih.
I do not know that man.

6. Distinction of Tones

1. 我 要 煙
Wǒ yào yēn.
I want tobacco, or, cigarettes.

我 要 鹽
Wǒ yào yén.
I want salt.

2. 我 要 湯
Wǒ yào t'āng.
I want soup.

我 要 糖
Wǒ yào t'áng.
I want sugar.

3. 我 要 買
Wǒ yào mǎi.
I want to buy.

我 要 賣
Wǒ yào mài.
I want to sell.

4. 那 是 誰?
Nà shìh shuí?
Who is that?

那 是 水
Nà shìh shuǐ.
That is water.

5. 我 不 打 他.
Wǒ pù tǎ t'a.
I do not whip him.

我 不 答 他.
Wǒ pù tá t'a.
I do not answer him.

6. 我 的 眼 睛.
Wǒ - tê yěn-chīng.
My eyes.

我 的 眼 鏡.
Wǒ - tê yěn-chìng.
My eye-glasses.

## Lesson 13 Review

1. Useful Phrases and Word Combinations

[The following useful phrases, if thoroughly discussed and practised in conversation, will help students not only to review their vocabulary but also to enhance their speaking ability in Chinese.]

| | | |
|---|---|---|
| 1. Two persons | Liăng-kê jến | 兩個人 |
| 2. Two months | Liăng-kê yüèh | 兩個月 |
| 3. Two years | Liăng nién | 兩年 |
| 4. Two classes | Liăng pān | 兩班 |
| 5. How many persons? | Chǐ-kê jến? | 幾個人? |
| 6. About ten persons | Shíh-lái-kề jến(1) | 十來個人. |
| 7. Ten-odd persons | Shíh-chǐ-kê jến(2) | 十幾個人. |
| 8. How many have you? | Ní yŭ tō-shăo? | 你有多少? |
| 9. Not very many | Méi-yŭ tō-shăo | 沒有多少. |
| 10. I have many (much) | Wó yú hĕn tō | 我有很多. |
| 11. I have many (much) | Wó yŭ pù shăo | 我有不少. |

| | | |
|---|---|---|
| 12. I have ten thousand | Wó yǔ í-wàn | 我有一萬. |
| 13. Is there much? (Are there many?) | Tō-pu-to? | 多不多? |
| 14. Not many (not much) | Pù tō | 不多. |
| 15. Not very many | Pù hěn tō | 不很多. |
| 16. Do you have it? | Ní yǔ-mei-yu? | 你有沒有? |
| 17. To have plenty | Yǔ-tê shìh | 有的是. |
| 18. Do you want it or not? | Ni yào-pu-yao? | 你要不要? |
| 19. I want this one, not that one | Wǒ yào chè-kê, pú yào nà-kê | 我要這個, 不要那個. |
| 20. This one is good, that one is not | Chè-kê hǎo, nà-kê pù hǎo | 這個好, 那個不好. |
| 21. How many days? | Chǐ t'iēn? Chǐ jìh? | 幾天? 幾日? |
| 22. For a good many days | Háo chǐ t'iēn | 好幾天. |
| 23. One or two days | Ì-liǎng t'iēn (3) | 一兩天. |
| 24. Two or three weeks | Liǎng-sān-kê lǐ-pài | 兩三個禮拜. |
| 25. More than two weeks | Liǎng-kê tō hsīng-ch'í | 兩個多星期. |
| 26. One week and a half | Í-kê pān hsīng-ch'í | 一個半星期 |
| 27. A teacher walks in front | Hsiēn-shêng tsǒu tsài ch'ién | 先生走在前 |
| 28. A student walks behind | Hsüéh-shêng tsǒu tsài hòu | 學生走在後 |
| 29. Two days before yesterday | Tà-ch'ién-t'ien | 大前天 |
| 30. Two days after tomorrow | Tà-hòu-t'ien | 大後天 |
| 31. To go up | Shàng-ch'ü | 上去 |
| 32. To come down | Hsià-lai | 下來 |
| 33. The first half-year | Shàng-pàn nién | 上半年 |
| 34. The second half-year | Hsià-pàn nién | 下半年 |
| 35. Week after next | Hsià-hsià lǐ-pài | 下下禮拜 |
| 36. Next time | Hsià huí | 下回 |
| 37. To come back | Huí-lai | 回來 |
| 38. To go back | Huí-ch'ü | 回去 |

| | | |
|---|---|---|
| 39. To return to one's own country | Huí kuó | 回國 |
| 40. To take a look | K'àn-i-k'an | 看一看 |
| 41. Good-looking, pretty | Hǎo-k'àn | 好看 |
| 42. Doesn't look well, ugly | Pù hǎo-k'àn | 不好看 |
| 43. Half a minute | Pàn fēn-chūng | 半分鐘 |
| 44. A minute and a half | Ì-fēn pàn chūng | 一分半鐘 |
| 45. Fifty-fifty, half and half | Í-pàn í-pàn | 一半一半 |
| 46. Too early | T'ài tsǎo | 太早 |
| 47. Too late | T'ài wǎn | 太晚 |
| 48. Neither early nor late | Pù tsǎo pù wǎn | 不早不晚 |
| 49. Just right | Chèng hǎo | 正好 |
| 50. Just correct, exactly | Chèng tuì | 正對 |
| 51. Sooner or later he will come | Tsáo-wǎn t'ā yào lái | 早晚他要來. |
| 52. Who comes? Who has come? | Shuí lái lê? | 誰來了? |
| 53. I come | Wǒ lái lê | 我來了. |
| 54. Who comes first? | Shuí hsiēn lái? | 誰先來? |
| 55. Who comes last? | Shuí hòu lái? | 誰後來? |
| 56. Who came first? | Shuí hsiēn lái-tê? | 誰先來的? |
| 57. Who came last? | Shuí hòu lái-tê? | 誰後來的? |
| 58. Who is the first to come (Whose coming [is] the first)? | Shuí lái-tê tì-ī? | 誰來的第一? |
| 59. Who said it? | Shuí shuō-tê? | 誰說的? |
| 60. I said it | Wǒ shuō-tê | 我說的. |
| 61. Isn't that right? | Pú tuì ma? | 不對嗎? |
| 62. Not much difference | Pú ch'à tō-shǎo | 不差多少. |
| 63. Great difference | Ch'à tō lê | 差多了. |
| 64. No difference whatever | Shén-mo yěh pú ch'à | 甚麼也不差. |
| 65. Not a minute's (cent's) difference | Ì-fēn yěh pú ch'à | 一分也不差. |
| 66. Very accurate | Hén chǔn | 很準 |
| 67. What happened today? | Chīn-t'ien yǔ shén-mo shìh? | 今天有甚麼事? |

| | | | |
|---|---|---|---|
| 68. | Nothing happened | Méi-yǔ shén-mo shìh | 沒有甚麼事 |
| 69. | Is there any joyful event? | Yǔ shén-mo hsǐ-shìh? | 有甚麼喜事? |
| 70. | New Year congratulations! | Pài nién, pài nién! | 拜年, 拜年! |
| 71. | Let's go together | Ì-t'úng ch'ü pa (4) | 一同去罷 |
| 72. | Schoolmate | T'úng-hsüéh | 同學 |
| 73. | Co-worker | T'úng-shìh | 同事 |
| 74. | Can't catch up with him | Chuī pú shàng t'a | 追不上他 |
| 75. | He is very stupid | T'ā hěn ch'ǔn | 他很蠢 |
| 76. | The Republic (China) | Mín-kuó | 民國 |
| 77. | Citizen, the people | Kuó-mín | 國民 |
| 78. | He is very tall and big | T'ā hěn kāo-tà | 他很高大 |
| 79. | Spring, summer, autumn, winter | Ch'ūn, hsià, ch'iū, tūng | 春夏秋冬 |
| 80. | I ask, you answer | Wǒ wèn, nǐ tá | 我問, 你答 |
| 81. | I ask you to sit down | Wǒ ch'ǐng ni tsò | 我請你坐 |
| 82. | Do you know (recognize) Mr. Wang? | Nǐ jèn-shih Wáng hsiēn-shêng ma? | 你認識王先生嗎? |
| 83. | I do not know him | Wǒ pú jèn-shih t'a | 我不認識他. |
| 84. | Too long | T'ài ch'áng lê | 太長了 |

2. Conversation

A. 王小姐, 你今天好嗎?
Wáng hsiáo-chieh, nǐ chīn-t'ien hǎo ma?

B. 李先生, 我很好, 謝謝.
Lǐ hsiēn-shêng, wǒ hěn hǎo, hsièh-hsieh.

A. 今天晚上八點半, 我要去看一個朋友. 你要同我去嗎?
Chīn-t'ien wǎn-shang pā tiěn pàn, wǒ yào ch'ü k'àn í-kê p'éng-yu. Nǐ yào t'úng wǒ ch'ü ma?

B. 好, 我同你去. 現在幾點了?
Hǎo, wǒ t'úng nǐ ch'ü. Hsièn-tsài chí tiěn lê?

A. 現在八點一刻了.
Hsièn-tsài pā tiěn í k'è lê.

| | |
|---|---|
| B. 你的表慢了罷? | Nǐ-tê piǎo màn lê pa? |
| A. 我的表不快也不慢, 很準. 我們快走罷. | Wǒ-tê piǎo pú k'uài yěh pú màn, hěn chǔn. Wǒ-mên k'uài tsǒu pa. |
| (In a friend's house) | |
| A (to C) 夏先生, 這是我的中國朋友, 王小姐. 這是夏先生. | Hsià hsiēn-shêng, chè shìh wǒ-tê Chūng-kuo p'ěng-yu, Wáng hsiáo-chieh. Chè shìh Hsià hsiēn-shêng. |
| B. 夏先生, 你好嗎? | Hsià hsiēn-shêng, ní hǎo ma? |
| C. 我很好, 謝謝. 你們請坐. | Wǒ hěn hǎo, hsièh-hsieh. Nǐ-mên ch'ǐng tsò. |
| B. 夏先生是新來中國的嗎? | Hsià hsiēn-shêng shìh hsīn lái Chūng-kuo tê ma? |
| C. 我是去年秋天來中國的. | Wǒ shìh ch'ǜ-nien ch'iū-t'ien lái Chūng-kuo tê. |
| A. 夏先生的中國話很好. | Hsià hsiēn-shêng-tê Chūng-kuo-huà hěn hǎo. |
| C. 謝謝. 李先生會說中國話嗎? | Hsièh-hsieh. Lǐ hsiēn-shêng huì shuō Chūng-kuo-huà ma? |
| A. 我會說一點兒. 我說的話不好懂罷. 昨天我去買煙, 那個人說他不賣鹽. 我去買糖, 那個賣糖的說他不是賣湯的. | Wǒ huì shuō ì-tiěn-êrh. Wǒ shuō-tê huà pu hǎo tǔng pa. Tsó-t'ien wǒ ch'ǜ mǎi yēn, nà-kê jén shuō t'ā pú mài yén. Wǒ ch'ǜ mǎi t'áng, nà-kê mài-t'áng-tê shuō t'ā pú shìh mài-t'āng-tê. |
| C. 是嗎? 那是因爲你不常說. | Shìh ma? Nà shìh yīn-wèi nǐ pù ch'áng shuō. |
| B. 夏先生, 在美國冬天冷不冷? | Hsià hsiēn-shêng, tsài Měi-kuo tūng-t'ien lěng-pu-lêng? |

C. 不很冷。
Pù hěn lěng.

B. 常下雪嗎?
Ch'áng hsià-hsüěh ma?

C. 不常下雪，常下雨。
Pù ch'áng hsià-hsüěh, ch'áng hsià-yǔ.

A. 夏先生，請問，美國有幾百萬人?
Hsià hsiēn-shêng, ch'ǐng wèn, Měi-kuo yǔ chí pǎi wàn jén?

C. 美國有一萬萬三千萬人。中國有三萬萬人嗎?
Měi-kuo yǔ í - wàn - wàn sān-ch'iēn-wàn(5) jén. Chūng-kuo yǔ sān-wàn-wàn jén ma?

B. 中國有六萬萬五千萬人。
Chūng-kuo yǔ liù - wàn - wàn wǔ-ch'iēn-wàn jén.

A. 第一個美國人是甚麼時候來中國的?
Tì - í - kê Měi - kuo jén shìh shén-mo shíh-hou lái Chūng-kuo tê?

B. 是在一千七百八十四年，對不對?
Shìh tsài ì-ch'iēn ch'ī-pǎi pā-shíh-ssǔ nién, tùi-pu-tui?

C. 不對罷；我們去問問王先生。
Pú tùi pa; wǒ - mên ch'ù wèn-wèn(6) Wáng hsiēn-shêng.

A. 王先生禮拜三有英文班，我們那天上午去問他，好不好?
Wáng hsiēn-shêng lǐ-pài-sān yǔ Yīng - wén pān, wǒ - mên nà t'iēn shàng - wǔ ch'ù wèn t'a, hǎo-pu-hao?

B. 好罷。
Hǎo pa.

C. 請問，一千九百四十八年是中華民國那一年?
Ch'ǐng wèn, ì-ch'iēn chiú - pǎi ssǔ-shíh-pā nién shìh Chūng-huá-mín-kuó nǎ-i nién?

A. 一千九百四十八年是民國三十七年。
Ì-ch'iēn chiú - pǎi ssǔ-shíh-pā nién shìh mín-kuó sān-shíh-ch'ī nién.

C. 這個禮拜下了有一尺多的雪。你們是走路來的嗎?
Chè - kê lǐ - pài hsià lê yǔ ì - ch'ǐh - tō - tê hsüěh. Nǐ - mên shìh tsǒu lù lái-tê ma?

| | |
|---|---|
| B. 是的. 路不好走. 我們走了兩里路. | Shìh - tê. Lù pù hǎo tsǒu. Wǒ-mên tsǒu lê liáng lǐ lù. |
| A. 人多, 路窄, 所以我們走的很慢. | Jén tō, lù chǎi, só-í wǒ-mên tsǒu-tê(7) hěn màn. |
| C. 你們太苦了. | Nǐ-mên t'ài k'ǔ lê. |
| A. 夏先生, 我們要走了. 現在我跟王小姐去買眼鏡. | Hsià hsiēn-shêng, wǒ-mên yào tsǒu lê. Hsièn-tsài wǒ kěn Wáng hsiáo-chieh ch'ù mái yěn-chìng. |
| B. 李先生的眼睛不好. | Lǐ hsiēn-shêng-tê yěn-ching pù hǎo. |
| C. 王小姐, 李先生, 謝謝你們來看我. | Wáng hsiáo-chieh, Lǐ hsiēn-shêng, hsièh-hsieh nǐ-mên lái k'àn wo. |
| A and B. 不客氣, 不客氣. | Pú k'ê - ch'i, pú k'ê - ch'i. |
| C. 請你們常來; 禮拜六再見罷. | Ch'íng ni-mên ch'áng lái; lǐ-pài-liù tsài chièn pa. |
| A and B. 再見, 再見. | Tsài chièn, tsài chièn. |

NOTES:

(1) See "lái" in the vocabulary of Lesson 8.

(2) See "chǐ" in the vocabulary of Lesson 8.

(3) No word corresponding to "or" is used in Chinese in such expressions as "ì-liǎng t'iēn" - "one or two days", and "wǔ-liù nién" - "five or six years".

(4) "T'úng" also means "together".

(5) The Chinese numerical system differs from that used in Western countries in that, in numbers having more than four decimal places, the grouping is by fours rather than by threes. That is, "ten thousand" is always called "wàn", never "shíh-ch'iēn", and numbers larger than ten thousand are read as so many "wàn". In Chinese, "one million" is "ì-pǎi-wàn", and "one hundred million", "í-wàn-wàn". "Í-wàn-wàn sān-ch'iēn-wàn jén" is "one hundred and thirty million people". Compare also Lesson 9, note 12.

(6) The repetition of "wěn" here is mainly for euphony, and "wěn-wěn" is an abbreviation of "wěn-i-wên".

(7) 的 used between a verb and an adverb is replaceable by 得.

In this use it has two functions: (1) euphony, and (2) denoting the manner of action. It has the idea of "so as to be" or "so that it is". This "tê" may be neglected in making a smooth translation. The sentence in the text may be rendered simply: "Since the people were numerous and the road narrow, therefore we walked very slowly." In accurate linguistic translation it should be: "[Since] people [were] many [and] the road narrow, we walked [in such a manner] as to be very slow." In the following sentences, 的 may be replaced by 得, and may be omitted in translation.

"T'ā shuō-tê hến hǎo" 他說的很好 - "He speaks (so as to be) very good", "His speaking is very good", or "He speaks very well".

"T'ā tsǒu lù tsǒu-tê t'ài màn" 他走路走的太慢 - "He walks (in such a manner as to be) too slow", "His walking is too slow", or "He walks too slowly".

3. Translate into Chinese:

1. This is standard time.
2. He speaks standard French.
3. Which year of the Chinese Republic was 1950?
4. There are 105 men in that class.
5. What day is today?
6. Today is September twenty-fifth.
7. What day of the week is this?
8. Is today Sunday?
9. No, today is Saturday.
10. Yesterday I went to see my Chinese friend.
11. It rained on Wednesday.
12. It will rain tomorrow.
13. What time is it?
14. It is half past ten.
15. It is a quarter past eight.
16. It is ten minutes past eight.
17. It is forty-seven minutes past eight.
18. It is a quarter of one.

19. It is five minutes of two.
20. It is seven p.m., not seven a.m.
21. What time is it by your watch, Mr. Li?
22. My watch is fast, your watch is slow, his watch is exactly right.
23. She will come to see me at half past ten.
24. I will go to see my friend this afternoon.
25. It is too early now.
26. It is too late now.
27. Yesterday he came late.
28. China is an ancient country.
29. January and February are frequently very cold; July and August are frequently very hot.
30. In summer it frequently rains.
31. The New Year is coming soon.
32. How much do you weigh?
33. I weigh a hundred and fifty pounds.
34. How tall are you?
35. I am five feet ten inches tall.
36. I don't know this man.
37. Do you know Mr. Li?
38. Has he come?
39. Are you coming to see me?
40. What do you want?
41. I do not understand what he said.
42. Let us walk a little faster.
43. You speak too slowly.
44. I want to buy two tons of salt and five pounds of sugar.
45. Ten inches make one foot.

CONVERSATIONAL CHINESE

PART III MEETING PEOPLE AND COMMON TOPICS

OF CONVERSATION

## Lesson 14 Making a Telephone Call

1. Vocabulary

| | | |
|---|---|---|
| 電 | tièn | Electric. |
| 電話 | tièn-huà | Telephone [í-kê tièn-huà]. |
| 局 | chǘ | Office, bureau [seldom used alone]. |
| 電話局 | tièn-huà-chǘ | Telephone office [í-kê tièn-huà-chǘ]. |
| 打電話 | tǎ tièn-huà | To make a telephone call. |
| 通 | t'ūng | To pass through. |
| 打通 | tǎ-t'ūng | To get [a telephone call] through, to make a passage through. |
| 掛 | kuà | To hang up. |
| 錯 | ts'ò | Wrong, bad. Mistake. |
| 等 | těng | To wait. |
| 聽 | t'īng | To hear, to listen. |
| 清 | ch'īng | Clear, pure. |
| 楚 | ch'ǔ | Clear, distinct [lit.]. |
| 清楚 | ch'īng-ch'u | Clear. Clearly. |
| 家 | chiā | Home, family. A numerative of shops. |
| 喂 | wèi (1) | Interjection used over telephone as Americans use "hello". |
| 着 | chó or cháo | A particle used with verbs to indicate progressive action or the attainment of an aim. |
| 哪 | nā (2) | A final particle denoting the present or progressive sense of a verb, and sometimes indicating an interrogative. |
| 叫 | chiào (3) | To call, to order. To be called, to be named. |
| 裏 | lǐ | Inside. |
| 這裏 | chê-li (4) | Here. This side. |
| 這兒 | chè-êrh | Here. This side. |
| 那裏 | nà-li | There. That side. |
| 那兒 | nà-êrh | There. That side. |

| | | |
|---|---|---|
| 那裏 | ná-li | Where? |
| 那兒 | nǎ-êrh | Where? |
| 位 | wèi | A numerative of persons (polite). A seat. |
| 張 | chāng | A surname. A numerative of tables, chairs, and flat objects such as papers and skins. |
| 本 | pěn | Root. Native, fundamental. A numerative of books, documents, etc. |
| 子 | tzǔ (5) | Child, son [lit.]. A suffix added for euphony to many nouns. |
| 本子 | pěn-tzǔ (6) | Notebook, book. |
| 館 | kuǎn | Lodging-house, residence [seldom used alone]. |
| 公館 | kūng-kuǎn (7) | Residence of an official. |
| 次 | tz'ǔ (8) | A time. Next. |
| 聲 | shěng | Noise, voice, tone, sound. |
| 語 | yǔ | Language, word. |
| 國語 | kuó-yǔ | The national language of China. |

2. Conversation

1. May I ask, is there a telephone here or not?

   Ch'ǐng wèn, chè-li yǔ tièn-huà méi - yǔ?

   請問，這裏有電話沒有？

2. There is no telephone here.

   Chè - li méi - yǔ tièn-huà.

   這裏沒有電話。

3. There is, over there.

   Yǔ, tsài nà - li.

   有，在那裏。

4. Have you a telephone directory?

   Ní yǔ tièn-huà pěn-tzǔ méi - yǔ?

   你有電話本子沒有？

5. Yes, [it is] also over there.

   Yǔ, yěh tsài nà - li.

   有，也在那裏。

6. Many thanks.

   Tō hsièh, tō hsièh.

   多謝，多謝。

7. [This is the] telephone office; what number (where) do you want to call?

Tièn-huà-chú; nǐ yào nǎ - êrh?

電話局；你要那兒？

8. I want number 1644.

Wǒ yào ì - ch'ien liù-pǎi ssǔ-shíh-ssǔ hào.

我要一千六百四十四號。

9. Someone is calling; please wait a moment.

Yǔ jén chiào; ch'íng ni těng - i - têng.

有人叫；請你等一等。

10. The call cannot go through; the line is busy.

Tièn-huà tǎ pù t'ūng; yǔ jén chiào-cho na.

電話打不通，有人叫着哪。

11. Hello, are you Mr. Wang?

Wèi, nǐ shìh Wáng hsiēn-shêng ma?

喂，你是王先生嗎？

12. No, my name is Chang.

Pú shìh, wǒ hsìng Chāng.

不是，我姓張。

13. What is your telephone number?

Nǐ - tê tièn-huà tō - shǎo hào?

你的電話多少號？

14. This (here) is number 1649.

Chè - li shìh í - liù-ssǔ-chiǔ (hào).

這裏是一六四九(號)。

15. Wrong [number]; please hang up.

Ts'ò lê; ch'íng ni kuà shàng pa.

錯了；請你掛上罷。

16. Hello, who are you? Who are you (polite form)?

Wèi, nǐ shìh shuí? Nǐ shìh nǎ - i - wèi?

喂，你是誰？你是那一位？

17. Where are you?

Ní nǎ - êrh?

你那兒？

18. This is the Wangs' residence.

Chè - li shìh Wáng kūng-kuǎn.

這裏是王公館。

19. I would like to speak to Mr. Wang, please.

Wǒ yào ch'ǐng Wáng hsien-shêng shuō-huà.

我要請王先生說話。

20. I do not hear clearly; please speak a little [more] slowly.
Wǒ t'īng pù ch'īng-ch'u; ch'íng ni shuō màn ì-tiĕn-êrh.
我聽不清楚；請你說慢一點兒。

21. Please speak a little louder. Please say [it] once more.
Ch'íng ni tà shĕng ì-tiĕn-êrh shuō. Ch'íng ni tsài shuō í tz'ŭ.
請你大聲一點兒說。請你再說一次。

22. Mr. Wang is not at home; please call again at three o'clock this afternoon.
Wáng hsiēn-shêng pú tsài chiā; hsià-wŭ sān-tiĕn-chūng ch'íng ni tsài tă pa.
王先生不在家；下午三點鐘請你再打罷。

23. Mr. Li, please wait a while; Mrs. Wang wants to speak to you.
Lǐ hsiēn-shêng, ch'íng ni tĕng-i-têng; Wáng t'ài-t'ai yào kĕn nǐ shuō-huà na.
李先生，請你等一等，王太太要跟你說話哪。

24. Mrs. Wang, how are you?
Wáng t'ài-t'ai, ní hăo ma?
王太太，你好嗎？

25. What you said is standard national language; I have heard [it] all clearly.
Nǐ shuō-tê huà shìh piāo-chŭn kuó-yŭ; wǒ tōu t'īng ch'īng-ch'u lê.
你說的話是標準國語，我都聽清楚了。

26. We shall come to see you on Saturday.
Lǐ-pài-liù wǒ-mên lái k'àn ni.
禮拜六我們來看你。

27. Goodby.
Tsài chièn.
再見。

NOTES:

(1) The word "wèi" is used in telephone calls and sometimes other-

wise, simply as an interjection to call attention, without specific meaning.

(2) The Use of "Nā"

"Nā" is now generally employed in the Peking dialect (but not in southern dialects) as an enclitic particle at the end of a sentence, usually interrogative. An enclitic particle is a word which, losing its own accent and having no meaning to be translated, aids the swing or rhythm of the sentence. "Nā" denotes the present or progressive sense of a verb. It is sometimes interchangeable with 呢 "ni", another final particle. Pronounced in the third tone, 哪 can be used as an interrogative interchangeably with 那 "nǎ".

(3) "Chiào", when followed by a name, means "to be named, to be called": "T'ā chiào Lǐ Ssù" 他叫李四 - "He is called Li Ssŭ"; when followed by an object with a verb complement, it means "to order, to call", as in ordering a car or calling a doctor to come.

(4) "Chè-li" and "nà-li" are interchangeable with "chè-êrh" and "nà-êrh", respectively. However, the former two terms are more commonly used in south China, the latter two in the north.

(5) The Use of "Êrh" and "Tzŭ" as Suffixes

The use of "êrh" and "tzŭ" as enclitic suffixes to nouns is one of the common methods by which monosyllabic words become polysyllabic and the number of possible meanings of a given word is limited. "Êrh" is usually used in the north, "tzŭ" in the south.

(6) "Pěn-tzŭ" is a colloquial term for something which looks like a book or a notebook. It is usually preceded by a qualifying word, as in "tièn-huà pěn-tzŭ" - "telephone directory".

(7) "Kūng-kuǎn", literally "public office", is a polite term referring to the residence of an official or other distinguished person. It should never be used in place of "wǒ-tê chiā" by an ordinary person.

(8) "Tz'ù" as a noun with the sense of "a time" can be used interchangeably with "huí" 回.

3. Tone and Pronunciation Drill

| | | | | | | | |
|---|---|---|---|---|---|---|---|
| huān | huán | huǎn | huàn | ch'ū | ch'ú | ch'ǔ | ch'ù |
| huā | huá | huǎ | huà | chǖ | chǘ | chǚ | chǜ |
| tēng | téng | těng | tèng | ch'ǖ | ch'ǘ | ch'ǚ | ch'ǜ |
| t'ēng | t'éng | t'ěng | t'èng | yū | yú | yǔ | yù |
| t'īng | t'íng | t'ǐng | t'ìng | yǖ | yǘ | yǚ | yǜ |
| t'ūng | t'úng | t'ǔng | t'ùng | | | | |

4. Exercises

a. "Fill-in" sentences

| | |
|---|---|
| 1. Wǒ yào ... ... ... ... hào. | I want number ... ... ... ... |
| 2. Chè-êrh shìh ... ... ... ... | This is ... ... ... ... |
| 3. Chè-êrh yǔ ... ... méi-yǔ? | Is there a ... ... here (or not)? |
| 4. Ní yǔ ... ... méi-yǔ? | Have you a ... ... or not? |
| 5. ... ... pú tsài chiā. | ... ... is not at home. |
| 6. Nǐ shuō-tê huà ... ... | All that you have said is (good, ... etc.) (bad, |

b. Translate into English:

1.(A) Wǒ yào ch'ǐng Wáng hsiēn-shêng shuō-huà. Wáng hsiēn-shêng, nǐ míng-t'ien yǔ shíh-hou kěn wǒ ch'ù k'àn Chāng hsiēn-shêng ma?

(B) Tùi pu ch'ǐ, wǒ míng-t'ien tsǎo-shang yào ch'ù New York. Wǒ-mên lǐ-pài-ssǔ ch'ù, hǎo-pu-hao?

(A) Hǎo, wǒ-mên chiù lǐ-pài-ssǔ ch'ù pa. Wáng t'ài-t'ai hǎo ma?

(B) T'ā hěn hǎo, hsièh-hsieh. T'ā shuō t'ā yào ch'íng Lǐ t'ài-t'ai shuō-huà.

2.(A) Lǐ hsiēn-shêng kěn Lǐ t'ài-t'ai tsài chiā ma?

(B) T'ā-mên tsài chiā pa. Ch'íng ni těng-i-têng, wǒ ch'ù k'àn-i-k'an. -- Tùi pu ch'ǐ, wǒ shuō ts'ò lê. T'ā-mên pú tsài chiā.

(A) Hǎo pa, wǒ-mên míng-t'ien tsài lái k'àn t'a-mên.

3. Wǒ-mên chè pān yǔ èrh-shíh-kè hsüéh-shêng.

4. T'ā shuō-huà t'ài k'uài; wǒ t'īng pù hěn ch'īng-ch'u.

c. Translate into Chinese:

1. He does not speak clearly.

2. My house does not have a telephone.

3. Whom do you want to speak to?

4. When will Mr. Li be at home?

5. He is at Mr. Wang's residence.

6. He will be at home at half past nine.

7. Thank you, I will call again at ten o'clock.

8. Mr. Wang's telephone is busy; I have called three times [but] I did not get through.

9. My telephone number is 2596.

10. Our teacher speaks the standard national language.

## Lesson 15 Making a Visit

1. Vocabulary

| | | |
|---|---|---|
| 名 | míng | Name, title. A numerative of persons. |
| 片 | p'ièn | Card, piece. A numerative of flat objects. |
| 名片 | míng-p'ièn | Visiting card [ì-chāng míng-p'ièn]. |
| 字 | tzǜ | Word, character. A special kind of personal name. |
| 名字 | míng-tzŭ (1) | Name, formal name [í-kê míng-tzŭ]. |
| 訴 | sù | To tell, to state. |
| 告訴 | kào-su | To tell. |
| 知 | chīh | To know, to understand [lit.]. |
| 道 | tào | Road, way. |
| 知道 | chīh-tao (2) | To know. |
| 一會兒 | ì-huǐ-êrh | A while, a few moments. |
| 忙 | máng | Busy. |
| 進 | chìn | To enter. |
| 進來 | chìn-lai (3) | Come in. |
| 出 | ch'ū | Out. To go out. |
| 出去 | ch'ū-ch'ü | To go out. |
| 吃 | ch'īh | To eat, to take, to smoke. |

| | | |
|---|---|---|
| 飯 | fàn | Cooked rice, food. |
| 吃飯 | ch'īh-fàn (4) | To take a meal, to eat. |
| 吃煙 | ch'īh-yēn | To smoke. |
| 喝 | hē̃ | To drink. |
| 茶 | ch'á | Tea. |
| 喝茶 | hē̃ ch'á | To drink tea. |
| 杯 | pēi | Cup [ì-pēi ch'á]. |
| 茶杯 | ch'á-pēi | Teacup [í-kê ch'á-pēi]. |
| 歡 | huān | To rejoice. Happy. [Lit.] |
| 喜歡 | hsǐ-huan | To delight in, to like. |
| 極 | chí | Very, extremely. |
| 希 | hsī | To hope [lit.]. |
| 望 | wàng | To look for, to gaze at [lit.]. |
| 希望 | hsī-wàng | To hope. |
| 可 | k'ě | However. May. |
| 可是 | k'ě-shih | But, however. |
| 東 | tūng | East. |
| 西 | hsī | West. |
| 東西 | tūng-hsi (5) | Thing. |

2. Conversation

1.(A) Is Mr. Wang at home? I want to see Mr. Wang.

Wáng hsiēn-shēng tsài chiā ma? Wǒ yào k'àn - i - k'an Wáng hsiēn-shēng.

王先生在家嗎？我要看一看王先生.

2.(B) What is your honorable name, sir?

Hsiēn-shēng kuèi hsìng?

先生貴姓？

3.(A) This is my visiting card.

Chè shìh wǒ - tê míng-p'ièn.

這是我的名片.

4.(B) Does Mr. Wang know you are coming to see him?

Wáng hsiēn-shêng chīh-tao nǐ lái k'àn t'a ma?

王先生知道你來看他嗎?

5.(A) He knows, because yesterday I telephoned to tell him

T'ā chīh-tao, yīn-wèi wǒ tsó-t'ien tǎ tièn-huà kào-

他知道,因爲我昨天打電話告

that I would come to see him today.

su t'a, wǒ chīn-t'ien lái k'àn t'a.

訴他,我今天來看他.

6.(B) Please wait a while, sir.

Hsiēn-shêng, ch'íng ni těng ì-huǐ-êrh.

先生,請你等一會兒.

7.(B) Mr. Wang, there is a guest [who] has come.

Wáng hsiēn-shêng, yǔ í-wèi k'è-jên lái lê.

王先生,有一位客人來了.

8.(C) Who is it?

Shìh shuí?

是誰?

9.(B) It is Mr. Hsia; this is his visiting card.

Shìh Hsià hsiēn-shêng; chè shìh t'ā-tê míng-p'ièn.

是夏先生;這是他的名片.

10.(C) Ask him to come in.

Ch'ǐng t'a chìn-lai pa.

請他進來罷.

11.(A) Are you busy, Mr. Wang?

Wáng hsiēn-shêng máng ma?

王先生忙嗎?

12.(C) I'm not busy - Please come in and sit down.

Pù máng - Ch'ǐng chìn-lai tsò-i-tso.

不忙 - 請進來坐一坐.

13.(A) Are your wife and daughter both at home?

T'ài-t'ai kěn hsiáo-chieh tōu tsài chiā ma?

太太跟小姐都在家嗎?

14.(C) They have gone out, but they will be back soon.

T'ā-mên ch'ū-ch'ü lê, k'ě-shih k'uài huí-lai lê (6).

他們出去了,可是快囘來了.

Mr. Hsia, do you smoke?

Hsià hsiēn-shêng ch'īh-yēn ma?

夏先生吃煙嗎?

15.(A) Thank you, I do not (literally, do not know how to) smoke; please go ahead.
Hsièh-hsieh, wǒ pú huì ch'īh-yēn, ní ch'ǐng pa.
謝謝，我不會吃煙，你請罷.

16.(C) Won't you have (literally, please drink) a cup of tea?
Ch'ǐng hē ì - pēi ch'á pa.
請喝一杯茶罷.

17.(A) Thank you. Is this Chinese tea? I hope it
Hsièh-hsieh. Chè shìh Chūng-kuo ch'á ma? Wǒ hsī-wàng
謝謝. 這是中國茶嗎? 我希望
is (Chinese tea), because I like very much to drink
shìh Chūng-kuo ch'á, yīn-wèi wó hěn hsǐ-huan hē Chūng-
是中國茶，因爲我很喜歡喝中
Chinese tea.
kuo ch'á.
國茶.

18.(C) We have here both what you hope for and what
Ní sǒ hsī-wàng kēn ní só hsǐ-huan tê tūng-hsi wǒ-
你所希望跟你所喜歡的東西，我
you like. You see this is Chinese
mên chè -li tōu yǔ (7). Nǐ k'àn chè shìh Chūng-kuo
們這裏都有. 你看這是中國
tea; this teacup also was bought in China.
ch'á; chè - kê ch'á-pēi yěh shìh tsài Chūng-kuo mǎi - tê (8).
茶；這個茶杯也是在中國買的.

19.(A) Beautiful indeed! I have a friend surnamed
Hǎo-k'àn chí lê! Wó yǔ í - kê p'éng -yu, hsìng
好看極了! 我有一個朋友，姓
Li, do you know [him]?
Lǐ, nǐ jèn-shih ma?
李，你認識嗎?

20.(C) Mr. Li? What is his personal name?
Lǐ hsiēn-shêng? T'ā chiào shén - mo míng-tzǔ(9)?
李先生? 他叫甚麼名字?

21.(A) His name is Li Ying.
T'ā chiào Lǐ Yīng(10).
他叫李英.

22.(C) I know of that man, but I am not acquainted with him.
Wǒ chīh-tao nà - kê jén, k'ě-shih wǒ pú jèn-shih t'a.
我知道那個人，可是我不認識他.

23.(A) He is my good friend. I am inviting him for

T'ā shìh wǒ - tê hǎo p'ếng - yu. Wó lǐ - pài - ī ch'ǐng

他是我的好朋友。我禮拜一請

dinner on Monday. Will you and your wife come too?

t'a ch'īh-fàn. Ch'íng ni kěn t'ài-t'ai tōu lái pa.

他吃飯。請你跟太太都來罷。

24.(C) Good, we'll both come. I hope to meet that

Hǎo, wǒ - mên tou lái. Wǒ hsī-wàng chièn-chièn nà-

好，我們都來。我希望見見那

Mr. Li.

wèi Lǐ hsiēn-shêng(11).

位李先生。

NOTES:

(1) "Míng-tzǔ": Chinese names are explained by Professor H.G. Creel in his Literary Chinese by the Inductive Method; Volume I, page 57, as follows: "The names by which a Chinese is known are more various and more complex than our own. The 姓 hsing$^4$ or surname is that of the family into which he is born or adopted; it usually consists of one character, but there are a few surnames composed of two or even more characters. The 名 ming$^2$ or personal name is usually two characters, but may be only one. The hsing and ming together make up the name by which a Chinese is formally known, and which he himself signs to documents. But for anyone but his parents, or one in a similar position of great superiority, to call him by his ming, or to address him so in a letter, would be very discourteous. For social purposes the ming is replaced by the 字 tzŭ$^4$ or 'style'. In addition to these names many Chinese have a 號 hao$^4$ or sobriquet, by which they may be quite generally known; this is acquired later in life than the other names, and may be chosen by the person himself or conferred upon him by others. In Chinese the surname is written first."

(2) The Distinction between "Chīh-tao" and "Jèn-shih"

"Chīh-tao", literally, "to know the road", means "to know, to be aware of, to understand". "Jèn-shih" primarily means "to recognize, to be acquainted with"; as a noun it means "acquaintance, recognition". An idiomatic expression is "Wǒ kěn t'ā jèn-shih" - "I am acquainted with him". It will save some confusion if students will remember that the most important meaning of "chīh-tao" is "to know, to understand", and of "jèn-shih" is "to recognize, to be acquainted with".

(3) "Chìn-lai", "ch'ū-ch'ü", and "huí-lai" belong to a class of compound verbs which are made up of a main verb and a co-verb*

*A co-verb is a separable verbal suffix. It differs from an auxiliary verb in that (a) it always follows the main verb, whereas

("lái", "ch'ǜ") which indicates the direction of the action of the main verb. "Lái" indicates motion toward the speaker, "ch'ǜ", motion from the speaker (Compare Lesson 8, note 6). Note that these are separable suffixes: i.e., other words may come between the main verb and the co-verb. For example: "Chìn chè-êrh lai" 進這兒來 - "Come in here"; "Ch'ū nà-êrh ch'ü" 出那兒去 - "Go out there"; "Huí chiā lai" 回家來 - "Come back home"; "Huí chiā ch'ü" 回家去 - "Go back home".

(4) "Ch'īh-fàn" and "ch'īh-yēn", like "shuō-huà" (see Lesson 5, note 7), are verb-noun phrases which contain their own object and are used only intransitively, as English uses the verbs "to eat" and "to smoke" intransitively. When "ch'īh" has another object in the sentence, "fàn" or "yēn" should be omitted; and when there are modifiers of "fàn" or "yēn", these should be inserted between the two parts of the verb-noun phrase. For example: "Wǒ ch'īh Chūng-kuo fàn" 我吃中國飯 - "I eat Chinese food" (never: "Wǒ ch'īh-fàn Chūng-kuo fàn").

(5) The use of "tūng-hsi", literally "east-west", to mean "a thing" requires some explanation. According to Chinese dictionaries, "things" are produced in the four directions, east, south, west, north; but by abbreviation only two directions are used to express the idea of "things", as only two seasons are mentioned in the term "ch'ūn-ch'iū" - "spring and autumn", representing a year.

(6) The particle "lê" here only gives emphasis to the idea that something is going to happen.

(7) A literal translation of this sentence would be "You that-which-hope and you that-which-like 's things, we here both have". See the note on the use of "sǒ" at the end of this lesson.

(8) Chinese verbs make no difference between active and passive voice, but the direction of action is usually implied in the context. The literal translation of this sentence obviously should be "This teacup also was bought in China".

(9) "Nǐ chiào shén-mo míng-tzǔ?" is much less polite than "Nǐ kuèi hsìng?", but when referring to a third person it is all right to say: "T'ā chiào shén-mo míng-tzǔ?"

(10) See note 8.

(11) The last phrase is a slight abbreviation of "chièn-i-chien nà-i-wèi Lǐ hsiēn-shêng"; the shorter form reads more smoothly.

3. Tone and Pronunciation Drill

a. Particular attention should be paid to the distinction between "hsǐ-huan" and "hsī-wàng", which is likely to be confusing to students. Listen carefully to your instructor's pronunciation of the following phrases:

---

an auxiliary verb precedes it; (b) a co-verb usually indicates the manner or direction of the main verb, while an auxiliary verb usually serves to conjugate the main verb, i.e., to express relations of persons and tenses. Cf. Jos. Mullie, The Structural Principles of the Chinese Language (Peiping, 1937), Vol. II, pp. 113-114.

| | |
|---|---|
| Wó hsǐ-huan | Wǒ hsī-wàng |
| Wó hsǐ-huan ch'ǜ | Wǒ hsī-wàng ch'ǜ |
| Wó hsǐ-huan hsià-yǚ | Wǒ hsī-wàng hsià-yǚ |

b. Tone drill

| | | | | | | | |
|---|---|---|---|---|---|---|---|
| chīh | chíh | chǐh | chìh | ch'ǖ | ch'ǘ | ch'ǚ | ch'ǜ |
| ch'īh | ch'íh | ch'ǐh | ch'ìh | ch'ū | ch'ú | ch'ǔ | ch'ù |
| shīh | shíh | shǐh | shìh | tzŭ̄ | tzŭ́ | tzŭ̌ | tzŭ̀ |
| jên̄ | jêń | jêň | jêǹ | p'iēn | p'ién | p'iěn | p'ièn |

4. Exercises

a. "Fill-in" sentences

| | |
|---|---|
| 1. Wǒ tsó-t'ien ch'ǐng t'a ... | Yesterday I invited him ... |
| 2. T'ā chiào ... ... | He is called ... ... |
| 3. Yǔ í-wèi ... ... lái k'àn ni. | There is a ... come to see you. |
| 4. Wǒ kào-su ni ... ... ... | I tell you ... ... ... |
| 5. Ch'íng ni ... -i- ... | Please (wait, sit, etc.) ... a ... |
| 6. T'ā-mên shén-mo shíh-hou ... ? | When will they (come, go, etc.) ... ? |
| 7. ... ... ... tsài chiā ma? | Is ... ... at home? |
| 8. Wǒ hsī-wàng ... yīn-wèi ... | I hope ... because ... |
| 9. Wó hsǐ-huan ... k'ě-shih ... | I like ... but ... |

b. Translate into English:

1. Shuí ch'íng Lǐ hsiēn-shêng ch'īh-fàn lê?
2. Hsià hsiēn-shêng ch'ǐng t'a lê, yéh ch'ǐng lê Wáng hsiēn-shêng.
3. Nǐ jèn-shih Lǐ hsiēn-shêng ma?
4. Hsià hsiēn-shêng ch'ǐng ch'īh-fàn, yú chǐ-wèi k'è-jên?
5. Hsièn-tsài Wáng hsiáo-chieh pú tsài chiā.
6. T'ā ssŭ-tiěn-chūng ch'ū-ch'ü lê; wǒ pù chīh-tao t'ā shén-mo shíh-hou huí-lai.
7. Wǒ pú tsài chiā, yǔ jén lái lê méi-yǔ?
8. Ch'ǐng chìn-lai.
9. Ch'ǐng wèn ni na, nà-kê tūng-hsi chiào shén-mo míng-tzŭ?
10. Tō-shǎo kūng-ch'ǐh hé ì kūng-lǐ?

c. Translate into Chinese:

1. Do you know at what time we are having dinner?

2. Do you know Mrs. Li? She had (drank) tea with us yesterday.

3. I do not (know how to) smoke.

4. There are two visiting cards; one is Miss Wang's [and] one is Miss Hsia's.

5. They like Chinese things.

6. They telephoned to tell me they wanted to come.

7. Please come in and sit down.

8. Wait a minute; we do not have time now.

9. What is your name? Do you have a visiting card?

10. Because you are very busy, therefore I should like to go away.

## On the Use of "Sŏ" 所

"Sŏ" is one of the most important particles in literary Chinese, and the influence of tradition causes it to be used to a considerable extent in refined spoken Chinese.

1. As a relative pronoun, "sŏ" is translated "that which, those who". It is usually followed by "tê" 的 and used in the possessive case, plural number, and past tense. The word order of a relative clause using "sŏ" is as follows: noun (or pronoun) - sŏ - verb - tê - noun. For example:

"T'ā sŏ-shuō-tê huà" 他所說的話 - "He that-which spoke 's words", i.e., "the words which he spoke".

"Tā sŏ-jèn-shih-tê jén" 他所認識的人 - "The people whom he knew".

Thus the word order in these clauses is just the opposite of that in English; in English the word modified by the relative expression comes before its modifier, in Chinese the modifier comes first.

2. Another common use of "sŏ" is in such expressions as fit the pattern "só-yŭ-tê - noun - tōu ... ". "Só-yŭ-tê" 所有的 means "all that there are" or simply "all"; "sŏ-shuō-tê", "all that [he] said"; etc.; and "tōu" after the noun gives particular emphasis on the idea of "all". For example:

"T'ā sŏ-shuō-tê huà tōu hĕn tuì" 他所說的話都很對 - "All that he said was correct".

"T'ā sǒ-mǎi-tê tūng-hsi tōu hǎo" 他所買的東西都好 - "All that he bought is good".

"Só-yǔ-tê jén tōu hěn k'è-ch'i" 所有的人都很客氣 - "All the people are very polite".

3. "Só-ǐ" 所以, literally "that by means of which", means "thereby, therefore"; it is a conjunction of consequence used after a subordinate clause. For example:

"Yīn-wèi tsó-t'ien hsià tà <u>hsüěh</u>, só-ǐ <u>chīn</u>-t'ien hěn lěng" 因為昨天下大雪，所以今天很冷 - "Because it snowed heavily yesterday, therefore today it is very cold".

## Lesson 16 What Is Your Occupation?

1. Vocabulary

| | | |
|---|---|---|
| 作 or 做 | tsò | To do, to make, to be. |
| 作事 | tsò-shìh | To work. |
| 教 | chiào | Teaching, instruction. |
| | chiāo | To teach. |
| 教書 | chiāo-shū | To teach. |
| 員 | yüán | Staff member, official [seldom used alone]. |
| 教員 | chiào-yüán | Teacher [í-kê or í-wèi chiào-yüán]. |
| 學校 | hsüéh-hsiào | School [í-kê hsüéh-hsiào]. |
| 大學 | tà-hsüéh | College, university [í-kê tà-hsüéh]. |
| 中學 | chūng-hsüéh | High school [í-kê chūng-hsüéh]. |
| 男 | nán | Male. Son. |
| 女 | nǚ | Female. Girl, woman. |
| 念 | nièn | To study, to read. |
| 念書 | nièn-shū | To study. |
| 寫 | hsiěh | To write. |
| 寫字 | hsiěh-tzǔ | To write characters. |
| 愛 | ài | To love, to like. |
| 每 | měi | Each, every. |

| | | |
|---|---|---|
| 定 | tìng | Certainly. To decide. |
| 一定 | í-tìng | Positively. Certain. |
| 到 | tào | To arrive at. To, until. |
| 德 | tế | Virtue. German. |
| 德國 | Tế-kuo | Germany. |
| 德文 | Tế-wến | German language. |
| 日本 | Jìh-pěn | Japan. |
| 日文 | Jìh-wến | Japanese language. |
| 只 | chǐh | Only, merely. |
| 談 | t'án (1) | To talk, to chat, to converse. |
| 過 | kuò (2) | To exceed, to pass through. Over, too much. A co-verb indicating the perfect tense. |
| 那麼 | nà-mo (3) | Then, well then, in that case. |

2. Conversation

1.(A) Where are you working?
Nǐ tsài ná - li tsò-shìh?
你在那裏作事?

2.(B) I am teaching in China University.
Wǒ tsài Chūng-kuo tà - hsüéh chiāo-shū.
我在中國大學教書.

3.(A) What are you teaching?
Nǐ chiāo shến - mo shū?
你教甚麼書?

4.(B) I teach English.
Wǒ chiāo Yīng-wến.
我教英文.

5.(A) How many students are there in your school?
Nǐ - mên hsüéh-hsiào yǔ tō - shǎo hsüéh-shêng?
你們學校有多少學生?

6.(B) There are a thousand and more students.
Yǔ ì - ch'iēn tō hsüéh-shêng.
有一千多學生.

7.(A) Is it co-educational?
Shìh nán - nǔ t'úng-hsüéh (4) ma?
是男女同學嗎?

8.(B) Yes. We have three hundred and more women students and

Shìh-tê. Wŏ-mên yŭ sān-păi tō nŭ hsüéh-shêng, ch'ī-

是的。我們有三百多女學生，七

seven hundred and more men students.

păi tō nán hsüéh-shêng.

百多男學生。

9.(A) How many teachers are there?

Yŭ tō-shăo chiào-yüán?

有多少教員？

10.(B) There are eighty and more.

Yŭ pā-shíh tō wèi.

有八十多位。

11.(A) How many students study English with you?

Tō-shăo hsüéh-shêng kĕn nĭ nièn Yīng-wén?

多少學生跟你念英文？

12.(B) There are thirty students, twenty men and ten

Yŭ sān-shíh-kè hsüéh-shêng, èrh-shíh-kè nán-tê(5), shíh-

有三十個學生，二十個男的，十

women.

kê nŭ-tê.

個女的。

13.(A) Do they all like to study English?

T'ā-mên tōu ài nièn Yīng-wén ma?

他們都愛念英文嗎？

14.(B) Some like to study, some do not like to study.

Yŭ-tê ài nièn, yŭ-tê pú ài nièn.

有的愛念，有的不愛念。

15.(A) Do they know both how to speak and how to write?

T'ā-mên tōu huì shuō huì hsiĕh ma?

他們都會說會寫嗎？

16.(B) They can do both a little.

T'ā-mên tōu huì ì-tiĕn-êrh.

他們都會一點兒。

17.(A) Do they have English class every day?

T'ā-mên mĕi t'iēn tōu yŭ Yīng-wén pān ma?

他們每天都有英文班嗎？

18.(B) No, they have only three hours every week.

Pū, t'ā-mên mĕi-kê lĭ-pài chíh yŭ sān-kê chūng-tiĕn.

不，他們每個禮拜只有三個鐘點。

19.(A) How many years have you taught English?
Nǐ chiāo lê chǐ nién Yīng-wén le?
你教了幾年英文了?

20.(B) I have taught for twenty years, fifteen years in high school and five years in college.
Wǒ chiāo lê èrh-shíh nién lê, shíh-wǔ nién tsài chūng-hsüéh, wǔ nién tsài tà-hsüéh.
我教了二十年了,十五年在中學,五年在大學.

21.(A) Well, you certainly must be a very good English teacher.
Nà-mo, nǐ í-tìng shìh í-kê hěn hǎo-tê Yīng-wén chiào-yüán.
那麽,你一定是一個很好的英文教員.

22.(B) Not necessarily. May I ask, what work do you do?
Yěh pù í-tìng. Ch'ǐng wèn, nǐ tsò shén-mo shih?
也不一定. 請問,你作甚麽事?

23.(A) I am a merchant. I came to China only five months ago.
Wǒ shìh tsò-mǎi-mài-tê. Wǒ lái Chung-kuo chih wǔ-kê yüèh.
我是作買賣的. 我來中國只五個月.

24.(B) Your Chinese is very good. Where did you learn it?
Nǐ-tê Chūng-kuo-huà hěn hǎo. Ni shih tsài ná-li hsüéh-tê?
你的中國話很好. 你是在那裏學的?

25.(A) I learned it in America.
Wǒ shìh tsài Měi-kuo hsüéh-tê.
我是在美國學的.

26.(B) Have you studied Japanese and German?
Nǐ hsüéh kuò Jìh-wén kěn Té-wén ma?
你學過日文跟德文嗎?

27.(A) I have not studied German, but when I was in Japan
Wǒ méi-yǔ hsüéh kuò Té-wén, k'ě-shih wǒ tsài Jìh-pěn
我沒有學過德文,可是我在日本

I learned a little Japanese.

tê shíh-hou, hsüéh kuò ì - tiěn-êrh Jìh-wěn.

的時候，學過一點兒日文。

28.(B) Please come to my house to have tea with me this Saturday

Chè lǐ - pài-liù hsià - wǔ ch'íng ni tào wǒ chiā - li hē

這禮拜六下午請你到我家裏喝

afternoon; we'll talk a little more, [is that] all right?

pēi ch'á; wǒ - mên tō t'án ì - huǐ-êrh, hǎo - pu - hao?

杯茶，我們多談一會兒，好不好？

29.(A) All right, I will certainly go. Thank you.

Hǎo pa, wǒ í - tìng ch'ù. Hsièh-hsieh.

好罷，我一定去. 謝謝.

NOTES:

(1) "T'án" and "shuō" are similar in meaning, but "t'án", which is a more informal word than "shuō", means "to talk, to chat, to carry on a conversation", while "shuō" usually means "to speak", or to say something specific.

(2) "Kuò" as a co-verb is an indicator of past tense which follows the main verb. It has the senses of "experienced, passed through"; sometimes it suggests the idea of "once" or "ever". "Kuò" and "lê" as indicators of past tense can usually be interchanged and are sometimes used together: "Ch'īh kuò lê" - "[I] have eaten". The difference is that while "lê" indicates general past tense or completed action, "kuò" denotes some elements involving both time and space, something in connection with action or changing of space, as in "passing through" or "experiencing".

(3) "Nà-mo", "well then, in that case, thus", is an unemphatic expression which is usually almost imperceptible in speech, but is used in maintaining continuity, or to mark a change to a new idea or the making of a decision.

(4) Literally, "male-female together-study", this expression conveys the idea of "co-education".

(5) "Tê" here is used as a pronoun meaning "one"; "nán-tê" and "nǔ-tê" might be translated literally "male ones" and "female ones". This use of "tê" as a pronoun, to avoid repetition of the noun, is common.

3. Tone and Pronunciation Drill

| | | | | | | | |
|---|---|---|---|---|---|---|---|
| mēi | méi | měi | mèi | hsüēh | hsüéh | hsüěh | hsüèh |
| nān | nán | nǎn | nàn | hsiāo | hsiáo | hsiǎo | hsiào |
| yüān | yüán | yüǎn | yüàn | hsiēh | hsiéh | hsiěh | hsièh |
| fā | fá | fǎ | fà | tē̂ | tế | tê̌ | tề |
| huā | huá | huǎ | huà | tā | tá | tǎ | tà |

4. Exercises

a. "Fill-in" sentences:

| | |
|---|---|
| 1. Wǒ chiāo ... ... | I teach ... ... |
| 2. Ní yǔ tō-shǎo ... ... ? | How many ... ... have you? |
| 3. Yǔ-tê ... ... , yǔ-tê ... ... | Some ... ... , some ... ... |
| 4. Nǐ chiāo lê chǐ nién ... lê? | How long have you taught ... ? |
| 5. Nǐ í-tìng shìh ... ... | You must certainly be ... ... |
| 6. T'ā-mên tōu ài ... ... ma? | Do they all like ... ... ? |
| 7. Nǐ huì shuō ... ... ma? | Can you speak (language) ... ? |
| 8. Só-yǔ-tê ... tōu ... | All the ... are ... |

b. Translate into English:

1. Wǒ shìh chiào-yüán.
2. Wǒ tsài í-kê hsüéh-hsiào chiāo-shū.
3. Ní yǔ tō-shǎo hsüéh-shêng?
4. Wó yǔ èrh-shíh-pěn shū: shíh-wú-pěn shìh Té-wén-tê, wú-pěn shìh Jìh-wén-tê.
5. Nǐ-tê hsüéh-shêng-mên ài nièn-shū ma?
6. T'ā-mên pú ài nièn-shū, t'ā-mên ài hsiěh-tzǔ.
7. T'ā-mên kěn ní nièn shén-mo?
8. Wǒ chiāo t'ā-mên Chūng-kuo-huà.
9. Ní měi t'iēn chiāo chí tiěn-chūng?
10. Pù í-tìng, yǔ-tê shíh-hou tō, yǔ-tê shíh-hou shǎo.

c. Translate into Chinese:

1. Do all your students like to study Chinese?
2. Yes, they all like to study it.
3. Are you a student?
4. Now I am a business man.
5. Do you have very much work to do?
6. I am very busy.

7. What is the matter?

8. There is nothing wrong (there is no matter).

9. I like to smoke.

10. I like to study Chinese, German, French, English, and Japanese.

## On the Use of "Tào" 到

1. As a main verb, "tào" means "to arrive".

"Wǒ shìh tsó-t'ien tào-tê" 我是昨天到的 - "I arrived yesterday".

"Tào-lê méi-yǔ?" 到了沒有? - "Has [he, it] arrived?"

"Tào-lê" 到了 - "[He] has arrived", "This is [our] destination".

"Shíh-hou tào-lê" 時候到了. - "The time has come" or "The time is up."

From the sense of "to arrive" are derived the meanings "to reach, to come to, to be present".

"Tào pu liǎo" 到不了 - "unable to reach".

"Yǔ tō-shǎo jến tào lê, tō-shǎo jến méi-yǔ tào?" 有多少人到了,多少人沒有到? - "How many people came, how many did not?" or "How many people were present, how many were absent?"

"T'ā chīn-t'ien méi-yǔ tào" 他今天沒有到 - "He was absent today".

2. As a co-verb, "tào" indicates that the action expressed by the main verb has been performed to a certain extent, or has been completed. It is a sign of the past tense or of the potential mood.

"Lái tào" 來到 - "[He] has come".

"Tsò tào" 作到 - "to have done [as much as to reach one's aim]".

"Tsò tế tào" 作得到 - "can be done".

"Tsò pu tào" 作不到 - "cannot be done".

"K'àn tế tào" 看得到 - "can be seen".

"K'àn tào lê" 看到了 - "has seen [it]".

"K'àn pu tào" 看不到 - "cannot be seen".

3. As a preposition, "tào" means "to, at, until".

"Nǐ tào nǎ-êrh ch'ù?" 你到那兒去? - "(To) where are you going?"

"Wǒ-mên ì-t'iēn máng tào wǎn" 我們一天忙到晚.- Literally, "We one day busy until night", i.e., "We are busy all day, [from morning] to night".

"Těng tào míng-t'ien tsài shuō" 等到明天再說.- "Wait until tomorrow to talk [about it] again".

Omission of "Tào" with "Chè-êrh", "Nà-êrh", and "Nǎ-êrh"

The meaning of "Where are you going?" can be expressed equally well in Chinese with or without "tào": "Nǐ tào nǎ-êrh ch'ü?" or "Nǐ ch'ǜ nǎ-êrh?" "You come here" can be expressed either by "Nǐ tào chè-êrh lai", or by "Nǐ lái chè-êrh". In each case, the first form is generally commoner, but the second is typically Pekingese. When "tào" is omitted, "lái" or "ch'ǜ" follows immediately after the subject.

## Lesson 17 Visiting a Family

1. Vocabulary

| | | |
|---|---|---|
| 親 | ch'īn | Parent, relative. Dear. [Lit.] |
| 父 | fù | Father [lit.]. |
| 父親 | fù-ch'in | Father [í-kê fù-ch'in]. |
| 爸爸 | pà-pa (1) | Papa. |
| 母 | mǔ | Mother [lit.]. |
| 母親 | mǔ-ch'in | Mother [í-kê mǔ-ch'in]. |
| 媽 | mā | Mother, old woman (familiar). |
| 媽媽 | mā-ma | Mama [í-kê mā-ma]. |
| 父母 | fù-mǔ | Parents. |
| 兄 | hsiūng | Elder brother [lit.]. |
| 弟 | tì | Younger brother [lit.]. |
| 兄弟 | hsiūng-tì (2) | Brothers. |
| 哥哥 | kē-kê | Elder brother [í-kê kē-kê]. |
| 弟弟 | tì-ti | Younger brother [í-kê tì-ti]. |
| 姐姐 | chiěh-chieh | Elder sister [í-kê chiěh-chieh]. |
| 妹妹 | mèi-mei | Younger sister [í-kê mèi-mei]. |
| 姐妹 | chiěh-mèi | Sisters. |

| | | |
|---|---|---|
| 孩 | hái | Child [seldom used alone]. |
| 孩子 | hái-tzŭ (3) | Child, children [í-kê hái-tzŭ]. |
| 歲 | suì | Age, year. |
| 老 | lăo | Old. Always. |
| 老先生 | lăo-hsiēn-shêng(4) | Venerable sir (polite form of address) [í-wèi or í-kê lăo-hsiēn-shêng]. |
| 老太太 | lăo-t'ài-t'ai | Venerable lady (polite form of address) [í-wèi or í-kê lăo-t'ài-t'ai]. Your mother. |
| 久 | chiŭ | For a long time. Long. |
| 仰 | yăng | To look up to, to rely on. |
| 久仰 | chiú-yăng (5) | I have long desired to meet you (conventional on being introduced to a famous person). |
| 介紹 | chièh-shào | To introduce. Introductory. |
| 最 | tsuì (6) | Most, extremely. |
| 奬 | chiăng | To praise. Prize. |
| 過奬 | kuò-chiăng | Over-complimentary, flattering. |
| 把 | pă | To take, to hold in the hand. An indicator of the objective case. |
| 給 | kĕi | To give to. To, for. |
| 爺 | yéh | Father. A term of respect applied to officials (not used alone). |
| 少爺 | shào-yeh (7) | Your son. |
| 可以 | k'ĕ-i | May, can, that will do. Sometimes used like "O.K." |

2. Conversation

1. How many people are there in your family?

   Nĭ(8) chiā yŭ tō - shăo jén?

   你 家 有 多 少 人?

2. There are eleven people in my family.

   Wŏ chiā yŭ shíh - í - kè jén.

   我 家 有 十 一 個 人.

3. Who are there in your family?

   Nĭ chiā yŭ shén - mo jén?

   你 家 有 甚 麽 人?

4. There are my parents, brothers, sisters, wife, and children.
Yú wǒ fù-mǔ, hsiūng-tì, chiěh-mèi, t'ài-t'ai, kěn hái-tzŭ-mên.
有我父母，兄弟，姐妹，太太，跟孩子們。

5. Please introduce me to the members of your family, [will that be] all right?
Ch'íng ni pá wo chièh-shào kéi(9) nǐ chiā-tê jén, hǎo-pu-hao?
請你把我介紹給你家的人，好不好？

6. All right, tomorrow afternoon at six o'clock please come to my home and have dinner. We can have a chat.
Hǎo, míng-t'ien hsià-wǔ, liù tiěn-chūng, ch'ǐng lái wǒ chiā ch'īh-fàn. Wǒ-mên k'ě-i t'án-i-t'an(10).
好，明天下午，六點鐘，請來我家吃飯。我們可以談一談。

7. Thank you, you are too generous.
Hsièh-hsieh, nǐ t'ài k'è-ch'i lê.
謝謝，你太客氣了。

8. Papa, mama, this is my American friend, Mr. Smith. This is my father, and [this is my] mother.
Pà-pa, mā-ma, chè shìh wǒ-tê Měi-kuo p'éng-yu, Smith hsiēn-shêng. Chè shìh wǒ fù-ch'in kěn mǔ-ch'in.
爸爸，媽媽，這是我的美國朋友 Smith 先生。這是我父親跟母親。

9. Venerable sir, Mr. Wang, venerable lady, Mrs. Wang, I have long desired to know you.
Wáng lǎo-hsiēn-shêng, Wáng lǎo-t'ài-t'ai, chiú-yǎng, chiú-yǎng.
王老先生，王老太太，久仰，久仰。

10. Mr. Smith, your Chinese is very good.
Smith hsiēn-shêng, nǐ-tê Chūng-kuo-huà hěn hǎo.
Smith 先生，你的中國話很好。

11. You are too complimentary, thank you.
Kuò-chiǎng, kuò-chiǎng, hsièh-hsieh.
過奬，過奬，謝謝。

12. Mr. Smith, this is my elder brother. This is my younger
Smith hsiēn-shêng, chè shìh wǒ kē - kê. Chè shìh wǒ tì -
Smith 先生，這是我哥哥。這是我弟
brother. That is my younger sister.
ti. Nà shìh wǒ - tê(11) hsiǎo mèi-mei.
弟。那是我的小妹妹。

13. How are you all? Is your wife at home?
Nǐ -mên tōu hǎo ma? Nǐ t'ài-t'ai tsài chiā ma?
你們都好嗎？你太太在家嗎？

14. I am sorry, she has something to do; after a while
Tùi pu ch'ǐ, t'ā yǔ ì - tiěn-êrh shìh; ì - hǔi - êrh
對不起，他有一點兒事；一會兒
(then) she will come out to meet you.
chiù ch'ū-lai chièn ni.
就出來見你。

15. Where are your daughters and sons (polite form)?
Nǐ - tê hsiáo-chieh kēn shào-yeh tsài ná - li?
你的小姐 跟少爺在那裏？

16. They have all gone out. They will soon be back.
T'ā-mên tōu ch'ū-ch'ü lê. Pù chiǔ chiù húi-lai.
他們都出去了。不久就囘來。

17. How many daughters and sons have you?
Ní yú chǐ-wèi hsiáo-chieh shào-yeh?
你有幾位小姐少爺？

18. I have three children, two boys [and] one
Wó yǔ sān - kê hái-tzŭ, liǎng - kê nán hái- tzŭ, í -
我有三個孩子，兩個男孩子，一
girl.
kê nǚ hái-tzŭ.
個女孩子。

19. How old are they?
T'ā-mên chǐ sùi lê?
他們幾歲了？

20. The oldest is ten years old, the second eight years old, the
Tsùi - tà - tê(12) shíh sùi, tì - èrh - kê pá sùi, tsùi-hsiǎo-
最大的 十歲，第二個八歲，最小
youngest five years old.
tê wǔ sùi.
的五歲。

21. Mr. Smith, how many people are there in your family?
Smith hsiēn-shêng, nǐ chiā yú chǐ - kê jén?
Smith 先生，你家有幾個人？

22. There are very few in my family; there are my wife and one small child.
Wǒ chiā - tê jén hén shǎo; yú wǒ t'ài-t'ai kēn í - kê hsiǎo hái-tzŭ.
我家的人很少；有我太太跟一個小孩子.

23. Where are they at present?
Hsièn-tsài t'ā-mên tsài ná - li?
現在他們在那裏？

24. They are in America.
T'ā-mên tsài Měi-kuo.
他們在美國.

25. Have you [any] sisters?
Ní yú chiěh-mèi méi - yŭ?
你有姐妹沒有？

26. I have an elder sister.
Wó yŭ í - kê chiěh-chieh.
我有一個姐姐.

27. Mr. Smith, here comes my wife.
Smith hsiēn-shêng, wǒ t'ài-t'ai lái lê.
Smith 先生，我太太來了.

28. How are you, Mrs. Wang?
Wáng t'ài-t'ai, ní hǎo ma?
王太太，你好嗎？

29. I am very well, thank you. I am sorry; because I was very busy I [could] not come out to talk with you.
Wó hén hǎo, hsièh-hsieh. Tuì pu ch'ǐ; yīn - wèi wó hěn máng, wǒ méi - yŭ ch'ū-lai kēn nǐ t'án-huà.
我很好，謝謝. 對不起；因爲我很忙，我沒有出來跟你談話.

30. Don't mention it. Mr. Wang told me that you were very busy.
Pú k'è-ch'i. Wáng hsiēn-shêng kào-su wo lê ní hěn máng.
不客氣. 王先生告訴我了你很忙.

31. Dinner is ready now, please come and eat.
Hsièn-tsài fàn té lê, ch'íng ni - mên ch'ù ch'īh-fàn pa.
現在飯得了；請你們去吃飯罷.

NOTES:

(1) "Pà-pa" and "mā-ma" are colloquial terms used in Chinese as in English by children to their parents and by husband and wife in addressing each other. The words "kē", "tì", "chiěh", and "mèi" are reduplicated in colloquial usage: "kē-kê", "tì-ti", and so forth. The more literary terms for father and mother are "fù-ch'in" and "mǔ-ch'in". The most polite forms for referring to members of one's own family in speaking to other people are "chiā-fù", "chiā-mǔ" (literally, "family father", "family mother"), and so on. There are many other polite or formal terms for addressing or referring to one's own or other people's relatives, but since modern educated Chinese no longer pay such strict attention to formality as formerly, foreigners may certainly be excused from memorizing all such specialized expressions.

(2) No numerative is needed before "hsiūng-tì" or "chiěh-mèi". For example: "Ní yú chǐ hsiūng-tì?"; "Wó yǔ sān hsiūng-tì".

(3) "Hái-tzŭ" means "child, children"; children are also called "hsiǎo hái" or "hsiǎo hái-tzŭ" - "small children".

(4) "Lǎo-hsiēn-shêng", "old sir, venerable sir", is a polite term of address to one who is really old or who is regarded as venerable or important.

(5) "Chiú-yǎng, chiú-yǎng" is a very polite expression used to one who is really well-known or to one whose name the speaker has heard before.

(6) The superlative of adjectives is formed in Chinese by the use of "tsuì" before and "tê" following the adjective, as in "tsuì-hǎo-tê", "the best"; "tsuì-tà-tê", "the largest".

(7) "Yéh" is a term of respect. "Lǎo-yeh" means an old gentleman, an official, or a master, and "shào-yeh" means a young gentleman or an official's son, and therefore is a polite term for someone else's son. It is used in speaking of a friend's son, or by a servant of his employer's son. "Yéh-yeh" is a childish expression, locally used for "papa".

(8) "Tê" 的 as a sign of the possessive is usually omitted when a possessive pronoun is used before a term of family relationship, before "chiā", and before a few other words meaning "house" or "room". "Nǐ chiā", "wó chiěh-chieh" mean the same as "nǐ-tê chiā", "wǒ-tê chiěh-chieh", but while the form with "tê" is more strictly grammatical, the form without it is more idiomatic. In spoken Chinese, it is best to be as idiomatic as possible.

(9) "Pǎ ... kěi" means literally "take ... to". See special note on "pǎ" at the end of this lesson.

(10) "T'án-i-t'an" means "talk for a while" or "have a talk". In the same way, "tsǒu-i-tsou" means "walk a while", "tsò-i-tso" - "sit a while", etc. Cf. Lesson 6, note 1.

(11) This sentence sounds much better with "tê", and is easier to pronounce.

(12) "Tê" must be used after an adjective in the superlative degree.

3. Tone and Pronunciation Drill

| | | | | | | | |
|---|---|---|---|---|---|---|---|
| tzū | tzú | tzǔ | tzù | hsiēn | hsién | hsiěn | hsièn |
| shāo | sháo | shǎo | shào | hsiūng | hsiúng | hsiǔng | hsiùng |
| suī | suí | suǐ | suì | hsiāo | hsiáo | hsiǎo | hsiào |

4. Exercises

a. "Fill-in" sentences

| | |
|---|---|
| 1. ... ... ... chǐ suì lê? | How old is ... ... ... ? |
| 2. Chè shìh wǒ ... ... | This is my ... ... |
| 3. Nǐ ... ... tsài chiā ma? | Is your ... ... at home? |
| 4. Wǒ chiā yǔ ... ... jén. | There are ... ... persons in my family. |
| 5. Ní yǔ ... ... méi-yǔ? | Have you ... ... (or not)? |
| 6. Tsuì-ch'áng-tê ... ... ; tsuì-tuǎn-tê ... ... | The longest is ... ... (feet, etc.); the shortest is ... ... |

b. Translate into English:

1. Ch'íng ni pá wo chièh-shào kéi nǐ fù-ch'in.
2. Mèi-mei, chè shìh Lǐ hsiēn-shêng.
3. Wó yǔ sān chiěh-mèi, liǎng hsiūng-tì.
4. T'ā yú liǎng-kê kē-kê, í-kê mèi-mei.
5. T'ā lǎo ài shuō-huà.
6. T'ā té lê tì-ì chiǎng.
7. Ní yú chǐ-wèi hsiūng-tì?
8. Nǐ jèn-shih nà-kê tzǔ ma?
9. Nà-kê tzǔ wǒ pú jèn-shih.
10. Wǒ tsài chè-li pù hěn chiǔ, t'ā tsài chè-li hěn chiǔ lê.

c. Translate into Chinese:

1. How many are there in your family?
2. There are ten persons in my family; some are older and some are

younger; some are larger and some are smaller.

3. Is your father at home?

4. Father, this is Mr. Wang.

5. That is my youngest sister.

6. She is seven years old.

7. My mother has gone out; she will be back at four o'clock.

8. Do you know that gentleman(hsiēn-shêng)?

9. Some students like to study; some students do not like to study.

10. Yesterday I had a very long talk with my friend.

## On the Use of "Pǎ" 把

"Pǎ", "to take, to take hold of", is used immediately before the object in an inverted construction in which the object precedes the main verb instead of following it. This use of "pǎ" emphasizes the subject. Examples:

"Wǒ pǎ t'ā-tê míng-tzǔ chiào ts'ò lê" 我把他的名字叫錯了 - "I took his name and called it incorrectly", i.e., "I called his name incorrectly".

"K'uài pǎ t'a ch'ǐng chìn-lai" 快把他請進來 - "Quickly take him and ask him to come in", i.e., "Ask him at once to come in".

"Wǒ pǎ t'a tǎ lê" 我把他打了 - "I took him and beat him", i.e., "I beat him".

Without "pǎ" these sentences would read:

"Wǒ chiào ts'ò lê t'ā-tê míng-tzǔ" - "I called his name incorrectly".

"K'uài ch'ǐng t'a chìn-lai" - "Quickly ask him to come in".

"Wǒ tǎ t'a" - "I beat him".

In this inverted construction, when no substantive or adverb follows the main verb, it should be followed by "lê", as in the last example above. Usually, however, this construction is employed when there is both an object and a complement or suffix to the main verb, and the order is: "pǎ - object - main verb - complement". Examples:

"Pǎ chè-kê kěi t'a" 把這個給他 - "Give this to him".

"Pǎ t'ā shuō-tê huà tsài shuō í tz'ǔ" 把他說的話再說一次 - "Take what he said and say it once more".

"Pá wǒ-tê míng-p'ièn kéi nǐ-tê hsiēn-shêng k'àn-k'an"把我的名片給你的先生看看 - "Give my visiting card to your master to look at".

"Ch'íng ni pá wo chièh-shào kéi nǐ-tê hsiēn-shêng"請你把我介紹給你的先生 - "Please introduce me to your teacher".

## On the Use of "Kěi" 給

給 is pronounced "chǐ" in literary Chinese, and "kěi" in colloquial.

1. As a principal verb, "kěi" means "to give". The word order is the same as the normal English order: subject - verb - indirect object - direct object. Examples:

"Wó kěi t'a sān-pěn shū" 我給他三本書 - "I give him three books".

"Chè-kê jén kěi hái-tzǔ t'áng ch'īh" 這個人給孩子糖吃 - "This man gives the child candy to eat".

2. As a co-verb, retaining something of the meaning of "to give to", "kěi" may be translated simply "to", or, often, not translated at all. It indicates the indirect object. The word order is: subject - main verb - kěi - indirect object - direct object. Examples:

"Wǒ mài kéi ni ì-pěn shū" 我賣給你一本書 - "I sell(to) you a book".

"Wó tǎ kéi ni í-kê tièn-huà" 我打給你一個電話 - "I made (to) you a telephone call" or "I telephoned to you".

3. As a preposition in the sense of "for, to", again, "kěi" indicates the dative case. When it is used in this way, the sentence order differs from the English in that the prepositional phrase precedes the main verb instead of following it. Examples:

"Wó kěi t'a hsiěh nà-kê tzǔ" 我給他寫那個字 - "I for him wrote that character".

"Wó kěi t'a tsò fàn" 我給他做飯 - "I for him make food", i.e., "I cook dinner for him".

"Chè-kê jén kěi hái-tzǔ mǎi t'áng" 這個人給孩子買糖 - "This man buys candy for the child".

NOTE (a) "Kěi" as a preposition may mean either "for, on behalf of", or "to" as in "to give to"; sometimes the exact meaning must be determined by the context. For example, "Wó kěi t'a hsiěh hsìn" 我給他寫信 may mean either "I write a letter to him" or "I write a letter for him", i.e., on his behalf; "Wó kĕi ni tă tièn-huà" 我給你打電話 may mean either "I telephone to you" or "I telephone for you".

NOTE (b) Sometimes the indirect object after "kĕi" is omitted as understood. For example: "Ch'ĭng míng-t'ien kéi măi lai" 請明天給買來 - "Please buy [it] for [me, him, etc.] tomorrow".

4. When used with a verb in the passive voice, "kĕi" means "by", and indicates the agent. Example:

> "Hái-tzŭ kĕi fù-ch'in tă lê" 孩子給父親打了 - "The child was beaten by [his] father".

NOTE: When "pă" 把 and "kĕi" appear in the same sentence, the word order is: pă - direct object - kĕi - indirect object - verb. For example: "Pă chè-pĕn shū kéi wo mài lê" 把這本書給我賣了 "Take this book for me sell it", i.e., "Sell this book for me".

## Lesson 18 In a Classroom

1. Vocabulary

| | | |
|---|---|---|
| 功 | kūng | Merit. |
| 課 | k'è | Lesson, class. |
| 功課 | kūng-k'è | Lesson [ì-mên 門 kūng-k'è]. |
| 堂 | t'áng | Hall, court. A numerative of periods of classroom work. |
| 一堂課 | ì-t'áng k'è | One period in which school work is conducted. |
| 課堂 | k'è-t'áng | Classroom [í-kê k'è-t'áng]. |
| 用 | yùng | To use, to employ. |
| 用功 | yùng-kūng (1) | Diligent. Diligently. To work hard. |
| 上 | shàng | To go up, to go over, to attend. See also page 61. |
| 下 | hsià | To go or come down, to quit. See also p. 55. |
| 講 | chiăng | To lecture, to explain. |
| 休 | hsiū | To rest, to resign [seldom used alone]. |
| 息 | hsī or hsí | To stop, to rest [seldom used alone]. |

| | | |
|---|---|---|
| 休息 | hsiū-hsi | Rest, as from toil. |
| 間 | chiēn | Space. Between, during, among. A numerative of rooms. |
| 時間 | shíh-chiēn(2) | Period, time [í-kê shíh-chiēn]. |
| 頁 | yèh (3) | Leaf, page. |
| 溫 | wĕ̃n | To warm up. Warm. |
| 習 | hsí | To practise. |
| 溫習 | wĕ̃n-hsí | To review. A review. |
| 考 | k'ǎo | To examine. |
| 試 | shìh | To try, to test. |
| 考試 | k'ǎo-shìh | Examination [í-kê k'ǎo-shìh]. |
| 黑 | hēi | Black, dark. |
| 板 | pǎn | Board [seldom used alone]. |
| 塊 | k'uài | Piece. A numerative of dollars, land, etc. |
| 黑板 | hēi-pǎn | Blackboard [í-k'uài hēi-pǎn]. |
| 紙 | chǐh | Paper [ì-chāng chǐh]. |
| 粉 | fĕ̃n | Powder. |
| 筆 | pǐ | Pen [ì-chīh pǐ]. A stroke. |
| 粉筆 | fén-pǐ | Chalk [ì-chīh fén-pǐ]. |
| 難 | nán | Difficult. |
| 容易 | júng-i | Easy. |
| 刷 | shuā | To brush. |
| 刷子 | shuā-tzŭ | A brush [í-kê shuā-tzŭ]. |
| 窗 | ch'uāng | Window [seldom used alone]. |
| 戶 | hù | Door. Family. [Lit.] |
| 窗戶 | ch'uāng-hu | Window [í-kê ch'uāng-hu]. |
| 開 | k'āi | To open, to serve, to drive, to operate. Boiled. |
| 拿 | ná | To take, to grasp, to carry. |
| 拿來 | ná-lai | To bring. |
| 椅子 | ǐ-tzŭ | Chair [ì-pá 把 ǐ-tzŭ]. |

| | | |
|---|---|---|
| 桌子 | chō-tzŭ | Table, desk [ì-chāng chō-tzŭ]. |
| 還 | hái | Still, furthermore. |
| 會話 | huì-huà | Conversation. |
| 夠 | kòu | Enough. |

2. Sentences

1. Today Mr. Wang went over the fifth lesson for us.
   Wáng hsiēn-shêng chīn-t'ien kéi wo-mên shàng(4) lê tì-wŭ k'è.
   王先生今天給我們上了第五課.
2. You are very diligent. He does not work very hard.
   Ní hĕn yùng-kūng. T'ā pù hĕn yùng-kūng.
   你很用功. 他不很用功.
3. Are you busy with your work?
   Nǐ-tê kūng-k'è máng-pu-mang?
   你的功課忙不忙?
4. How many classes did you have yesterday?
   Nǐ tsó-t'ien yú chǐ-t'áng k'è?
   你昨天有幾堂課?
5. Where is our classroom?
   Wŏ-mên-tê k'è-t'áng tsài ná-li?
   我們的課堂在那裏?
6. After each class they have ten minutes' recess (literally, rest-time).
   T'ā-mên mĕi hsià ì-t'áng k'è yŭ shíh fĕn-chūng-tê hsiū-hsi shíh-chiēn.
   他們每下一堂課有十分鐘的休息時間.
7. To which page has [the teacher] explained today?
   Chīn-t'ien chiăng tào nă-i yèh lê?
   今天講到那一頁了?
8. We have explained as far as page three.
   Wŏ-mên chiăng tào tì-sān yèh lê.
   我們講到第三頁了.
9. What lesson shall we review tomorrow?
   Wŏ-mên míng-t'ien wĕn-hsí tì-chǐ k'è?
   我們明天溫習第幾課?

10. Mr. Wang said that lesson five is a review.
Wáng hsiēn-shêng shuō tì - wǔ k'ề shìh wến-hsí.
王先生說第五課是溫習。

11. Today I didn't do well in the examination.
Chīn-t'ien wó k'ǎo tê pù hǎo.
今天我考得不好。

12. Students do not like examinations [to be] too difficult; teachers do not expect examinations [to be] too easy.
Hsüéh-shêng pù hsǐ-huan k'ǎo-shìh t'ài nán; hsiēn-shêng pù hsī-wàng k'ǎo-shìh t'ài júng - i.
學生不喜歡考試太難；先生不希望考試太容易。

13. The teacher writes characters on the blackboard.
Hsiēn-shêng tsài hēi-pǎn shàng hsiěh tzǜ.
先生在黑板上寫字。

14. When [one] uses the blackboard, then [one] doesn't use paper.
Yùng-hēi-pǎn - tê shíh-hou, chiù pú yùng chǐh.
用黑板的時候，就不用紙。

15. Use [a piece of] chalk to write characters on the blackboard.
Tsài hēi-pǎn shàng hsiěh tzǜ yùng fến - pǐ.
在黑板上寫字用粉筆。

16. Is there a blackboard eraser (literally, brush) in this classroom?
Chề - kê k'ề-t'áng lí yǔ hēi-pǎn shuā-tzǔ ma?
這個課堂裏有黑板刷子嗎？

17. Please open the window.
Ch'íng ni pǎ ch'uāng - hu k'āi-k'ai(5).
請你把窗戶開開。

18. Are our chairs enough?
Wǒ - mên - tê ǐ - tzǔ kòu - pu - kou?
我們的椅子夠不夠？

19. Someone has taken away the chairs of this classroom.
Yǔ jến pǎ chề - kê k'ề-t'áng - tê ǐ - tzǔ ná tsǒu lê.
有人把這個課堂的椅子拿走了。

20. Who wrote your Chinese book?
Nǐ - tê Chūng-wến shū shìh shuí tsò - tê(6)?
你的中文書是誰作的？

21. My "Chinese Conversation" was written by the teacher.
Wǒ nà - pěn "Chūng-wến Huì-huà" shìh hsiēn-shêng tsò - tê.
我那本『中文會話』是先生作的。

22. Sometimes our teacher sits on the desk to explain the
Yǔ - tê shíh-hou, wǒ - mên - tê chiào-yüan tsò tsài chō-tzŭ
有的時候，我們的教員 坐在桌子
lesson.
shàng chiǎng shū.
上講書.

23. Tonight I still have to study "Chinese Conversation";
Wǒ chīn-t'ien wǎn-shang hái yào nièn "Chūng-wến Huì - huà";
我今天晚上還要念『中文會話』;
tomorrow Mr. Li is likely to test me.
míng-t'ien Lǐ hsiēn-shêng huì(7) k'áo wo.
明天李先生會 考我.

NOTES:

(1) "Yùng-kūng" means literally "to spend effort", hence "diligent".

(2) "Shíh-chiēn" and "shíh-hou" 時候 are occasionally confused. "Shíh-chiēn" means "a space of time, a period", while "shíh-hou" denotes a special, small unit of time, usually referring to a certain hour in the day.

(3) The Distinction between "Chāng" 張 and "Yèh" 頁

"Chāng" means a piece of paper, "yèh" a leaf or a page of a book. Occasionally the two words may be used interchangeably.

(4) "Shàng" here has the special meaning of "to go over".

(5) "K'āi-k'ai" means "open wide". The repetition is chiefly for euphony. If "pǎ" were not used here, one would say "Ch'íng ni k'āi ch'uāng-hu".

(6) This and the following sentence, literally translated, are in the passive voice and would read: "Your Chinese book is made by whom?" and "That 'Chinese Conversation' [book] of mine is made by the teacher".

(7) "Huì" in this place does not mean "know how to", but is an indicator of the future tense. "Yào" 要 is used in the same way to indicate future. Both are used as auxiliaries before the verb, but "yào" indicates desire or intention, while "huì" indicates a possibility.

3. Exercises

a. "Fill-in" sentences

1. Nǐ ì t'iēn yǔ ... ... ... ... (How many) classes do you have
k'è? in one day?

| | |
|---|---|
| 2. Nǐ-tê shū ...-pu-... ? | Have you (many) ... books? |
| 3. Nǐ ... ... pu ... ... chè-i k'è? | Do you (understand) ... this lesson? |
| 4. Wǒ-mên-tê ǐ-tzŭ ...-pu-... ? | Have we (enough) ... chairs? |
| 5. Pă (object) ... hsüéh (complement) ... | Take ... learn ... |
| 6. Pă ... kéi wo (verb) ... | Take ... for me. |
| 7. Wó kĕi t'a ... ... | I give him ... ... |

b. Translate into English:

1. Ní k'è-i pă chè-pěn shū ná ch'ü.
2. Wǒ hsièn-tsài pú yùng hēi-păn.
3. Nǐ hùi hsiĕh Chūng-kuo tzǔ ma?
4. K'è-t'áng lǐ yú chǐ-kê hsüéh-shêng?
5. Chīn-t'ien-tê k'ăo-shìh nán-pu-nan?
6. Wǒ yào hsiū-hsi ì-huǐ-êrh.
7. Ch'íng ni ná ì-chāng chǐh kéi wo.
8. Chè-pěn shū shìh t'ā tsò-tê.
9. Wǒ-mên shén-mo shíh-hou shàng k'è?
10. Hsièn-tsài shíh-hou tào lê, wǒ-mên hsià k'è(leave class) pa.

c. Translate into Chinese:

1. I want to learn Chinese conversation.
2. Who wrote this book?
3. Would you please get me a piece of chalk?
4. Please give me that eraser and chalk.
5. I shall have an examination tomorrow.
6. The classroom is too big.
7. I study at this table.
8. There are fifty students in a class.
9. Do you know who is speaking?
10. I have three classes in the morning.

## PART III, LESSON 18

### On the Particle "Chiù" 就

"Chiù", "to accomplish, to follow, according to", is one of the most important particles in spoken Chinese. Its various uses and meanings include the following:

1. With the sense of "immediately, at once", it indicates immediate future and connotes resolution. Examples:

"Wǒ chiù lái" 我就來 - "I will come at once".

"Ì-huǐ-êrh chiù té" 一會兒就得 - "In a moment it will be ready".

2. With the sense of "and, and then, thereupon", it indicates a relationship of cause and effect:

"T'ā ch'īh kuò fàn, chiù tsǒu lê" 他吃過飯就走了 - "He ate, and then left".

"T'ā lái, wǒ chiù ch'ǜ" 他來,我就去 - "[If] he comes, then I'll go".

3. Sometimes it means "only":

"Wǒ chiù yǔ ì-pěn shū" 我就有一本書 - "I have only one book".

4. Used in a subordinate clause followed by a main clause using "yěh" 也, it may mean "even if, even when". Examples:

"Chiù-shih wǒ ch'ǜ ch'ǐng t'a, t'ā yěh pú huì kěn wǒ í-k'uài-êrh huí-lai" 就是我去請他,他也不會跟我一塊兒回來 - "Even if I go to ask him, he still cannot come back together with me".

"T'ā chiù pù ch'íng wo, wó yěh yào ch'ǜ" 他就不請我,我也要去 - "Even if he does not invite me, I would like to go".

5. "Chiù" is used with "shìh" 是 with the following meanings:

(a) "Only, except that". Example:

"Chè-pěn shū hěn hǎo, chiù-shih t'ài kuèi" 這本書很好,就是太貴 - "This book is very good, only it is too expensive".

(b) "Is just, is equal to". Examples:

"Nǐ yào-tê chiù-shih chè-pěn shū" 你要的就是這本書 - "This book is just what you want".

"Shíh-wǔ fěn chiù-shih í-k'è-chūng" 十五分就是一刻鐘 -

"Fifteen minutes is equal to a quarter of an hour (or, is just a quarter of an hour)".

(c) "All right, very well", usually used as an affirmative reply.

"Chiù-shih lê" 就是了 - "It is so".

"Chè chiù-shih lê" 這就是了 - "This is it" or "This will be all right".

"Nà chiù-shih lê" 那就是了 - "That is it" or "That will be all right".

(d) "Namely, that is". Example:

"Wǒ yào kào-su ni sān-chièn shìh: chiù-shih, ī ... èrh ... " 我要告訴你三件事：就是一... 二 ... - "I want to tell you three things: namely, one ... two ... "

## Lesson 19 Review

1. Useful Phrases and Word Combinations

| | | | |
|---|---|---|---|
| 1. | 不錯 | pú ts'ò | Not bad, not wrong. |
| 2. | 錯了 | ts'ò lê | Wrong. |
| 3. | 你錯了 | Nǐ ts'ò lê | You are wrong. |
| 4. | 打聽 | tǎ-t'īng | To make an inquiry. |
| 5. | 貴姓 | Kuèi hsìng? | [Your] honorable surname? |
| 6. | 大名 | Tà míng? | [Your] great personal name? |
| 7. | 有名的 | yǔ-míng-tê | Famous. |
| 8. | 你知道不知道？ | Nǐ chīh-tao pu chīh-tao? | Do you know? |
| 9. | 我不知道 | Wǒ pù chīh-tao | I don't know. |
| 10. | 吃早飯 | ch'īh tsǎo-fàn | To eat breakfast. |
| 11. | 吃晚飯 | ch'īh wǎn-fàn | To eat supper [or dinner], the evening meal. |
| 12. | 吃飽了 | ch'īh pǎo lê | To have eaten enough. |
| 13. | 沒吃飽 | méi ch'īh pǎo | Did not eat enough, not satiated. |
| 14. | 吃過了 | ch'īh kuò lê | To have eaten. |
| 15. | 還沒吃 | hái méi ch'īh | Not yet eaten. |

| | | | |
|---|---|---|---|
| 16. | 中學教員 | chūng-hsüéh chiào-yüán | Middle school (high school) teacher. |
| 17. | 小學教員 | hsiǎo-hsüéh chiào-yüán | Grade school teacher. |
| 18. | 小學生 | hsiǎo hsüéh-shêng | Grade school pupil. |
| 19. | 中學生 | chūng hsüéh-shêng | Middle school (high school) student. |
| 20. | 大學生 | tà hsüéh-shêng | College student. |
| 21. | 生日 | shēng-jìh | Birthday. |
| 22. | 愛人 | ài-jén | Lover, sweetheart. |
| 23. | 愛國 | ài-kuó | Patriotic. To love one's country. |
| 24. | 他很愛國 | T'ā hěn ài-kuó | He is very patriotic. |
| 25. | 親愛的 | ch'īn-ài-tê | Dear. |
| 26. | 親愛的父親 | ch'īn-ài-tê fù-ch'in | Dear father. |
| 27. | 走路來 | tsǒu lù lái | To come on foot. |
| 28. | 走路去 | tsǒu lù ch'ǜ | To go on foot. |
| 29. | 講堂 | chiǎng-t'áng | Classroom [í-kê chiǎng-t'áng]. |
| 30. | 大禮堂 | tà-lǐ-t'áng | Auditorium [í-kê tà-lǐ-t'áng]. |
| 31. | 教堂 | chiào-t'áng | Church [í-kê chiào-t'áng]. |
| 32. | 黑人 | hēi-jén | Negro. |
| 33. | 可不可以 | k'ě-pù-k'ě-i? | May or not? |
| 34. | 不可以 | pù k'ě-i | May not. |
| 35. | 溫水 | wēn shuǐ | Warm water. |
| 36. | 開水 | k'āi shuǐ | Boiled water. |
| 37. | 開不開 | k'āi pù k'āi | Cannot open. |
| 38. | 難過 | nán-kuò | To feel uneasy or sad; difficult to pass through. |
| 39. | 過得去 | kuò-tê-ch'ǜ | Passable. |
| 40. | 過年 | kuò-nién | The New Year period; to pass the New Year. |
| 41. | 過去 | kuò-ch'ǜ | Past. |
| 42. | 他過去了 | T'ā kuò-ch'ǜ lê | He has passed away (died). |
| 43. | 過問 | kuò wèn | To interfere, to inquire into. |

| | | | |
|---|---|---|---|
| 44. | 不要你過問 | pú yào ni kuò wèn | Doesn't like you to interfere. |
| 45. | 第二課 | tì-èrh k'è | Second lesson, Lesson two. |
| 46. | 上課 | shàng k'è | To attend class. |
| 47. | 下課 | hsià k'è | To dismiss class, to leave class (when it is over). |
| 48. | 課本 | k'è-pěn | Textbook. |
| 49. | 上月 | shàng-yüèh | Last month. |
| 50. | 下月 | hsià-yüèh | Next month. |
| 51. | 本月 | pěn yüèh | This month, instant. |
| 52. | 這個月 | chè-kê yüèh | This month. |
| 53. | 上等 | shàng těng | Good quality (of goods or conduct). First class. |
| 54. | 下等 | hsià těng | Bad quality (of goods or conduct). Lower class. |
| 55. | 認不出來 | jèn pu ch'ū-lai | Cannot make out. |
| 56. | 認不清楚 | jèn pu ch'īng-ch'u | Cannot recognize clearly. |
| 57. | 說來就來 | shuō lái chiù lái | Speak of coming and come at once ("no sooner said than done"). Can come at once. |
| 58. | 說走就走 | shuō tsǒu chiù tsǒu | Can go at once. |
| 59. | 說到 | shuō tào | To speak of. |
| 60. | 說不過他 | shuō pu kuò t'a | Cannot get the better of him in talk. |
| 61. | 說不過去 | shuō pu kuò ch'ü | Cannot be said, cannot gloss over. |
| 62. | 說不來 | shuō pu lái | Unable to explain, unable to speak out. |
| 63. | 我說錯了 | Wǒ shuō ts'ò lê | I spoke mistakenly. |
| 64. | 不一定 | pù í-tìng | Uncertain. |
| 65. | 一定不 | í-tìng pū | Certainly not. |
| 66. | 快到時候了 | k'uài tào shíh-hou lê | The time is almost up. |
| 67. | 你還要說甚麼? | Nǐ hái yào shuō shén-mo? | What do you still want to say? |
| 68. | 夠多了 | kòu-tō lê | Plenty. |
| 69. | 夠用了 | kòu yùng lê | Enough for use. |
| 70. | 容易極了 | júng-i chí lê | Very easy. |

2. Narrative to be translated into English

王先生是一位教員．他在一個中學教書．那個學校裏有六百多學生．王先生有兩個孩子．他的兒子叫國英，他的女兒叫美英．他們兩個人都在那個學校裏念書．

王太太今天很忙，因爲今天是國英的生日．王先生跟王太太請了二十位客人來喝茶．他們很愛國英，因爲他很用功，愛念書，常常溫習功課．在他的班裏他是第一個好學生．他們今天給國英一個很好的表．

下午四點半，客人都來了．客人們

Wáng hsiēn-shêng shìh í-wèi chiào-yüán. T'ā tsài í-kê chūng-hsüéh chiāo-shū. Nà-kê hsüéh-hsiào lí yǔ liù-pǎi tō hsüéh-shêng. Wáng hsiēn-shêng yú liǎng-kê hái-tzǔ. T'ā-tê érh-tzǔ chiào Kuó-yīng, t'ā-tê nǚ-êrh chiào Měi-yīng. T'ā-mên liǎng-kê jén tōu tsài nà-kê hsüéh-hsiào lǐ nièn-shū.

Wáng t'ài-t'ai chīn-t'ien hěn máng, yīn-wèi chīn-t'ien shìh Kuó-yīng-tê shēng-jìh. Wáng hsiēn-shêng kēn Wáng t'ài-t'ai ch'ǐng lê èrh-shíh-wèi k'è-jên lái hē ch'á. T'ā-mên hěn ài Kuó-yīng, yīn-wèi t'ā hěn yùng-kūng, ài nièn-shū, ch'áng-ch'áng wēn-hsí kūng-k'è. Tsài t'ā-tê pān lǐ t'ā shìh tì-í-kê hǎo hsüéh-shêng. T'ā-mên chīn-t'ien kěi Kuó-yīng í-kê hén hǎo-tê piǎo.

Hsià-wǔ ssù-tiěn-pàn, k'è-jên tōu lái lê. K'è-jên-mên

問王太太:『今天是少爺的生日, 他現在幾歲了?』

國英的母親說:『他現在是十六歲了. 他今年秋天就要進大學了. 王先生的美國朋友, Smith 先生, 今年秋天回美國去. 他說最好國英跟他去美國念書.』

在這時候, 美英進來問他哥哥:『現在就喝茶嗎?』國英說:『妹妹, 等一會兒罷. Smith 先生打電話告訴我他現在有一點兒事, 要來晚一點兒.』

有一位客人問:『美英, 你也去美國嗎?』美英說:『我不知道. 母親說我太

wèn Wáng t'ài-t'ai: "Chīn-t'ien shìh shào-yeh-tê shēng-jìh, t'ā hsièn-tsài chǐ suì lê?"

Kuó-yīng-tê mǔ-ch'in shuō: "T'ā hsièn-tsài shìh shíh-liù suì lê. T'ā chīn-nien ch'iū-t'ien chiù yào chìn tà-hsüéh lê. Wáng hsiēn-shêng-tê Mĕi-kuo p'éng-yu, Smith hsiēn-shêng, chīn-nien ch'iū-t'ien huí Mĕi-kuo ch'ü. T'ā shuō tsuì hăo Kuó-yīng kēn t'ā ch'ü Mĕi-kuo nièn-shū."

Tsài chề shíh-hou, Mĕi-yīng chìn-lai wèn t'ā kê̄-kê: "Hsièn-tsài chiù hē ch'á ma?" Kuó-yīng shuō: "Mèi-mei, tĕng ì-huǐ-êrh pa. Smith hsiēn-shêng tă tièn-huà kào-su wo t'ā hsièn-tsài yŭ ì-tiĕn-êrh shìh, yào lái wăn ì-tiĕn-êrh."

Yŭ í-wèi k'è-jên wèn: "Mĕi-yīng, ní yĕh ch'ǜ Mĕi-kuo ma?" Mĕi-yīng shuō: "Wŏ pù chīh-tao. Mŭ-ch'in shuō wŏ t'ài

小，等兩年去也不晚.』

五點鐘 Smith 先生來到了. 王先生說:『Smith 先生, 請進來.』Smith 先生說:『王太太, 王先生. 你們都好嗎? 對不起, 我來晚了.』

王先生說:『國英! 你把 Smith 先生介紹給我們的朋友罷. 美英! 請你快給 Smith 先生一杯茶.

有一位客人問 Smith 先生:『請問, 先生來中國有幾年了?』Smith 先生告訴他:『我來中國十年了.』國英說:『你的中國話很好. 你說的跟我們的差不多.』Smith 先生說:『過獎, 過獎.』

hsiǎo, těng liǎng nién ch'ǜ yěh pù wǎn."

Wú-tiěn-chūng, Smith hsiēn-shêng lái tào lê. Wáng hsiēn-shêng shuō: "Smith hsiēn-shêng, ch'ǐng chìn-lai." Smith hsiēn-shêng shuō: "Wáng t'ài-t'ai, Wáng hsiēn-shêng, nǐ - mên tōu hǎo ma? Tuì pu ch'ǐ, wǒ lái wǎn lê."

Wáng hsiēn-shêng shuō: "Kuó-yīng! Ní pǎ Smith hsiēn-shêng chièh-shào kéi wǒ - mên - tê p'éng - yu pa. Měi-yīng! Ch'íng ni k'uài kěi Smith hsiēn-shêng ì-pēi ch'á."

Yǔ í - wèi k'è - jên wèn Smith hsiēn-shêng: "Ch'ǐng wèn, hsiēn-shêng lái Chūng-kuo yú chǐ nién lê?" Smith hsiēn-shêng kào - su t'a: "Wǒ lái Chūng-kuo shíh nién lê." Kuó-yīng shuō: "Nǐ - tê Chūng-kuo-huà hěn hǎo. Nǐ shuō - tê kēn wǒ - mên - tê ch'á - pu - tō." Smith hsiēn-shêng shuō: "Kuò-chiǎng, kuò-chiǎng."

有幾個客人問Smith先生美國的事. 有的人問:『美國的學校多嗎? 學校的課堂很大嗎? 學生喜歡考試嗎?』有的人問:『美國的小姐們喜歡吃煙嗎? 美國人吃甚麼飯?』Smith先生都很清楚的告訴他們.

Yú chǐ-kê k'è-jên wèn Smith hsiēn-shêng Měi-kuo-tê shìh. Yǔ-tê jến wèn: "Měi-kuo-tê hsüéh-hsiào tō ma? Hsüéh-hsiào-tê k'è-t'áng hến tà ma? Hsüéh-shêng hsǐ-huan k'ǎo-shìh ma?" Yǔ-tê jến wèn: "Měi-kuo-tê hsiáo-chieh-mên hsǐ-huan ch'īh-yēn ma? Měi-kuo jến ch'īh shến-mo fàn?" Smith hsiēn-shêng tōu hến ch'īng-ch'u-tê kào-su t'a-mên.

六點半, 有一位客人說:『時候不早了. 我們要走了.』王先生跟王太太說:『謝謝你們來. 有時候請你們常來.』客人們說:『多謝. 多謝. 再見, 再見.』

Liù-tiěn-pàn, yǔ í-wèi k'è-jên shuō: "Shíh-hou pù tsǎo lê. Wǒ-mên yào tsǒu lê." Wáng hsiēn-shêng kěn Wáng t'ài-t'ai shuō: "Hsièh-hsieh nǐ-mên lái. Yǔ shíh-hou ch'íng ni-mên ch'áng lái." K'è-jên-mên shuō: "Tō hsièh, tō hsièh. Tsài chièn, tsài chièn."

3. Exercises

a. Translate into Chinese:

1. Where is your telephone?
2. I want to telephone Miss Wang.
3. I want to invite her to dinner on Wednesday.

4. The weather was very fine, and not very hot.
5. Mr. Smith said: "Miss Wang, my friend Mrs. Li tells me you want to go to America next year."
6. Yes, I am going to college there.
7. What are you going to study?
8. I want to study English, because I want to come back to China [and] teach English.
9. Your English conversation is very good.
10. Thank you. I want to learn some more and read many books under famous teachers.
11. Do you know German and French?
12. I have studied a little French. I do not understand German.
13. I have some friends in America. I will ask them to go [and] see you.
14. Thank you, that will be fine. I do not know many people in your honorable country.
15. The people of my humble country are all very polite. Miss Wang, when you arrive, will you please go to see my mother?
16. I will certainly go. Are there many people in your family?
17. Not very many. There are my father and mother, an elder sister, a younger sister, and an elder brother.
18. What do your brother and sisters do?
19. My brother is working. He has a wife and two children. My elder sister is working too. She is a teacher.
20. Is your younger sister also a teacher?
21. No, she is studying at college. She is very pretty, and has many friends.
22. She will introduce you to her friends.

b. Conversation demonstration in the classroom

[The following simple dialogue is to be spoken in Chinese by four students before the class.]

Smith: How are you, Mr. Wang?

Wang: I'm fine, Mr. Smith. Have you eaten?

Smith: No, I'm going to Mr. Li's house for dinner.

Wang: I am going too. What time do they have dinner?

Smith: At eight o'clock. It is 7:45 now. Let's hurry.

Li: Mr. Wang, Mr. Smith, please come in.

Smith: Are we late?

Li: No, you are not late. These are my brother and his wife, and their little daughter.

Wang: She is very pretty. How old is she?

Li: She is four years old.

Mrs. Li: Mr. Smith, do you smoke?

Smith: Thank you, I have my cigarettes. Do you smoke, Mrs. Li?

Mrs. Li: Please go ahead, Mr. Smith. I do not (know how to) smoke.

Li: The guests have all arrived. Let us have dinner.

Mrs. Li: I am sorry, the table is small, and we need two more chairs.

Li: There are two more chairs. Will you please open the window a little, because there are too many people.

Mrs. Li: Mr. Smith, do you like to eat Chinese food?

Smith: I like [it] very much. Thank you for asking me to come.

CONVERSATIONAL CHINESE

PART IV FOOD AND DRINK

Lesson 20 The Three Meals

1. Vocabulary

| | | |
|---|---|---|
| 頓 | tùn | A numerative of meals. A time. |
| 一頓飯 | í-tùn fàn | A meal. |
| 餐 | ts'ān (1) | Meal. A numerative of meals. |
| 西餐 | hsī-ts'ān (2) | Western meal, Western-style food. |
| 午飯 | wǔ-fàn | Lunch, noon meal. |
| 剛 | kāng | Just now. Stiff, stuborn. |
| 才 | ts'ái (3) | Then, just now. Talent, ability. |
| 剛才 | kāng-ts'ái | A moment ago. |
| 渴 | k'ě | Thirsty. |
| 餓 | è | Hungry. |
| 心 | hsīn | Heart, mind, core [ì-k'ě hsīn]. |
| 燙 | t'àng | To scald, to iron. |
| 嘴 | tsuǐ | Lip, mouth, beak of a bird [ì-chāng tsuǐ]. |
| 曉 | hsiǎo | To know. Dawn. |
| 曉得 | hsiǎo-tê (4) | To know, to comprehend. |
| 筷子 | k'uài-tzǔ | Chopstick [ì-chīh or ì-shuāng k'uài-tzǔ]. |
| 碗 | wǎn | Bowl [í-kê wǎn]. |
| 能 | nếng (5) | To be able to. Can. |
| 不謝，不謝 | pú hsièh, pu hsieh | You're welcome, don't mention it, there is no need to thank me. |
| 粥 | chōu | Rice boiled to gruel, porridge, congee. |
| 匙子 | ch'íh-tzǔ | Spoon [í-kê ch'íh-tzǔ]. |
| 涼 | liáng | Cool, cold. |
| 外 | wài | Outside, foreign. |
| 外國 | wài-kuó | Foreign nation(s). |
| 俄國 | Ế-kuo | Russia. |
| 還有 | hái yǔ ... | There is still ... |

還是 hái shìh Still is. Or.

爲甚麽 wèi shén-mo Why? What for?

抽 ch'ōu To draw out, to pull up, to smoke (tobacco).

2. Sentences

1. I am thirsty. I am very thirsty.
Wó k'ě lê. Wó k'ě chí lê.
我渴了. 我渴極了.

2. I want to drink cold boiled water.
Wǒ yào hē liáng k'āi shuǐ.
我要喝涼開水.

3. I am hungry. I am extremely hungry.
Wǒ è lê. Wǒ è chí lê.
我餓了. 我餓極了.

4. I want to eat. I want to eat Chinese food.
Wǒ yào ch'īh-fàn. Wǒ yào ch'īh Chūng-kuo fàn.
我要吃飯. 我要吃中國飯.

5. I do not want to eat Western food.
Wǒ pú yào ch'īh hsī-ts'ān.
我不要吃西餐.

6. Why are you extremely hungry?
Nǐ wèi shén-mo è chí lê?
你爲甚麽餓極了?

7. I had breakfast at seven o'clock this morning.
Wǒ chīn-t'ien tsǎo-shang ch'ī-tiěn-chūng ch'īh tê tsǎo-fàn.
我今天早上七點鐘吃的早飯.

8. Now it is three o'clock in the afternoon, [and] I still haven't had lunch.
Hsièn-tsài shih hsià-wǔ san-tiěn lê, wǒ hái méi-yǔ ch'īh wǔ-fàn na.
現在是下午三點了, 我還沒有吃午飯哪.

9. How many meals do you have in a day?
Nǐ ì t'iēn ch'īh chǐ-tùn fàn?
你一天吃幾頓飯?

10. I have three meals a day: one in the morning, one at
Wǒ ì t'iēn ch'īh sān tùn: tsǎo-shang í tùn, chūng-wǔ
我一天吃三頓: 早上一頓, 中午

noon, and one in the evening.
í tùn, wǎn-shang í tùn.
一頓，晚上一頓.

11. When did you eat breakfast?
Nǐ shìh shén-mo shíh-hou ch'īh tê tsǎo-fàn?
你是甚麼時候吃的早飯？

12. At six o'clock in the morning.
Tsǎo-shang liù-tiěn.
早上六點.

13. When will dinner be served (When is dinner served)?
Shén-mo shíh-hou k'āi wǎn-fàn?
甚麼時候開晚飯？

14. I do not know.
Wǒ pù hsiǎo-tê or Wǒ pù chīh-tao.
我不曉得. 我不知道.

15. Do you know how to hold chopsticks?
Nǐ hùi ná k'uài-tzŭ ma?
你會拿筷子嗎？

16. I can. I (already) learned it in America.
Wǒ hùi. Wǒ tsài Měi-kuo chiù hsüéh hùi lê.
我會. 我在美國就學會了.

17. Do you like the Chinese spoon?
Ní hsǐ-huan Chūng-kuo-tê ch'íh-tzŭ ma?
你喜歡中國的匙子嗎？

18. I like the Chinese spoon, because when I eat (lit. drink) hot soup, it will not scald [my] lips.
Wó hsǐ-huan Chūng-kuo-tê ch'íh-tzŭ, yīn-wèi hē jè t'āng tê shíh-hou, pú t'àng tsuǐ.
我喜歡中國的匙子，因爲喝熱湯的時候，不燙嘴.

19. Have you had your lunch (or, dinner)?
Nǐ ch'īh kuò fàn lê ma(6)?
你吃過飯了嗎？

20. I have eaten. I have just eaten. I have not yet eaten.
Wǒ ch'īh kuò lê. Wǒ kāng-ts'ái ch'īh kuò. Wǒ hái méi-yǔ ch'īh(7).
我吃過了. 我剛才吃過. 我還沒有吃.

21. Have you had enough? (Literally, have you eaten your fill?)
Nǐ ch'īh pǎo lê ma?
你吃飽了嗎？

22. [I have had] enough; I have eaten two bowls of rice.
Pǎo lê; wǒ ch'īh lê liáng wǎn fàn lê.
飽了；我吃了兩碗飯了。

23. Please have some cake.
Ch'ǐng ch'īh ì - tiěn-êrh tiěn-hsīn(8) pa.
請吃一點兒點心罷。

24. Please drink a bowl of congee.
Ch'íng ni hē ì - wǎn chōu pa(9).
請你喝一碗粥罷。

25. I have had enough of everything; I can't eat any more, thank you.
Wǒ tōu kòu lê; pù néng tsài ch'īh lê, hsièh-hsieh.
我都夠了；不能再吃了，謝謝。

26. Do you like to eat Russian food, or do you like to eat French food?
Ní hsǐ-huan ch'īh Ế-kuo fàn, hái-shìh(10) hsǐ-huan ch'ih Fà-kuo fàn?
你喜歡吃俄國飯，還是喜歡吃法國飯？

27. I don't like either very much. I like best to eat Chinese food.
Wǒ tōu pù hén hsǐ-huan. Wǒ tsuì ài ch'īh Chūng-kuo fàn.
我都不很喜歡。 我最愛吃中國飯。

28. Will you have another cup of tea now, [and] smoke a cigarette?
Hsièn-tsài ch'íng ni tsài hē ì-pēi ch'á, ch'ōu ì-chīh yēn pa(11), hǎo-pu-hao?
現在請你再喝一杯茶，抽一枝煙罷，好不好？

29. Yes, thank you. Don't thank me (Don't mention it).
Hǎo, hsièh-hsieh. Pú hsièh, pu hsieh.
好，謝謝。 不謝，不謝。

NOTES:

(1) "Tùn" and "ts'ān" as numeratives of meals can be used interchangeably, but "tùn" is more common in northern China and "ts'ān" in the south.

(2) "Hsī-ts'ān" and "wài-kuó fàn" are commonly used interchangeably of Western food.

(3) 才 , "talent, ability", is used as an abbreviation of 纔 "ts'ái", "just now, a moment ago". "Ts'ái" in this sense is interchangeable with "kāng". Sometimes the phrase "kāng-ts'ái" is used to express the same idea. "Ts'ái" is also used with the meaning of "wait until ... and then ... " or "not until", as in "Těng t'ā lái lê, wǒ ts'ái tsǒu tê" - "I waited until he came, and then went away"; or "Míng-t'ien t'ā ts'ái lái" - "He is not coming until tomorrow".

(4) "Hsiǎo-tê" and "chīh-tao" may be used interchangeably, but "hsiǎo-tê" is more commonly used in the south.

(5) "Néng" should not be confused with "hùi" 會, although they may sometimes be used interchangeably in the sense of "to be able", as in "Nǐ hùi-pu-hui tsò?" 你會不會作? - "Can you do it?"; "Wǒ hùi tsò" 我會作 - "I can". But it should be remembered that "hùi" means "to be able" in the sense of "to know how to", while "néng" means "to be able" in the sense of physical ability. Also, "hùi" is used as an indicator of the future tense (see Lesson 18, note 7); "néng" has no such use.

(6) This question is a common form of greeting, to which one usual reply is "Ch'īh kuò lê" - "[I] have eaten".

(7) "Lê" 了 is seldom used after a verb which follows "méi" or "méi-yǔ".

(8) "Tiěn-hsīn" is used to mean cakes, pastry, or light refreshment taken between meals, and sometimes a light supper.

(9) "Chōu" or congee is usually the main diet of poor Chinese. Well-to-do people occasionally use it, mixed with chicken soup or other delicacies, as an after-dinner or midnight dish.

(10) "Hái-shìh" means "[either] or"; it indicates a choice between alternatives, or an indirect question.

(11) The meaning of "ch'ōu yēn" and "ch'īh yēn" is the same, but the former is more commonly used in north China, while the latter is commoner in the south.

3. Exercises

a. "Fill-in" sentences

| | |
|---|---|
| 1. Wǒ hái méi-yǔ ch'īh ... ... | I haven't had (lunch / dinner etc.) yet. |
| 2. Wǒ ... chí lê. | I am very (hungry, thirsty, etc.) ... |
| 3. Ch'íng ni tsài ... ì-tiěn-êrh. | Please (eat, drink) ... a little more. |
| 4. Míng-t'ien ... ... ... ch'íng wo ... ... | Tomorrow ... ... invites me (to his house, to dinner) ... ... |

| | |
|---|---|
| 5. Nǐ shến-mo shíh-hou lái kê̌n wǒ ... ... ... ? | When will you come to have (tea, ... dinner, foreign food) ... ... with me? |
| 6. Nǐ wèi shến-mo ... ... ? | Why do you ... ... ? |
| 7. Wǒ yào ch'īh ... ... fàn. | I want to eat (Chinese, American, ... French, German, Russian) ... ... food. |
| 8. Shến-mo shíh-hou k'āi ... ? | When will ... be served? |

b. Translate into English:

1. Chề shìh shến-mo tiěn-hsīn?
2. Nǐ kê̌n nǐ-tê p'ếng-yu tōu ài ch'īh Chūng-kuo fàn ma?
3. Ní hsǐ-huan ch'ōu yēn, hái-shìh hsǐ-huan hê̌ ch'á?
4. Wáng hsiēn-shêng shuō, t'ā yào ch'íng wo-mên ch'īh hsī-ts'ān.
5. Nǐ ề-pu-ê? Ní k'ê̌-pu-k'ê?
6. Wǒ hsièn-tsài pú ề, yěh pù k'ê̌.
7. Hǎo, wǒ-mên wǎn ì-tiěn-êrh ch'īh-fàn pa.
8. Nǐ hái yào shến-mo? Wǒ hái yào hê̌ ì-wǎn chōu.
9. Wǒ hái yào hê̌ ì-pēi ch'á, yěh yào ch'ōu ì-chīh yēn.
10. Yǔ-fàn-ch'īh-tê jến pú ề; ề-tê jến méi fàn ch'īh.

c. Translate into Chinese:

1. May I ask [whether] you have foreign food here?
2. Do you have Russian food here?
3. My friend can speak English, German, French, Russian, Japanese, and Chinese.
4. I want to have (translate: eat) a foreign meal.
5. Do you know (hsiǎo-tê) whether the Chinese food here is good?
6. We will eat Chinese food this evening.
7. I do not like to drink hot tea, because it scalds [my] lips.
8. What did you eat for breakfast?
9. You are in a foreign country; I am in China.
10. Please give me a pair of chopsticks and a spoon.

## PART IV, LESSON 20

### On the Use of "Kuò" 過

1. As a main verb, "kuò" means "to pass, to pass over or through, to experience, to exceed, to transgress, to cross". Examples:

"Kuò hé" 過河 - "to cross a river".

"Kuò tê ch'ü" 過得去 - "can be passed, passable, tolerable".

"Kuò pu ch'ü" 過不去 - "cannot be passed, intolerable, very bad".

"Kuò liǎng t'iēn tsài shuō" 過兩天再說 - "After (passing) two days, let's talk again".

"Kuò-nién-tê shíh-hou, wǒ pú nièn-shū" 過年的時候,我不念書 - "At New Year's time (passing the year) I don't study".

"T'ā chīn-nien kuò pu ch'ü" 他今年過不去 - "He cannot pass this year", i.e., "He cannot live beyond this year".

"T'ā fù-ch'in tsǎo kuò ch'ü lê" 他父親早過去了 - "His father passed away long ago".

2. As a co-verb, "kuò" is used (a) as an indicator of the past or perfect tense, with a sense of "ever, once, formerly, experienced". In this use "kuò" follows immediately after the main verb. Examples:

"Wǒ ch'īh kuò lê" 我吃過了 - "I have eaten".

"Wǒ ch'ü kuò Chūng-kuo" 我去過中國 - "I have (or, had) been in (gone to) China".

"Wǒ nièn kuò Té-wén" 我念過德文 - "I have studied German".

"Wǒ méi-yǔ huì kuò t'a" 我沒有會過他 - "I have never met him".

As a co-verb, "kuò" is also used (b) with a spatial rather than a temporal meaning of "over, through, to pass". In this sense, it is a separable suffix to the main verb. Examples:

"Ní tsǒu pú kuò ch'ü" 你走不過去 - "You cannot pass through".

"T'ā kāng tsǒu kuò ch'ü" 他剛走過去 - "He has just walked over".

"T'ā ì-huǐ-êrh tsǒu kuò lai, ì-huǐ-êrh tsǒu kuò ch'ü" 他一會兒走過來,一會兒走過去 - "He came over for a while, and [then] went back".

"Chè-li-tê kūng-k'è t'ài tō, wǒ máng pu kuò lái" 這裏的功課太多,我忙不過來 - "The work here is too much, I cannot get through it".

3. "Kuò" is frequently translated "after, beyond". Examples:

"Kuò lê pàn nién, wǒ chiù hǎo lê" 過了半年我就好了 - "After half a year, I shall be all right".

"Kuò lê ssǔ-tiěn, wǒ chiù yào tsǒu lê" 過了四點我就要走了 - "After four o'clock, I must go".

"Kuò shíh-hou lê" 過時候了 - "Beyond time".

"Kuò chùng" 過重 - "Beyond [the limit of] weight".

4. As a noun, "kuò" means "transgression, fault". For example:

"Chè shìh wǒ-tê kuò-ts'ò" 這是我的過錯 - "This is my fault".

NOTE: "Kuò", like "lê" 了, indicates past tense, but it should be borne in mind that "kuò" has the fundamental meaning of "to pass", and indicates or suggests passage or movement from one place to another, or from one time to another, while "lê" is a more general indicator of completed action, without such connotations. For emphasis, "kuò" and "lê" are used together to stress the past tense or completion of action.

## Lesson 21 In a Restaurant

1. Vocabulary

| | | |
|---|---|---|
| 飯館 | fàn-kuǎn | Restaurant [í-kê fàn-kuǎn]. |
| 房 | fáng | Room, house, building [ì-chiēn fáng]. |
| 茶房 | ch'á-fáng (1) | Waiter [í-kê ch'á-fáng]. |
| 面 | mièn | Face, front, side. A numerative of flags, mirrors, etc. |
| 前面 | ch'ién-mien | Before, in front of. |
| 以前 | ǐ-ch'ién (2) | Formerly. |
| 菜 | ts'ài | Vegetable. Food (in general). |
| 單 | tān | Alone, single, odd. A single sheet of paper. A bill, a check. |
| 菜單 | ts'ài-tān | Menu [ì-chāng ts'ài-tān]. |
| 牛 | niú | Ox, cow [ì-chīh niú]. |
| 牛奶 | niú-nǎi (3) | Cow's milk. |
| 排 | p'ái | To arrange in order. Row, rank. |
| 牛排 | niú-p'ái | Beef steak [í-k'uài niú-p'ái]. |

| | | |
|---|---|---|
| 雞 or 鷄 | chī | Chicken [í-kê or ì-chīh chī]. |
| 雞子兒 | chī-tzŭ-êrh | Egg [í-kê chī-tzŭ-êrh]. |
| 肉 | jòu | Meat, flesh (especially pork). |
| 猪 | chū | Pig [í-kê or ì-chīh chū]. |
| 猪肉 | chū-jòu | Pork. |
| 牛肉 | niú-jòu | Beef. |
| 羊 | yáng | Sheep [ì-chīh yáng]. |
| 羊肉 | yáng-jòu | Mutton. |
| 魚 | yǘ | Fish [ì-t'iáo yǘ]. |
| 青 | ch'īng | Green, the color of nature, blue. |
| 青菜 | ch'īng-ts'ài | Green vegetable. |
| 白 | pái | White. |
| 白菜 | pái-ts'ài | Celery cabbage, cabbage. |
| 紅 | húng | Red. |
| 紅茶 | húng ch'á | Red tea (what is called in English "black tea). |
| 西紅柿 | hsī-húng-shìh | Tomato [í-kê hsī-húng-shìh]. |
| 綠 | lǜ | Green. |
| 炒 | ch'ǎo | To fry, to roast, to sauté. |
| 酒 | chiǔ | Liquor (usually translated "wine"). |
| 黃 | huáng | Yellow, brown. |
| 黃酒 | huáng-chiǔ | Yellow wine ("Chinese sherry"). |
| 燒 | shāo | To burn, to bake. |
| 燒酒 | shāo-chiǔ | Distilled spirit ("Chinese whiskey"). |
| 呢 | ni | An emphatic and interrogative particle. |
| 壺 | hú | Pot. |
| 想 | hsiǎng | To think about, to expect. |
| 意 | ì | Idea, opinion, intention, meaning (not used alone). |
| 利 | lì | Profit, advantage, interest on money. Sharp. |
| 意大利 | ì-tà-lì | Italy. |

2. Sentences

1. May I ask, where is the restaurant?
Ch'ǐng wèn, fàn-kuǎn tsài nǎ - êrh?
請問，飯館在那兒？

2. Do you want to eat foreign food, or (to eat) Chinese food?
Nǐ yào ch'īh wài-kuó fàn, hái-shìh ch'īh Chūng-kuo fàn(4)?
你要吃外國飯，還是吃中國飯？

3. Are there any foreign restaurants here? Are there French restaurants and Italian restaurants?
Chè - li yǔ wài-kuó fàn-kuǎn méi - yǔ? Yǔ Fà - kuo fàn-kuǎn kēn Ì - tà - lì fàn-kuǎn ma?
這裏有外國飯館沒有？有法國飯館跟意大利飯館嗎？

4. We have no French and Italian restaurants here. Formerly there were a German restaurant and an American restaurant, but now there are none. Do you like Chinese food?
Wǒ - mên chè - li méi - yǔ Fà -kuo kēn Ì - tà - lì fàn-kuǎn. Ǐ - ch'ién yǔ í - kê Té - kuo fàn-kuǎn t'úng í - kê Měi-kuo fàn-kuǎn, k'ě-shìh hsièn-tsài tōu méi - yǔ lê. Ní hsǐ-huan ch'īh Chūng-kuo fàn ma?
我們這裏沒有法國跟意大利飯館。以前有一個德國飯館同一個美國飯館，可是現在都沒有了。你喜歡吃中國飯嗎？

5. I like to eat Chinese food.
Wǒ ài ch'īh Chūng-kuo fàn.
我愛吃中國飯。

6. There is a very good Chinese restaurant over there.
Nà - li yǔ í - kê hěn hǎo - tê Chūng-kuo fàn-kuǎn.
那裏有一個很好的中國飯館。

7. Thank you for telling me.
Hsièh-hsieh ni kào - su wo.
謝謝你告訴我。

8. Waiter: Sir, how are you? What would you like to eat?
Ch'á-fáng: Hsiēn-shêng, ní hǎo ma? Ní hsǐ - huan ch'īh shén - mo?
茶房：『先生，你好嗎？ 你喜歡吃甚麼？』

9. Do you have a menu? Where is the menu?

Ní yǔ ts'ài-tān ma? Ts'ài-tān tsài ná - li?

你有菜單嗎? 菜單在那裏?

10. Sir, this is the menu. Please write down all the dishes that you would like to eat.

Hsiēn-shêng, chè shìh ts'ài-tan. Ch'íng pá nǐ ài ch'īh - tê ts'ài hsiěh-hsia lai(5).

先生, 這是菜單. 請把你愛吃的菜寫下來.

11. I am sorry, I cannot write.

Tuì pu ch'ǐ, wǒ pú huì hsiěh.

對不起, 我不會寫.

12. Sir, would you like to eat beef?

Hsiēn-shêng, ní hsǐ-huan ch'īh niú-jòu ma?

先生, 你喜歡吃牛肉嗎?

13. I would like to eat beef steak; I also like mutton.

Wó hsǐ-huan ch'īh niú-p'ái; yéh hsǐ-huan ch'īh yáng-jòu.

我喜歡吃牛排; 也喜歡吃羊肉.

14. I'm sorry, there is no beef or mutton here; would you like to eat chicken? We have chicken, we have pork, and we have fish.

Tuì pu ch'ǐ, chè - li méi - yǔ niú-jòu, méi - yǔ yáng-jòu; ní hsǐ-huan ch'īh chī ma? Wǒ - mên yǔ chī, yǔ chū-jòu, yéh yǔ yǘ.

對不起. 這裏沒有牛肉, 沒有羊肉; 你喜歡吃雞嗎? 我們有雞, 有猪肉, 也有魚.

15. Chicken, very good. I also want a little vegetable.

Chī, hěn hǎo. Wó yěh yào ì - tiěn-êrh ch'īng-ts'ài.

鷄, 很好. 我也要一點兒青菜.

16. Will cabbage be all right? Cabbage sautéed with pork [and] tomatoes sautéed with eggs are both good dishes.

Pái-ts'ài hǎo - pu - hao? Pái-ts'ài ch'ǎo chū-jòu, hsī-húng-shìh ch'ǎo chī-tzǔ-êrh, tōu shìh hěn hǎo - tê ts'ài.

白菜好不好? 白菜炒猪肉, 西紅柿炒鷄子兒, 都是很好的菜.

17. I want cabbage sautéed with pork. Is there some wine here?

Wǒ yào pái-ts'ài ch'ǎo chū-jòu. Chè - li yú chiǔ méi - yǔ?

我要白菜炒猪肉. 這裏有酒沒有?

18. Sir, do you want to drink wine?
Hsiēn-shêng, nǐ yào hē̌ chiǔ ma?
先生，你要喝酒嗎？

19. I want to drink wine, and also want to drink milk.
Wǒ yào hē̌ chiǔ, yěh yào hē̌ niú-nǎi.
我要喝酒，也要喝牛奶。

20. We have no milk. What wine do you want to drink,
Wǒ-mên méi-yǔ niú-nǎi. Nǐ yào hē̌ shến-mo chiǔ,
我們沒有牛奶。你要喝甚麼酒，
yellow wine or spirits?
huáng-chiǔ ni(6) hái-shìh shāo-chiǔ ni?
黃酒呢還是燒酒呢？

21. I want to drink yellow wine.
Wó hsiǎng hē̌ huáng-chiǔ.
我想喝黃酒。

22. Because I am very busy, and also very hungry, please hurry a little.
Yīn-wèi wó hěn máng, yéh hěn è, ch'íng ni k'uài ì-tiěn-êrh.
因爲我很忙，也很餓，請你快一點兒。

23. Yes, sir, it will come right away.
Shìh-tê, hsiēn-shêng, chè chiù lái.
是的，先生，這就來。

24. Hello! Waiter, please give me a pot of tea first.
Wèi! Ch'á-fáng, ch'íng ni hsiēn kéi wo ì-hú ch'á.
喂！茶房，請你先給我一壺茶。

25. Do you want black tea or green tea?
Nǐ yào hē̌ húng ch'á hái-shìh hē̌ lǜ ch'á?
你要喝紅茶還是喝綠茶？

26. I want to drink green tea.
Wǒ yào hē̌ lǜ ch'á.
我要喝綠茶。

27. Well, please bring the food first.
Hǎo lê, ch'íng ni hsiēn pǎ ts'ài ná-lai pa.
好了，請你先把菜拿來罷。

NOTES

(1) "Chá-fáng", which literally means "tea room", is used to mean

a tea attendant in a restaurant or on a ship.

(2) "Ĭ-ch'ién" at the beginning of a sentence, or directly following the subject, means "formerly". For example: "Ĭ-ch'ién wǒ shìh hsüéh-shêng" - "Formerly I was a student". When it means "before", as in "Before I was a teacher, I was a student", "Ĭ-ch'ién" must come at the end of the phrase: "Wǒ shìh chiào-yüán ĭ-ch'ién - - ". This difference from the English word order should be carefully noted.

(3) With names of liquids, such as milk or tea, names of containers or nouns denoting quantity are used as numeratives. For example: "ì-pēi niú-nǎi" - "a cup of milk"; "í-pàng niú-nǎi" - "a pound of milk", "ì-pēi ch'á" - "a cup of tea", "ì-wǎn ch'á" - "a bowl of tea", "ì-hú ch'á" - "a pot of tea". Thus no specific numerative will be given in the vocabularies with nouns meaning liquids. The same applies to some other things, such as sugar and noodles, which are measured rather than counted.

(4) In an interrogative sentence offering an alternative, as in "Do you want to eat foreign food or Chinese food?", Chinese, for purposes of emphasis or clarity, repeats the verb where English does not.

(5) In the phrase "hsiěh-hsia lai", "lai" is an indicator of direction, meaning "here"; the phrase thus means "write down here". In this use, "lai" is an atonic separable suffix.

(6) The Use of "Ni"

"Ni" is an emphatic and interrogative particle. Unlike "ma", it can be added to a sentence which already contains an interrogative expression such as "shén-mo" or "ná-li". A special use of "ni" is to indicate a question offering a selection of two or three alternatives, as: "Nǐ ài ch'īh chī ni, ch'īh yú ni, hái-shìh ch'īh jòu ni?" - "Would you like to eat chicken, fish, or pork?" Another special use is to express impatience or helplessness. For instance, if one wished to go to a theater and found all seats taken, he might say: "Wǒ-mên tào ná-li ch'ǜ ni?" - "Where shall we go?" "Ni" also sometimes indicates surprise, as in "How many children has he?" - "He has eighteen!" - "T'ā yǔ shíh-pá-kè ni!" Or if one is asked to go to a theater when he is very hungry, he might say "Wǒ hái méi ch'īh-fàn ni!" In the last two examples, "na" 哪 (see Lesson 14, note 2) can be used in place of "ni".

3. Exercises

a. "Fill-in" sentences

| | |
|---|---|
| 1. Wǒ yào ch'ǜ ... ... ... ch'īh-fàn. | I want to go to a ... ... for dinner. |
| 2. Chè-êrh-tê ... ... hén hǎo. | The ... ... here is very good. |
| 3. Nǐ ài ch'īh ... ... ma? | Do you like to eat ... ... ? |
| 4. T'ā shìh ... ... ma? | Is he the ... (waiter, etc.)? |

| | |
|---|---|
| 5. Wǒ-mên hsiăng ch'īh ... ... | We would like to eat ... ... |
| 6. Chè-kê fàn-kuăn-tê ts'ài ... ... ... | The food in this restaurant is (very good, bad, etc.) ... ... |
| 7. Nǐ ài ch'īh ... ... hái-shìh ài ch'īh ... ... ? | Do you like to eat ... ... or ... ... ? |

b. Translate into English:

1. Lǐ hsiēn-shêng ch'ǐng t'ā-tê Měi-kuo p'éng-yu ch'ù fàn-kuăn ch'īh-fàn.
2. Smith hsiēn-shêng ch'ǐng t'ā-tê Chūng-kuo p'éng-yu ch'īh hsī-ts'ān; t'ā-mên ch'īh niú-p'ái, hē niú-năi.
3. Wǒ ài ch'īh ch'īng-ts'ài, k'ě-shih wǒ pú ài ch'īh chū-jòu.
4. Chè-kê fàn-kuăn-tê ts'ài hăo ma?
5. Hăo chí lê. Nǐ ài ch'īh shén-mo ts'ài?
6. Wǒ ài ch'īh chī kĕn yű, k'ě-shih wǒ pú ài ch'īh yáng-jòu.
7. Wǒ-mên hē ì-pēi chiŭ pa.
8. Tuì pu ch'ǐ, wǒ pù hē chiŭ; wǒ hē ì-pēi niú-năi hăo lê.
9. Míng-t'ien wăn-shang wó ch'íng ni ch'ù ch'īh wài-kuó fàn, hăo-pu-hao?
10. Hén hăo. Wǒ-mên tào ná-li ch'ù ch'īh?

c. Translate into Chinese:

1. Waiter, please give me the menu.
2. Would you like to have beef or pork?
3. I would like to have steak, green vegetables, tomato, egg soup, and milk.
4. Is there any Western restaurant here?
5. Would you like to go to a Chinese restaurant with me?
6. That restaurant is too small; I would like to go to a big restaurant.
7. Every morning I eat two eggs and drink a glass of milk.

8. Would you like to eat fish, or would you like to eat chicken?

9. I like both (tōu).    I like neither.

10. I know how to say "red, brown, blue, white, and black".

The Distinction between "Hái" 還, "Yěh" 也, and "Tsài" 再

To help the student avoid confusion, the meanings and idiomatic uses of "hái", "yěh", and "tsài" will be analyzed one by one. Each of these three words intensifies the meaning of the sentence in which it is used by marking something extra, and each usually precedes the verb.

"Hái" means "still, yet", referring in a general way to duration or repetition of action, but not in the sense of "a second time".

1. The primary meaning of "hái" is "still". Examples:

"Chè hái pù hǎo ma?" 這還不好嗎? - "Is this still not good?"

"Nǐ hái méi ch'īh pǎo ma?" 你還沒吃飽嗎? - "Have you still not eaten enough?"

"Hái yào liǎng-sān t'iēn ts'ái tsò-tê hǎo" 還要兩三天才作得好 - "Two or three days will still be required before it can be finished".

2. "Hái" may sometimes be translated "more", "again", or "yet", but in such cases the literal meaning remains "still". Examples:

"Hái yǔ-mei-yu?" 還有沒有? - "Is there still some?" or "Is there any more?"

"Hái yǔ" 還有 - "There is still some".

"Hái yào-pu-yao?" 還要不要? - "Do [you] still want some?" or "Do you want any more?"

"Nǐ míng-t'ien hái lái ma?" 你明天還來嗎? - "Are you still coming tomorrow?" or "Are you coming again tomorrow?"

"Hái méi tào ch'īh-fàn-tê shíh-hou" 還沒到吃飯的時候 - "It is not yet time for dinner".

"Wǒ hái méi shuō na!" 我還沒說哪! - "I haven't spoken yet!"

"Yěh" means "also, and, even". It indicates something additional, but without any implication concerning time or duration. Examples:

1. In the sense of "also":

"Yào-shih ní <u>mǎi</u>, t'ā yéh <u>mǎi</u>" 要是你買，他也買 - "If you buy, he also buys".

"Nǐ ch'ù, wó yěh <u>ch'ù</u>" 你去，我也去 - "If you go, I also will go".

2. In the sense of "and", "yěh" differs from "kēn" 跟 and "hé" 和, which are used between substantives, in that it is used to connect predicates. Thus, in sentences such as "I can speak English and French", if "yěh" is used as the conjunction, the verb must be repeated. For example:

"Wǒ huì <u>shuō</u> Yīng-wén yěh huì <u>shuō</u> Fà-wén" 我會說英文，也會說法文 - "I can speak English and (can speak) French".

"Wǒ chè-li yǔ <u>chī</u> yéh yǔ yú" 我這裏有鷄也有魚 - "I have here chicken and fish".

3. In the sense of "even", giving emphasis and usually following "shén-mo", "yěh" can be used like "tōu". In this use it may often be omitted in translation. Examples:

"T'ā <u>shén</u>-mo <u>yěh</u> (or, <u>tōu</u>) néng ch'īh" 他甚麽也(都)能吃 - literally, "He whatever [thing] even can eat", i.e., "He can eat anything".

"T'ā <u>shén</u>-mo <u>yěh</u> néng shuō" 他甚麽也能說 - "He can say anything".

"T'ā <u>shén</u>-mo jén <u>yěh</u> pú chièn" 他甚麽人也不見 - "He will not see anyone at all".

"T'ā <u>í</u>-kè yěh méi-yǔ" 他一個也沒有 - "He has not a single one".

"<u>Shuí</u> yěh pù chīh-tao" 誰也不知道 - "Whoever even does not know", i.e., "No one at all knows".

"<u>Tsài</u>"

1. "Tsài" means "again, for the second time (or, another time), more". It is used for action which is to be repeated in the future, not for action in the present or the past. Examples:

"Nǐ shén-mo shíh-hou tsài <u>lái</u>?" 你什麽時候再來? - "When will you come again?"

"Wǒ pù néng <u>tsài</u> hē lê" 我不能再喝了 - "I cannot drink any more".

2. "Tsài" sometimes may be translated "then, and then", when it indicates one action following another, or the postponement of intended action, as when one has been advised to wait until something

has happened, or until a certain time, before acting. Examples:

> "Wǒ hsiēn ch'ǜ k'àn ni, tsài ch'ǜ k'àn t'a" 我先去看你，再去看他 - "I'll go to see you first, and then go to see him".
>
> "Těng tào míng-t'ien tsài shuō" 等到明天再說 - "Wait until tomorrow and then [let us] talk again".

NOTE the distinction between "tsài" and "ts'ái" 才 . "Tsài" means a repetition or continuation of something that has been done before; "ts'ái", used to introduce the second part of a conditional statement, means that "not until" something has happened will something else begin.

> "Těng wǒ lái nǐ ts'ái ch'ǜ" 等我來你才去 - "Wait until I come before you go".
>
> "Hsià k'è ǐ-hou ts'ái ch'īh-fàn" 下課以後才吃飯 - "[Wait] until after class, and then [we'll] eat".

In conclusion, it may be repeated that the most important meaning of "hái" is "still", of "yěh" is "also", and of "tsài" is "again".

## Lesson 22 In a Restaurant (continued)

1. Vocabulary

| | | |
|---|---|---|
| 麵 | mièn | Noodles. Wheat flour. |
| 麵包 | mièn-pāo | Bread [í-p'ièn or í-k'uài mièn-pāo]. |
| 烤 | k'ǎo | To toast, to roast, to bake. |
| 烤麵包 | k'ǎo mièn-pāo | Toasted bread [í-p'ièn or í-k'uài k'ǎo mièn-pāo]. |
| 油 | yú | Oil, fat, grease. To paint, to varnish. |
| 黃油 | huáng-yú | Butter [í-p'ièn or í-k'uài huáng-yú]. |
| 牛油 | niú-yú | Butter [í-p'ièn or í-k'uài niú-yú]. |
| 辣 | là | Acrid, hot, severe. |
| 醬 | chiàng | Bean sauce. Pickled. |
| 醬油 | chiàng-yú | Soy sauce. |
| 醋 | ts'ù | Vinegar. |
| 胡椒 | hú-chiāo | Pepper. |

| | | |
|---|---|---|
| 胡椒麵 | hú-chiāo-mièn | Ground pepper. |
| 薑 | chiāng | Ginger. |
| 味 | wèi | Taste, flavor. |
| 瓜 | kuā | Melon, gourd, cucumber [seldom used alone]. |
| 黃瓜 | huáng-kua | Cucumber [ì-t'iáo huáng-kua]. |
| 冬瓜 | tūng-kua | A kind of pumpkin [í-kê tūng-kua]. |
| 西瓜 | hsī-kua | Watermelon [í-kê hsī-kua]. |
| 桃子 | t'áo-tzŭ | Peach [í-kê t'áo-tzŭ]. |
| 豆 | tòu | Bean, pea [ì-k'ē̂ tòu]. |
| 腐 | fŭ | Curd. Rotten. |
| 豆腐 | tòu-fu (1) | Bean-curd [í-k'uài tòu-fu]. |
| 蔴 | má | Hemp. |
| 煩 | fán | To trouble, to annoy. |
| 蔴煩 | má-fan | Troublesome, complicated. To bother. |
| 香 | hsiāng | To smell good. Fragrant. |
| 根 | kē̂n | Root, foundation. A numerative of long slender things, including sticks, poles, bamboos, ropes, strings. |
| 洋 | yáng | Ocean. Foreign. Dollar. |
| 火 | huŏ | Fire. |
| 洋火 | yáng-huŏ | Match [ì-kē̂n yáng-huŏ]. |
| 腿 | t'uĭ | Leg, thigh [ì-t'íao t'ui]. |
| 火腿 | huó-t'uĭ | Ham [ì-chīh huó-t'uĭ]. |
| 鴨子 | yā-tzŭ | Duck [ì-chīh yā-tzŭ]. |
| 錢 | ch'ién | Money, copper coin. |
| 酒錢 | chiŭ-ch'ien | Literally, "wine money", i.e., a tip. |
| 賬 | chàng | Account, bill, debt. To charge. |
| 賬單 | chàng-tān | Bill [í-kê chàng-tān]. |
| 行 | hsíng | To walk, to do. |
| 些 | hsiēh (2) | A little, some. Rather, slightly. |
| 這些 | chè-hsiēh (3) | These. |

| | | |
|---|---|---|
| 或 | huò | Perhaps, or [lit.]. |
| 者 | chě | One who, that which. An emphatic particle. [Lit.] |
| 或者 | huò-chě (4) | Perhaps. Or. |

2. Sentences

1. The food is ready, sir.
   Hsiēn-shêng, ts'ài tế lê.
   先生，菜得了.
2. Very good. Please bring it quickly.
   Hǎo chí lê. Ch'íng ni k'uài ná-lai pa.
   好極了. 請你快拿來罷.
3. Would you like to eat rice or noodles?
   Nǐ yào ch'īh fàn hái-shìh yào ch'īh mièn?
   你要吃飯還是要吃麵?
4. I want to eat toast. Do you have bread and butter here?
   Wǒ yào ch'īh k'ǎo mièn-pāo. Nǐ-mên chè-li yǔ mièn-pāo kēn huáng-yú ma?
   我要吃烤麵包. 你們這裏有麵包跟黃油嗎?
5. We don't have them here, but I can go out and buy [some].
   Wǒ-mên chè-li méi-yǔ, k'ě-shih wó k'ě-i ch'ū-ch'ü mǎi.
   我們這裏沒有，可是我可以出去買.
6. That's too much trouble. Rice will do.
   Nà t'ài má-fan lê. Ch'īh-fàn chiù hsíng lê.
   那太麻煩了. 吃飯就行了.
7. This is the chicken you ordered.
   Chè shìh nǐ-yào-tê chī.
   這是你要的鷄.
8. This dish smells very good. What is the name of that dish?
   Chè-kê ts'ài hsiāng chí lê. Nà-kê ts'ài chiào shén-mo?
   這個菜香極了. 那個菜叫甚麼?
9. This is bean-curd soup. That is ham and pumpkin soup.
   Chè shìh tòu-fu t'āng. Nà shìh huó-t'uǐ tūng-kua t'āng.
   這是豆腐湯. 那是火腿冬瓜湯.

10. This is barbecued pork. That is roast duck.
Chè shìh hung-shāo jòu. Nà shìh k'ǎo yā - tzǔ.
這是紅燒肉. 那是烤鴨子.

11. All these dishes are very delicious.
Chè-hsieh ts'ài tōu hěn hǎo ch'īh.
這些菜都很好吃.

12. Please eat slowly (i.e., please enjoy your dinner).
Ch'íng ni màn-mān - tê ch'īh pa.
請你慢慢的吃罷.

13. Please give me some salt.
Ch'íng ni kéi wo ì - tiěn(5) yén.
請你給我一點鹽.

14. Sir, [when you] eat Chinese food, it is a little better to use soy sauce.
Hsiēn-shêng, ch'īh Chūng-kuo ts'ài, yùng chiàng - yú hǎo ì-tiěn-êrh.
先生, 吃中國菜, 用醬油好一點兒.

15. Well then, give me the soy sauce.
Nà - mo, kéi wo chiàng - yú pa.
那麽給我醬油罷.

16. Do you still want anything?
Nǐ hái yào shén - mo?
你還要甚麽?

17. I still want some pepper and vinegar.
Wǒ hái yào hú - chiāo-mièn kěn ts'ù.
我還要胡椒麵跟醋.

18. These are pepper and vinegar. I'll come again in a little while.
Chè shìh hú - chiāo-mièn kěn ts'ù. Wǒ ì - hǔi - êrh tsài lái.
這是胡椒麵跟醋. 我一會兒再來.

19. Waiter, I still want a pot of tea.
Ch'á-fáng, wǒ hái yào ì - hú ch'á.
茶房, 我還要一壺茶.

20. Do you have cigarettes or not?
Ní yǔ yēn méi - yǔ?
你有煙沒有?

21. I have none; please buy a package of cigarettes for me.
Wǒ méi - yǔ; ch'íng ni kéi wo mǎi ì - pāo yēn pa.
我沒有；請你給我買一包煙罷.

22. Do you want matches?
Nǐ yào yáng-huǒ ma?
你要洋火嗎?

23. No, thank you, because I still have a good many.
Wǒ pú yào, hsièh-hsieh, yin-wèi wǒ hái yú hǎo-hsiēh.
我不要，謝謝，因爲我還有好些.

24. What thing is this? What is that thing called in Chinese?
Chè shìh shén - mo tūng-hsi? Nà - kê tūng-hsi Chūng-kuo-huà chiào shén - mo?
這是甚麼東西?那個東西中國話叫甚麼?

25. That is called a teapot. This is called a teacup.
Nà - kê chiào ch'á - hú. Chè - kê chiào ch'á-pēi.
那個叫茶壺. 這個叫茶杯.

26. This is pickled cucumber; that is ginger.
Chè shìh chiàng huáng-kua; nà shìh chiāng.
這是醬黃瓜；那是薑.

27. Ginger has a very good flavor, but a little hot.
Chiāng - tê wèi-êrh hén hǎo, k'ě-shih là ì - tiěn-êrh.
薑的味兒很好，可是辣一點兒.

28. Sir, have you had enough?
Hsien-shêng, kòu lê ma?
先生，夠了嗎?

29. Everything is sufficient, but I still would like to eat a little dessert.
Tōu kòu lê, k'ě-shih wǒ hái hsiǎng ch'īh ì - tiěn-êrh tiěn-hsīn.
都夠了，可是我還想吃一點兒點心.

30. What kind of dessert do you want to eat?
Nǐ yào ch'īh shén - mo tiěn-hsīn ni?
你要吃甚麼點心呢?

31. Give me whatever you have.
Ní yǔ shén - mo chiù kéi wo shén - mo.
你有甚麼就給我甚麼.

32. Would watermelon or peaches be all right?

Hsī-kua huò-chě t'áo-tzŭ hǎo - pu - hao?

西瓜或者桃子好不好?

33. Watermelon is very good.

Hsī-kua hǎo chí lê.

西瓜好極了.

34. How much money? Give me a check, please.

Tō - shǎo ch'ién? Ch'íng kéi wo chàng-tān.

多少錢? 請給我賬單.

35. Sir, it is just four dollars.

Hsiēn-shêng, kāng-kāng ssŭ k'uài-ch'ién.

先生, 剛剛四塊錢.

36. Very good indeed. This is a little tip that I give you.

Hǎo chí lê. Chè shìh wǒ kéi ni tê ì - tiĕn- êrh chiŭ-ch'ién.

好極了. 這是我給你的一點兒酒錢.

37. Thank you. Please come often.

Hsièh-hsieh. Ch'íng ni ch'áng lai.

謝謝. 請你常來.

NOTES:

(1) On Chinese restaurant menus, "tòu-fu" is usually written in the abbreviated or vulgar form 豆付 (付 "fù" - "to pay").

(2) The Distinction between "Yŭ-tê" and "Hsiēh" or "Ì-hsiēh"

Both "yŭ-tê" and "hsiēh" (or "ì-hsiēh") may be translated "some", but the exact meaning of "yŭ-tê" is "there are those who" or "there are those which", while "hsiēh", a sign of the plural, is used in the same way as "some" in English. For example: "Yŭ-tê jén kāo, yŭ-tê jén ăi" 有的人高, 有的人矮 - "There are people who are tall, there are people who are short", i.e., "Some people are tall, some are short"; "Yŭ-tê piáo chŭn, yŭ-tê piǎo pù chŭn" 有的表準, 有的表不準 - "Some watches are accurate, some are inaccurate". "Hsiēh" is usually used to indicate the plural number, as: "í-kê jén, ì-hsiēh jén" - "a man, some men (or, some people)"; "ì-pěn shū, ì-hsiēh shū" - "a book, some books". "Hsiēh" is never used at the beginning of a sentence.

(3) "Chè-hsieh" may be regarded as the plural of "chè-kê", and "nà-hsieh" as the plural of "nà-kê".

(4) In the sense of "or", "huò-chě" can be replaced by "huò-shìh" 或是.

"Huò-chě" and "huò-shìh" should be distinguished from "hái-shìh" in the sense of "or". "Huò-chě" indicates a selection between two subjects or two predicates, while "hái-shìh" offers an alternative between parallel interrogative sentences (see Lesson 20, note 10). Examples:

"Tsó-t'ien ní chiěh-chieh huò-ché nǐ mèi-mei tă tièn-huà lai, ch'íng ni húi chiā" 昨天你姐姐或者你妹妹打電話來，請你回家 - "Yesterday your elder sister or younger sister telephoned here, asking you to go home".

"Ch'íng ni ch'īh í-k'uài t'áng, huò-chě ch'ōu ì-chīh yēn" 請你吃一塊糖，或者抽一枝煙 - "Please eat a piece of candy, or smoke a cigarette".

(5) The "êrh" of "i-tiĕn-êrh" is slurred in speech, and in writing is often omitted for brevity.

3. Exercises

a. "Fill-in" sentences

| | |
|---|---|
| 1. Ch'ing ni pă ... kéi wo. | Please pass me the ... |
| 2. Nǐ yào ... hái-shìh yào ... ? | Do you want ... or ... ? |
| 3. Wó hsiăng chè-êrh-tē ... ... í-tìng hăo. | I think the ... ... here must certainly be good. |
| 4. Ch'íng ni pă yēn kĕn ... ... kĕi t'a. | Please give him the cigarettes and ... |
| 5. Ts'ài-tān shàng yŭ ... , yŭ ... , yéh yŭ ... | There is ... [and] ... [and] also ... on the menu. |
| 6. Nà-kê ... ... chiào shén-mo? | What is that ... called? |

b. Translate into English:

1. Ch'īh Chūng-kuo fàn yào yùng chiàng-yú.
2. Chè-kê chū-jòu ch'ăo pái-ts'ài hăo-ch'īh ma?
3. Nǐ ài hĕ tòu-fu t'āng, huò-chĕ tūng-kua t'āng ma?
4. Wŏ ài hĕ tòu-fu t'āng, k'ĕ-shih chè-êrh-tê tòu-fu t'āng pù hăo hĕ.
5. Nà-kê ch'á-hú t'ài hsiăo; wó k'ĕ-i kéi ni măi í-kê tà-tê.
6. Má-fan pu má-fan? Pù má-fan.

7. Hsíng-pu-hsing? Pù hsíng.

8. Wǒ pú ài ch'īh <u>là</u>-tê tūng-hsi.

9. Chè-kê, <u>Chūng</u>-kuo-huà <u>chiào</u> shén-mo?

10. Yú hǎo-hsiēh jén pù hsǐ-huan ch'īh <u>yú</u> <u>hsiā</u>.

11. Wǒ <u>huò</u>-chě ch'ù, <u>huò</u>-chě pú ch'ù.

c. Translate into Chinese:

1. Whether you come or not, please tell me first.

2. We have bread, but we don't have butter.

3. Well then, let's have a meal of Chinese food.

4. Have you [any] money? I want to buy some things.

5. Please drink one more cup of tea, or smoke one more cigarette.

6. You may use my money, but I do not have very much.

7. Some people have some very good friends.

8. I ate two eggs, two pieces of toast, and two cups of black tea.

9. This is very delicious.

10. An ox has four legs, but a man has only two legs.

## On the Particle "Tê" 的

The particle 的, which is pronounced "ti" in literary Chinese, and "tê" in the national language, especially in north China, is of great importance in the Chinese spoken language, and is used in the following ways:

1. To indicate the possessive case (in which use it is often translated by "of", but corresponds in position to "'s").

"Wǒ-tê piǎo" 我的表 - "my watch".

"Fáng-tzŭ-tê tà-hsiǎo" 房子的大小 - "the size of the room".

"Ch'ù-nien-tê t'iēn-ch'i" 去年的天氣 - "last year's weather".

In the last two examples, "tê" is used to indicate that what precedes it modifies what follows it. Its function still resembles that of "'s". When we speak of "the room's size" or "last year's weather", there is no question of ownership; we simply mean that the size and the weather are qualified by the room and by last year.

2. To indicate past tense. "Tê" may be used after a verb to express definite past time, and the absence of "tê" indicates either present or future time.

"T'ā [shìh] shén-mo shíh-hou lái-tê?" 他[是]什麼時候來的? - "What time did he come?"

"T'ā shén-mo shíh-hou lái?" 他什麼時候來? - "What time is he coming?" or "When will he come?"

3. To connect adjectives or modifiers with that which they modify. Often, the modifier is best translated as a relative clause.

"Nién-lǎo-tê jén" 年老的人 - "[an] old man".

"Hén-hǎo-tê fàn" 很好的飯 - "very good rice (food)".

"Tsó-t'ien lái-tê nà-kê jén shìh wǒ-tê p'éng-yu" 昨天來的那個人,是我的朋友 - "That man who came yesterday is my friend".

4. To form participles.

"Chè shìh wó hsiěh-tê" 這是我寫的 - "This is my writing" or "This was written by me".

5. Combined with a repeated adjective, the particle "tê" usually forms a compound adverb.

"Màn-mān-tê" 慢慢的 - "slowly".

"Nǐ k'uài-k'uāi-tê shuō" 你快快的說 - "Speak quickly".

6. Used with a verb-noun phrase, it indicates an agent or occupation.

"Chiāo-shū-tê" 教書的 - "teacher".

"K'ān-hsiǎo-hái-tê" 看小孩的 - "nursemaid", one who looks after small children.

7. "Tê" is used after an adjective in the superlative degree, or after an adjective preceded by an adverb, when the adjective is not used predicatively.

"Tsuì-hǎo-tê" 最好的 - "the best" or "the best one".

"Hén hǎo-tê pǐ" 很好的筆 - "[a] very good pen".

8. "Tê", following a noun antecedent, is used in the sense of "one" or "it", in order to avoid repetition.

"Yǔ sān-shíh-kè hsüéh-shêng, èrh-shíh-kè nán-tê, shíh-kè nǚ-tê" 有三十個學生,二十個男的,十個女的 - "There are thirty students, twenty male ones, ten female ones".

"Hǎo-tê méi-yǔ lê" 好的沒有了 - "There are no good ones".

9. "Yǔ-tê ... yǔ-tê ... " is used in parallel constructions presenting a contrast.

"Yǔ-tê shíh-hou tō, yǔ-tê shíh-hou shǎo" 有的時候多,有的時候少 - "Sometimes more, sometimes less".

"Tê" is usually omitted:

1. When an adjective and a noun which it modifies are monosyllabic.

"Jè t'iēn" 熱天 - "hot weather".
"Lěng t'iēn" 冷天 - "cold weather".
"Hǎo jén" 好人 - "good man".

2. When a noun or pronoun is followed by a term of relationship, a word meaning "family", or an indicator of direction or location.

"Wǒ fù-ch'in" 我父親 - "my father".
"Wǒ chiā" 我家 - "my family".
"T'ā ch'ién-mien" 他前面 - "in front of him".
"Chō-tzǔ shàng-mien" 桌子上面 - "on top of the table, on the table".

Exercises in the Use of the Particle "Tê"

1. 我的錢不多.
Wǒ - tê ch'ién pù tō.

2. 這是誰的東西?
Chè shìh shuí - tê tūng-hsi?

3. 我要大的, 不要小的.
Wǒ yào tà - tê, pú yào hsiǎo - tê.

4. 我看小的也不錯.
Wǒ k'àn hsiǎo - tê yěh pú ts'ò.

5. 這班裏的學生都很好.
Chè pān lǐ tê hsüéh-shêng tōu hěn hǎo.

6. 昨天來的那一位是我哥哥.
Tsó-t'ien lái - tê nà - i - wèi shìh wǒ kē - kê.

7. 他說的中國話很好.
T'ā shuō - tê Chūng-kuo-huà hěn hǎo.

8. 你說的也不錯.
Nǐ shuō - tê yěh pú ts'ò.

9. 有的人好，有的人不好.
Yǔ - tê jén hǎo, yǔ - tê jén pù hǎo.

10. 這本書，你在那裏買的？
Chè-pěn shū, nǐ tsài ná - li mǎi - tê?

11. 你快快的寫吧.
Nǐ k'uài-k'uāi - tê hsiěh pa.

12. 他是念書的，我是做事的.
T'ā shìh nièn-shū - tê, wǒ shìh tsò-shìh - tê.

13. 這本書是誰念的？
Chè-pěn shū shìh shuí nièn - tê?

14. 那家飯館裏的東西都很好.
Nà -chiā fàn-kuán lǐ tê tūng-hsi tōu hěn hǎo.

## Lesson 23 Invitation to a Banquet

1. Vocabulary

| | | |
|---|---|---|
| 席 | hsí | Seat, mat. Feast. |
| 酒席 | chiǔ-hsí | Feast, banquet [ì-chō 桌 chiǔ-hsí). |
| 房間 | fáng-chiēn(1) | Room [ì-chiēn fáng-chiēn]. |
| 各 | kè (2) | Every one, each. Various. |
| 座 | tsò (3) | Seat, stand. A numerative of mountains, cities, pagodas, houses, etc. |
| 上座 | shàng-tsò | Head of the table, place of honor. |
| 遠 | yüǎn | Far, far away, distant. |
| 讓 | jàng | To let, to yield. |
| 份 | fèn | A share, a set. Duty. |
| 刀 | tāo | Knife [ì-pǎ tāo]. |
| 叉 | ch'ā (4) | Fork, prong [ì-pǎ ch'ā]. |
| 碟 | tiéh | Saucer, plate. A numerative of dishes. |
| 碟子 | tiéh-tzǔ | Saucer, plate [í-kê tiéh-tzǔ]. |
| 隨 | suí | To follow, to accompany. According to. |
| 便 | pièn | Convenient, handy, cheap. Then, in that case. |

| | | |
|---|---|---|
| 隨便 | suí-pièn | To follow [one's] convenience. As one pleases, at pleasure. Informal. |
| 冰 | pīng | Ice [í-k'uài pīng]. |
| 冰激凌 | pīng-chi-líng | Ice cream [ì-pēi pīng-chi-líng]. |
| 骨 | kŭ | Bone, rib. |
| 排骨 | p'ái-kŭ | Spare ribs. |
| 敢 | kăn | To dare, to venture. |
| 當 | tāng | Just then. Ought. To take charge, to act as. To face. |
| 不敢當 | pù kăn tāng(5) | You do me too much honor (literally, I dare not face [this honor]). |
| 敬酒 | chìng chiŭ | To honor with wine, to give a toast. |
| 站 | chàn | To stand, to stop. A station. |
| 起來 | ch'ĭ-lai (6) | To get up, to rise. |
| 乾 | kān | Dry. |
| 乾杯 | kān pēi | To dry the [wine] cup. |
| 龍 | lúng | Dragon [ì-t'iáo lúng]. |
| 龍蝦 | lúng-hsiā | Lobster [ì-chīh lúng-hsiā]. |
| 別 | piéh (7) | Other. To separate. Do not. |
| 醉 | tsùi | Drunk. |
| 果 | kuŏ | Fruit, result [seldom used alone]. |
| 水果 | shuí-kuŏ | Fruit, fresh fruit. |
| 梨 | lí | Pear [í-kê lí]. |
| 蘋果 | p'íng-kuŏ | Apple [í-kê p'íng-kuŏ]. |
| 橘子 | chű-tzŭ | Orange [í-kê chű-tzŭ]. |
| 恐 | k'ŭng | To fear, to frighten. |
| 怕 | p'à | To fear. Lest, perhaps. |
| 恐怕 | k'ŭng-p'à (8) | To be afraid. |
| 葉 | yèh | Leaf. |
| 茶葉 | ch'á-yèh | Tea leaves. |
| 井 | chĭng | Well [í-kê chĭng]. |
| 龍井 | Lúng-chĭng | "Dragon Well" tea, the name of a popular green tea produced in the West Lake region, Hangchow. |

| | | |
|---|---|---|
| 香片 | hsiāng-p'ièn | Jasmine tea (literally, fragrant leaves). |
| 擱 | kē | To put, to place, to lay. |
| 濃 | núng | Strong, thick, rich. |
| 淡 | tàn | Weak, tasteless, dull, fresh. |

2. Conversation

1.Chang (to restaurant attendant)
My name is Chang. I am a guest of Mr. Li
Wǒ hsìng Chāng. Wǒ shih Li Kuó-ying hsien-shêng - tê
我姓張。 我是李國英先生的
Kuo-ying.
k'è - jên.
客人。

2.Attendant: Mr. Li's banquet is in room number three.
Lǐ hsiēn-shêng - tê chiǔ-hsí tsài sān hào fáng-chiēn.
李先生的 酒席在三號房間。

3.Waiter: Mr. Li, your foreign guest has come.
Lǐ hsiēn-shêng, nǐ - tê wài-kuó k'è-jên lái lê.
李先生，你的外國客人來了。

4.Host: Ask him to come in.
Ch'ǐng t'a chìn-lai.
請他進來。

5.Chang: I am sorry, Mr. Li, I come late.
Tuì pu ch'ǐ, Lǐ hsiēn-shêng, wǒ lái wǎn lê.
對不起，李先生，我來晚了。

6.Host: Don't mention it. You come just on time.
Pú k'è-ch'i. Nǐ lái tê chèng shìh shíh-hou(9).
不客氣。 你來的正是時候。

7.Host: Mr. Chang, today I ask you to sit in the place of
Chāng hsiēn-shêng, chīn-t'ien wǒ ch'íng ni tsò shàng
張先生， 今天我請你 坐上
honor, because you are a guest from far away.
tsò, yīn-wèi nǐ shìh yüǎn k'è.
座，因爲你是遠客。

8.Chang: You do me too much honor. Please let another venerable gentleman take that seat.
Pù kǎn tang. Ch'ǐng jàng piéh - tê lǎo-hsiēn-shêng tsò pa.
不敢當。請讓別的老先生坐罷。

9.Host: Let us not stand on ceremony; please sit down.
Pú yào k'ĕ-ch'i; ch'ĭng tsò-hsia pa.
不要客氣； 請坐下罷.

10.Host: Waiter, please bring a plate and a (set of)
Ch'á-fáng, ch'íng ni ná í-kê tiéh-tzŭ kĕn í fĕn
茶房，請你拿一個碟子跟一份
knife and fork. I am afraid this guest does not
tāo ch'ā lai(10). Wó k'ŭng-p'à chè-wèi k'ĕ-jên pú
刀叉來. 我恐怕這位客人不
know how to use chopsticks.
huì yùng k'uài-tzŭ.
會用筷子.

11.Chang: I can use chopsticks; please don't bring me knife
Wŏ huì yùng k'uài-tzŭ; ch'ĭng pú yào kéi wo ná tāo
我會用筷子，請不要給我拿刀
and fork.
ch'ā lê.
叉了.

12.Host: Please drink some wine. Please eat anything at
Ch'íng ni-mên hĕ chiŭ. Ch'íng ni-mên suí-pièn ch'īh
請你們喝酒. 請你們隨便吃
your pleasure.
ts'ài pa.
菜罷.

13.A guest: Mr. Chang is our American friend,
Chāng hsiēn-shêng shìh wŏ-mên-tê Mĕi-kuo p'ĕng-yu,
張先生 是我們的美國朋友,
let us honor him with a cup of wine.
wŏ-mên chìng t'a ì-pēi chiŭ pa.
我們敬他一杯酒罷.

14.Host: Good. Let us all stand up. Please dry your cups.
Hăo. Wŏ-mên tōu chàn ch'ĭ-lai pa. Ch'ĭng kān pēi.
好. 我們都站起來罷. 請乾杯.

15.Chang: Thank you. Let me also give a toast to my Chinese
Hsièh-hsieh. Jàng wo yĕh chìng wŏ-tê Chūng-kuo p'ĕng-
謝謝. 讓我也敬我的中國朋
friends. Please dry your cups.
yu-mên ì-pēi chiŭ. Ch'ĭng kān pēi.
友們一杯酒. 請乾杯.

16.Host: This is roast duck; that is lobster. Mr. Chang,
Chè shìh shāo yā; nà shìh lúng-hsiā. Chāng hsiēn-
這是燒鴨；那是龍蝦．張先
do you like (to eat) [it]?
shêng, ní hsǐ-huan ch'īh ma?
生，你喜歡吃嗎？

17.Chang: [It is] very good, I like [it] very much.
Hến hǎo, wó hến hsǐ-huan.
很好，我很喜歡．

18.Host: That is sweet and sour spare ribs.
Nà shìh t'áng ts'ù p'ái-kǔ.
那是糖醋排骨．

19.Guests: That is our favorite dish.
Nà shìh wǒ-mên hến hsǐ-huan ch'īh tê ts'ài.
那是我們很喜歡吃的菜．

20.Host: Mr. Wang, let us not eat rice just now.
Wáng hsiēn-shêng, wǒ-mên hsièn-tsài pú yào ch'īh fàn.
王先生，我們現在不要吃飯．
Let us drink three more cups of wine.
Tsài hễ sān-pēi chiǔ pa.
再喝三杯酒罷．

21.Wang: I am drunk. I cannot drink any more.
Wǒ tsuì lê. Pù nếng tsài hễ lê.
我醉了．不能再喝了．

22.Host: Today we have no ice cream, but [we] have
Chīn-t'ien méi-yǔ pīng-chi-líng, k'ễ-shih yú shuí-
今天沒有冰激淩，可是有水
fruit: there are pears, apples, and oranges.
kuǒ: yǔ lí, yǔ p'íng-kuǒ, yéh yǔ chú-tzǔ.
果：有梨，有蘋果，也有橘子．
Please eat some as you like.
Ch'íng ni-mên suí-pièn ch'īh ì-tiěn pa.
請你們隨便吃一點罷．

23.Wang: I have eaten too much. I do not want to eat fruit,
Wǒ ch'īh tê t'ài pǎo lê. Wǒ pú yào ch'īh shuí-kuǒ,
我吃的太飽了．我不要吃水果，
I want to drink some tea; may I?
wǒ yào hễ ì-tiěn ch'á; k'ễ-i ma?
我要喝一點茶，可以嗎？

24.Host: Of course, of course. Mr. Chang, do you want to put
K'ě - i, k'ě - i. Chāng hsiēn-shêng, nǐ hē ch'á
可以，可以。張先生，你喝茶
sugar in your tea?
yào kē t'áng ma?
要擱糖嗎？

25.Chang: I do not want (to put) sugar, thank you.
Wǒ pú yào kē t'áng, hsièh-hsieh.
我不要擱糖，謝謝。

26.Host: Do you like [your] tea strong or weak?
Ní hsǐ-huan ch'á núng ì - tiěn-êrh hái-shìh tàn ì -
你喜歡茶濃一點兒還是淡一
tiěn-êrh?
點兒？

27.Chang: I like to drink medium tea.
Wǒ ài hē pù núng pú tàn tê ch'á.
我愛喝不濃不淡的茶。

28.Wang: These tea leaves are very fragrant. Is this black
Chè - kê ch'á-yèh hěn hsiāng. Chè shìh húng ch'á
這個茶葉很香。這是紅茶
or green tea?
hái-shìh lǜ ch'á?
還是綠茶？

29.Host: This pot is Dragon Well tea, that pot is jasmine
Chè - i hú shìh Lúng-chǐng, nà - i hú shìh hsiāng-
這一壺是龍井，那一壺是香
tea. These are both green teas.
p'ièn. Chè tōu shìh lǜ ch'á.
片。這都是綠茶。

30.Wang: I am sorry; because I have something to do, I have to
Tuì pu ch'ǐ; yīn-wèi wó yǔ shìh, wǒ yào tsǎo
對不起；因爲我有事，我要早
go a little early.
ì - tiěn-êrh tsǒu.
一點兒走。

31.Guests: We have to go, too.
Wǒ - mên yěh yào tsǒu lê.
我們也要走了。

32.Chang: Today the feast was very good, also I have made many
Chīn-t'ien tê chiǔ-hsí hěn hǎo, wó yěh jèn-shih lê
今天的酒席很好，我也認識了
acquaintances; thank you, thank you.
hěn tō - tê jên; hsièh-hsieh, hsièh-hsieh.
很多的人；謝謝，謝謝．

33.Host: Please don't mention it. Goodby, goodby, every-
Ch'ǐng pú yào k'è-ch'i. Tsài chièn, tsài chièn, kè-
請不要客氣．再見，再見，各
body, goodby.
wèi, tsài chièn.
位，再見．

NOTES:

(1) Another word for "room" is "wū-tzǔ" 屋子 .

(2) The Distinction between "Kè" and "Měi"

While "kè" and "měi" are often used interchangeably, there are some differences. "Měi" has only the meanings "each, every"; "kè" has also the senses "all, the various". "Měi" is used in such expressions as "měi nién" 每年 , "měi yüèh" 每月 , "měi jìh" 每日 , "měi shíh" 每時 ; "kè" is never used with these words denoting time.

(3) The Distinction between "Hsí", "Tsò", "Tsò-wei" 座位 , and "Wèi-tzǔ" 位子

"Hsí" originally meant a mat, such as was used to sit on before the invention of chairs. It is now used to mean a formal seat at a banquet, a congress, etc. The following combinations are used:

"Tsò hsí" 坐席 - "to take a place at a table".
"T'úng hsí" 同席 - "at the same banquet".
"Ch'ū hsí" 出席 - "to go to a meeting".
"Pěn hsí" 本席 - "this chair, I" (used by a speaker at a congress or conference in referring to himself).

"Tsò" 座 , etymologically "to sit" 坐 under a cover or shelter, is now used to mean "seat, throne, base, stand", and as a numerative of cities, villages, houses, pagodas, and mountains.

"Tsò-wei" and "wèi-tzǔ" are synonymous in the sense of "a seat", but "tsò-wei" is not used figuratively, while "wèi-tzǔ" may mean "a position" in the sense of employment. Examples:

"Tsài k'è-t'áng lǐ, měi-i-kè hsüéh-shêng yǔ í-kê tsò-wei(or, wèi-tzŭ)" 在課堂裏每一個學生有一個座位 (or, 位子) - "In a classroom, every student has a seat".

"Chè-kê tsò-wei (or, wèi-tzŭ) yŭ jén lê" 這個座位(or,位子)有人了 - "This place has been taken".

"Ch'íng ni suí-pièn kĕi t'a í-kê wèi-tzŭ pa" 請你隨便給他一個位子吧 - "Please give him a position as you see fit".

Thus, in brief, "hsí" means a seat, usually in connection with a banquet; "tsò" means a seat in any ordinary place, also in a palace or temple, or a stand for a vase, clock, or similar object; and "tsò-wei" and "wèi-tzŭ" are synonyms for a seat in a classroom, theater, living room, etc.

(4) When the terms for "knife" and "fork" are used separately, people sometimes say "tāo-tzŭ" and "ch'ā-tzŭ".

(5) "Pù kăn tāng" means literally "I dare not face [such an honor]", "I dare not undertake [such responsibility]", or "I dare not occupy [such a high place]". It is a conventional phrase used in the sense of "you do me too much honor, you flatter me", etc.

(6) "Ch'ĭ-lai", in the sense of "up, to start, at the beginning [of an action], whenever", is used as a co-verb with many verbs, somewhat in the way "up" is used in such English expressions as "stand up", "take up the fight". Very often, the sense of "lai", which is usually not translatable, is like that of the German "her" - "here, hither". The object of the main verb may come between the two syllables of "ch'ĭ-lai". Examples of its use: "chàn ch'ĭ-lai" - "to stand up"; "tsò ch'ĭ shìh lai" - "whenever [one] works"; "Wŏ hái méi-yŭ tào, t'ā-mên chiù ch'īh ch'ĭ fàn lai lê" - "They started to eat before I arrived" (literally, "I hadn't yet arrived, they had already started to eat").

(7) "Piéh" in the sense of "other, another" is usually followed by "tê" as a suffix, as in "Wŏ yào piéh-tê shū" - "I want other books". When used in the sense of "do not, should not, is not to be", it forms an imperative. For example: "piéh tsò" - "don't do it"; "Nĭ piéh tōu ch'īh lê" - "Don't eat it all".

(8) The phrase "k'ŭng-p'à" consists of two words with similar meanings. It is commonly used in the sense of "to be [mildly] apprehensive", as in "I am afraid I cannot come"; while "p'à" alone means "to fear" as in "I fear robbers". The object of "k'ŭng-p'à" is usually a clause, that of "p'à" a substantive.

(9) "Chèng", when it means "just", frequently denotes a progressive sense of the verb which follows, signifying that the action is, was, or will be going on at the time indicated, as in "Wŏ chèng k'àn shū" - "I was just reading a book". Very often it is used with "tsài" 在, as in "T'ā lái-tê shíh-hou, wŏ chèng-tsài ch'īh-fàn" - "At the time when he came, I was just eating".

(10) In the expressions "ná-lai" and "ná-ch'ù" 拿去, "lai" and "ch'ü" are separable co-verbs denoting direction, "here" and "there" respectively. "Ná chìn lai" 拿進來 - "Bring it in"; "Ná ch'ū

ch'ü" 拿出去 - "Take it out"; "Ch'íng ni ná tào chè-êrh lai" 請你拿到這兒來 - "Please bring it here"; "Ch'íng ni ná tào nà-êrh ch'ü" 請你拿到那兒去 - "Please take it there".

3. Exercises

a. "Fill-in" sentences

| | |
|---|---|
| 1. Ch'á-fáng, kéi wo í fèn ... | Waiter, give me a set of ... |
| 2. T'ā ... tê shíh-hou, wǒ chèng-tsài ... ... | When he (came, went) ..., I was just (eating, studying, etc.) ... ... |
| 3. Ch'á-fáng, ch'íng ni ná ... ... lai. | Waiter, please bring me (water, tea, etc.) ... ... |
| 4. Ch'íng ni-mên suí-pièn ... ... pa. | Please (you) (eat, walk, talk, etc.) ... ... as you please. |
| 5. Nǐ hē ... tê shíh-hou, yào kē ... ma? | When you drink (tea, wine, soup) ... do you like to put (sugar, salt, sauce) ... ... in it? |
| 6. Wǒ-tê ... kē tsài ... shàng. | My (pen, book) ... was laid on the (table, chair) ... |

b. Translate into English:

1. Tsó-t'ien Lǐ hsiēn-shêng ch'íng wo-mên ch'īh chiǔ-hsí; yǔ lúng-hsiā, yā-tzŭ, hái yú hěn tō piéh-tê ts'ài.
2. Wǒ-mên tōu chǐng lê Smith hsiēn-shêng ì-pēi chiǔ.
3. Ch'íng ni pá wǒ-tê chiǔ-pēi kē tsài chō-tzŭ shàng, yīn-wèi wǒ tsuì lê.
4. Nǐ hái yào ch'ǐng shén-mo piéh-tê k'è-jên?
5. Jàng wo hsiǎng-i-hsiang.
6. Wǒ-mên kěi Smith hsiēn-shêng mǎi shén-mo tūng-hsi?
7. Suí-pièn pa. Tsuì hǎo kěi t'a mái yǔ-yùng-tê tūng-hsi.
8. Wǒ yào mǎi í pàng Lúng-chǐng, pàn pàng hsiāng-p'ièn.
9. Sān-pēi núng ch'á tāng ì-pēi chiǔ.

10. Chè hú ch'á t'ài tàn lê, ch'íng ni tsài kě ì-tiěn-êrh ch'á-yèh pa.

11. Tsài Chūng-kuo hǎo-hsiēh jén hē chíng-shuǐ.

12. Pīng-chi-líng kěn shuí-kuǒ (lí, chú-tzū, p'íng-kuǒ), tōu k'ě-i tāng tsò fàn-hòu-tê tiěn-hsīn (dessert).

c. Translate into Chinese:

[The instructor may desire to have the students translate the following paragraph in class, in order to train their power of interpretation.]

Yesterday was old Mrs. Wang's birthday. Her sons invited very many guests. They went to the biggest restaurant [and] ate a very good banquet. There were more than ten dishes. A guest said, "Mr. Wang, you are too formal. There are too many dishes." Mr. Wang said, "The food (ts'ài) is not enough. Please eat a little more." Mrs. Li said, "I want to drink a toast to old Mrs. Wang." Mrs. Wang said, "You do me too much honor. I want to thank you for coming." There was an American at the banquet, whose Chinese name was Chang. His Chinese was very good. He said he learned the Chinese language in only six months.

## On the Uses of "Liǎo" ("Lê") 了

The word 了 has been defined as a verbal suffix indicating completed action, and as a final particle. Without going into the intricacies of grammatical terms, we may say that in general it has several major uses.

1. To indicate completed action.

a. Simple past:

"T'ā-mên lái lê ì-huǐ-êrh" 他們來了一會兒 - "They came [for] a little while".

b. Present perfect:

"T'ā-mên tōu ch'ū-ch'ü lê" 他們都出去了 - "They have all gone out".

c. Past perfect:

"Nà shíh-hou wó ǐ-ching kào-su lê t'a" 那時候我已經告訴了他 - "At that time I had already told him".

d. Future perfect:

"<u>Těng</u> ì-huǐ-êrh nǐ chiù tōu <u>hsüéh</u> huì lê" 等一會兒你就都學會了 - "In a little while you will have learned everything well".

2. To round out and give emphasis to a verb in the imperative.

"Piéh tsǒu lê" 別走了 - "Don't go!"

3. Used with some verbs and other parts of speech, it indicates the categorical affirmative of the present conditions.

"Hsíng lê" 行了 - "This will do!"
"Ts'ò lê" 錯了 - "[It is] wrong!"

4. Used with 不 and a verb, it indicates a categorical negation in the future.

"Wǒ pú nièn lê" 我不念了 - "I will not study" (although formerly I intended to study, or, although I have studied).

5. Used with 得 or 不 and a verb, it denotes the possibility or impossibility of the completion of the action (in this use it is pronounced "liǎo").

"Tsò té liǎo" 作得了 - "It can be done".
"Hē pù liǎo" 喝不了 - "[I] can't drink it [all]".
"Liǎo pu liǎo" 了不了 - "unable to finish, cannot be done".
"Liǎo-pu-tê" 了不得 - "This will never do; terrible; very".

6. In an interrogative sentence in which the interrogative has the double verb form negated by "méi", and the verb is without an object or modifiers, "lê" is frequently used after the unnegated verb to give smooth, natural phrasing.

"T'ā <u>nièn</u> lê méi nièn?" 他念了沒有? - "Has he read [it] or not?"

"T'ā <u>tsò</u> lê méi tsò?" 他做了沒有? - "Has he done [it] or not?"

NOTE that is is not always necessary to use the particle "lê" to show that a verb is in the past tense. Frequently the presence in a sentence of such an expression of time as "yesterday" or "last month" sufficiently indicates past time.

To become proficient in the use of "lê" the student, in addition to learning the above rules, should observe closely its use in Chinese texts and in the speech of native Chinese. This is something which, like genders in French or the use of prepositions in English, can hardly be completely covered by exact grammatical rules.

Further Exercises in the Use of "Liǎo" ("Lê")

1. 他拿了這本書就走.
T'ā ná lê chè-pěn shū chiù tsǒu.

2. 你說了沒有?
Nǐ shuō lê méi - yǔ?

3. 我看不了那麼多的書.
Wǒ k'àn pù liǎo nà - mo tō - tê shū.

4. 太難了; 別看錯了.
T'ài nán lê; piéh k'àn ts'ò lê.

5. 我不進去了.
Wǒ pú chìn-ch'ü lê.

6. 他講到那裏了?
T'ā chiǎng tào ná - li lê?

7. 我餓了, 有什麼東西吃?
Wǒ è lê, yǔ shén - mo tūng-hsi ch'īh?

8. 我不能再寫了.
Wǒ pù néng tsài hsiěh lê.

## Lesson 24 Review

1. Useful Phrases and Word Combinations

| | | | |
|---|---|---|---|
| 1. | 好吃不好吃? | hǎo-ch'īh pu hǎo-ch'īh? | Does it taste good? |
| 2. | 吃不得 | ch'īh-pu-tê | Not fit to eat. |
| 3. | 吃不來 | ch'īh pù lái | I cannot eat it. |
| 4. | 吃不了 | ch'īh-pu-liǎo | I cannot eat it all. |
| 5. | 做飯 | tsò fàn | To prepare food. |
| 6. | 做菜 | tsò ts'ài | To cook. |
| 7. | 你吃過中國飯沒有? | Nǐ ch'īh kuò Chūng-kuo fàn méi-yǔ? | Have you ever eaten Chinese food? |
| 8. | 這是我第一次吃中國飯 | Chè shìh wǒ tì - í tz'ǔ ch'īh Chūng-kuo fàn | This is the first time I have eaten Chinese food. |
| 9. | 天天吃中國飯 | t'iēn-t'ien ch'īh Chūng-kuo fàn | To eat Chinese food every day. |

| | | |
|---|---|---|
| 10. 天天喝茶 | t'iēn-t'ien hē ch'á | To drink tea every day. |
| 11. 可愛 | k'ě-ài | Lovable. |
| 12. 可能 | k'ě-néng | Possible, probable. |
| 13. 不可能 | pù k'ě-néng | Impossible. |
| 14. 可靠 | k'ě-k'ào | Trustworthy, reliable. |
| 15. 不可靠 | pù k'ě-k'ào | Unreliable. |
| 16. 可了不得 | k'é-liǎo-pu-tê | Terrible; extremely. |
| 17. 可不是 | k'ě-pú-shìh | To be sure, certainly. |
| 18. 可不是麽? | k'ě-pú-shìh mo? | Is it not right? Of course. |
| 19. 還可以 | hái k'ě-i | Still passable, fair, not so bad. |
| 20. 房東 | fáng-tūng | Landlord, landlady ("tūng" in the sense of "master, host"). |
| 21. 房錢 | fáng-ch'ien | Room rent. |
| 22. 面子 | mièn-tzŭ | The face, social standing. |
| 23. 外面很好看 | wài-mien hěn hǎo-k'àn | The outside (surface) is lovely. |
| 24. 單雙 | tān-shuāng | Single and double, odd and even. |
| 25. 單日雙日 | tān-jìh shuāng-jìh | The odd and even days. |
| 26. 單位 | tān-wèi | A unit. |
| 27. 白話 | Pái-huà | The colloquial language ("plain speech"). |
| 28. 白天 | pái-t'ien | Bright day, daytime. |
| 29. 想起來 | hsiáng-ch'ǐ-lai | To call to mind. |
| 30. 想不起來 | hsiǎng-pu-ch'ǐ-lai | Cannot recall. |
| 31. 想不到 | hsiǎng-pu-tào | Unanticipated, unexpected. |
| 32. 想望 | hsiǎng-wàng | Expectation. |
| 33. 利錢 | lì-ch'ien | Interest, profit. |
| 34. 利不利? | lì-pu-li? | Is it sharp or not? Is it advantageous or not? |
| 35. 對我很不利 | tùi wó hěn pú lì | Very disadvantageous to me, very bad for me. |
| 36. 香水 | hsiāng-shuǐ | Liquid scent, perfume. |

| | | |
|---|---|---|
| 37. 香煙 | hsiāng-yēn | Cigarette. |
| 38. 根本 | kěn-pěn | Root, source, origin. |
| 39. 根本就錯了 | kěn-pěn chiù ts'ò lê | Fundamentally wrong. |
| 40. 根本就不對 | kěn-pěn chiù pú tuì | Fundamentally incorrect. |
| 41. 便是 | pièn-shìh | That is, then it is ... |
| 42. 不是 A ,便是 B | Pú shìh A, pièn-shìh B | If it is not A, then it is B. |
| 43. 不便說話 | pú pièn shuō-huà | Not convenient to talk, not in a position to talk. |
| 44. 當中 | tāng-chūng | In the middle. |
| 45. 在這班人當中, A 先生最好 | Tsài chè pān jén tāng-chūng, A hsiēn-shēng tsuì hǎo | In this class of people, Mr. A is the best. |
| 46. 當天 | tāng t'iēn | On that very day, on that day. |
| 47. 當時 | tāng shíh | At that time, at this time, instantly. |
| 48. 當面 | tāng-mièn | Face to face, personally, openly. |
| 49. 請你當面告訴他 | Ch'íng ni tāng-mièn kào-su t'a | Please tell him personally. |
| 50. 擱下 | kē-hsia | To put down. |
| 51. 擱不下 | kē-pu-hsià | Unable to put down. |
| 52. 擱開 | kē-k'ai | To put aside. |
| 53. 冷淡 | lěng-tàn | Indifferent, cold. |
| 54. 多半 | tō-pàn | More than half. For the most part, probably. |
| 55. 多嘴 | tō-tsuǐ | Very loquacious, meddlesome. |
| 56. 人人都知道 | jén-jén tōu chīh-tao | Everybody knows. |

## 2. Useful Phrases Which Should Be Memorized

[Languages are hard to learn but easy to forget. For the purpose of a general rapid review, we recapitulate the useful phrases given in previous lessons in the order in which they have appeared, and without romanization so that students may be sure of learning the characters thoroughly. These expressions should be recognized in reading and used in speech without hesitation. They will be very useful in reading newspapers and other modern literature.]

i. Greetings

好嗎? 你好嗎? 你好不好?

我好, 謝謝. 我很好, 你呢?

ii. Introductions and Polite Expressions

貴姓? 你貴姓? 請問, 先生貴姓? 你姓甚麼? 敝姓王.

大名? 你叫甚麼名字?

請給我們介紹介紹.

請你把我介紹給你的朋友.

這是王先生. 這是李先生.

請坐. 王先生請坐.

這是誰? 這是我的朋友.

你的朋友貴姓? 他姓張.

貴國是那國? 請問, 貴國是那國?

你是那國人? 敝國是美國.

我是美國人. 他是英國人.

我們都是好朋友.

你的中國話很好. 過獎, 過獎.

你是這班最好的學生. 不敢當.

謝謝. 多謝. 不謝, 不謝.

不客氣. 不要客氣.

再見. 再會. 明天見.

禮拜五再見.

iii. Talking about Languages

你懂中國話嗎? 你懂法文跟德文嗎?

我懂. 我不懂. 我懂一點兒.

請問, 你會說中國話嗎?

我會說中國話. 我不會說中國話.

我會說一點兒. 我會說, 可是不會寫.

你說甚麼? 請慢慢的說.

請你說慢一點兒. 請再慢一點兒說. 請寫一寫.

請用中文寫.

請用英文寫. 請用俄文寫.

請你再說一次. 現在我懂了, 謝謝.

這是甚麼? 那是甚麼? 對不起, 我不知道. 他也不曉得.

這是誰的? 這是我的.

這個叫甚麼? 這是甚麼東西?

那個東西中國話叫甚麼?

日文跟德文難不難學?

不很容易.

甚麼話最容易學?

恐怕英文最容易學.

誰會說英文? 我們都會說英文.

誰會說意大利文? 誰也不會說意大利文.

iv. Week and Month

今天是禮拜幾? 今天是禮拜一.

今天是那一天? 今天是幾號?

今天是八月十五.

我們要學十二個月的中國話.

正月, 二月, 三月, 四月, 五月, 六月, 七月, 八月, 九月, 十月, 十一月, 十二月.

v. Year and Season

一年有四季: 春, 夏, 秋, 冬.

貴國夏天很熱嗎? 敝國夏天不很熱.

春天的天氣多半是不冷也不熱. 夏天常下雨.

我也不喜歡冬天, 因為太冷.

一千九百五十年是中華民國三十九年.

今天天氣好嗎? 今天天氣很好.

今天天氣熱不熱? 今天天氣冷不冷?

今天天氣好極了, 因為不冷也不熱.

我最喜歡春天. 我也喜歡秋天.

我不喜歡夏天, 因為太熱.

天晴了. 下雨了.

vi. Time of Day

現在是甚麼時候? 現在是幾點鐘?

現在幾點了? 你的表幾點了? 幾點了?

現在是一點一刻. 現在是兩點半.

現在是差一刻三點.

你的表對嗎? 你的表對不對?

我的表慢一點兒. 我的表快一點兒.

我的表很對. 我的表很準.

你甚麼時候回家?

時候不早了, 我要走了.

請你走快一點兒.

對不起, 我來晚了. 我明天準來.

vii. Weights and Measures, etc.

一尺有十寸, 一寸有十分.

我家有五畝地. 他家很有錢.

從*這裏到那裏有三里路遠. 這是標準尺.

得寸進尺.

一噸有多少磅?

高, 矮, 長, 短, 寬, 窄, 都是很有用的字.

我五尺八高, 一百四十磅重.

---

*Ts'ung, see p. 188.

我每天吃三頓飯.

追, 吹, 飽, 跑, 準, 蠢, 沙, 蝦, 都是要念的很清楚的.

告, 靠, 古, 苦, 誰, 水, 也是不好念的字.

蝦裏有沙. 我鞋裏有沙.

每一個人要吃鹽, 不一定要吃煙.

喝茶要擱糖, 喝湯不要擱糖.

我是作買賣的.

書擱在椅子上.

眼鏡在眼睛上.

viii. Making a Telephone Call

請問, 這兒有電話沒有?

我要一六四四號.

喂, 你是誰? 你是那一位? 你那兒?

你是王先生嗎?

我要請王先生說話.

我聽不清楚. 請你大聲一點兒說.

你的電話是多少號?

錯了, 請你掛上罷.

ix. Making a Visit

你有名片嗎? 請你給我一張名片罷.

這是我的名片.

你認識一位李先生嗎?

你知道嗎? 我知道. 我不知道.

請你等一會兒. 請你等一等.

有一位客人來了. 是誰?

請進來. 請他進來罷.

請進來坐一坐. 好久沒見了.

你忙嗎? 我很忙. 我不忙.

你抽 (吃) 煙嗎?

我抽煙. 我不抽煙. 那麼, 請喝一杯茶罷.

麻煩不麻煩? 一點兒不麻煩.

x. What Is Your Occupation?

你在那裏作事? 請問, 你作甚麼事?

我教英文.

你們學校有多少學生?

你每天教幾點鐘書?

不一定. 有的時候多, 有的時候少.

你每天作幾點鐘事?

我每天作八點鐘事.

你去不去? 我一定去. 你那兒去?

我去作事. 甚麼事? 沒有甚麼.

xi. In a Family

你家有多少人? 你家有甚麽人?

你有多少兄弟? 你有幾姐妹?

你有孩子沒有? 你有幾位小姐跟少爺?

王老先生, 久仰, 久仰.

這是我的哥哥. 那是我最小的妹妹.

你弟弟在家嗎? 他不在家.

他一會兒就回來. 不久就回來.

xii. In a Classroom

你的功課忙不忙?

你今天有幾堂課?

我們甚麽時候有考試?

昨天先生講到那一課, 那一頁?

這個課堂裏有桌子, 椅子, 黑板, 跟黑板刷子, 可是沒有粉筆.

時候到了, 我們去上課罷.

現在我們下課.

xiii. Foods and Drinks

我渴了. 我渴極了.

我要喝水. 我要喝茶. 我要喝酒.

我要吃飯. 我要吃中國飯.

你一天吃幾頓飯? 你吃早飯了嗎?

你是甚麼時候吃的早飯?

你甚麼時候吃午飯?

甚麼時候開晚飯? 晚飯甚麼時候開?

你會拿筷子嗎? 我會. 我不會.

你吃飯了嗎? 我吃過了. 我剛才吃過.

你吃飽了嗎? 我吃飽了.

我不能再吃了.

你早飯吃了甚麼? 我喝了粥.

我喝了一杯牛奶, 吃了一片麵包跟兩個鷄子.

我吃了一個梨, 一個蘋果, 跟一片西瓜.

我吃了一個橘子.

你餓不餓? 你餓了嗎? 我現在不餓.

飯得了. 飯好了.

你還要甚麼? 我還要喝一杯茶.

你愛喝濃茶還是喝淡茶? 我愛喝不濃不淡的茶.

這壺茶太濃了, 請你對一點兒水罷.

這壺茶太淡了, 請你擱一點兒茶葉罷.

你喝茶, 要擱糖跟牛奶嗎? 中國人喝茶不擱糖. 我喝紅茶的時候, 要擱一點兒糖.

xiv. In a Restaurant

請問, 飯館在那兒? 請問, 那裏有飯館? 那裏有西餐館? ·

這裏沒有. 這裏有一家. 謝謝你告訴我.

我們走罷. 我們去吃飯罷.

你喜歡吃甚麼? 你要吃甚麼?

你有菜單嗎? 菜單在那兒?

你要喝甚麼? 你要喝酒嗎?

給我茶罷. 我不喝酒. 水就行了.

請給我一杯水. 請給我一壺茶.

請給我鹽跟胡椒麵.

請給我醋跟醬油.

這兒有酒沒有? 這兒有酒.

你要喝黃酒還是喝燒酒?

請你快一點兒. 一會兒就來.

菜好了. 菜得了. 請你快拿來罷.

你要豆腐湯, 還是火腿冬瓜湯?

這是糖醋排骨. 這是白菜炒猪肉. 這很好吃.

很好. 好極了. 這些菜都很好吃.

你還要吃甚麼? 我不要吃甚麼.

請乾杯. 我醉了. 我不能再喝了.

因爲我有事, 我要早一點兒走.

行不行? 行. 不行.

不對. 差不多.

沒有甚麼. 是嗎? 是的.

你有甚麼就給我甚麼.

多少錢? 要給酒錢嗎? 隨你便罷.

3. Aural Drill

[The following method has been found useful in conducting aural drill, and some instructors may wish to use it. Before the students read the following humorous anecdote, it has been read aloud to the class by the instructor. The students listen carefully, and then write down the general idea of the story in English. When this has been done, the instructor reads the story again and allows the students to make corrections. After this, the students read the story as it appears in Chinese in characters and romanization on the following pages, but for best results they should not yet read the translation. On the next day, the instructor reads the story to the class a third time, and a careful translation is worked out by the students. The translation given at the end of this lesson is used only to check results after this has been done.

Note that the key expression of this anecdote is the figure of speech ".. chiù-shih wǒ-tê mìng 命 (life, fate)" - "[It] is my life"; i.e., "I love it as much as my life".]

## 豆腐就是我的命

### TÒU-FU CHIÙ-SHIH WǑ-TE MÌNG

有一個人請一位先生到他的家裏教他的兒子. 在這位先生來的第一天, 他想要做一頓好飯

Yǔ í - kê jến ch'ǐng í-wèi hsiēn-shêng tào t'ā-tê chiā-li chiāo t'ā - tê ḗrh - tzǔ. Tsài chḕ-wèi hsiēn-shêng lái-tê tì - ì t'iēn, t'ā hsiǎng yào tsò í-tùn hǎo fàn

給先生吃．可是他想，吃肉罷，太貴了！吃鷄子罷，也很貴！最後他想豆腐不貴，所以只好做豆腐給先生吃．先生來的時候，他們談了一會兒，就請吃飯．在吃飯的時候，他就問先生說：『先生！你喜歡吃豆腐嗎？』先生囘答說：『我很喜歡吃豆腐；豆腐就是我的命．』那個人，一聽先生愛吃豆腐，就很喜歡．因爲吃豆腐不要用很多的錢，所以他每天做豆腐給先生吃．先生吃多了，不想再吃了，可是不便說出來．

有一天，過年了．

kěi hsiēn-shêng ch'īh. K'ě-shih t'ā hsiǎng, ch'īh jòu pa, t'ài kuèi lê! Ch'īh chī-tzǔ pa, yéh hěn kuèi! Tsuì hòu t'ā hsiǎng tòu-fu pú kuèi, só-ǐ chíh hǎo tsò tòu-fu kěi hsiēn-shêng ch'īh. Hsiēn-shêng lái-tê shíh-hou, t'ā-mên t'án lê ì-huǐ-êrh, chiù ch'ǐng ch'īh-fàn. Tsài ch'īh-fàn-tê shíh-hou, t'ā chiù wěn hsiēn-shêng shuō: "Hsiēn-shêng! Ní hsǐ-huan ch'īh tòu-fu ma?" Hsiēn-shêng huí tá shuō: "Wǒ hěn hsǐ-huan ch'īh tòu-fu; tòu-fu chiù-shih wǒ-tê míng." Nà-kê jén, ì t'īng hsiēn-shêng ài ch'īh tòu-fu, chiù hěn hsǐ-huan. Yīn-wèi ch'īh tòu-fu pú yào yùng hěn tō-tê ch'ién, só-ǐ t'ā měi t'iēn tsò tòu-fu kěi hsiēn-shêng ch'īh. Hsiēn-shêng ch'īh tō lê, pù hsiǎng tsài ch'īh lê, k'ě-shih pú pièn shuō-ch'ū-lai.

Yǔ ì t'iēn, kuò nién lê.

| | |
|---|---|
| 那個人做了一碗肉. | Nà - kê jến tsò lê ì - wǎn jòu. |
| 他想先生很喜歡吃 | T'ā hsiǎng hsiēn-shêng hến hsǐ-huan ch'īh |
| 豆腐, 所以再做了 | tòu - fu, só - ǐ tsài tsò lê |
| 一碗豆腐. 在吃飯 | ì - wǎn tòu-fu. Tsài ch'īh-fàn- |
| 的時候, 先生只吃 | tê shíh-hou, hsiēn-shêng chǐh ch'īh |
| 肉, 不吃豆腐. 他 | jòu, pù ch'īh tòu - fu. T'ā |
| 就問先生說:『先生! | chiù wền hsiēn-shêng shuō: "Hsiēn-shêng! |
| 你不是說豆腐就是 | Nǐ pú shìh shuō tòu-fu chiù-shih |
| 你的命嗎? 你爲甚 | nǐ - tê míng ma? Nǐ wèi shến- |
| 麼今天只吃肉不吃 | mo chīn-t'ien chǐh ch'īh jòu pù ch'īh |
| 豆腐呢?』先生說: | tòu - fu ni?" Hsiēn-shêng shuō: |
| 『對了, 因爲我看見 | "Tùi lê, yīn-wèi wǒ k'àn-chien |
| 了肉, 就不要命了.』 | lê jòu, chiù pú yào míng lê." |

## TRANSLATION

### "Bean-Curd Is My Life"

There was a man who invited a teacher to come to his home to teach his son. On the first day that the teacher came, he wanted to prepare a good meal for the teacher to eat. But he thought, to eat meat was too expensive! To eat eggs, also very expensive! At last he thought that bean-curd was not expensive, and so he had better prepare bean-curd for the teacher to eat. When the teacher came, they talked for a while, and then [the man] invited [the teacher] to eat. While eating, he asked the teacher: "Sir, do you like to eat bean-curd?" The teacher replied: "I like to eat bean-curd very much; bean-curd is my life." That man, the moment he heard that the teacher loved to eat bean-curd, was delighted. Because to eat bean-curd it is not necessary to spend much money, therefore every day he prepared bean-curd for the teacher to eat. The teacher, eating so much, did not want to eat any more. But he was not in a position to speak out.

One day, it was the New Year. That man prepared a bowl of meat. He thought that the teacher liked to eat bean-curd, so he again prepared a bowl of bean-curd. When eating, the teacher ate only meat and did not eat bean-curd. He asked the teacher: "Sir, didn't you say that bean-curd is your life? Why do you only eat meat without eating bean-curd today?" The teacher said: "That's right, because when I saw the meat, I no longer wanted life."

CONVERSATIONAL CHINESE

PART V TERMS USED IN TRAVELING

Lesson 25 Asking Directions

1. Vocabulary

| | | |
|---|---|---|
| 手 | shǒu | Hand, arm [ì-chīh shǒu]. |
| 找 | chǎo (1) | To look for, to find. To repay (as money). |
| 怎麼 | tsěn-mo | In what way? How? What? |
| 着 | cháo | To order, to send. To catch, to suffer. See also p. 89. |
| 南 | nán (2) | South. |
| 北 | pěi | North. |
| 左 | tsǒ | Left. |
| 右 | yù | Right. |
| 往 | wǎng | To go to. Past. |
| | wàng | To, toward. |
| 街 | chiēh | Street [ì-t'iáo chiēh]. |
| 路過 | lù-kuò | To pass by or through. <u>En</u> <u>route</u>. |
| 邊 | piēn | Side, edge. |
| 旁 | p'áng | Side. By the side of. Other. |
| 旁邊 | p'áng-piēn | The side. At the side. |
| 明白 | míng-pai | To understand. |
| 直 | chíh | Straight, directly. Upright. |
| 一直 | ì-chíh | Straight ahead. |
| 緊 | chǐn | Tight, urgent, important, strict. |
| 急 | chí | Anxious, impatient. Haste. |
| 緊急 | chǐn-chí | Urgent, pressing. |
| 警 | chǐng | To warn. Alarm. |
| 察 | ch'á | To examine into, to observe. |
| 警察 | chǐng-ch'á | Policeman [í-kê chǐng-ch'á]. |
| 近 | chìn | Near, recent. |
| 弄 | nùng | To do, to make. |
| 對面 | tùi-mièn | Opposite, face to face. |

| | | |
|---|---|---|
| 方 | fāng | Square. Side, direction, method. |
| 地方 | tì-fang | Place [í-kê tì-fang, a place; í-k'uài tì-fang, a piece of land]. |
| 向 | hsiàng | Toward. |
| 方向 | fāng-hsiang | Direction. |
| 離 | lí | Apart, far from, from. |
| 離開 | lí-k'ai | To leave, to part from. |
| 從 | ts'úng | From, since. To follow. |
| 拐 | kuǎi | To turn, to kidnap. |
| 彎 | wān | To curve. Curved. Corner [í-kê wān]. |
| 拐彎 | kuǎi wān | To turn a corner. |
| 四川 | Ssǔ-ch'uan | Szechwan Province. |
| 門 | mén | Gate, door. |
| 牌 | p'ái | Signboard, placard, tablet. |
| 門牌 | mén-p'ái | Door-plate. |
| 山 | shān | Hill, mountain [í-tsò shān]. |

2. Conversation

[From this point on, translation of the reading material will be placed in a separate section, following the notes. The student should first work out a careful translation of his own, in order to develop his ability to do independent work, and only afterwards check with the translation in the book, to discover his errors. In reading these sentences, the student should study the Chinese characters and refer only when necessary to the romanization, which is furnished as a help to the beginner, on which he should not however permit himself to become too dependent.]

1.(A) 先生，請你告訴我中國大學在那兒？
Hsiēn-shêng, ch'íng ni kào-su wo Chūng-kuo Tà-hsüéh tsài nǎ-êrh?

2.(B) 對不起，我也是剛來這兒的；這兒的路我都不認識。請你問別人罷。
Tùi pu ch'ǐ, wó yěh shìh kāng lái chè-êrh tê; chè-êrh-tê lù wǒ tōu(3) pú jèn-shih(4). Ch'ing ni wèn piéh jén pa.

3.(A) 好，謝謝。 老先生，你知道
Hǎo, hsièh-hsieh. - Lǎo-hsiēn-shēng, nǐ chīh-tao
中國大學在那兒嗎？
Chūng-kuo Tà-hsüéh tsài nǎ-êrh ma(5)?

4.(C) 讓我想一想。我沒有去過，可
Jàng wo hsiǎng-i-hsiang. Wǒ méi-yǔ ch'ù kuò(6), k'ě-
是我知道在四川路。
shih wǒ chīh-tao tsài Ssǔ-ch'uan Lù.

5.(A) 四川路離這兒遠嗎？
Ssǔ-ch'uan Lù lí chè-êrh yüǎn(7) ma?

6.(C) 不遠，離這兒很近。從這兒一
Pù yüǎn, lí chè-êrh hěn chìn. Ts'úng(8) chè-êrh ì-
直往東走，到了第三條街，
chíh wàng tūng tsǒu, tào lê ti-sān t'iáo chiēh,
再往南走就是。
tsài(9) wàng nán tsǒu chiù-shih.

7.(A) 東南西北的方向我還沒弄清
Tūng nán hsī pěi tê fāng-hsiang wǒ hái méi nùng ch'īng-
楚呢。
ch'u ni.

8.(C) 我們現在對面的方向是東，右
Wǒ-mên hsièn-tsài tuì-mièn tê fāng-hsiang shìh tūng, yù-
手是南邊，左手是北邊。
shǒu shìh nán-pien, tsó-shǒu shìh pěi-pien.

9.(A) 現在我明白了。多謝，多謝。
Hsièn-tsài wǒ míng-pai lê. Tō hsièh, tō hsièh.

10.(C) 不客氣。
Pú k'è-ch'i.

(In Mr. Wang's office)

11.(A) 我要看王先生；他在這兒嗎？
Wǒ yào k'àn Wáng hsiēn-shēng; t'ā tsài chè-êrh ma?

12.(D) 王先生剛回家。你可以到他家
Wáng hsiēn-shēng kāng huí chiā. Ní k'ě-i tào t'ā chiā
去找他。
ch'ü chǎo t'a.

13.(A) 他家在甚麼地方？
T'ā chiā tsài shén-mo tì-fang?

14.(D) 你有很緊急的事，要到他家去
Ní yǔ hěn chǐn-chí-tê shìh, yào tào t'ā chiā ch'ù

找他嗎？
chǎo t'a ma?

15.(A) 我們是很老的朋友，可是好些
Wǒ - mên shìh hěn lǎo - tê p'éng - yu, k'ě-shih hǎo-hsiēh
年沒見面了。我現在路過這
nién méi chièn mièn lê. Wǒ hsièn-tsài lù - kuò chè-
個地方，今天晚上就要離開。
kê tì - fang, chīn-t'ien wǎn-shang chiù yào lí - k'ai.
所以我要到他家裏去找他。
Só - i wǒ yào tào t'ā chiā - li ch'ù chǎo t'a.

16.(D) 那麼，我告訴你罷。他家在中
Nà - mo, wǒ kào - su ni pa. T'ā chiā tsài Chūng-
山路，門牌二百十四號。
shān Lù(10), mén-p'ái(11) èrh-pǎi shíh-ssǔ hào.

17.(A) 中山路離這兒遠嗎？
Chūng-shān Lù lí chè-êrh yüǎn ma?

18.(D) 中山路離這兒很近。
Chūng-shān Lù lí chè-êrh hěn chìn.

19.(A) 請你告訴我從這兒怎麼走。
Ch'íng ni kào - su wo ts'úng chè-êrh tsěn - mo tsǒu.

20.(D) 我也不很清楚。那兒有一個警
Wó yěh pù hěn ch'īng-ch'u. Nà - êrh yǔ í - kê chǐng-
察；最好你去問他罷。
ch'á; tsuì hǎo nǐ ch'ù wèn t'a pa.

21.(A, to policeman) 請問，去中山路怎麼走？
Ch'ǐng wèn, ch'ù Chūng-shān Lù tsěn - mo tsǒu?

22.(E) 從這兒往北走，過了兩條街往
Ts'úng chè-êrh wàng péi tsǒu, kuò lê liǎng-t'iáo chiēh wàng
右拐。走到一個外國飯館；
yù kuǎi. Tsǒu tào í - kê wài-kuó fàn-kuǎn;
你再拐一個彎兒，就到了。
nǐ tsài kuǎi í - kê wān-êrh, chiù tào lê.
你要找門牌多少號？
Nǐ yào chǎo mén-p'ái tō - shǎo hào?

23.(A) 我要找二百十四號。
Wǒ yào chǎo èrh-pǎi shíh-ssǔ hào.

24.(E) 二百十四號是在一個女子中學
Èrh-pǎi shíh-ssǔ hào shìh tsài í - kê nǚ - tzǔ chūng-hsüéh-

的 旁 邊.
tê p'áng-piēn.

25.(A) 我 恐 怕 找 不 着.
Wó k'ŭng-p'à chǎo pù cháo(12).

26.(E) 你 看 着 街 走, 不 會 走 錯 的.
Nǐ k'àn-cho(13) chiēh tsǒu, pú huì tsǒu ts'ò tê.

27.(A) 麻 煩 你 了, 謝 謝.
Má - fan ni lê, hsièh-hsieh.

28.(E) 一 點 兒 不 麻 煩; 再 見.
Ì - tiěn-êrh pù má - fan; tsài chièn.

NOTES:

(1) Care should be taken to distinguish the form of 找 "chǎo" from that of 我 "wǒ"; and also the pronunciation of "chǎo" from that of 叫 "chiào".

(2) In naming directions, Chinese reverses the English order and says "tūng-pěi", "east-north"; "hsī-nán", "west-south", etc.

(3) "Tōu pù" means "all not", or "none at all". "Tōu" may be translated "all", "entirely", or sometimes "even" (for example: "Nǐ chè tōu pù tŭng ma?" - "Don't you understand even this?"). It precedes verbs and adjectives and follows nouns and pronouns.

(4) "Jèn-shih lù" means "to recognize the way" or "to know the directions".

(5) This sentence consists of a question within a question. One question is: "Nǐ chīh-tao ma?"; the other "Chūng-kuo Tà-hsüéh tsài nǎ-êrh?"

(6) See the note on "kuò" as a co-verb, Lesson 20, page 141.

(7) "Lí ... yüǎn" expresses the idea of distance or separation; for example: "Nǐ chiā lí wǒ chiā yŭ tō yüǎn?" - "How far is your house (separated) from mine?"; "Lí chè-li pù yüǎn, yŭ ì-chiā fàn-kuǎn" - "Not far from here, there is a restaurant". Sentence 17 of this lesson is another illustration.

(8) "Ts'úng ... tào ..." is commonly used to indicate motion from one place to another. The basic formula for this construction is: "subject - ts'úng - place - tào - place - lái (or, ch'ü)". For example: "Wǒ ts'úng Chūng-kuo tào Měi-kuo lai". Note that if there is a verb indicating the kind of motion, it follows the "ts'úng" phrase and precedes the "tào" phrase; for example: "Wǒ ts'úng chè-li tsǒu tào nà-li ch'ü".

(9) Here, "tsài" means "then". See section 2 of note on the uses of "tsài" at the end of Lesson 21 (page 150).

(10) Thoroughfares in Chinese cities are often named "Chung-shan Road" in honor of Sun Chung-shan (Sun Yat-sen), the founder of the Chinese Republic.

(11) "Mḗn-p'ái" means a door-plate on which the street and number are inscribed.

(12) "Chǎo pù cháo" means "look for [and] not succeed [in finding]", i.e., to look for and not find.

(13) 着 is pronounced "cho" or "chê" when it is used with verbs as a suffix indicating a progressive sense: "Wǒ tsò-cho" - "I sit" or "I am sitting". "K'àn-cho chiēh" means "watching the streets".

3. Translation

1.(A) Sir, please tell me where China College is.

2.(B) I'm sorry, I am a newcomer here too (literally, I too have just come here). I do not know the way hereabouts (literally, I do not recognize the roads here at all). Please ask someone else.

3.(A) All right, thank you. - Venerable sir, do you know where China College is?

4.(C) Let me think. I have not been (gone) there, but I know [it] is on Szechwan Road.

5.(A) Is Szechwan Road far from here?

6.(C) Not far, it is very near (from) here. Go straight ahead to the east from here, [and when you] arrive at the third street, then [turn] to the south and there you are.

7.(A) The directions of east, south, west, north, I have not yet made clear [to myself].

8.(C) The direction we are now facing is east, the right-hand side is south, the left-hand side is north.

9.(A) Now I understand. Many thanks, many thanks.

10.(C) Don't mention it.

11.(A) I want to see Mr. Wang; is he here?

12.(D) Mr. Wang has just gone home. You can go to his house to look for him.

13.(A) Where is his house (literally, His house is at what place)?

14.(D) Have you some very urgent business, [so that] you must go to his house to look for him?

15.(A) We are very old friends, but for a good many years we have not seen [each other's] face. Now I am passing through this place, and this evening I must leave. Therefore I want to go to his house to look for him.

16.(D) Well then, I'll tell you. His house is at number 214 Chung-shan Road.

17.(A) Is Chung-shan Road far from here?

18.(D) Chung-shan Road is very near here.

19.(A) Please tell me how to go from here.

20.(D) I too am not very clear [about it]. There is a policeman; [it would be] best [for] you to go and ask him.

21.(A) May I ask how to go to Chung-shan Road?

22.(E) Go north from here, past two streets, [then] turn to the right. Walk [on till you] arrive at a foreign restaurant, then turn a corner and you are there. What house (door) number are you looking for?

23.(A) I want to find number 214.

24.(E) Number 214 is at the side of a girls' high school.

25.(A) I am afraid I won't find it.

26.(E) Watching the streets as you go, [you] cannot go wrong.

27.(A) Thank you for your trouble (literally, I have bothered you, thank you).

28.(E) No trouble at all; goodby.

4. Exercises

a. "Fill-in" sentences.

| | |
|---|---|
| 1. Ch'ǐng wèn ... ... ... tsài nǎ-êrh? | May I ask, where is ... ... ... ? |
| 2. Nǐ chīh-tao Ssǔ-ch'uan Lù ... ... ... ma? | Do you know ... ... ... Szechwan Road? |
| 3. Ts'úng chè-êrh tào ... ... ... ... tsǒu? | ... ... ... go from here to ... ... ? |
| 4. T'ā chiā tsài ... ... ... , mén-p'ái ... ... ... | His house is on ... ... ... , number ... ... ... |
| 5. Chè-t'iáo ... shàng yú chǐ-kê ... ... ? | How many ... ... are there on this ... ? |
| 6. ... ... lí ... ... (yüǎn) / (chìn). | (Place) ... is (far from) / (near) here. |
| 7. Tsǒu tào tì-èrh-t'iáo chiēh, ... ... kuǎi. | [When you] arrive at the second street, turn ... ... |
| 8. ... ... tsǒu. | Go (direction) ... ... |
| 9. ... ... ts'úng ... tào ... ... (lai) / (ch'ü). | ... (comes) / (goes) from ... to ... |

b. Translate into English:

1. Chè-êrh-tê lù, nĭ tōu jèn-shih ma?
2. Wŏ tōu jèn-shih, yīn-wèi wŏ lái lê yŭ liù nién lê.
3. Nà-mo, ch'íng ni kào-su wo, Ssŭ-ch'uan Lù tsài ná-li?
4. Ssŭ-ch'uan Lù lí chè-êrh yüăn cho na.
5. Ts'úng chè-êrh tsĕn-mo tsŏu?
6. Wŏ pù chīh-tao, yīn-wèi wó yĕh méi-yŭ ch'ǜ kuò.
7. Wŏ yào ch'ǜ chăo í-wèi Chūng-kuo Tà-hsüéh-tê chiào-yüán.
8. K'ĕ-shih wŏ pú jèn-shih lù, tsĕn-mo hăo?
9. Wó kéi ni wèn-i-wên chĭng-ch'á, hăo-pu-hao?
10. Nĭ piéh kuò-wèn piéh-jén-tê shìh.
11. Wŏ yào lí-k'ai Chūng-kuo.

c. Translate into Chinese:

1. Turn to the left and you'll see the school.
2. Let us walk toward the south.
3. I think [it would be] best to walk straight ahead.
4. What did the policeman say?
5. He asked me, "What street are you looking for?"
6. I told him, "We are looking for Chung-shan Road."
7. Can you tell me how to go from here?
8. I have not yet found the place of which he spoke.
9. By the side of the road there is an auditorium (see page 127).
10. In that place there are many indifferent people.

## Special Drill on the Word 着

The word 着 has three different principal uses and two pronunciations.

1. Used as a main verb meaning "to catch, to suffer", it is pronounced "cháo". Examples of this use:

"Cháo liáng" 着凉 - "to catch cold".

"Cháo chí" 着急 - "to become impatient, to be worried".

"Cháo huŏ" 着火 - "to catch fire, to be burned".

2. Used as a co-verb denoting the attainment of an aim, it is pronounced "cháo". For example:

"Wó chăo-cháo lê" 我找着了 - "I found it (was successful in finding it)".

"Nà-kê tūng-hsi wó măi-cháo lê" 那個東西我買着了 - "I bought (succeeded in buying) that object".

NOTE that "cháo" in this sense is used after the main verb and is followed by "lê". If preceded by "pù", it indicates impossibility or failure of the action. Examples:

"Wó chăo pù cháo" 我找不着 - "I am unable to find it".

"Nà-kê tūng-hsi wó măi pù cháo" 那個東西我買不着 -"I cannot buy that thing".

3. Used as a co-verb denoting a state of affairs or continued action, it is pronounced "cho". For example:

"Tĕng-cho" 等着 - "waiting, while waiting, to wait".

"Hsiēn-shêng chàn-cho chiăng; hsüéh-shêng tsò-cho t'īng" 先生站着講，學生坐着聽 - "The teacher, standing, lectures; the students, sitting, listen".

"Cho" is also often used after adjectives and adverbs, for euphony.

"Hái tō-cho na" 還多着哪 - "There is still much" ("na" is a final particle which gives strong emphasis to an assertion or declaration).

"T'iēn hái tsăo-cho na" 天還早着哪 - "It is still early".

Exercises in the Use of 着

1. 王小姐着我到這兒來拿粉筆.

2. 我着了一個人去買東西.

3. 我找不着我的片子.

4. 我着涼了.

5. 不要着急.

6. 那個房子着火了.

7. 你在這兒站着作什麼?

8. 請你在這兒等着我.

9. 你們關*着門作什麽?

10. 我得不着準時候.

11. 那個東西我找了半天找不着.

12. 這個蘋果還生着哪.

13. 我再說一次, 請你聽着.

14. 時候還早着哪, 請你不要忙着下課.

## Lesson 26 Using Various Vehicles

1. Vocabulary

| | | |
|---|---|---|
| 車 | ch'ê̄ | Wheeled vehicle, cart, car. |
| 輛 | liàng | A numerative of vehicles. |
| 洋車 | yáng-ch'ê̄ | Ricksha [í-liàng yáng-ch'ê̄]. |
| 夫 | fū | Laborer, man, husband [seldom used alone]. |
| 車夫 | ch'ê̄-fū (1) | Ricksha puller, driver of a cart or of any vehicle [í-kê ch'ê̄-fū]. |
| 汽 | ch'ì | Steam, vapor. |
| 汽車 | ch'ì-ch'ê̄ | Automobile, taxicab [í-liàng ch'ì-ch'ê̄]. |
| 司 | ssū | To manage, to preside. Department. |
| 機 | chī | Machine, mechanism, opportunity. |
| 司機 | ssū-chī (2) | Chauffeur (one who manages a machine) [í-kê ssū-chī]. |
| 共 | kùng | All, together. To share. |
| 公共汽車 | kūng-kùng ch'ì-ch'ê̄ | Public bus [í-liàng kūng-kùng ch'ì-ch'ê̄]. |
| 電車 | tièn-ch'ê̄ | Street car, trolley car [í-liàng tièn-ch'ê̄]. |
| 園 | yüán | Garden, park, yard. A term applied to tea houses, theaters, etc. |
| 公園 | kūng-yüán | Public park [í-kê kūng-yüán]. |
| 雇 | kù | To hire. |
| 停 | t'íng | To stop, to delay. |



*Kuān To shut, to close, see p. 215.

-196-

| | | |
|---|---|---|
| 忘 | wàng | To forget. |
| 記 | chì | To remember, to record. |
| 興 | hsìng | Joyful. To prosper, to use. |
| 高興 | kāo-hsìng | To like, to be delighted. Glad to. In high spirits. |
| 啊 | ā | An exclamation. |
| 毛 | máo | Hair, fur, feather, wool. Ten cents. |
| 一毛錢 | ì-máo-ch'ién (3) | Ten cents. |
| 一分錢 | ì-fēn-ch'ién | One cent. |
| 元 | yüán (4) | Dollar. First, original. |
| 圓 | yüán | Round, circular. Dollar. |
| 角 | chiǎo | The horn of an animal. Corner, angle. A ten-cent piece. |
| 朵 | tǒ | Lobe, cluster. A numerative of flowers and pendants. |
| 花 | huā | Flower[ì-tǒ huā]. To spend (money or time). |
| 棵 | k'ē | A numerative of trees and plants. |
| 草 | ts'ǎo | Grass, herb [ì-kēn or ì-k'ē ts'ǎo]. |
| 樹 | shù | Tree [ì-k'ē shù]. |
| 木 | mù | Tree, wood [seldom used alone]. |
| 竹子 | chú-tzǔ | Bamboo [ì-kēn chú-tzǔ]. |
| 一塊兒 | í-k'uài-êrh | Together. |
| 方便 | fāng-pièn | Convenient,advantage. |
| 宜 | í | Proper, right, fit. |
| 便宜 | p'ién-i | Cheap. Advantage. |
| 交 | chiāo | To hand over, to pay, to exchange. |
| 交通 | chiāo-t'ūng | Communication, traffic. |
| 眞 | chēn (5) | Real, true, genuine. Really. |
| 樓 | lóu | Upper storey, high building [í-tsò lóu]. |
| 平 | p'íng | Peace. Even, equal. |
| 北平 | Pěi-p'íng | Peiping. |

2. Conversation

1.(A) 今天天氣很好. 你高興去公園走一走罷?
Chīn-t'ien t'iēn-ch'i hĕn hăo. Nĭ kāo-hsìng ch'ù kūng-yüán tsŏu - i - tsou pa?

2.(B) 我很高興去, 因爲我還沒有去過公園. 我們怎麼去?
Wó hĕn kāo-hsìng ch'ù, yīn - wèi wŏ hái méi - yŭ ch'ù kuò kūng-yüán. Wŏ - mên tsĕn - mo ch'ù?

3.(A) 公園離這裏很近. 我們可以坐洋車去.
Kūng-yüán lí chè - li hĕn chìn. Wŏ - mên k'ĕ - i tsò yáng-ch'ē ch'ü.

4.(B) 那麼, 請你等一等, 我先去雇車.
Nà - mo, ch'íng ni tĕng - i - têng, wŏ hsiēn ch'ù kù ch'ē.

5.(A) 洋車! 從這裏到公園你要多少錢?
Yáng-ch'ē! Ts'úng chè - li tào kūng-yüán (nĭ) yào tō-shăo ch'ién?

6.(C) 兩毛錢.
Liăng máo ch'ién.

7.(A) 我們有兩個人去. 你多給我雇一輛車.
Wŏ - mên yú liăng - kê jén ch'ü. Nĭ tō kéi wo kù í - liàng ch'ē.

8.(B) 車夫, 請你停一停. 我要買一包煙.
Ch'ē - fū, ch'íng ni t'íng - i - t'ing. Wŏ yào măi ì-pāo yēn.

9.(A) 到了, 我們下車罷.
Tào lê, wŏ - mên hsià ch'ē pa.

10.(B) 讓我給錢罷.
Jàng wo kĕi ch'ién pa.

11.(A) 不客氣. 我這兒有. 車夫, 我給你一塊錢, 你有零錢找給我嗎?
Pú k'è-ch'i. Wŏ chè-êrh yŭ. Ch'ē-fu, wó kéi ni í-k'uài-ch'ién, ní yŭ líng-ch'ién chăo(6) kéi wo ma?

12.(C) 讓 我 看 一 看. 我 這 兒 有 六 毛 錢.
Jàng wo k'àn - i - k'an. Wǒ chè - êrh yǔ liù - máo - ch'ién.

13.(A) 那 邊 有 很 多 的 花 草, 樹 木, 跟 竹 子, 你 想 去 看 一 看 嗎?
Nà - pien yú hěn tō - tê huā ts'ǎo, shù - mu, kěn chú - tzǔ, ní hsiǎng ch'ǜ k'àn - i - k'an ma?

14.(B) 好 罷. 那 些 花 都 開 了. 眞 好 看.
Hǎo pa. Nà - hsieh huā tōu k'āi lê. Chěn hǎo-k'àn.

15.(A) 這 些 花 香 極 了. 樹 木 跟 竹 子 的 綠 葉, 也 很 可 愛.
Chè-hsieh huā hsiāng chí lê. Shù - mu kěn chú - tzǔ - tê lǜ yèh, yěh hěn k'ě - ài.

16.(B) 你 看. 前 面 那 個 人 不 是 王 竹 園 先 生 嗎?
Nǐ k'àn. Ch'ién-mien nà - kê jén pú shìh Wáng Chú-yüán hsiēn-shêng ma?

17.(A) 王 竹 園 是 誰? 我 忘 了.
Wáng Chú-yüán shìh shuí? Wǒ wàng lê.

18.(B) 王 竹 園 是 我 的 朋 友. 去 年 我 們 在 一 塊 兒 吃 過 好 幾 次 飯. 你 就 忘 了 嗎?
Wáng Chú-yüán shìh wǒ - tê p'éng - yu. Ch'ǜ-nien wǒ - mên tsài í - k'uài-êrh ch'īh kuò háo chǐ tz'ù fàn. Nǐ chiù wàng lê ma?

19.(A) 現 在 我 記 起 來 了. 我 們 叫 他 罷.
Hsièn-tsài wǒ chì ch'ǐ-lai lê. Wǒ - mên chiào t'a pa.

20.(B) 喂, 王 先 生!
Wèi, Wáng hsiēn-shêng!

21.(D) 啊, 李 先 生, 你 甚 麼 時 候 來 北 平 的?
Ā, Lǐ hsiēn-shêng, nǐ shén - mo shíh-hou lái Pěi-p'íng tê?

22.(B) 我 是 昨 天 來 的.
Wǒ shìh tsó-t'ien lái tê.

23.(D) 你 是 坐 公 共 汽 車 來 的 嗎?
Nǐ shìh tsò kūng-kùng ch'ì-ch'ē lái tê ma?

24.(B) 是 的.
Shìh - tê.

25.(A) 我們想在公園走一走，就去吃一頓外國飯. 王先生，請你也去罷.
Wǒ-mên hsiǎng tsài kūng-yüán tsǒu-i-tsou, chiù ch'ü ch'īh í-tùn wài-kuó fàn. Wáng hsiēn-shêng, ch'íng ni yěh ch'ü pa.

26.(D) 好罷，謝謝. 我的汽車在外面. 我們可以坐車去. 請你告訴司機的去那個飯館罷.
Hǎo pa, hsièh-hsieh. Wǒ-tê ch'ì-ch'ē tsài wài-mien. Wǒ-mên k'ě-i tsò ch'ē ch'ü. Ch'íng ni kào-su ssū-chī-tê ch'ü nǎ-kê fàn-kuǎn pa.

27.(A) 我們去大美樓，好不好?
Wǒ-mên ch'ü Tà-měi-lóu, hǎo-pu-hao?

28.(D) 好. 司機，我們現在去大美樓.
Hǎo. Ssū-chī, wǒ-mên hsièn-tsài ch'ü Tà-měi-lóu.

29.(B) 這裏的交通眞方便. 有電車，公共汽車，跟洋車.
Chè-li-tê chiāo-t'ūng chēn fāng-pièn. Yǔ tièn-ch'ē, kūng-kùng ch'ì-ch'ē, kēn yáng-ch'ē.

30.(A) 對了. 坐電車很便宜. 我們花幾分錢，就可以坐到很遠的地方.
Tuì lê. Tsò tièn-ch'ē hěn p'ién-i. Wǒ-mên huā chǐ fēn-ch'ién, chiù k'ě-i tsò tào hěn yüǎn-tê tì-fang.

31.(B) 這條路眞不窄.
Chè-t'iáo lù chēn pù chǎi.

32.(A) 這是我們最寬的一條街.
Chè shìh wǒ-mên tsuì-k'uān-tê ì-t'iáo chiēh(7).

NOTES:

(1) A ricksha puller is also called "yáng-ch'ē-fū".

(2) A chauffeur was formerly called "ch'ì-ch'ē-fū" 汽車夫, but at present the more polite term "ssū-chī" is more commonly used of one who drives an automobile.

(3) A synonym for "ì-máo-ch'ién" is "ì-chiǎo-ch'ién" 一角錢. The former is more commonly used in north China, the latter in the south.

(4) In business usage, the expression for one dollar is "ì-yüán-

ch'ién" 一圓錢 or "ì-yüán", and 元 is often used as an abbreviation for 圓 . In the spoken language, "í-k'uài-ch'ién" 一塊錢 is the common term for a dollar.

(5) Care should be taken not to confuse the characters 真 and 直 .

(6) "Chǎo" means "to give [coins or stamps] in exchange". "Chǎo ch'ién" means "to change money"; "chǎo tō-shǎo?" - "How much [do I owe you] in change?" If A owes B sixty cents and gives him one dollar, A may say: "Chǎo kéi wo ssǔ-máo-ch'ién" - "Give me forty cents in change".

(7) "Tsuì-hǎo-tê" means "the best"; "tsuì-hǎo-tê í-kè" or "í-kè tsuì-hǎo-tê" means "one of the best". To express the idea of "one of the best" or "two of the best", etc., a numerative is used either before or after the superlative form of the adjective. For example, "one of the widest streets" may be expressed either as "tsuì-k'uān-tê ì-t'iáo chiēh", or as "ì-t'iáo tsuì-k'uān-tê chiēh".

3. Translation

1.(A) Today the weather is very fine. Would you like to go to the park to take a walk?

2.(B) I shall be delighted to go, because I haven't been to the park yet. How shall we go?

3.(A) The park is very near here. We can go by ricksha.

4.(A) Well, please wait a moment; I'll first go to hire a ricksha.

5.(A) Ricksha! How much money do you want to go from here to the park?

6.(C) Twenty cents.

7.(A) There are two of us going. Will you hire one more ricksha for me?

8.(B) Ricksha man, please stop a moment. I want to buy a package of cigarettes.

9.(A) [We have] arrived. Let's get down [from] the rickshas.

10.(B) Let me pay.

11.(A) Please don't be formal. I have [it] here. Ricksha man, [if] I give you a dollar do you have small change to give me (in change)?

12.(C) Let me see. I have sixty cents here.

13.(A) There are many flowers, trees, and bamboos over there; would you like to go and look?

14.(B) All right. Those flowers are all open. [They are] really pretty.

15.(A) These flowers are very fragrant. The green leaves of the trees and bamboos are also very lovely.

16.(B) Look. Isn't that man in front [of us] Mr. Wang Chu-yüan?

17.(A) Who is Wang Chu-yüan? I have forgotten.

18.(B) Wang Chu-yüan is my friend. Last year we ate together many times. Have you forgotten?

19.(A) Now I recall (literally, remember up). Let's call him.

20.(B) Hello, Mr. Wang!

21.(D) Ah, Mr. Li, when did you come to Peiping?

22.(B) I came yesterday.

23.(D) Did you come by bus?

24.(B) Yes.

25.(A) We thought of taking a walk in the park, and then going to have a meal of foreign food. Mr. Wang, will you please go too?

26.(D) All right, thank you. My car is outside, we can ride over (literally, sit [in the] car go). Please tell the driver which restaurant to go to.

27.(A) Shall we go to Ta-mei-lou?

28.(D) Good. Driver, we are going to Ta-mei-lou now.

29.(B) The communications here are really convenient. There are trolley cars, buses, and rickshas.

30.(A) That's right. To ride in a street car is very cheap. We spend a few cents, then [we] can ride to a very distant place.

31.(B) This avenue is really not narrow (emphatic way of saying that it is very wide).

32.(A) This is one of our widest streets.

4. Exercises

a. "Fill-in" sentences

| | |
|---|---|
| 1. Ts'úng chè-êrh tào ... ... nǐ yào tō-shǎo ch'ién? | How much money do you want to go from here to ... ... ? |
| 2. Í-k'uài-ch'ién t'ài ... lê. | A dollar is too ... (much, expensive) |
| 3. Chè shìh shén-mo ... ... ? | What ... ... is this? |
| 4. Ssū-chī, k'āi ... ... ... | Driver, drive (a little slower / faster). |
| 5. Ch'íng ni cháo kéi wo ... | Please give me ... in change. |
| 6. Chè-t'iáo ... hěn ... | This ... is very ... |
| 7. Wǒ chiā lí hsüéh-hsiào hěn ... | My home is very ... from school. |

b. Translate into English:

1. 車夫、拐了彎、停一停、

2. 坐電車便宜、坐汽車貴、

3. 他家太遠了、我走不到、

4. 可是我沒有錢坐車.

5. 這裏的交通方便嗎?

6. 你家離這裏很近,還是很遠?

7. 在這裏那一條街最寬,那一條街最窄?

8. 我們可以慢慢兒的走,因為時候還多着哪.

9. 下課的時候,先生走在先,學生走在後.

10. 我有一張圓桌子.他有一張方桌子.

c. Translate into Chinese:

1. Is that place very far from here, or very near?
2. To go by taxi (literally, ride taxi go) is very convenient.
3. Some places do not have taxis; [they] have trolley cars.
4. Driver, please stop; I want to buy something.
5. This pair of chopsticks is made not of wood but of bamboo.
6. Go past two streets, turn a corner, [and] then you're there (arrived).
7. I like red flowers and green grass.
8. This university is one of the best in America.
9. Chang San is the best student in his class.
10. We two share a room.

CONVERSATIONAL CHINESE

## Special Exercises in the Uses of "Tào" 到, "Lí" 離, and "Ts'úng" 從

When "tào" is used alone, it means "to reach, to arrive at, to attain to; to, at, till". Examples of these uses:

"Wǒ ts'ái tào tê" 我才到的 - "I have just arrived".

"T'ā měi t'iēn máng tào wǎn" 他每天忙到晚 - "He is busy every day till night".

"Těng tào k'ǎo-shìh-tê shíh-hou ts'ái nièn-shū, nà chiù wǎn lê" 等到考試的時候才念書，那就晚了 - "If you wait until examination time before studying, then it will be [too] late".

"Wǒ tsò pú tào" 我作不到 - "I can't do [it] (i.e., can't attain to doing it)".

"Nǐ tào nǎ-êrh ch'ü?" 你到那兒去 - "Where are you going (to)?"

When "tào" is used as a co-verb, it imparts to the principal verb the idea of completion of the action.

"Chièn-tào" 見到 - "to have seen".

"Hsiǎng-tào" 想到 - "to think of, to anticipate".

"Nǐ chièn-tào t'a tê shíh-hou, ch'íng ni kéi wo wèn hǎo" 你見到他的時候，請你給我問好 - "When you see him, please give him my regards".

"Méi hsiǎng-tào chīn-t'ien hsià-hsüěh" 沒想到今天下雪 - "I didn't think it would snow today".

"K'ǔng-p'à tsò pú tào" 恐怕做不到 - "I am afraid it can't be done".

"Lí" means "from, apart from, far from; to leave, to separate". Examples:

"Chè-kê tì-fang lí nà-kê tì-fang tō yüǎn?" 這個地方離那個地方多遠？ - "How far is this place from that place?"

"Hsüéh-hsiào lí chè-êrh pù yüǎn" 學校離這兒不遠 - "The school is not far from here".

"Nǐ-tê hsüéh-hsiào lí wǒ chiā hěn yüǎn" 你的學校離我家很遠 - "Your school is very far from my home".

"Lí chiā" 離家 - "to leave home".

"Lí pu k'āi" 離不開 - "unable to separate".

"Ts'úng" is usually used as a preposition meaning "from, since, through". Examples:

"Ts'úng tsăo tào wăn" 從早到晚 - "from morning till night".

"Wŏ ts'úng hsiăo jèn-shih t'a" 我從小認識他 - "I have known him since childhood".

"Nĭ ts'úng nă-êrh lái-tê?" 你從那兒來的？ - "Where do you come from?"

"Wŏ ts'úng hsüéh-hsiào lai" 我從學校來 - "I come from school".

## Lesson 27 At a Railway Station

1. Vocabulary

| | | |
|---|---|---|
| 火車 | huŏ-ch'ē | Railway train [í-liàng huŏ-ch'ē] |
| 車站 | ch'ē-chàn | Railway station [í-kê ch'ē-chàn]. |
| 處 | ch'ù | Place, point, office. |
| 問事處 | wèn-shìh-ch'ù (1) | Information desk. |
| 海 | hăi | Sea. |
| 上海 | Shàng-hăi | Shanghai. |
| 天津 | T'iēn-chin | Tientsin. |
| 查 | ch'á | To investigate, to examine, to inquire. |
| 票 | p'iào | Ticket, bank note [ì-chāng p'iào]. |
| 查票員 | ch'á-p'iào-yüán | Conductor [í-kê ch'á-p'iào-yüán]. |
| 李 | lĭ | Plum. One of the commonest Chinese surnames. |
| 行李 | hsíng-li (2) | Baggage, luggage [í-chièn hsíng-li]. |
| 皮 | p'í | Skin, leather, fur. Covering, wrapper. |
| 皮包 | p'í-pāo | Suitcase, briefcase [í-kê p'í-pāo]. |
| 箱 | hsiāng | Box, case, trunk [seldom used alone] |
| 箱子 | hsiāng-tzŭ | Trunk, box, case [í-kê hsiāng-tzŭ]. |
| 腳 | chiăo | Foot, leg. Bottom, base. [Í-kê chiăo]. |
| 腳夫 | chiăo-fu | Porter [í-kê chiăo-fu]. |
| 趕 | kăn | To pursue, to drive, to expel. |

| | | |
|---|---|---|
| 趕上 | kăn-shang | To catch (a train, bus, etc.). |
| 換 | huàn | To change, to exchange, to replace. |
| 特 | t'è | Special. |
| 特別 | t'è-piéh | Special, peculiar, unusual. |
| 特別快車 | t'è-piéh k'uài-ch'ē̆ | Express train [í-liàng t'è-piéh k'uài-ch'ē̆]. |
| 睡 | shuì | To sleep, to go to bed. |
| 睡車 | shuì-ch'ē̆ | Sleeping car [í-liàng shuì-ch'ē̆]. |
| 飯車 | fàn-ch'ē̆ | Dining car [í-liàng fàn-ch'ē̆]. |
| 來回票 | lái-huí-p'iào | Round trip ticket [ì-chāng lái-huí-p'iào]. |
| 頭 | t'óu | Head, top, chief, end. In front. |
| 頭等 | t'óu-tĕ̌ng | First-class. |
| 鋪 | p'ù | Bed, berth, shop, store. |
| | p'ū | To spread out, to arrange. |
| 上鋪 | shàng-p'ù | Upper berth. |
| 下鋪 | hsià-p'ù | Lower berth. |
| 時間表 | shíh-chiēn-piăo | Time table [ì-chāng shíh-chiēn-piăo]. |
| 限 | hsièn | Limit, boundary. To limit. |
| 限期 | hsièn-ch'í | Time limit. To fix a limit of time. |
| 身 | shē̆n | The body, the person. Personal. [Seldom used alone]. |
| 帶 | tài | Belt, girdle, zone. To take with one, to wear on the head. |
| 隨身帶 | suí shē̆n tài | To carry with one, to carry on the person. |
| 收 | shōu | To receive, to collect. |
| 收條 | shōu-t'iáo | Receipt, check [í-kê shōu-t'iáo]. |
| 室 | shìh | House, room [seldom used alone]. |
| 候車室 | hòu-ch'ē̆-shìh | Waiting room [ì-chiēn hòu-ch'ē̆-shìh]. |
| 借 | chièh (3) | To lend, to borrow. |
| 光 | kuāng | Light. Only. Bare. |
| 借光 | chièh-kuāng | By your leave, allow me to pass, excuse me, please (literally,"to borrow light"). |

2. Conversation

1.(A, to by stander) 先生，請你告訴我問事處在甚麼地方？
Hsiēn-shēng, ch'íng ni kào-su wo wèn-shìh-ch'ù tsài shén-mo tì-fang?
Or, 借光，問事處在那兒？
Chièh-kuāng, wèn-shìh-ch'ù tsài nǎ-êrh? (4)

2.(B) 問事處就在車站前門的右邊。
Wèn-shìh-ch'ù chiù tsài ch'ē-chàn ch'ién mén-tê yù-pien.

3.(A, to information clerk) 請問，從這兒去上海的車，一天有幾次？
Ch'ǐng wèn, ts'úng chè-êrh ch'ù Shàng-hǎi tê ch'ē, ì t'iēn yú chǐ tz'ǔ?

4.(C) 今天早上有一次慢車．下午有兩次快車．
Chīn-t'ien tsǎo-shang yǔ í-tz'ǔ màn-ch'ē. Hsià-wǔ yú liǎng-tz'ǔ k'uài-ch'ē.

5.(A) 上午沒有快車嗎？
Shàng-wǔ méi-yǔ k'uài-ch'ē ma?

6.(C) 有，可是那次車不一直到上海；到了天津(你)要換車．
Yǔ, k'ě-shih nà-tz'ǔ ch'ē pú ì-chíh tào Shàng-hǎi; tào lê T'iēn-chin (nǐ) yào huàn ch'ē.

7.(A) 那太麻煩了．
Nà t'ài má-fan lê.

8.(C) 今天晚上有一次特別快車；要是先生可以等到晚上，坐那次車最好．
Chīn-t'ien wǎn-shang yǔ í-tz'ǔ t'è-piéh k'uài-ch'ē; yào-shih hsiēn-shēng k'ě-i těng tào wǎn-shang, tsò nà-tz'ǔ ch'ē tsùi hǎo.

9.(A) 那次車有睡車嗎？
Nà-tz'ǔ ch'ē yǔ shùi-ch'ē ma?

10.(C) 有睡車也有飯車．先生要買上鋪還是買下鋪？
Yǔ shùi-ch'ē yéh yǔ fàn-ch'ē. Hsiēn-shēng yào mǎi shàng-p'ù hái-shih mǎi hsià-p'ù?

11.(A) 下鋪．我要買一張頭等來回票．
Hsià-p'ù. Wǒ yào mǎi ì-chāng t'óu-těng lái-huí-p'iào.

不知道限期多久.
Pù chīh-tao hsièn-ch'í tō chiù.

12.(C) 限期三個月.
Hsièn-ch'í sān - kê yüèh.

13.(A) 甚麼時候開車?
Shến - mo shíh-hou k'āi ch'ễ?

14.(C) 晚上八點鐘. 讓我給你一張
Wǎn-shang pā - tiěn-chūng. Jàng wo kéi ni ì - chāng
時間表.
shíh-chiēn-piǎo.

15.(A, at 7:40, to porter) 腳夫, 現在 請你快把這
Chiǎo -fu, hsièn-tsài ch'íng ni k'uài pǎ chề
四件行李拿到第六號車. 我
ssǔ-chièn hsíng - li ná tào tì - liù hào ch'ễ. Wǒ
要趕這次車.
yào kǎn chề-tz'ǔ ch'ễ.

16.(D) 這三個皮包, 一個箱子, 先生
Chề sān - kê p'í-pāo, í - kê hsiāng-tzū, hsiēn-shêng
都要隨身帶嗎?
tōu yào suí shến tài ma?

17.(A) 最小的皮包 我要隨身帶, 別的
Tsùi-hsiǎo - tê p'í-pāo wǒ yào suí shến tài, piéh - tê
行李可以拿到行李車.
hsíng - li k'ễ - i ná tào hsíng- li -ch'ễ.

18.(D) 先生, 這是你的行李收條. 還
Hsiēn-shêng, chề shìh nǐ - tê hsíng - li shōu-t'iáo. Hái
有幾分鐘, 你要去候車室坐
yú chǐ fễn-chūng, nǐ yào ch'ù hòu-ch'ễ-shìh tsò -
一坐嗎?
i - tso ma?

19.(A) 我恐怕趕不上車; 不去候車室
Wó k'ǔng-p'à kǎn pu shàng ch'ễ; pú ch'ù hòu-ch'ễ-shìh
了. 這是你的酒錢.
lê. Chề shìh nǐ - tê chiǔ-ch'ien.

20.(E, a fellow-passenger on the train) 你知道飯車在那兒嗎?
Nǐ chīh-tao fàn-ch'ễ tsài nǎ - êrh ma?

21.(A) 我也不知道. 查票員來了. 我
Wó yěh pù chīh-tao. Ch'á-p'iào-yüán lái lê. Wǒ -
們問他罷.
mên wên t'a pa.

22. (F, the conductor) 請把票給我.
Ch'íng pă p'iào kéi wo.

23. (E) 請問,飯車在那兒?
Ch'ǐng wèn, fàn-ch'ē tsài nă-êrh?

24. (F) 在第三輛車. 就在前面.
Tsài tì-sān-liàng ch'ē. Chiù tsài ch'ién-mien.

25. (E) 謝謝. 我們去吃飯罷.
Hsièh-hsieh. Wǒ-mên ch'ù ch'īh-fàn pa.

26. (A) 借光, 借光, 讓我過去罷.
Chièh-kuāng, chièh-kuāng, jàng wo kuò-ch'ü pa.

27. (E) 對不起,現在飯車裏的人太多, 請你先去罷.
Tuì pu ch'ǐ, hsièn-tsài fàn-ch'ē lǐ tê jén t'ài tō, ch'íng ni hsiēn ch'ù pa.

28. (A) 你現在餓不餓?
Nǐ hsièn-tsài è-pu-ê?

29. (E) 我現在不餓,我要過半點鐘才去.
Wǒ hsièn-tsài pú è, wǒ yào kuò pàn-tiěn-chūng ts'ái ch'ü.

30. (A) 好,囘頭見.
Hǎo, huí-t'óu chièn(5).

NOTES:

(1) "Wèn-shìh-ch'ù" means literally "ask information office (or bureau)".

(2) The term "hsíng-li" as a name for "baggage" is said to have been derived from an ancient custom of taking a basket of plums as a gift when one traveled to visit friends.

(3) When "chièh" means "to lend", it is followed by "kěi"; when it means "to borrow", "kěi" is not used. Examples of the first use:

"Wǒ chièh kéi ni wǔ-k'uài-ch'ién" 我借給你五塊錢 - "I lend you five dollars".

"T'ā chièh kéi wo ì-pěn shū" 他借給我一本書 - "He lends me a book".

"Nǐ chièh kěi t'a ì-chīh pǐ" 你借給他一枝筆 - "You lent him a pen".

In the sense of "to borrow", "chièh" is used in two ways. One may say:

"Wǒ chièh t'a wǔ-k'uài-ch'ién" 我借他五塊錢 - "I borrowed five dollars [from] him".

But it is clearer to express it as follows:

"Wǒ hsiàng t'ā chièh wǔ-k'uài-ch'ién" 我向他借五塊錢, which means literally "I, facing him, borrowed five dollars".

Another example:

"T'ā hsiàng wǒ chièh ì-pěn shū" 他向我借一本書 - "He borrowed a book from me".

(4) These two sentences have the same meaning, but the second is more idiomatic.

(5) "Huí-t'óu chièn", literally meaning "turn the head see", is used to mean "see you later" or "I'll see you again".

3. Translation

1.(A) Sir, please tell me, where is the information desk?
(or, Excuse me, please, where is the information desk?)

2.(B) The information desk is just at the right of the front door of the station.

3.(A) May I ask, how many trains a day are there from here to Shanghai?

4.(C) There is one slow train this morning. This afternoon there will be two fast trains.

5.(A) Isn't there a fast train in the morning?

6.(C) Yes, but that train does not go directly to Shanghai; you have to change trains at Tientsin.

7.(A) That's too much trouble.

8.(C) This evening there is an express train. If you can wait till evening, sir, it would be best to go on that train.

9.(A) Is there a sleeper on that train?

10.(C) There is a sleeper and a diner. Would you like to buy an upper or a lower berth?

11.(A) A lower berth. I would like to get a round-trip ticket, first class. I don't know what the time limit is.

12.(C) The time limit is three months.

13.(A) When does the train leave?

14.(C) Eight p.m. Let me give you a time table.

15.(A) Porter, please hurry now to take these four pieces of baggage to train number six. I must catch this train.

16.(D) These three suitcases and one trunk, do you want to take them all with you, sir?

17.(A) I want to take (or, keep) the smallest suitcase with me. You may take the rest of the baggage to the baggage car.

18.(D) Sir, this is your baggage check. There are still a few minutes, would you like to go and sit in the waiting room?

19.(A) I am afraid I won't catch the train; I won't go to the waiting room. This is your tip.

20.(E) Do you know where the diner is?

21.(A) I don't know either. The conductor is coming. Let's ask him.

22.(F) Please give me your tickets.

23.(E) May I ask, where is the diner?

24.(F) It is in the third car. Right ahead.

25.(E) Thank you. Let's go to eat.

26.(A) Excuse me, please let me pass.

27.(E) I beg your pardon; there are too many people in the dining car now; will you please go first?

28.(A) Are you hungry now?

29.(E) At present I am not hungry; after half an hour I will go in.

30.(A) All right, I'll see you later.

4. Exercises

a. "Fill-in" sentences

| | |
|---|---|
| 1. Ts'úng ... tào ... yǔ tō yüǎn? | How far is it from ... to ... ? |
| 2. ... ... lí ... yǔ tō yüǎn? | How far is ... from ... ? |
| 3. Wǒ yào mǎi ì-chāng ... p'iào. | I want to buy a ... ticket. |
| 4. Chí tiěn-chūng k'āi ... ...? | What time (is ... served / does ... leave)? |
| 5. Ch'íng pǎ hsiāng-tzǔ ná tào ... ... | Please take the trunk to the ... ... |
| 6. Ch'íng ni chièh kéi wo ... | Please lend me ... ... |
| 7. Wǒ chièh t'a ... ... | I borrowed ... ... from him. |
| 8. Hsià ch'ē tê shíh-hou, pú yào wàng lê nǐ-tê ... ... | When you get off the train, don't forget your ... ... |
| 9. ... těng ch'ē-p'iào shìh ... k'uài ... máo ... fēn-ch'ién. | A ... class ticket is ... ... dollars and ... cents. |

b. Translate into English:

1. 我恐怕趕不上車.

2. 他的行李太多了.
3. 請你給我叫一個脚夫.
4. 這兩個皮包我要隨身帶.
5. 你給了我六件行李,這是你的收條.
6. 問事處在那兒?
7. 查票員,請你告訴我,我們什麼時候到上海?
8. 還要一個半點鐘.
9. 先生可以去飯車吃一點兒點心.
10. 借光你哪,請問這兒有姓李的嗎?

c. Translate into Chinese:

1. I want to go on the express train.
2. The conductor is [over] there. Ask him.
3. Put these trunks in the baggage car.
4. Which suitcase is mine?
5. Where is the porter?
6. I want a round-trip ticket.
7. You must change trains at Tientsin.
8. There are too many people in the diner.
9. I bought a lower berth because it is more convenient (convenient a little).
10. Excuse me, please let me go out.

## PART V, LESSON 27

### Particles Indicating Direction

Particles or suffixes indicating direction are usually used in combination with "tsài" 在. Therefore, it is necessary to discuss "tsài" first.

"Tsài" is sometimes used as a verb corresponding to a combination of verb and preposition in English: "to be in, to be on, to be at"; and sometimes simply as a preposition.

"T'ā-mên tsài <u>chiā</u> ma?" 他們在家嗎? - "Are they at home?"

The common words indicating direction are:

| | |
|---|---|
| "t'óu" 頭 "head, end, side" | "ch'ién" 前 "before" |
| "mièn" 面 "face, side" | "hòu" 後 "behind" |
| "piēn" 邊 "line, side" | "tsǒ" 左 "left" |
| "shàng" 上 "upper part" | "yù" 右 "right" |
| "hsià" 下 "lower part" | "lǐ" 裏 "inside" |
| "wài" 外 "outside" | "nèi" 內 "inside" |
| "chūng" 中 "middle" | "chūng-chiēn 中間 "middle" |
| "tūng" 東 "east" | "hsī" 西 "west" |
| "nán" 南 "south" | "pěi" 北 "north" |

Of the above listed words, the first three, "t'óu", "mièn", and "piēn", can be used interchangeably in the following combinations:

"lǐ-t'ou" 裏頭, "lǐ-mien" 裏面, "lǐ-pien" 裏邊, all of which mean "inside".

"tsài lǐ-t'ou", "tsài lǐ-mien", "tsài lǐ-pien", all of which mean "within (in the inside)".

"tsài ... lǐ-t'ou", "tsài ... lǐ-mien", "tsài ... lǐ-pien", all of which mean "within ..., inside of ... ".

Examples:

"Fáng-tzŭ lǐ-t'ou shìh hēi-tê" 房子裏頭是黑的 - "Inside the room, it is dark".

"Shū-fáng tsài lǐ-t'ou, huā-yüán tsài wài-t'ou" 書房在裏頭. 花園在外頭 - "The study is inside, the flower garden is outside".

In any such sentences, "lǐ-t'ou" can be replaced by "lǐ-mien" or "lǐ-pien" without changing the meaning.

Other combinations of "tsài" with direction indicators are listed below:

| | |
|---|---|
| 在上 | 在……………上(面) |
| 在下 | 在……………下(面) |
| 在前 | 在………(的)前(面) |
| 在後 | 在………(的)後(面) |
| 在左 | 在………(的)左邊 |
| 在右 | 在………(的)右邊 |
| 在中 | 在………(的)中間 |
| 在東 | 在………(的)東邊 |
| 在南 | 在………(的)南邊 |
| 在西 | 在………(的)西邊 |
| 在北 | 在………(的)北邊 |

Examples of their use:

"T'iēn tsài shàng" 天在上 - "Heaven is above".
"Tì tsài hsià" 地在下 - "Earth is below".
"Jén tsài chūng" 人在中 - "Man is in the middle".
"Wǒ tsài ch'ién" 我在前 - "I am in front".
"Nǐ tsài hòu" 你在後 - "You are behind".
"T'ā tsài chūng-chiēn" 他在中間 - "He is in the middle".
"Tsài wǒ méi-yǔ lái ǐ-ch'ién" 在我沒有來以前 - "Before I came ... "
"Tsài t'ā tsǒu lê ǐ-hòu" 在他走了以後 - "After he left ... "
"Wǒ chàn tsài nǐ-tê ch'ién-mien" 我站在你的前面 - "I stand in front of you".
"Nǐ tsò tsài wǒ-tê hòu-mien" 你坐在我的後面 - "You sit behind me".
"T'ā tsò tsài wǒ-mên-tê chūng-chiēn" 他坐在我們的中間 - "He sits between us".
"Nà-kê jén tsài wǒ-tê ch'ién-t'ou" 那個人在我的前頭 - "That person is in front of me".
"Jìh-t'ou tsài tūng-pien ch'ū-lai" 日頭在東邊出來 - "The sun rises in the east".

"Hsī-pien yŭ í-tsò tà fáng-tzŭ" 西邊有一座大房子 - "There is a large house on the west side".

"Fáng lĭ-t'ou jén hĕn tō; wŏ-mên tào wài-t'ou ch'ù pa" 房裏頭人很多；我們到外頭去吧 - "There are very many people in this room; let's go outside".

"Wŏ pú tsài nèi" 我不在内 - "I am not on the inside" (i.e., I am not involved).

"Chiŭ-ch'ien tsài wài" 酒錢在外 - "The tip is extra".

"Chiŭ-ch'ien tsài nèi" 酒錢在内 - "The tip is included".

"Wŏ chù tsài lóu-shàng" 我住在樓上 - "I live upstairs".

"T'ā chù tsài lóu-hsià" 他住在樓下 - "He lives downstairs".

"Wŏ-tê p'éng-yu chù tsài tì-sān lóu" 我的朋友住在第三樓 - "My friend lives on the third floor".

## Lesson 28 Journey by Sea

1. Vocabulary

| | | |
|---|---|---|
| 船 | ch'uán | Ship, boat [ì-t'iáo ch'uán]. |
| 岸 | àn | Shore, river bank. |
| 碼 | mă | Yard (measure), sign, figure. Pier. (See also page 68.) |
| 碼頭 | mă-t'óu | Pier [í-kê mă-t'óu]. |
| 艙 | ts'āng | Cabin, hold of a ship [seldom used alone]. |
| 艙房 | ts'āng-fáng | Cabin [í-kê ts'āng-fáng]. |
| 口 | k'ŏu | Mouth, hole, opening [í-kê k'ŏu]. A numerative of persons, etc. |
| 海口 | hái-k'ŏu | Harbor, port [í-kê hái-k'ŏu]. |
| 水手 | shuí-shou | Seaman, sailor [í-kê shuí-shou]. |
| 檢 | chiĕn | To examine. |
| 檢查 | chiĕn-ch'á | To examine, to censor. |
| 關 | kuān | Pass, custom-house. Connection. To shut. Concerned with. |
| 海關 | hăi-kuān | Custom-house. |
| 鐘頭 | chūng-t'óu (1) | Hour [í-kê chūng-t'ou]. |
| 船面 | ch'uán-mièn | Deck. |

| | | |
|---|---|---|
| 完 | wán | To finish. Completed. The end. |
| 玩 | wán | To amuse oneself, to play with. |
| 樣 | yàng | Manner, sort, style. Sample, pattern. |
| 救 | chiù | To rescue, to help, to save. |
| 救生帶 | chiù-shēng-tài | Life-belt [í-kê chiù-shēng-tài]. |
| 危 | wéi | To be in danger. To endanger. |
| 險 | hsiěn | Dangerous. |
| 危險 | wéi-hsiěn | Danger. Dangerous. |
| 接 | chiēh | To receive, to meet, to connect. |
| 舒 | shū | Comfortable [lit.]. |
| 服 | fú | Clothes. To submit, to serve [lit.]. To swallow. A dose. |
| 舒服 | shū-fu | Comfortable. |
| 稅 | shuì | Tax, customs duty. |
| 風 | fēng | Wind. Custom, rumor. |
| 浪 | làng | Wave, billow. Profligate [lit.]. |
| 旅 | lǔ | To travel. Traveling. [Lit.]. A unit of an army. |
| 旅行 | lǔ-hsíng | Journey. To travel. |
| 旅客 | lǔ-k'è | Passenger, traveler [í-kê lǔ-k'è]. |
| 練 | lièn | To practise, to drill, to choose. |
| 練習 | lièn-hsi | To practise. |
| 樂 | lè<br>yüèh | Happy. Pleasure, joy.<br>Music. |
| 快樂 | k'uài-lê | Happy, glad. |
| 打牌 | tǎ-p'ái | To play cards. |
| 機會 | chī-hui | Opportunity [í-kê chī-hui]. |

2. Narrative

[Beginning with this lesson, the reading material will be arranged with characters on one side of the page and romanization on the other, to make it easier for students to read the characters alone as far as possible, referring to the romanization only when in need of help.]

我有一個朋友昨天從美國來．我到碼頭去接他．他坐的這條船很大．有幾百個艙房，兩千多旅客．

Wó yǔ í-kê p'éng-yu tsó-t'ien ts'úng Měi-kuo lai. Wǒ tào mǎ-t'óu ch'ù chiēh t'a. T'ā tsò tê chè-t'iáo ch'uán hěn tà. Yú chí-pǎi-kê ts'āng-fáng, liǎng-ch'iēn tō lǚ-k'è.

我的朋友上岸的時候，行李很多．在海關檢查很麻煩．他等了兩個鐘頭，才檢查完了．因爲他帶了很多的東西海關抽了他不少的稅．

Wǒ-tê p'éng-yu shàng àn tê shíh-hou, hsíng-li hěn tō. Tsài hǎi-kuān chiěn-ch'á hěn má-fan. T'ā těng lê liǎng-kê chūng-t'óu, ts'ái chiěn-ch'á wán lê. Yīn-wèi t'ā tài lê hěn tō-tê tūng-hsi, hǎi-kuān ch'ōu lê t'ā pù shǎo-tê shuì.

他告訴我，這次旅行很舒服．一路上，沒有一點風浪．他認識了很多的人；每天他們都在船面上玩．男的女的常

T'ā kào-su wo, chè-tz'ù lǚ-hsíng hěn shū-fu. Í lù shàng, méi-yǔ ì-tiěn fēng làng. T'ā jèn-shih lê hěn tō-tê jén; měi t'iēn t'ā-mên tōu tsài ch'uán-mièn shàng wán. Nán-tê nǚ-tê ch'áng

在一塊兒走路，談話，喝茶．有的時候，他們也打牌．因爲在海上常有危險，他們在船上練習了兩次怎麼樣用救生帶．每次船停在海口的時候，他們都上岸去到各地方玩，喝酒，買東西，看好看的地方…玩得快樂極了．

tsài í-k'uài-êrh tsǒu lù, t'án-huà, hē ch'á. Yǔ-tê shíh-hou, t'ā-mên yéh tǎ-p'ái. Yīn-wèi tsài hǎi shàng ch'áng yǔ wéi-hsiěn, t'ā-mên tsài ch'uán shàng lièn-hsi lê liǎng tz'ǔ tsěn-mo yàng yùng chiù-shēng-tài. Měi tz'ǔ ch'uán t'íng tsài hái-k'ǒu tê shíh-hou, t'ā-mên tōu shàng àn ch'ǜ tào kè tì-fang wán, hē chiǔ, mǎi tūng-hsi, k'àn hǎo-k'àn-tê tì-fang ... wán-tê k'uài-lê chí lê.

那天我在碼頭上，看見了各國的水手．有幾個人過來跟我說話．他們都很快樂，因爲他們這次看見了很多特別的地方，過着很舒服的日子．

Nà t'iēn wǒ tsài mǎ-t'óu shàng, k'àn-chien(2) lê kè kuó-tê shuí-shou. Yú chǐ-kê jén kuò-lái kēn wǒ shuō-huà. T'ā-mên tōu hěn k'uài-lê, yīn-wèi t'ā-mên chè tz'ǔ k'àn-chien lê hěn tō t'è-piéh-tê tì-fang, kuò-cho hěn shū-fu-tê jìh-tzǔ.

我還沒有坐過海船，希望不久能有一個坐船的機會．

Wǒ hái méi-yǔ tsò kuò hǎi-ch'uán, hsī-wàng pù chiǔ néng yǔ í-kê tsò-ch'uán-tê chī-hui.

NOTES:

(1) "Chūng-t'óu", unlike "tiĕn-chūng", is used with a numerative. People say "ì tiĕn-chūng", but "í-kê chūng-t'óu".

(2) "K'àn" means "to look, to see"; "chièn" means "to see, to perceive". Used together, they indicate intention or effort to see. Thus "k'àn-chien" means "to see"; "k'àn-tê-chièn", "is able to see"; and "k'àn pu chièn", "is unable to see". In somewhat the same way, since "t'īng"聽 means "to listen, to hear", "t'īng-chien" means "to listen and hear", thus "to hear"; "t'īng-tê-chièn" means "is able to hear"; and "t'īng pu chièn", "is unable to hear".

The use of "chièn" as a suffix to "k'àn" and "t'īng" serves euphony as well as clarity of meaning.

3. Translation

I have a friend who came from America yesterday. I went to the pier to meet him. The ship which he took was very large. There were several hundred cabins [and] more than two thousand passengers.

When my friend came ashore, he had a lot of baggage. The examination [of baggage] at the custom-house was very troublesome. He waited more than two hours, before the examination was finished. Because he had brought a great many things, the custom-house [authorities] charged him not a little customs duty.

He told me that the trip was very comfortable. All the way, there wasn't a bit of wind or waves (i.e., stormy weather). He knew very many people; every day they amused themselves on deck. Men and women frequently walked together, talking and drinking tea. Sometimes they also played cards. Because there is often danger on the seas, they twice practised the use of life-belts. Every time the ship stopped at a harbor, they went ashore and went to various places to amuse themselves, drinking wine, shopping, looking at beautiful places ... they amused themselves so that they were very happy.

That day at the pier I saw sailors of every nation. A few of them came over to talk to me. They were all very happy, because this time they had seen many strange places and spent very comfortable days.

I have not yet been on an ocean-going ship, and hope that before long I can have an opportunity to go on a ship.

4. Exercises

a. "Fill-in" sentences

| | |
|---|---|
| 1. Tsò ch'uán ... ... ma? | Is it {dangerous / comfortable etc.) to travel on a ship? |
| 2. Wó těng lê ... ... chūng-t'óu; t'ā ts'ái ... ... | I waited . . . hours; he then {came back / went out etc.) |

| | |
|---|---|
| 3. Nǐ shàng ... ... lê méi-yǔ? | Did you go (ashore / upstairs) etc.)? |
| 4. Wǒ-mên hsièn-tsài ... ... Chūng-kuo-huà. | We are now (learning to speak) / (practising) Chinese. |
| 5. Yǔ ... ... tê shíh-hou, wǒ chiù ... ... | When I have (opportunity) ..., then I (speak Chinese / play cards etc.). |
| 6. Wǒ hsī-wàng wó yǔ chī-hui ch'ü ... ... | I hope I shall have a chance to go ... ... |

b. Translate into English:

1. 船面上有很多可玩的東西.
2. 沒有風浪的時候，我到船面上去玩.
3. 你有機會跟水手們説話嗎？
4. 我看他們都快樂極了.
5. 你喜歡旅行嗎？
6. 你的行李在海關檢查了嗎？
7. 他們抽了多少錢的稅？
8. 你是在那一個海口上船的？
9. 我在碼頭上等你，好不好？
10. 不，你可以上船來接我.

c. Translate into Chinese:

1. Do you often have an opportunity to travel?
2. Was your cabin comfortable?
3. I want to go on deck, because today there is no wind [or] waves.
4. When shall we have life-belt drill (drill in the use of life-belts)?

5. I'm afraid the trip will be a little dangerous.

6. Will you go ashore this time?

7. No, I think my friends will come aboard to see me.

8. Do you have friends in every port?

9. Every time they examine my baggage, [they] then impose a lot of duty.

10. That is because you bring too many things.

## On the Particle "ǐ" 以

Besides other meanings that are used in literary Chinese, the particle "ǐ" is used as a fixed point, usually in connection with the following particles of direction, to express time or place.

a. "ǐ-shàng" 以上 - "above".

"ǐ-shàng-tê huà tōu shìh pú-tùi-tê" 以上的話都是不對的 - "The above statements are all incorrect".

b. "ǐ-hsià" 以下 - "below".

"Shíh sùi ǐ-hsià-tê hsiǎo hái pù nêng k'āi ch'ē" 十歲以下的小孩不能開車 - "A child under ten years old cannot drive a car".

c. "ǐ-ch'ién" 以前 - "before".

"Wǒ ǐ-ch'ién méi-yǔ ch'ǜ kuò" 我以前沒有去過 - "I have not been there before".

d. "ǐ-hòu" 以後 - "afterward".

"Wǒ ǐ-hòu ch'áng ch'ǜ k'àn t'a" 我以後常去看他 - "Afterwards I often went to see him"

e. "ǐ-nèi" 以內 - "within".

"Tsài í-kê yüèh ǐ-nèi, wǒ yào nièn wán chè-pěn shū" 在一個月以內，我要念完這本書 - "Within a month, I shall finish reading this book".

f. "ǐ-wài" 以外 - "beyond, outside".

"K'è-t'áng ǐ-nèi pù nêng ch'ōu yēn, k'è-t'áng ǐ-wài k'ě-i ch'ōu" 課堂以內不能抽煙，課堂以外可以抽 - "In the classroom [one] cannot smoke, outside the classroom [one] may smoke".

(Other combinations using "ǐ-wài" will be introduced later when we have the necessary vocabulary.)

g. "ǐ-lái" 以來 - "using a given point to come, ever since, until now".

"Ts'úng ch'ǜ-nien pá-yüèh ǐ-lái, wó hěn máng" 從去年八月以來，我很忙 - "Since last August, I have been very busy".

## Lesson 29 Aviation

1. Vocabulary

| | | |
|---|---|---|
| 空 | k'ūng | Air, sky. Empty. In vain. |
| | k'ùng | Leisure. |
| 航 | háng | To navigate, to sail. |
| 航空 | háng-k'ūng | Aviation. |
| 運 | yǜn | To transport, to convey. Luck. |
| 輸 | shū | To transport, to introduce, to lose, to be beaten. |
| 運輸 | yǜn-shū | Transportation. |
| 種 | chǔng | Kind, sort, race. Seed. |
| | chùng | To sow, to plant. |
| 架 | chià | A frame. A numerative of airplanes, clocks, etc. |
| 飛 | fēi | To fly. |
| 飛機 | fēi-chī | Air-plane [í-chià fēi-chī]. |
| 場 | ch'ǎng | Ground, area, place. |
| 飛機場 | fēi-chī-ch'ǎng | Airfield [í-kê fēi-chī-ch'ǎng]. |
| 陸 | lù | Land. |
| 比 | pǐ | To compare. |
| 公司 | kūng-ssū | Company, commercial corporation [í-kê kūng-ssū]. |
| 般 | pān | Sort, manner. The same. |
| 一般 | ì-pān | One sort. The average, the general. |
| 工 | kūng | Work. To work. |

| | | |
|---|---|---|
| 具 | chǜ | Utensil. To furnish. [Lit.] |
| 工具 | kūng-chǜ | Tool, instrument. |
| 定座位 | tìng tsò-wei | To reserve a seat. |
| 過磅 | kuò-pàng | To weigh, to be weighed. |
| 雲 | yǘn | Cloud [ì-tǒ or í-p'ièn yǘn]. |
| 霧 | wù | Fog, mist, vapor. |
| 不過 | pú-kuò | Not exceeding. Only, but. |
| 最近 | tsuì-chìn | Most recent. Recently. |
| 無 | wú | Not. Without. |
| 線 | hsièn | Thread, wire, line [ì-kēn hsièn]. |
| 無線電 | wú-hsièn-tièn | Wireless telegraph, radio. |
| 發 | fā | To send forth, to issue, to distribute. |
| 發明 | fā-míng | To discover, to invent. |
| 減 | chiěn | To diminish, to reduce. |
| 減少 | chién-shǎo | To decrease, to lessen, to reduce. |
| 導 | tào | To lead, to guide. |
| 指 | chǐh | To point out. Finger. |
| 指導 | chǐh-tào | To guide, to conduct. |
| 按 | àn | To lay hands on, to press down. According to. |
| 空間 | k'ūng-chiēn | Space. |
| 更 | kēng | To change [lit.]. |
| | kèng | Still more, further, even. |
| 縮 | sō | To shrink, to contract. |
| 景 | chǐng | Appearance [seldom used alone]. |
| 風景 | fēng-chǐng | View, landscape. |
| 海味 | hǎi-wèi | Sea delicacy, sea food. |
| 音 | yīn | Sound. News [lit.]. |
| 音樂 | yīn-yüèh | Music. |
| 夜 | yèh | Night [í yèh]. |
| 半夜 | pàn-yèh | Midnight. |

| | | |
|---|---|---|
| 將 | chiāng | To take, to hold. About to. |
| 將來 | chiāng-lái | In future. Thereafter. |
| 戲 | hsì | Play, game [í-kê hsì]. |
| 密 | mì | Secret, confidential, close, dense. |
| 降 | chiàng | To descend, to send down, to come down. |
| 落 | lò | To fall, to drop. |
| 傘 | sǎn | Umbrella, parasol [ì-pá sǎn]. |
| 降落傘 | chiàng-lò-sǎn | Parachute. |
| 跳 | t'iào | To jump, to dance, to skip over. |
| 住 | chù | To live, to dwell, to cease. Firm. |
| 法 | fā | Method. |
| | fǎ | Law. (See Lesson 5, note 6.) |
| 沒有法子 | méi-yǔ fá-tzǔ | There is no help for it. |

2. Exposition

運輸有三種：水，陸，空．水上用船，陸上用車，空中用飛機．一般人都知道電車比洋車快，汽車比電車快，可是最快的還是飛機．

Yǜn-shū yǔ sān chǔng: shuǐ, lù, k'ūng. Shuǐ shàng yùng ch'uán, lù shàng yùng ch'ê̄, k'ūng chūng yùng fēi-chī(1). Ì-pān jén tōu chīh-tao tièn-ch'ê̄ pǐ yáng-ch'ê̄ k'uài(2), ch'ì-ch'ê̄ pǐ tièn-ch'ê̄ k'uài, k'ê̌-shih tsuì-k'uài-tê hái-shìh fēi-chī.

飛機是一種最新的運輸工具．坐飛機比坐火車跟坐船貴，可是快多了．你要是坐飛機旅行，

Fēi-chī shìh ì chǔng tsuì-hsīn-tê yǜn-shū kūng-chǜ. Tsò fēi-chī pǐ tsò huǒ-ch'ê̄ kēn tsò ch'uán kuèi, k'ê̌-shih k'uài tō lê. Nǐ yào-shih tsò fēi-chī lǚ-hsíng,

一定先要去航空公司買票，定坐位。上飛機的那天，航空公司有汽車來接旅客，把他們一直開到飛機場。沒有上飛機以前，先要把行李過磅，因爲坐飛機不能帶很多的行李。

飛機飛得很高很快，可以飛過高山大海，白雲密霧。天氣好的時候，可以很清楚的從空中看到地上的山水跟房子。坐飛機多半很舒服，可是雲霧多的時候，有一點危險。要是沒有法子的時候，開飛機的要用降落傘跳下來，危險更要大一點。

í-tìng hsiēn yào ch'ǜ háng-k'ūng kūng-ssū mǎi p'iào, tìng tsò-wei. Shàng fēi-chī tê nà t'iēn, háng-k'ūng kūng-ssū yǔ ch'ì-ch'ē lái chiēh lǚ-k'è, pǎ t'ā-mên ì-chíh k'āi tào fēi-chī-ch'ǎng. Méi-yǔ shàng fēi-chī ǐ-ch'ién, hsiēn yào pǎ hsíng-li kuò pàng(3), yīn-wèi tsò fēi-chī pù néng tài hěn tō-tê hsíng-li.

Fēi-chī fēi-tê(4) hěn kāo hěn k'uài, k'ě-i fēi kuò kāo shān tà hǎi, pái yǘn mì wù. T'iēn-ch'i hǎo-tê shíh-hou, k'ě-i hěn ch'īng-ch'u-tê ts'úng k'ūng chūng k'àn tào tì-shàng-tê shān-shuǐ kēn fáng-tzū. Tsò fēi-chī tō-pàn hěn shū-fu, k'ě-shih yǘn wù tō-tê shíh-hou, yǔ ì-tiěn wéi-hsiěn. Yào-shih méi-yǔ fá-tzǔ tê shíh-hou, k'āi-fēi-chī-tê yào yùng chiàng-lò-sǎn t'iào hsià lai, wéi-hsiěn kèng yào tà ì-tiěn.

不過最近有了無線電的各種新發明以後，飛機在空中的危險減少很多了．開飛機的，有了無線電的指導，他就可以按着一定的空中路線走．這樣子，他就不會走錯方向；不會因爲雲霧多出事了．

Pú-kuò(5) tsùi-chìn yǔ lê wú-hsièn-tièn-tê kè chǔng hsīn fā-míng ǐ-hòu(6), fēi-chī tsài k'ūng-chūng tê wéi-hsiěn chién-sháo hěn tō lê. K'āi - fēi - chī - tê, yǔ lê wú-hsièn-tièn-tê chǐh-tào, t'ā chiù k'ě - i àn-cho í - tìng-tê k'ūng-chūng lù-hsièn tsǒu. Chè yàng-tzū, t'ā chiù pú huì tsǒu ts'ò fāng-hsiang; pú huì yīn-wèi yún wù tō ch'ū-shìh(7) lê.

飛機把空間跟時間縮短了．我們試想一想，要是我們有一架飛機，我們早上可以從Chicago飛到Niagara Falls去看風景，中午在Boston吃海味，下午在New York聽戲．晚上回到Chicago休息．住在英國的人，早上可以在法國吃早餐，下午在德國聽音樂，晚

Fēi-chī pǎ k'ūng-chiēn kěn shíh-chiēn sō tuǎn lê. Wǒ-mên shìh hsiǎng-i-hsiang, yào-shih wǒ-mên yǔ í - chià fēi - chī, wǒ - mên tsǎo-shang k'ě-i ts'úng Chicago fēi tào Niagara Falls ch'ǜ k'àn fěng-chǐng, chūng-wǔ tsài Boston ch'īh hǎi-wèi, hsià-wǔ tsài New York t'īng hsì, wǎn-shang huí tào Chicago hsiū-hsi. Chù tsài Yīng-kuo tê jén, tsǎo-shang k'ě-i tsài Fà-kuo ch'īh tsǎo-ts'ān, hsià-wǔ tsài Té-kuo t'īng yīn-yüèh, wǎn-

上在意大利聽戲,半夜再回到英國休息.你看這不是很方便嗎?

shang tsài Ì-tà-lì t'īng hsì, pàn-yèh tsài huí tào Yīng-kuo hsiū-hsi. Nǐ k'àn chè pú shìh hěn fāng-pien ma?

不久的將來,飛機一定不會賣得太貴,買飛機的人一定很多.那麽,遠地旅行的機會要更多了.

Pù-chiŭ-tê chiāng-lái(8), fēi-chī í-tìng pú hùi mài-tê t'ài kuèi, mǎi-fēi-chī-tê jén í-tìng hěn tō. Nà-mo, yüǎn-tì lǚ-hsíng-tê chī-hui yào kèng tō lê.

NOTES:

(1) Omission of Subject in Chinese Sentences

Note that this sentence lacks a subject. In Chinese the subject is frequently not expressed in statements about oneself, in dialogue and brief narration where the subject is obvious, in such general statements as this in the text, and in sentences describing the weather and other natural phenomena (see also Lesson 10, note 5).

(2) See note on the comparative degree, at the end of this lesson.

(3) "Kuò pàng" means "to pass over the (pound) scales", hence "to weigh, to be weighed".

(4) See Lesson 13, note 7.

(5) The Distinction between "Pú-kuò" and "K'ě-shih" 可是

"Pú-kuò", "not passing, merely, just, however, nevertheless", can be used both as an adverb and as a conjunction. In the sense of "however, nevertheless", it may stand as an introductory word at the beginning of a sentence or paragraph, linking it with what has gone before. "K'ě-shih", "but, however", is used as a conjunction linking two clauses, with an emphatic sense of contrast.

(6) A literal translation of this phrase might be "most recently having radio's various kinds of new inventions by-means-of-which after". "Ī" is used here as a fixed point of time, and the object is "fā-míng". The words preceding "fā-míng" are modifiers. In making a smooth translation, the student should always be able to distinguish the real object and modifiers, and to put the modifiers into an adjectival phrase or clause.

(7) "Ch'ū-shìh", literally "produce something", means "something happened", or "an incident".

(8) Literally, "not-long's future", i.e., "before long", or "in the near future".

3. Translation

There are three types of transportation - land, sea, air. On the sea [we] use ships, on land [we] use [land] vehicles, in the air [we] use airplanes. People in general all know that the trolley car is faster than the ricksha, the automobile is faster than the trolley, but still faster is the airplane.

The airplane is one of the newest kinds of means of transportation. It is more expensive to go by plane than to go by train or by boat, but it is much faster. If you travel by plane, you must first go to the aviation company to buy a ticket and reserve a seat. On the day that you board the plane, the aviation company has a car come to get the passengers and drive them directly to the airfield. Before boarding the plane, the baggage must first be weighed, because on a plane [you] cannot take very much baggage with you.

The airplane flies very high and very fast; [it] can fly over high mountains [and] great oceans, white clouds [and] thick fog. In good weather it is possible to see very clearly from the air down to the mountains, rivers, and buildings on the earth. It is generally very comfortable on a plane, but in foggy or cloudy weather it is somewhat dangerous. If, at a time when there is nothing [else] to be done, the pilot of a plane must use a parachute to jump down, the danger is still greater.

But recently, since various new inventions in radio have [been made], the dangers to airplanes in the sky have been greatly reduced. One who flies a plane, having the guidance of the radio, then can travel according to a certain route in the sky. In this way, he will not go in a wrong direction, and will not have accidents because of clouds or fog.

The airplane has reduced space and time. Let us try to imagine: if we had a plane we could fly in the morning from Chicago to Niagara Falls to look at the scenery, at noon we could eat sea food in Boston, in the evening we could hear an opera in New York, and at night we could return to Chicago to rest. People who live in England could eat breakfast in the morning in France, in the afternoon listen to music in Germany, in the evening hear an opera in Italy, [and] at midnight return to England to rest. Don't you think that would be very convenient?

In the near future, airplanes certainly will not be sold at too high [a price], [and] those who buy airplanes will certainly be very many. Then, opportunities for long-distance travel will be even more numerous.

4. Exercises

a. "Fill-in" sentences

1. Nǐ ch'áng t'īng ... ... ma? Do you often listen to (radio / music / opera)?

| | |
|---|---|
| 2. Yào-shih nǐ àn-cho í-tìng-tê ... ... nǐ pú huì ... ... | If you (verb) ... according to a certain (route / time), you will not be (wrong / busy). |
| 3. Chè yàng-tzŭ, chiù ... ... ... | In this manner [it] will be (correct / all right). |
| 4. Méi-yŭ fá-tzŭ tê shíh-hou, wŏ chiù ... ... | When I cannot help it, then I will ... ... |
| 5. Chè shìh tsuì-hsīn-tê ì chŭng ... ... | This is the newest kind of ... ... |
| 6. Tsò fēi-chī ... ... ma? | Is it ... ... on an airplane? |
| 7. Pù-chiŭ-tê chiāng-lái, ... ... í-tìng ... ... | In the near future ... ... will certainly ... ... |
| 8. Yào-shih wŏ yùng-kūng, wŏ-tê ... ... kèng ... ... | If I work hard, my ... will be even more ... ... |
| 9. Chè-kê ... pù hăo, nà-kê ... ... kèng ... ... | This ... is not good, that one is even ... |

b. Translate into English:

1. 我們去中國可以坐船，也可以坐飛機.
2. 我們比一比？我比不上你,不能比.
3. 你會開飛機嗎？
4. 因為有警察在大街上指導來往的車輛跟行人，所以減少了很多的危險.
5. 坐飛機比坐頭等火車貴，所以我

不常坐飛機.

6. 我旅行的機會很少，所以我有很多的地方沒有去過.

7. 下雨天用雨傘.

8. 我最愛聽無線電，可是我沒有多少時候聽.

9. 她長†得很好看，不過高一點兒.

10. 龍蝦很好吃，可是很貴.

c. Translate into Chinese:

1. Please reserve a seat on the plane for me tomorrow.
2. Where will the baggage be weighed?
3. The car from the aviation company will come to get the passengers.
4. There are very high mountains in the northwest of America.
5. The population* of Shanghai is very dense.
6. The view of Niagara Falls is very beautiful.
7. I like to eat sea food, but I don't like to eat too much pork.
8. After the invention of new means of communication, the distance between China and America has been reduced.
9. I like to hear opera, and I also like to listen to music from the radio.
10. The people who live upstairs frequently talk in loud voices at midnight.

## Comparison of Adjectives and Adverbs

1. The comparative degree is expressed in the following ways:

---

†Chăng: to grow, or "is growing to be."

*Jén-k'ou 人口

a. By the use of "hsiēh" 些, "tiěn" 點, "ì-tiěn" 一點, or "tō" 多. Examples:

"Tsǒu k'uài hsiēh" 走快些 - "Walk faster".

"Chè-kê jén kāo hsiēh" 這個人高些 - "This man is taller".

"Chè-kê hǎo ì-tiěn" 這個好一點 - "This is better (This is good by a little)".

"T'ā hǎo tō lê" 他好多了 - "He is much better".

b. Where two objects or actions are compared, "kèng" 更 indicates an emphatic comparative.

"Wǒ k'āi ch'ē k'āi-tê k'uài, t'ā k'āi-tê kèng k'uài" 我開車開的快，他開的更快 - "I drive (a car) fast, [but] he drives even faster".

"Wǒ-tê ch'ì-ch'ē hǎo, t'ā-tê ch'ì-ch'ē kèng hǎo" 我的汽車好，他的汽車更好 - "My automobile is good, his is even better".

c. "Pǐ" 比 is used in the comparison of two objects according to the formula: "substantive - pǐ - substantive - adjective".

"Tièn-ch'ē pǐ yáng-ch'ē k'uài" 電車比洋車快 - "The street car is faster than the ricksha".

"Wó pǐ t'ā tà sān suì" 我比他大三歲 - "I am three years older than he".

"Wó tsǒu-tê pǐ ní tsǒu-tê k'uài" 我走的比你走的快 - "My walking is faster than your walking", i.e., "I walk faster than you".

d. Where two actions are compared, a slightly different formula may be used: "substantive - pǐ - substantive - verb - adverb".

"Ní pǐ wó tsǒu-tê k'uài" 你比我走得快 - "You walk faster than I".

"T'ā pí wǒ shuō-tê hǎo" 他比我說的好 - "He speaks better than I".

e. In negative comparison, "pù pǐ" is not often used in spoken Chinese; instead, people use such phrases as "kǎn-pu-shàng" 趕不上 - "unable to overtake, unable to match", "pǐ-pu-tê" 比不得 - "not to be compared with", or "méi-yǔ ... nà-mo ... " 沒有 ... 那麽 ... - "not so ... ". For example:

"Wǒ-tê Yīng-wén kǎn-pu-shàng nǐ-tê" 我的英文趕不上你的 - "My English cannot catch up with yours", i.e., is inferior to yours".

"Wǒ-tê pí pǐ-pu-tê nǐ-tê pǐ nà-mo hǎo-k'àn" 我的筆比不得你的筆那麽好看 - "My pen is not so pretty as yours".

"Chè-kê méi-yǔ nà-kê hǎo" 這個沒有那個好 - "This one is not so good as that one".

2. Equality is expressed by the use of "í-yàng" 一樣 - "one sort, the same manner", "ì- pān-êrh" 一般兒 - "in the same manner, equally", or "yěh ... nà-mo" 也 ... 那麽 - "also ... so". For example:

"Wǒ-tê piǎo kěn nǐ-tê piǎo í-yàng-tê hǎo" 我的表跟你的表一樣的好 - "My watch with your watch is equally good", i.e., "My watch is as good as yours".

"Wǒ-tê hsüéh-shêng kěn nǐ-tê hsüéh-shêng ì-pān-êrh tō" 我的學生跟你的學生一般兒多 - "My students are as many as yours".

"Wó yěh yú nǐ nà-mo tō ch'ién" 我也有你那麽多錢 - "I also have as much money as you".

3. The superlative degree is expressed:

a. By prefixing to the adjective one of the following adverbs: "tsuì" 最, or "tǐng" 頂 - "head, top, very". These two words can be used interchangeably, but "tǐng" is more colloquial. Examples:

"Nà-kê jén tsuì hǎo" 那個人最好 - "That man is the best".

"Chè-kê tì-fang tíng hǎo" 這個地方頂好 - "This place is the best".

"Tíng háo nǐ hsiēn ch'ù" 頂好你先去 - "[It] is best [for] you to go first".

b. By naming a class, singling out one member of the class, and applying to that member the adjective, which may be preceded by "hái-shìh". Examples:

"Tsài chè-pān jén lǐ-t'ou, hái-shìh t'ā hǎo" 在這班人裏頭,還是他好 - "In this class, he is still the best".

"Chè-hsieh jén chūng, hái-shìh t'ā yùng-kūng" 這些人中, 還是他用功 - "Among these men, he is the most diligent".

Examples of the Use of the Comparative and Superlative Degrees

"Nǐ-tê Chūng-kuo-huà hǎo, Wáng hsiēn-shêng-tê kèng hǎo, Lǐ

hsiēng-shêng-tê <u>tsuì</u> hǎo" 你的中國話好，王先生的更好，李先生的最好 - "Your Chinese is good, Mr. Wang's is even better, Mr. Li's is the best".

"Ch'ì-ch'ē <u>k'uài</u>, huǒ-ch'ē <u>kèng</u> k'uài, k'ě-shih fēi-chī <u>tsuì</u> k'uài" 汽車快，火車更快，可是飛機最快 - "The automobile is fast, the train is even faster, but the airplane is the fastest".

## Lesson 30 Review

1. Useful Phrases and Word Combinations

| | | | |
|---|---|---|---|
| 1. | 四方 | ssǔ fāng | The four directions. Square. |
| 2. | 東，南，西，北 | tūng,nán,hsī,pěi | East, south, west, north. |
| 3. | 西南，西北 | hsī-nán, hsī-pěi | Southwest, northwest. |
| 4. | 東南，東北 | tūng-nán, tūng-pěi | Southeast, northeast. |
| 5. | 往南，往北 | wàng-nán, wàng-pěi | Southward, northward. |
| 6. | 路南，路北 | lù-nán, lù-pěi | On the south side of [the] road, on the north side of [the] road. |
| 7. | 東南風 | tūng-nán fěng | Southeast wind. |
| 8. | 西北風 | hsī-pěi fěng | Northwest wind. |
| 9. | 南方，北方 | nán-fāng, pěi-fāng | Southern part, northern part; south China, north China. |
| 10. | 南房，北房 | nán-fáng, pěi-fáng | South room (room facing south), north room. |
| 11. | 一班學生 | ì-pān hsüéh-shêng | A class of students. |
| 12. | 一般學生 | ì-pān hsüéh-shêng | Students in general. |
| 13. | 一般重 | ì-pān chùng | The same weight. |
| 14. | 手指，腳指 | shóu-chǐh, chiáo-chǐh | Finger [í-kê shóu-chǐh], toe [í-kê chiáo-chǐh]. |
| 15. | 買東西 | mǎi tūng-hsi | To shop, to buy commodities. |
| 16. | 做買賣的 | tsò-mǎi-mài-tê | Businessman. |
| 17. | 幾塊錢? | chǐ k'uài-ch'ién? | How many dollars? |
| 18. | 一塊錢 | í-k'uài-ch'ién | One dollar. |
| 19. | 半塊錢 | pàn-k'uài-ch'ién | Half a dollar. |

| | | | |
|---|---|---|---|
| 20. | 五毛錢 | wǔ-máo-ch'ién | Fifty cents. |
| 21. | 兩毛五分錢 | liǎng-máo wǔ-fēn-ch'ién | Twenty-five cents. |
| 22. | 兩塊半錢 | liǎng-k'uài-pàn-ch'ién | Two dollars and a half. |
| 23. | 三塊九毛五 | sān-k'uài chiǔ-máo-wǔ | Three dollars and ninety-five cents. |
| 24. | 一百塊錢 | ì-pǎi-k'uài-ch'ién | One hundred dollars. |
| 25. | 不遠，不近 | pù yüǎn, pú chìn | Not far away, not near. |
| 26. | 很遠，很近 | hěn yüǎn, hěn chìn | Very far away, very near. |
| 27. | 多遠? | tō yüǎn? | How far? |
| 28. | 不很遠，<br>不大近 | pù hěn yüǎn,<br>pú tà chìn | Not very far away,<br>not very near. |
| 29. | 離這兒遠 | lí chè-êrh yüǎn | Far from here. |
| 30. | 一輛車，車輛 | í-liàng ch'ē, ch'ē-liàng | A vehicle, carts. |
| 31. | 書鋪，酒鋪 | shū-p'ù, chiǔ-p'ù | Bookstore, wine shop. |
| 32. | 樓上，樓下 | lóu-shàng, lóu-hsià | Upstairs, downstairs (ground floor). |
| 33. | 上樓，下樓 | shàng lóu, hsià lóu | To go upstairs, to go downstairs. |
| 34. | 火車站 | huǒ-ch'ē-chàn | Railway station. |
| 35. | 電車站 | tièn-ch'ē-chàn | Street car stop. |
| 36. | 頭等，二等 | t'óu-těng, èrh-těng | First class, second class. |
| 37. | 好機會 | hǎo chī-hui | Good opportunity. |
| 38. | 沒有機會 | méi-yǔ chī-hui | No opportunity. |
| 39. | 開會 | k'āi hùi | To open a meeting. |
| 40. | 會客室 | hùi-k'è-shìh | Reception room, living room. |
| 41. | 睡不着，<br>睡着了 | shùi-pu-cháo,<br>shùi cháo lê | Could not sleep,<br>fell asleep. |
| 42. | 空房間 | k'ūng fáng-chiēn | Unoccupied room. |
| 43. | 空跑了一次 | k'ūng p'ǎo lê í tz'ù | To run in vain. |
| 44. | 你有空沒有? | Ni yǔ k'ùng méi-yǔ? | Have you unoccupied time? |
| 45. | 我沒有空 | Wǒ méi-yǔ k'ùng | I have no time. |
| 46. | 火警，警告 | huó-chǐng, chǐng-kào | Fire alarm, to warn. |

| | | |
|---|---|---|
| 47. 忘了 | wàng lê | Forgot, forgotten. |
| 48. 忘記了 | wàng-chi lê | Forgot, forgotten. |
| 49. 忘不了 | wàng-pu-liǎo | Cannot forget, unforgettable. |
| 50. 記起來了 | chì ch'ǐ-lai lê | Recalled. |
| 51. 開門, 關門 | k'āi mén,kuān mén | Open the door, close the door. |
| 52. 他愛玩, 不愛念書 | T'ā ài wán, pú ài nièn-shū | He likes to play, does not like to study. |
| 53. 聽說 | t'īng shuō | I have heard, hearsay. |
| 54. 說不定 | shuō pú tìng | Cannot say for certain, cannot be sure. |
| 55. 明天我去不去, 還說不定 | Míng-t'ien wǒ ch'ü-pu-ch'ü, hái shuō pú tìng. | Whether I shall go tomorrow or not, I still cannot be sure. |

2. Conversation

王: 我的朋友下個禮拜要從美國來. 我想去接他.

李: 他在那兒下船?

王: 在上海.

李: 你要去上海接他的船, 還是等他來到北平才去車站接他?

王: 我想去接船, 因爲這是他第一次來中國. 有很多的事他都不很知道.

李: 他要是從美國來, 行李一定很多. 在海關檢查起來一定很麻煩.

王: 我這次想坐晚車去上海, 在車上睡一晚上, 就到了.

李: 還有誰跟你去?

王: 我想把我的女兒帶到上海去進中學.

李: 你的小姐幾歲了?

王: 她十二歲了.

李: 才十二歲就要進中學了, 她一定是一個很好的學生.

王: 她是很愛念書的. 李先生最近去過上海嗎?

李: 我上個月爲公事去了一次.

王: 你坐船去過上海沒有?

李: 我沒有坐過, 可是我聽別人說坐船也很舒服, 就是慢一點兒.

王: 我很喜歡坐船, 就怕有風浪. 坐大船還好, 坐小船眞不舒服.

李: 你的美國朋友是來這兒玩的嗎?

王: 對了. 他很喜歡旅行, 看各地方的風景.

李: 聽說不久我們的老朋友Smith先生也要來, 對不對?

王: 對了. 他不久就要來.

李: Smith 先生到了以後, 請你告訴我. 我們幾個人可以玩一玩.

王: 好罷. 我一定告訴你. 你要我在上海給你買甚麼東西嗎? 我可以給你帶來.

李：謝謝，我想沒有甚麼罷．你回來以後給我打電話．我要請你跟你的朋友到我家來吃飯．

3. Aural Drill

[The purpose of the aural drill is to help the students acquire ability not only to carry on simple conversations, but also to understand long discussions and to listen to lectures or radio broadcasts in Chinese. Although interpretation may be difficult at first, practice in listening to connected narrative or discourse in Chinese will increase the students' ability in aural comprehension and also their ability to remember what they hear and render it into English. Although it is difficult to tell a good story with a strictly limited vocabulary, the instructor may wish to give the students further practice by telling them other stories similar to the following example. A method of use of the aural drill has been suggested in Lesson 24, section 3.]

## 一個看羊的孩子

兩千年以前，有一個看羊的孩子，名叫路溫舒．他家沒有甚麼錢，他父親只靠着做工過日子[1]．路溫舒有的時候跟着他父親做工，有的時候到外面去看羊．一天到晚，一點空兒也沒有．他很想念書，可是沒有機會，也沒有錢買書．他看見人家念書，常常站在旁邊聽，聽得很高興．

有一天，他想，我快要十歲了，一定要念書了．可是沒有機會念書，也沒有錢買書，怎麼得了呢？[2]看羊這樣的事，可以做到老[3]嗎？

路溫舒想了很久，想到工是一定要做的，因爲不做工，就沒有飯吃；書是不能不念的，因爲不念書就沒有學問[4]. 將來不能夠[5]做很大的事. 所以他最後想出來的法子, 就是做工不忘念書.

天氣很溫和[6], 春風吹在路溫舒的面上. 他跟着幾隻羊, 在綠草上慢慢的走, 心裏正在想他怎樣才可以念書. 一會兒走到一個有水的地方, 他就不走了, 站在岸上.

他看見岸上長了一種樹, 樹上的綠葉, 很長很寬. 他想:『好, 這東西乾了的時候, 就可以用作書本了[7].』他就把很多的樹葉擱在一塊兒, 很高興的拿回家去了. 他把樹葉擱在一塊, 跟書的樣子差不多. 他向他的小朋友, 借到了很多的書本. 晚上有空的時候, 拿來一頁一頁的寫在樹葉上面.

從這個時候起, 路溫舒在外面看羊的時候, 手裏老[8]是拿着一本樹葉做的書, 慢慢的念. 念完一本, 再寫一本, 因爲樹葉是不要花錢買的.

不到十年, 他念的書很不少了. 後來他是一個有學問的人.

NOTES:

[No translation will be given here. The instructor may wish to assign translation of the above story as a written exercise, after oral practice in the classroom. A few special expressions are explained below.]

(1) "Kuò jìh-tzŭ" - "to pass the days, to spend time". "Tzŭ" here

is a suffix without any particular meaning.

(2) "Tsěn-mo tế liǎo ni?" may be rendered "What can be done?", or "How can [we] obtain the end [in view]?"

(3) "Tsò tào lǎo" - "to work until old age".

(4) "Hsüéh-wèn", literally "to study and ask" (the way to acquire knowledge), means "learning, knowledge". "T'ā hến yǔ hsüéh-wèn" and "T'ā-tê hsüéh-wèn hến hǎo" both mean "He is a good scholar".

(5) "Néng-kòu" means "can"; "kòu" is added for euphony.

(6) "Wēn-hê" - "warm, genial, mild".

(7) During the period of the Former Han Dynasty (B.C. 206-8 A.D.), when Lu Wēn-shu lived, paper had not yet been invented and the materials used for writing, such as bamboo slips, flat pieces of wood, and silk, were all bulky and expensive.

(8) "Lǎo" here means "always".

CONVERSATIONAL CHINESE

PART VI VARIOUS BUSINESS TRANSACTIONS

## Lesson 31 In a Hotel

1. Vocabulary

| | | |
|---|---|---|
| 旅館 | lǘ-kuǎn | Hotel [í-kê lǘ-kuǎn]. |
| 店 | tièn | Shop, inn [seldom used alone]. |
| 飯店 | fàn-tièn (1) | Hotel [í-kê fàn-tièn]. |
| 經 | chīng | Already. A classic. To pass through. |
| 理 | lǐ | To govern, to manage, to pay attention. Reason, principle. |
| 經理 | chīng-lǐ | Manager [í-kê chīng-lǐ]. |
| 已 | ǐ | Already. Finished. To stop. |
| 已經 | ǐ-ching | Already. |
| 層 | ts'ếng | Storey, layer. A numerative of storeys. |
| 梯 | t'ī | Ladder, steps, stairs. |
| 樓梯 | lóu-t'ī | Stairs, stairway [í-kê lóu-t'ī]. |
| 電梯 | tièn-t'ī | Elevator [í-kê tièn-t'ī]. |
| 客廳 | k'ề-t'īng | Reception room, sitting room [ì-chiēn k'ề-t'īng]. |
| 飯廳 | fàn-t'īng | Dining room [ì-chiēn fàn-t'īng]. |
| 臥 | wò | To lie down. |
| 臥房 | wò-fáng | Bedroom [ì-chiēn wò-fáng]. |
| 澡 | tsǎo | Bath [í-kê tsǎo]. |
| 澡房 | tsǎo-fáng | Bathroom [ì-chiēn tsǎo-fáng]. |
| 洗 | hsǐ | To wash. |
| 洗澡 | hsí-tsǎo | To take a bath. |
| 廁所 | tz'ǜ-sǒ | Toilet, privy [ì-chiēn tz'ǜ-sǒ]. |
| 燈 | tēng | A light. |
| 亮 | liàng | Bright, clear, transparent. |
| 鑰 | yào | Lock, key [seldom used alone]. |
| 鑰匙 | yào-shih | Key [í-kê yào-shih]. |
| 預 | yǜ | To prepare. Beforehand. [Seldom used alone in colloquial]. |

| | | |
|---|---|---|
| 備 | pèi | Complete. To prepare, to furnish. [Not used alone in colloquial]. |
| 預備 | yǜ-pei | To make ready, to prepare. |
| 平常 | p'íng-ch'áng | Usually, ordinarily. |
| 安 | ān | Peace, quiet [seldom used alone in colloquial]. |
| 靜 | chìng | Quiet, calm, silent. |
| 安靜 | ān-ching | Quiet, peacefulness. |
| 封 | fēng | To seal. A numerative of letters. |
| 信 | hsìn | Letter [ì-fēng hsìn]. Sincerity. To believe, to trust. |
| 幫 | pāng | To help. |
| 北京 | Pěi-chīng | Peking. |
| 太陽 | t'ài-yang | Sun. |
| 月亮 | yüèh-liang | Moon. |
| 朝 | ch'áo | To face. Dynasty. |
| | chāo | Morning. |
| 床 | ch'uáng | Bed [í-p'ù or ì-chāng ch'uáng] |
| 被 | pèi | Quilt, coverlet, bedclothes [ì-t'iáo pèi]. To suffer. By [indicating agent with passive voice. |
| 被單子 | pèi-tān-tzŭ | Sheet (of a bed), coverlet [ì-t'iáo pèi-tān-tzŭ]. |
| 毯子 | t'ǎn-tzŭ | Blanket [ì-chāng or ì-t'iáo t'ǎn-tzŭ]. |
| 枕頭 | chěn-t'ou | Pillow [í-kê chěn-t'ou]. |
| 套 | t'ào | Case, wrapper, covering. A numerative for things worn. |
| 滿 | mǎn | Full. |
| 玻璃 | pō-li | Glass [í-k'uài pō-li]. |
| 鬧 | nào | Noisy. To make a disturbance. |
| 鬧鐘 | nào-chūng | Alarm-clock [í-kê nào-chūng]. |
| 小心 | hsiǎo-hsin | Be careful. To take care. |

2. Conversation

[By this time students should have acquired a sense of the rhythm of Chinese sentences; underlining of stressed words is therefore discontinued as no longer helpful.]

| | |
|---|---|
| 1.Wáng: 你這次去北平要住在那一個旅館? | Nǐ chè tz'ù ch'ù Pěi-p'íng yào chù tsài nǎ-i-kê lǘ-kuǎn? |
| 2. Lǐ: 我不知道. 那一個好? | Wǒ pù chīh - tao. Nǎ - i - kê hǎo? |
| 3.Wáng: 我住過一個很大的旅館, 在東長安街. 那個地方的交通方便, 房間也很舒服. | Wǒ chù kuò í - kê hěn tà - tê lǘ-kuǎn, tsài Tūng-ch'áng-ān Chiēh. Nà - kê tì - fang - tê chiāo-t'ūng fāng-pièn, fáng-chiēn yéh hěn shū-fu. |
| 4. Lǐ: 那裏安靜嗎? | Nà - li ān - ching ma? |
| 5.Wáng: 安靜極了, 一點兒不鬧. 你要是去, 最好先寫信去定房間. | Ān - ching chí lê, ì - tiěn - êrh pú nào. Nǐ yào - shih ch'ù, tsuì hǎo hsiēn hsiěh hsìn ch'ù tìng fáng-chiēn. |
| 6. Lǐ: 那個旅館叫甚麼名字? | Nà - kê lǘ-kuǎn chiào shén-mo míng-tzǔ? |
| 7.Wáng: 叫交通旅館. 還有一個旅館也不錯, 叫北京飯店. 要是交通旅館沒有房間, 你可以到那個飯店去. | Chiào Chiāo - t'ūng Lǘ-kuǎn. Hái yǔ í - kê lǘ - kuǎn yěh pú ts'ò, chiào Pěi-chīng Fàn-tièn. Yào-shih Chiāo-t'ūng Lǘ-kuǎn méi-yǔ fáng-chiēn, ní k'ě - i tào nà - kê fàn-tièn ch'ü. |

(在旅館)

(Tsài lǘ-kuǎn)

8. Lǐ: 借光，那一位是經理？

Chièh - kuāng, nǎ - i - wèi shìh chīng-lǐ?

9. Chāng: 我就是．先生有甚麽事要我幫忙嗎？

Wǒ chiù-shìh. Hsiēn-shêng yǔ shén-mo shìh yào wǒ pāng-máng(2) ma?

10. Lǐ: 經理先生，我是從上海來的．姓李．

Chīng - lǐ hsiēn - shêng, wǒ shìh ts'úng Shàng-hǎi lái-tê. Hsìng Lǐ.

11. Chāng: 李先生，上禮拜你寫信來定房間．我們已經給你預備好了．

Lǐ hsiēn-shêng, shàng lǐ - pài ní hsiěh hsìn lái tìng fáng-chiēn. Wǒ - mên ǐ - ching kéi ni yǜ-pei hǎo lê.

12. Lǐ: 謝謝你．我的房間在那一層樓？多少錢一天？

Hsièh - hsieh ni. Wǒ - tê fáng-chiēn tsài nǎ-i ts'ếng-lóu? Tō-shǎo ch'ién ì t'iēn?

13. Chāng: 在第三層樓．我們給你預備了一間臥房，一間客廳，一間澡房．每天的房錢只要十塊五毛錢．

Tsài tì - sān ts'ếng - lóu. Wǒ - mên kéi ni yǜ - pei lê ì-chiēn wò-fáng, ì-chiēn k'ề-t'īng, ì-chiēn tsǎo-fáng. Měi t'iēn-tê fáng-ch'ién chǐh yào shíh-k'uài wǔ-máo-ch'ién.

14. Lǐ: 好極了．這兒的飯廳早上幾點鐘

Hǎo chí lê. Chề - êrh-tê fàn-t'īng tsǎo-shang chí tiěn-chūng

| | |
|---|---|
| 開門? 因爲我明天早上八點鐘以前要出去. | k'āi mén? Yīn-wèi wǒ míng-t'ien tsǎo-shang pā-tiěn chūng ǐ-ch'ién yào ch'ū-ch'ü. |
| 15. Chāng: 飯廳平常八點才開門. 可是茶房可以把早飯給你拿到房間去. 這是你房間的鑰匙. | Fàn-t'ǐng p'íng-ch'áng pā-tiěn ts'ái k'āi mén. K'ě-shih ch'á-fáng k'ě - i pá tsǎo - fàn kéi ni ná tào fáng-chiēn ch'ü. Chè shìh nǐ fáng-chiēn-tê yào-shih. |
| 16. Lǐ: 那兩個箱子我現在不用, 可以晚一點兒給我拿上來. | Nà liǎng - kê hsiāng-tzǔ wǒ hsièn-tsài pú yùng, k'ě - i wǎn ì-tiěn-êrh kéi wo ná shàng lai. |
| 17. Chāng: 茶房, 把這個小皮包給李先生拿到三四三號房. | Ch'á - fáng, pǎ chè - kê hsiǎo p'í-pāo kéi Lǐ hsiēn-shêng ná tào sān-ssǜ-sān hào fáng. |
| 18. Lǐ: 我也要請你告訴我電梯在那裏? | Wó yěh yào ch'íng ni kào-su wo tièn - t'ī tsài ná - li? |
| 19. Ch'á-fáng: 先生, 好了, 我拿這件行李到你的房間去了. 電梯在這邊. | Hsiēn - shêng, hǎo lê, wǒ ná chè-chièn hsíng-li tào nǐ-tê fáng chiēn ch'ǜ lê. Tièn-t'ī tsài chè-pien. |
| 20. 一位旅客: 茶房, 請你告訴我, 這層樓有廁所嗎? | Í-wèi lǚ - k'è: Ch'á - fáng, ch'íng ni kào-su wo, chè ts'éng-lóu yǔ tz'ǜ-sǒ(3) ma? |
| 21. Ch'á-fáng: 有, 就在樓梯 | Yǔ, chiù tsài lóu - t'ī - |

的左邊. tê tsǒ-pien.

22.Ch'á-fáng: 先生要我給你開電燈嗎? Hsiēn-shêng yào wo kéi ni k'āi tièn-tēng ma?

23. Lǐ: 現在還早, 這個房間夠亮了, 不用開燈. 請你給我開一個窗罷, 因爲房間太熱了. Hsièn-tsài hái tsǎo, chè-kê fáng-chiēn kòu liàng lê, pú yùng k'āi tēng. Ch'íng ni kéi wo k'āi í-kê ch'uáng pa, yīn-wèi fáng-chiēn t'ài jè lê.

24.Ch'á-fáng: 這個房間最好. 朝東, 早上滿房都是太陽光. 這邊是客廳, 那邊是臥房, 洗澡房就在後面. 這個房間的東西都是新的. 床上的被單子, 枕頭套, 毯子, 都是今天早上換過的. Chè-kê fáng-chiēn tsuì hǎo. Ch'áo tūng, tsǎo-shàng mǎn fáng tōu shìh t'ài-yang kuāng. Chè-pien shìh k'è-t'īng, nà-pien shìh wò-fáng, hsí-tsǎo-fáng chiù tsài hòu-mien. Chè-kê fáng-chiēn-tê tūng-hsi tōu shìh hsīn-tê. Ch'uáng-shàng-tê pèi-tān-tzŭ, chěn-t'ou-t'ào, t'ǎn-tzŭ, tōu shìh chīn-t'ien tsǎo-shang huàn kuò tê.

25. Lǐ: 那好極了. 回頭你拿那兩個箱子上來的時候, 請你小心一點兒, 因爲裏面有很多玻璃的東西. Nà hǎo chí lê. Huí-t'óu nǐ ná nà liǎng-kê hsiāng-tzŭ shàng lai tê shíh-hou, ch'íng ni hsiǎo-hsin ì-tiěn-êrh, yīn-wèi lǐ-mien yú hěn tō(4) pō-li-tê tūng-hsi.

| | |
|---|---|
| 26.Ch'á-fáng:剛才先生說明天八點鐘要出去.我七點半把早餐拿到你房間來好嗎? | Kāng-ts'ái hsiēn-shēng shuō míng-t'ien pā tiĕn-chūng yào ch'ū-ch'ü. Wŏ ch'ī-tiĕn-pàn pá tsăo-ts'ān ná tào nǐ fáng-chiēn lai hăo ma? |
| 27. Lǐ: 好極了.你不說我可忘了一件事.你們旅館有沒有鬧鐘?最好借來給我用用.我恐怕明天早上不能那麼早起來. | Hăo chí lê. Nǐ pù shuō wó k'ĕ(5) wàng lê í-chièn shìh. Nǐ-mên lú-kuán yŭ-mei-yu nào-chūng? Tsuì hăo chièh lai kéi wo yùng-yung. Wó k'ŭng-p'à míng-t'ien tsăo-shang pù nếng nà-mo tsáo ch'ǐ-lai. |
| 28.Ch'á-fáng:回頭我拿來給你.先生還要甚麼嗎? | Huí-t'óu wŏ ná-lai kéi ni. Hsiēn-shêng hái yào shến-mo ma? |
| 29. Lǐ: 不要甚麼了,謝謝你. | Pú yào shến-mo lê, hsièh-hsieh ni. |
| 30.Ch'á-fáng:你要甚麼就叫我好了.我一天到晚都在這裏. | Nǐ yào shến-mo chiù chiào wo hăo lê. Wŏ ì-t'iēn-tào-wăn(6) tōu tsài chè-li. |

NOTES:

(1) "Lú-kuăn", literally "lodging-house", is an expression usually used in Peking for a small or old-fashioned hotel. "Fàn-tièn", "eating-house", is an expression for a modern, Western-style hotel. However, in south China "lú-kuăn" and "fàn-tièn" are used interchangeably. Note the distinction between "fàn-tièn", "hotel", and "fàn-kuăn", "restaurant".

(2) "Pāng-máng", literally "to help [when] busy", is generally used in the sense of "to help, to give assistance", and "máng" is

the usual object of "pāng". When "pāng" is used alone it means "to help, to defend", and must have an object.

(3) Usually "tz'ǔ-sǒ" means "men's room", while the "women's room" is called "nǚ tz'ǔ-sǒ".

(4) "Tê" 的 is omitted here in order to avoid repetition.

(5) "K'ě" is used as an adversative adverb, meaning "however, nevertheless", and giving emphasis to the contrary effect. In making a smooth translation, the meaning of "k'ě" is frequently neglected.

(6) "Ì-t'iēn-tào-wǎn" means "from morning till night".

3. Translation

1. Wang: This time you go to Peiping, which hotel are you going to stay in?
2. Li: I don't know. Which one is good?
3. Wang: I have stayed in a very large hotel, on Tung-ch'ang-an Street. The communications of that area are convenient, and the rooms are very comfortable.
4. Li: Is it quiet there?
5. Wang: Very quiet, not noisy at all. If you are going, it would be best to write to reserve a room first.
6. Li: What's the name of that hotel?
7. Wang: It's called the Chiao-t'ung Hotel. There is [another] hotel [which is] also not bad, called the Peking Hotel. If there is no room [available] at the Chiao-t'ung Hotel, you can go to that hotel.

(At the hotel)

8. Li: Please excuse me; who is the manager?
9. Chang: I am. Do you want me to help you, sir?
10. Li: Mr. Manager, I have come from Shanghai. My name is Li.
11. Chang: Mr. Li, you wrote last week to reserve rooms. We have already prepared the rooms for you.
12. Li: Thank you. On which floor is my room? How much a day?
13. Chang: On the third floor. We have prepared for you a bedroom, a sitting room, and a bathroom. It is only ten dollars and fifty cents a day.
14. Li: Fine! At what time in the morning does the dining room here open? Because I have to go out before eight o'clock tomorrow morning.
15. Chang: Ordinarily the dining room doesn't open till eight o'clock. But the boy can take breakfast to your room. This is your room key.
16. Li: I don't need those two trunks now; [they] can be brought up to me later.
17. Chang: Boy, take this small suitcase to room number 343 for Mr. Li.

18. Li: I must also ask you to tell me where the elevator is.

19. Boy: All right, sir. I am taking this baggage to your room. The elevator is over here.

20. A guest: Boy, please tell me, is there a men's room on this floor?

21. Boy: Yes, it's just at the left of the stairs.

22. Boy: Sir, would you like me to turn on the electric light for you?

23. Li: It's still early; this room is bright enough, no need to turn on the light. Please open a window for me, because the room is too warm.

24. Boy: This room is the best. [It] faces east, in the morning the room is full of sunshine. The sitting room is on this side, the bedroom is on that side, the bathroom is at the back. The things in this room are all new. The sheets, pillow-cases, [and] blankets on the bed were all changed this morning.

25. Li: Very good. Later, when you bring those two trunks up, please be a little careful, because there are many glass things inside.

26. Boy: You said just now, sir, [that you] want to go out at eight o'clock tomorrow. Shall I bring breakfast to your room at half past seven?

27. Li: Very good. [If] you hadn't spoken, I might have forgotten something. Has your hotel an alarm-clock? It would be best to lend it to me to use. I'm afraid [I] won't be able to get up so early tomorrow.

28. Boy: Later I'll bring it to you. What more do you want, sir?

29. Li: I don't want anything more, thank you.

30. Boy: [If] you want anything, just call me. I'm here all day long (literally, all day till night).

4. Exercises

a. "Fill-in" sentences

| | |
|---|---|
| 1. Chề-kê pǐ nà-kê ... ... ... | This, compared to that, is (larger / better) etc.). |
| 2. Wǒ ... tê pí nǐ ... tê ... ... | My (speaking / walking etc.) is (better / faster etc.) than yours. |
| 3. Ní pí wǒ ... ... | You are (taller / older etc.) than I. |
| 4. Chê-kê ... ... méi-yǔ nà-kê ... ... | This ... is not so (good / small etc.) as that one. |
| 5. Wǒ shìh ts'úng ... ... lái-tê. | I come from ... ... |

| | |
|---|---|
| 6. Měi-i-chiēn wò-fáng tōu yǔ ... ... ma? | Does every bedroom have ... ... ? |
| 7. Chè-êrh-tê ... ... shìh wǒ-tê lǎo p'éng-yu. | The ... here is my old friend. |
| 8. ... ... tō-shǎo ch'ién i ... ? | How much a (hour / day / month etc.) for a (house / room / worker etc.)? |

b. Translate into English:

1. 太陽沒有下去，月亮就出來了。
2. 這條路滿地都是花。
3. 那條被單被我的朋友拿走了。
4. 我現在住的房子有一間客廳，一間臥房，一間澡房。
5. 那個旅館有六層樓，可是沒有電梯。
6. 我住過一次，以後就不想再去了。
7. 那個地方一定很不方便。
8. 我可以幫你找一個舒服一點兒的地方住。
9. 北京飯店的房錢很貴。
10. 你別鬧了，我帶你出去玩玩。

c. Translate into Chinese:

1. Has my friend come to reserve rooms for me?

2. I don't know. Let me ask the manager.
3. Yes, the rooms are all ready (prepared).
4. Please take my suitcase up for me first. I will go up in a few minutes.
5. Where is the men's room?
6. Be careful of the glass when you bring the baggage to me.
7. How much a day for this room?
8. The dining room doesn't open (its doors) till eight-fifteen. Will that be too late?
9. Please change the sheets and pillow-cases, because a guest will stay here tonight.
10. I want to wash my hands before I go to eat.

## Lesson 32 In a Post Office

1. Vocabulary

| | | |
|---|---|---|
| 郵 | yú | Mail. A post station. Postal. [Seldom used alone.] |
| 政 | chèng | Government, administration [seldom used alone]. |
| 郵政局 | yú-chèng-chű | Post office [í-kê yú-chèng-chű]. |
| 信箱 | hsìn-hsiāng | Mail-box [í-kê hsìn-hsiāng]. |
| 郵差 | yú-ch'āi | Postman [í-kê yú-ch'āi]. |
| 信差 | hsìn-ch'āi(1) | Postman [í-kê hsìn-ch'āi]. |
| 剩 | shèng | Left over. Remainder. |
| 管 | kuǎn | Tube. To control, to manage. A numerative of tubular things. |
| 墨 | mò | Ink. |
| 瓶 | p'íng | Bottle [í-kê p'íng]. |
| 墨水 | mò-shuǐ | Ink [ì-p'íng mò-shuǐ]. |
| 墨水筆 | mò-shuí-pǐ | Pen [ì-kuǎn or ì-chīh mò-shuí-pǐ]. |
| 信封 | hsìn-fēng | Envelope [í-kê hsìn-fēng]. |

| | | |
|---|---|---|
| 郵票 | yú-p'iào | Stamp [i-chang yú-p'iào]. |
| 普 | p'ǔ | General. Everywhere. All, vast. [Seldom used alone.] |
| 普通 | p'ǔ-t'ūng | Common, general, ordinary. |
| 厚 | hòu | Thick, heavy. |
| 薄 | pó | Thin. |
| 掛號信 | kuà-hào-hsìn | Registered letter [ì-fēng kuà-hào-hsìn]. |
| 丟 | tiū | To lose, to throw away, to get rid of. |
| 快信 | k'uài-hsìn | Special delivery [ì-fēng k'uài-hsìn]. |
| 明信片 | míng-hsìn-p'ièn | Post-card [ì-chāng míng-hsìn-p'ièn]. |
| 保 | pǎo | To insure, to guarantee, to protect, to care for. |
| 保險 | páo-hsiěn | To insure. |
| 挖 | wā | To dig out, to scoop out. |
| 破 | p'ò | To break. Broken, worn out. |
| 窟窿 | k'ū-lung | Hole [í-kê k'ū-lung]. |
| 布 | pù | Cloth [í-k'uài or ì-t'iáo pù]. |
| 裹 | kuǒ | To wrap up, to bandage, to enclose. A numerative of small packages. |
| 包裹 | pāo-kuǒ | Parcel [í-kê pāo-kuǒ]. |
| 題 | t'í | Topic, theme, heading, title. |
| 問題 | wèn-t'í | Question, problem, difficulty, topic [í-kê wèn-t'í]. |
| 要緊 | yào-chǐn | Important, urgent. |
| 寄 | chì | To send, to deposit. To lodge at. |
| 址 | chǐh | Foundation [seldom used alone]. |
| 住址 | chù-chǐh | Address [í-kê chù-chǐh]. |
| 自 | tzǜ | From. Self. Naturally. |
| 己 | chǐ (2) | Self. Private. |
| 自己 | tzǜ-chǐ | Oneself. |
| 攪 | chiǎo | To stir up, to excite, to interrupt. |
| 打攪 | tá-chiǎo | To disturb, to interrupt. |
| 送 | sùng | To send, to give, to escort. |

2. Conversation

| | |
|---|---|
| 1.(A) 寄一封信，要幾分郵票? | Chì ì - fēng hsìn, yào chǐ fēn yú-p'iào? |
| 2.(B) 普通信，國內五分，國外兩毛五. | P'ǔ - t'ūng hsìn, kuó nèi wǔ-fēn, kuó wài liǎng - máo - wǔ. |
| 3.(A) 寄一封航空信到美國要多少郵票? | Chì ì-fēng háng-k'ūng hsìn tào Měi - kuo yào tō - shǎo yú - p'iào? |
| 4.(B) 要一塊兩毛五的郵票．可是你這封信太重了，要兩塊半錢. | Yào í - k'uài liǎng-máo-wǔ - tê yú-p'iào. K'ě-shih nǐ chè-fēng hsìn t'ài chùng lê, yào liǎng-k'uài-pàn ch'ién. |
| 5.(A) 這封信看起來很薄，怎麼會過重呢? 好罷．我還有一封信是國內的．我要寄快信. | Chè-fēng hsìn k'àn ch'ǐ-lai hěn pò, tsěn - mo huì kuò chùng ni? Hǎo pa. Wǒ hái yǔ ì-fēng hsìn shìh kuó - nèi - tê. Wǒ yào chì k'uài-hsìn. |
| 6.(B) 先生，這封信要掛號嗎? | Hsiēn-shêng, chè-fēng hsìn yào kuà-hào(3) ma? |
| 7.(A) 我這封信很要緊，請你給我掛號罷. | Wǒ chè-fēng hsìn hěn yào-chǐn, ch'íng ni kéi wo kuà - hào pa. |
| 8.(B) 那麼，請你把你自己的住址也寫在信封上．這兒有一管墨水筆. | Nà - mo, ch'íng ni pá nǐ tzǔ-chǐ-tê chù-chǐh yéh hsiěh tsài hsìn-fēng shàng. Chè-êrh yǔ i-kuǎn mò-shuí-pǐ. |

| | |
|---|---|
| 9.(A) 謝謝．這封信也不輕罷? | Hsièh-hsieh.  Chè-fēng hsìn yĕh pù ch'īng pa? |
| 10.(B) 還沒過重．信裏有錢沒有? | Hái méi kuò chùng.  Hsìn lí yŭ ch'ién méi - yŭ? |
| 11.(A) 沒有錢，可是有要緊的事．所以我要掛號．剩下來的錢你不用找給我，我用來買一分的郵票． | Méi - yŭ ch'ién, k'ĕ - shih yŭ yào - chĭn - tê shìh, só - í wŏ yào kuà-hào.  Shèng-hsia lái-tê ch'ién ni pú yùng chăo kéi wo, wŏ yùng lái măi ì - fĕn - tê yú-p'iào. |
| 12.(A) 郵政局幾點鐘關門? 我要寄一個包裹，不知道趕得上嗎? | Yú-chèng-chŭ chí tiĕn-chūng kuān mén?  Wŏ yào chì í - kê pāo-kuŏ, pù chīh-tao kăn - tê shàng ma? |
| 13.(B) 下午六點．你那個包裹大不大? | Hsià - wŭ liù tiĕn.  Nĭ nà-kê pāo - kuŏ tà - pu - ta? |
| 14.(A) 不很大．我想用厚的黃紙包就行了罷? | Pù hĕn tà.  Wó hsiăng yùng hòu-tê huáng chĭh pāo chiù hsíng lê pa? |
| 15.(B) 你還沒預備好嗎? 請你快一點罷，因為六點鐘的時候人很多．還有，你不要用紙包，因為一 | Nĭ hái méi yù - pei hăo ma?  Ch'íng ni k'uài ì-tiĕn pa, yīn-wèi liù-tiĕn-chūng-tê shíh-hou jén hĕn tō.  Hái - yŭ, nĭ pú yào yùng chĭh pāo, yin-wèi í |

| | |
|---|---|
| 不小心，挖破一個窟窿，裏面的東西就丢了。 | pù hsiǎo - hsīn, wā - p'ò í - kê k'ū-lung, lǐ - mien - tê tūng-hsi chiù tiū lê. |
| 16.(A) 那麽，我用布包就行了．寄包裹要保險嗎? | Nà - mo, wǒ yùng pù pāo chiù hsíng lê. Chì pāo-kuǒ yào páo-hsiěn ma? |
| 17.(B) 最好是保險． | Tsuì hǎo shìh páo-hsiěn. |
| 18.(A) 多謝你告訴我．我差一點忘了；我還要買幾張明信片． | Tō - hsièh nǐ kào - su wo. Wǒ ch'à ì - tiěn wàng lê; wǒ hái yào mái chǐ-chāng míng-hsìn-p'ièn. |
| 19.(B) 多少張? | Tō - shǎo chāng? |
| 20.(A) 十四張．對不起，我還有一個問題．請問，信差一天開幾次信箱? | Shíh-ssǔ-chāng. Tuì pu ch'ǐ, wǒ hái yǔ í - kê wèn - t'í. Ch'ǐng wèn, hsìn-ch'āi ì t'iēn k'āi chǐ tz'ǔ hsìn-hsiāng? |
| 21.(B) 一天六次．最晚的是晚上十二點，所以你甚麽時候寄信都趕得上． | Ì t'iēn liù tz'ǔ. Tsuì-wǎn-tê shìh wǎn-shang shíh-èrh-tiěn, só - í nǐ shén - mo shíh-hou chì hsìn tōu kǎn - tê-shàng. |
| 22.(A) 好了．你很忙，我不再打攪你了． | Hǎo lê. Ní hěn máng, wǒ pú tsài tá - chiǎo ni lê. |
| 23.(B) 不要緊，不要緊．先生，這是你掛號信的收條，別丢了． | Pú yào-chin, pú yào-chin(4). Hsiēn-shêng, chè shìh nǐ kuà-hào-hsìn-tê shōu-t'iáo, piéh tiū lê. |

這是你買明信片剩下來的錢。 Chè shìh ní mǎi míng-hsìn-p'ièn shěng-hsia lái - tê ch'ién.

24.(A) 謝謝，再見。 Hsièh-hsieh, tsài chièn.

NOTES:

(1) Colloquially, a postman is also called "sùng-hsìn-tê" 送信的 "one who carries letters, letter-carrier".

(2) Note carefully the distinction between "chǐ" 己 and "ǐ" 已.

(3) "Kuà-hào", literally "to hang a number", usually means "to register" a letter, or "to register" (in a hospital).

(4) "Pú yào-chǐn", "it is unimportant", is used idiomatically in the sense of "never mind, it doesn't matter".

3. Translation

1.(A) How much postage is needed to send a letter?

2.(B) An ordinary letter, within the country, five cents, outside the country, twenty-five cents.

3.(A) How much postage is needed to send an airmail letter to America?

4.(B) [You] need $1.25 postage, but this letter of yours is too heavy, [it] will need $2.50.

5.(A) This letter looks very thin, how can it be overweight? All right. I have another letter, domestic mail. I want to send it special delivery.

6.(B) Sir, do you want to register this letter?

7.(A) This letter of mine is very important. Please register it for me.

8.(B) In that case, please write your own address on the envelope too. Here is a pen.

9.(A) Thank you. This letter isn't light either, is it?

10.(B) It still isn't overweight. Is there money in the letter?

11.(A) There is no money, but it contains important business, so I want to register [it]. The money left over you needn't pay me; I'll use it to buy one-cent stamps.

12.(A) What time does the post office close its doors? I have a package to send; I wonder whether I'll catch the post.

13.(B) Six p. m. Is your package large?

14.(A) Not very large. I think it will be all right to wrap it in heavy brown paper, won't it?

15.(B) Haven't you got it ready yet? Please hurry a little, because at six o'clock there are lots of people. And also, you shouldn't use paper to wrap [it], because the moment you're not careful and make a hole, the things inside will be lost.

16.(A) Then I'll use cloth to wrap [it] and it will be all right. To send a package, must it be insured?

17.(B) It is best to insure it.

18.(A) Many thanks for telling me. I almost forgot; I still want to buy a few postcards.

19.(B) How many?

20.(A) Fourteen. I'm sorry, I still have another question. May I ask, how many times a day does the postman open the mail-boxes? (How many collections -- ?)

21.(B) Six times a day. The latest is at twelve at night, so no matter when you mail a letter you will still catch the post.

22.(A) Good. You are very busy; I won't disturb you any more.

23.(B) It doesn't matter. Sir, here's the receipt for your registered letter, don't lose it. This is the money left over from the postcards you bought.

24.(A) Thank you. Goodby.

4. Exercises

a. "Fill-in" sentences.

| | |
|---|---|
| 1. Chì ì-fē̂ng ... ... hsìn yào chǐ fē̂n ... ... ? | How much ... is needed to send a ... letter? |
| 2. Chề-fē̂ng hsìn, wǒ yào ... ... | I want to ... this letter. |
| 3. Chề shìh ì-fē̂ng ... hsìn. | This is a ... letter. |
| 4. Chì pāo-kuǒ yào ... ... ma? | Is it necessary to ... a parcel [when you] send it? |
| 5. Hsìn-hsiāng ... ... ... ? | ... is the mail-box? |
| 6. Ch'ing pǎ ... ... hsiěh tsài ... ... shàng. | Please write the ... on the ... |
| 7. Chề-fē̂ng hsìn hê̌n ... ... | This letter is very ... ... |
| 8. Piéh pǎ shōu-t'iáo ... lê. | Don't ... the receipt. |
| 9. Wǒ tiū lê ... ... | I lost ... ... |

b. Translate into English:

1. 這個問題很要緊、

2. 普通的包裹不一定要保險、

3. 他喜歡用明信片寫信.
4. 他給了我一管墨水筆.
5. 寄航空信可以用普通的信封嗎?
6. 這是普通的,那是特別的.
7. 他現在很忙,別打攪他了.
8. 我自己的事還沒作,所以不能幫你的忙.
9. 你給我的住址,我恐怕丟了.
10. 今天送信的來了沒有?

c. Translate into Chinese:

1. Please send this letter for me.
2. Do you want to send [it as an] airmail letter?
3. No, special delivery will do.
4. But don't forget to register it.
5. Do you have anything else to take to the post office?
6. Do you have letter paper and envelopes?
7. The postage on this envelope is not enough, because the letter is heavy.
8. My watch is lost; [it] cannot be found.
9. Is there a mail-box on this street?
10. My shoes are worn out.

## Lesson 33 Telegraph and Radio

1. Vocabulary

| | | |
|---|---|---|
| 報 | pào | To report. Newspaper. |
| 電報 | tièn-pào | Telegraph. Telegram [í-kê tièn-pào]. |
| 電報局 | tièn-pào-chű | Telegraph office [í-kê tièn-pào-chű]. |
| 電報本子 | tièn-pào-pěn-tzŭ | Telegraph code book [ì-pěn tièn-pào-pěn-tzŭ]. |
| 國家 | kuó-chiā | Nation, state [í-kê kuó-chiā]. National. |
| 明碼 | míng-mǎ | Public code. |
| 密碼 | mì-mǎ | Private (secret) code. |
| 成 | ch'ếng | To become, to accomplish, to succeed. |
| 得 | těi | Ought, must (see also page 87). |
| 翻 or 繙 | fān | To translate, to turn over. A numerative of troubles and happenings. |
| 底 | tǐ | The bottom. Below. Low. |
| 海底電報 | hái-tǐ-tièn-pào | Submarine cable [í-kê hái-tǐ-tièn-pào]. |
| 故 | kù | Old. Cause. Therefore. [Lit.] |
| 故事 | kù-shih | Story ("old affairs") [í-kê kù-shih]. |
| 開心 | k'āi-hsīn | To feel happy. To make fun of another. |
| 無線電報 | wú-hsièn-tièn-pào | Radiogram. |
| 廣 | kuǎng | Wide, large. To enlarge. |
| 播 | pò | To broadcast, to sow, to make known. |
| 廣播 | kuǎng-pò | To broadcast. |
| 台 | t'ái | Platform, tower, stage, terrace. |
| 廣播電台 | kuǎng-pò-tièn-t'ái | Broadcasting station [í-kê kuǎng-pò-tièn-t'ái]. |
| 波 | pō or p'ō | Wave, breaker. |
| 短波 | tuǎn-pō | Short-wave. |
| 收音機 | shōu-yīn-chī | Radio receiver [í-kê shōu-yīn-chī]. |
| 燈泡子 | tēng-p'ào-tzŭ | Lamp bulb, electron tube [í-kê tēng-p'ào-tzŭ]. |
| 於 | yű | With, at, to, in. |
| 關於 | kuān-yű | Regarding, concerning. |

| | | |
|---|---|---|
| 聖 | shèng | Sage. Sacred, divine. |
| 誕 | tàn | Birthday. To give birth to. |
| 聖誕 | Shèng-tàn | Christmas. |
| 節 | chiéh | Joint of bamboo. Festival. |
| 賀 | hè | To congratulate. Greetings. |
| 消 | hsiāo | To melt, to consume, to disperse. |
| 消息 | hsiāo-hsi | News, report, rumor [í-kê hsiāo-hsi]. |
| 提 | t'í | To remind, to mention, to lift in the hand. |
| 醒 | hsǐng | To wake up. |
| 提醒 | t'í-hsǐng | To remind, to arouse. |
| 聞 | wén | To hear, to smell. News. |
| 新聞 | hsīn-wén (1) | News [í-kê or í-chièn hsīn-wên]. |
| 工夫 | kūng-fu | Leisure, time. |
| 不管 | pù-kuǎn | Regardless. |
| 應 | yīng | Ought, should. Proper. To deserve [seldom used alone]. |
| | yìng | To answer, to correspond to. |
| 應當 | yīng-tāng | Ought, should, must. |
| 覺 | chüéh | To perceive, to feel. |
| 覺得 | chüéh-tê | To feel, to be inclined to think. |
| 哦 | ó | An exclamation. |
| 情 | ch'íng | The passions, affections. Facts, circumstances. [Seldom used alone.] |
| 事情 | shìh-ch'ing | Affair, business [í-chièn shìh-ch'ing]. |

2. Conversation

| | |
|---|---|
| 1.(A) 借光，電報局在那裏? | Chièh-kuāng, tièn-pào-chǘ tsài ná - li? |
| 2.(B) 離這裏最近的電報局在交通大樓的對面. | Lí chè - li tsùi-chìn-tê tièn-pào-chǘ tsài Chiāo-t'ūng-tà-lóu - tê tùi mièn(2). |

3.(A) 國內跟國外的電報都能在那裏打嗎？

Kuó-nèi kěn kuó-wài-tê tièn-pào tōu néng tsài nà-li tǎ ma?

4.(B) 我想可以罷，因爲這個電報局很大。

Wó hsiáng k'ě-i pa, yīn-wèi chè-kê tièn-pào-chú hěn tà.

5.(A) 打英文電報是跟打中文電報一樣嗎？

Tǎ Yīng-wén tièn-pào shìh kěn tǎ Chūng-wén tièn-pào í-yàng(3) ma?

6.(B) 打英文電報很容易．打中文的就麻煩了。

Tǎ Yīng-wén tièn-pào hěn júng-i. Tǎ Chūng-wén-tê chiù má-fan lê.

7.(A) 我還沒有打過中文的電報．請你告訴我怎麼打罷。

Wǒ hái méi-yǔ tǎ kuò Chūng-wén-tê tièn-pào, ch'íng ni kào-su wo tsěn-mo tǎ pa.

8.(B) 打中文電報的時候，每個字都得翻成號碼。

Tǎ Chūng-wén tièn-pào tê shíh-hou, měi-kê tzù tōu těi fān ch'éng hào-mǎ.

9.(A) 那麼，怎麼知道應當用甚麼號碼呢？

Nà-mo, tsěn-mo chīh-tao yīng-tāng yùng shén-mo hào-mǎ ni?(4)

10.(B) 查電報本子就知道了．可是電報本子有兩種，一種是明碼的，一種是密碼的。

Ch'á tièn-pào-pěn-tzū chiù chīh-tao lê. K'ě-shih tièn-pào-pěn-tzū yú liáng chǔng, ì chǔng shìh míng-mǎ-tê, ì chǔng shìh mì-mǎ-tê.

11.(A) 明天是聖誕節；我要給我家打一個

Míng-t'ien shìh Shèng-tàn-chiéh; wǒ yào kéi wǒ chiā tǎ í-kê

| | |
|---|---|
| 賀電. 那應當用密碼, 還是用明碼? | hè - tièn. Nà yīng-tāng yùng mì-mǎ, hái - shìh yùng míng - mǎ? |
| 12.(B) 這是普通的事情; 用明碼就成了. | Chè shìh p'ǔ-t'ūng-tê shìh-ch'ing; yùng míng-mǎ chiù ch'éng lê(5). |
| 13.(A) 我打海底電報好, 還是無線電報好? | Wó tǎ hái - tǐ - tièn-pào hǎo, hái-shìh wú-hsièn-tièn-pào hǎo? |
| 14.(B) 我想一樣罷. 我們去問一問電報局. | Wó hsiǎng í - yàng pa. Wǒ - mên ch'ù wèn - i - wên tièn-pào-chǘ. |

(On the way to the telegraph office)

| | |
|---|---|
| 15.(A) 今天的消息怎麽樣? | Chīn-t'ien-tê hsiāo-hsi tsěn-mo yàng? |
| 16.(B) 我還沒有看見今天的新聞, 可是我昨天晚上聽了無線電, 消息很好. | Wǒ hái méi-yǔ k'àn-chien chīn-t'ien - tê hsīn-wén, k'ě-shih wǒ tsó-t'ien wǎn-shang t'īng lê wú-hsièn-tièn, hsiāo-hsi hěn hǎo. |
| 17.(A) 你那個無線電收音機有短波嗎? | Nǐ nà - kê wú-hsièn-tièn shōu-yīn - chī yú tuǎn - pō ma? |
| 18.(B) 長短都有. 我昨天聽見的消息是從美國廣播來的. | Ch'áng tuǎn tōu yǔ. Wǒ tsó-t'ien t'īng-chien-tê hsiāo-hsi shìh ts'úng Měi - kuo kuǎng-pò lái - tê. |
| 19.(A) 是那一個廣播電台? | Shìh nǎ - i - kê kuǎng-pò-tièn-t'ái? |
| 20.(B) 是 N. B. C. | Shìh N. B. C. |
| 21.(A) 你常聽無線電嗎? | Nǐ ch'áng t'īng wú-hsièn-tièn ma? |

| | |
|---|---|
| 22.(B) 我常聽. 不快樂的時候，我愛聽無線電裏的故事，開開心. | Wǒ ch'áng t'īng. Pú k'uài-lê-tê shíh-hou, wǒ ài t'īng wú-hsièn-tièn lǐ tê kù-shih, k'āi-k'ai hsīn. |
| 23.(A) 聽過以後，你就覺得好了嗎? | T'īng kuò ǐ-hòu, nǐ chiù chüéh-tê hǎo lê ma? |
| 24.(B) 聽了以後，我心裏就覺得好過了. | T'īng lê ǐ-hòu, wǒ hsīn-lǐ chiù chüéh-tê hǎo-kuò(6) lê. |
| 25.(A) 關於國家大事的消息，你聽不聽? | Kuān-yǘ kuó-chiā tà shìh tê hsiāo-hsi, nǐ t'īng-pu-t'ing? |
| 26.(B) 關於國家大事的新聞，我也聽. | Kuān-yǘ kuó-chiā tà shìh tê hsīn-wén, wó yěh t'īng. |
| 27.(A) 那麼，你每天還看報嗎? | Nà-mo, ní měi t'iēn hái k'àn pào ma? |
| 28.(B) 不一定，有工夫就看，沒有就不看. | Pù í-tìng, yǔ kūng-fu chiù k'àn, méi-yǔ chiù pú k'àn(7). |
| 29.(A) 我跟你不一樣. 要是我們有好消息的時候，不管怎麼忙我也要看一看報. | Wǒ kēn nǐ pù í-yàng. Yào-shih wǒ-mên yú hǎo hsiāo-hsi tê shíh-hou, pù-kuán(8) tsěn-mo máng wó yěh yào k'àn-i-k'àn pào. |
| 30.(B) 無線電報告要緊的消息，比新聞紙早，所以我就不要看報了. 哦，我差 | Wú-hsièn-tièn pào-kào yào-chǐn-tê hsiāo-hsi, pǐ hsīn-wén-chíh tsǎo, só-í wǒ chiù pú yào k'àn pào lê. Ó, wǒ ch'à- |

| | | |
|---|---|---|
| | 不多忘了買收音機的燈泡子. 回頭打完電報, 請你提醒我. | pu-tō wàng lê mǎi shōu-yīn-chī-tê tēng-p'ào-tzŭ. Huí-t'óu tǎ wán tièn-pào, ch'íng ni t'í-hsíng wo. |
| 31.(A) | 好, 回頭我提醒你一下. 你看, 這不是電報局嗎? | Hǎo, huí-t'óu wǒ t'í - hsíng ni í - hsià(9). Nǐ k'àn, chè pú shìh tièn - pào - chǘ ma? |
| 32.(B) | 我們快進去罷. | Wǒ - mên k'uài chìn - ch'ü pa. |

NOTES:

(1) "Hsīn-wến" and "hsiāo-hsi" can be used interchangeably in the sense of daily "news". But "hsīn-wến", literally "newly heard", is a formal expression for news or for new ideas discovered by research, while "hsiāo-hsi" may mean a rumor, or confidential information.

(2) "Tuì mièn" means "opposite, the opposite side, face to face".

(3) "Í-yàng", "the same, the same manner, of the same kind, alike", is a common idiom. The phrase is used as an adjective, adverb, or noun.

(4)The subject is omitted in this sentence, which may be translated literally as follows: "Well, how do [you] know [that one] should use what numbers?"

(5) "Ch'éng lê" and "hsíng lê" 行了 both mean "that will do, that will be all right, and can be used interchangeably.

(6) "Hǎo-kuò", literally "easy to pass [the time]", means "comfortable, happy".

(7) Note that "kūng-fu" is omitted after "méi-yǔ", in order to avoid repetition. In this construction, as in English, a slight pause usually marks the omission.

(8) "Pù-kuǎn" has the sense of "regardless, no matter, in spite of". Used as a verb, it means "not to care, not to be responsible". For example: "Wǒ pù kuǎn" - "I don't care" or "It's none of my business".

(9) "Í-hsià" is a colloquial expression for "one time, one moment, one blow". For example: "Tǎ t'a í-hsià" - "Strike him a blow".

3. Translation

1.(A) Please tell me, where is the telegraph office?

2.(B) From here, the nearest telegraph office is across the street from the Communications Building.

3.(A) Can [one] send both foreign and domestic telegrams from there?

4.(B) I think [one] can, because this telegraph office is very large.

5.(A) Is sending an English telegram the same as sending a Chinese one?

6.(B) It's very easy to send an English telegram. To send a Chinese one is troublesome.

7.(A) I have never yet sent a Chinese telegram; please tell me how to send [one].

8.(B) To send a Chinese telegram, it is necessary to translate each word into a number.

9.(A) In that case, how [does one] know which numbers should be used?

10.(B) Consult a telegraph code book, then you will know. But there are two kinds of telegraph code book. One kind is the public code, one kind is the private (or, secret) code.

11.(A) Tomorrow is Christmas; I want to send a telegram of greetings to my family. [For] that should [I] use the private code or the public code?

12.(B) This is an ordinary matter; it will be all right just to use the public code.

13.(A) Which would be better for me to send, a cable or a radiogram?

14.(B) I think it's the same. Let's go to ask at the telegraph office.

15.(A) How's today's news?

16.(B) I haven't seen today's paper yet, but last night I listened to the radio. The news is very good.

17.(A) Does that radio receiver of yours have short-wave?

18.(B) Both long and short. The news that I heard yesterday was broadcast from America.

19.(A) Which broadcasting station was it?

20.(B) It was N.B.C.

21.(A) Do you often listen to the radio?

22.(B) I frequently do. When I'm unhappy, I like to listen to the stories in the radio, to cheer [myself] up.

23.(A) After listening, do you immediately feel better?

24.(B) After listening, in my heart (or, mind) I feel happy.

25.(A) Do you listen to news concerning great affairs of the nation?

26.(B) I also listen to news concerning great affairs of the nation.

27.(A) Well then, do you still read newspapers every day?

28.(B) Not always (literally, not certainly); [when I] have time then [I] read [them], [when I] haven't, then [I] don't read.

29.(A) You and I are not the same. (If) when we have good news, no matter how busy [I am], I still want to take a look at the newspaper.

30.(B) The radio reports important news earlier than the newspapers do, so I don't want to read the newspapers. Oh, I nearly forgot to buy radio receiver tubes. Later, after sending the telegram, please remind me.

31.(A) All right, later I'll remind you. Look, isn't this the telegraph office?

32.(B) Let's go in quickly.

4. Exercises

a. "Fill-in" sentences

| | |
|---|---|
| 1. Wǒ yào tǎ ... ... tièn-pào. | I want to send a ... telegram. |
| 2. Wǒ chīn-t'ien chüéh-tê ... | I feel ... today. |
| 3. Nǐ hùi k'àn Chūng-wến ... ma? | Can you read Chinese ... ? |
| 4. T'ā ch'áng t'īng ... ... | He often listens to ... ... |
| 5. Měi-kuo yǔ tō-shǎo .. ... ... (t'ái)? | How many ... ... (stations) are there in America? |
| 6. ... ... kuǎng-pō pù hěn ch'īng-ch'u. | ... ... broadcasts are not very clear. |
| 7. Ní měi t'iēn tōu ... ... ? | Do you ... ... every day? |

b. Translate into English:

1. 中國話容易學還是難學？
2. 你們應當常練習說中國話.
3. 我很喜歡聽無線電,報告國家大事.
4. 今天的消息好不好？
5. 請你開開無線電,我們聽聽音樂.
6. 他在廣播電台作事.
7. 請你跟我去電報局打一個電報.

8. 我要給Smith先生打一個賀電,因為今天是他的生日.

9. 你今天覺得怎麼樣?

10. 請你不要拿我開心.

11. 不管我怎麽忙,我每天都要看幾分鐘報.

c. Translate into Chinese:

1. When you have time, please send this telegram for me.
2. I want to send a cable to my brother.
3. Shall I go to visit a friend, or [stay] at home to study?
4. [For] a telegram that is not important, [you] may use the public code.
5. Please come to my house to listen to the news.
6. He gets up earlier than I do every day.
7. Please remind me to buy lamp bulbs, because these bulbs are broken.
8. Buy me a Chinese newspaper, and help me to translate it into English.
9. If you help me, after two months I shall be able to read a Chinese newspaper.
10. This thing is too heavy; I cannot lift it up.
11. I have many good friends here; I feel very happy (k'āi-hsīn).

PART VI, LESSON 34

## Lesson 34 In a Bank

1. Vocabulary

| | | |
|---|---|---|
| 銀 | yín | Silver, money. |
| 銀行 | yín-háng | Bank [ì-chiā yín-háng or í-kê yín-háng]. |
| 款 | k'uǎn | Fund, money, sum. Item. [ì-pí 筆 k'uǎn, an amount of money.] |
| 支 | chīh | Branch. To pay, to draw money. |
| 支票 | chīh-p'iào | Check [ì-chāng chīh-p'iào]. |
| 存 | ts'ún | To keep, to deposit. Alive. |
| 以爲 | ǐ-wéi | To consider, to regard as, to think, to presume. |
| 現錢 | hsièn-ch'ién | Ready money, cash. |
| 會 | k'uài | To calculate. See also p. 30. |
| 計 | chì | To count, to calculate. |
| 會計 | k'uài-chì | Cashier [í-kê k'uài-chì]. |
| 市 | shìh | Market, fair, city. Municipal. [Seldom used alone.] |
| 行市 | háng-shih | Rate of exchange, market rate. |
| 簽 | ch'iēn | To sign, to endorse. Label. A bamboo slip for divination. |
| 簽字 | ch'iēn-tzǜ | Signature. To endorse, to sign one's name. |
| 簽名 | ch'iēn-míng | Signature. To endorse, to sign one's name. |
| 數 | shǔ<br>shù | To count.<br>Number, amount. |
| 匯 | huì | To remit, to advance money. |
| 匯票 | huì-p'iào | Draft [ì-chāng huì-p'iào]. |
| 存款 | ts'ún-k'uǎn | To deposit money. A deposit [ì-pǐ ts'ún-k'uǎn]. |
| 辦 | pàn | To do, to manage, to transact. |
| 辦法 | pàn-fǎ | Measure, method of transacting business [í-kê pàn-fǎ]. |
| 票子 | p'iào-tzǔ | Paper money [ì-chāng p'iào-tzǔ]. |
| 金 | chīn | Gold. |
| 美金 | Měi-chīn | Gold dollars, American money. |
| 招 | chāo | To hail, to beckon, to call. |

| | | |
|---|---|---|
| 待 | tài<br>tāi | To wait for, to treat.<br>To stay at a place. |
| 招待 | chāo-tài | To entertain, to treat, to wait upon, to serve. |
| 取 | ch'ǚ | To take, to choose. |
| 算 | suàn | To calculate, to take into account, to regard as. |
| 打算 | tǎ-suan | To plan, to intend. |
| 旅行支票 | lǚ-hsíng chīh-p'iào | Traveler's check [ì-chāng lǚ-hsíng chīh-p'iào]. |
| 社 | shè | Society, company. |
| 中國旅行社 | Chūng-kuo Lǚ-hsíng Shè | China Tourist Bureau. |
| 青年 | ch'īng-nién | Youth ("green years"). |
| 青年會 | Ch'īng-nién-hùi | Youth Association, the Young Men's Christian Association. |
| 熟 | shóu | Well acquainted with. Ripe, cooked. |
| 立 | lì | To establish, to stand. Instantly. |
| 立刻 | lì-k'è | Immediately. |
| 既 | chì | Already, since [seldom used alone]. |
| 然 | ján | However, but, yes [seldom used alone]. |
| 既然 | chì-ján | Since, whereas. This being the case ... |
| 許 | hsǚ | Perhaps. About. To allow, to promise. |
| 也許 | yéh-hsǚ (1) | Perhaps. |
| 指教 | chǐh-chiào | To teach, to instruct. Advice. |
| 除 | ch'ú | To deduct, to take away, to get rid of. |
| 以外 | ǐ-wài | Besides, beyond. See also p. 221. |
| 除了.....以外 | ch'ú lê ... ǐ-wài | Besides, except. |
| 肯 | k'ěn | To be willing to. |
| 並 | pìng | Together with. Two together [seldom used alone]. Also. Definitely (before a negative). |
| 且 | ch'iěh | Moreover, and. |
| 並且 | pìng-ch'iěh | Moreover, besides. |
| 方法 | fāng-fǎ | Means, method [í-kê fāng-fǎ]. |

2. Conversation

1.(A) 這個地方我不熟;你知道那一個銀行好?請你介紹一家給我.

Chè-kê ti-fang wǒ pù shóu; nǐ chīh-tao nǎ-i kê yín-háng hǎo? Ch'íng ni chièh-shào ì-chiā kéi wo.

2.(B) 我的錢是存在大陸銀行.我認識那兒的經理.你要是想在那兒存錢,我可以跟你去見他.

Wǒ-tê ch'ién shìh ts'ún tsài Tà-lù Yín-háng(2). Wǒ jèn-shih nà-êrh-tê chīng-lǐ. Nǐ yào-shih hsiǎng tsài nà-êrh ts'ún ch'ién, wó k'ě-i kēn nǐ ch'ǜ chièn t'a.

3.(A) 我有五百多塊錢要存在銀行.你以爲存在大陸銀行好嗎?

Wó yǔ wú-pǎi tō k'uài-ch'ién yào ts'ún tsài yín-háng. Ní ǐ-wéi ts'ún tsài Tà-lù Yín-háng hǎo ma?

4.(B) 你存了以後,是不是常要取錢?

Nǐ ts'ún lê ǐ-hòu, shìh-pu-shih ch'áng yào ch'ǚ ch'ién?

5.(A) 不,我不常要取錢.我打算把這一筆款存兩年.

Pū, wǒ pù ch'áng yào ch'ǚ ch'ién. Wó tǎ-suan pǎ chè-i-pí k'uǎn ts'ún liǎng nién.

6.(B) 既然你想存兩年,也許存在交通銀行好.

Chì-ján ní hsiǎng ts'ún liǎng nién, yéh-hsǚ ts'ún tsài Chiāo-t'ūng Yín-háng hǎo.

7.(A) 爲甚麼?

Wèi shén-mo?

8.(B) 因爲他們給的利

Yīn-wèi t'ā-mên kěi-tê lì-

| | |
|---|---|
| 錢高一點，也很可靠. | ch'ién kāo ì - tiĕn, yéh hĕn k'ĕ-k'ào. |
| 9.(A) 我還有一件事要請你指教. | Wŏ hái yŭ í - chièn shìh yào ch'íng ni chĭh-chiào. |
| 10.(B) 不要客氣，甚麽事? | Pú yào k'è - ch'i, shén - mo shìh? |
| 11.(A) 除了這筆錢以外，我有一張匯票，兩張支票. 不知道他們肯不肯給我換現錢. | Ch'ú lê chè-pĭ ch'ién ĭ - wài, wó yŭ ì - chāng huì-p'iào, liăng-chāng chīh-p'iào. Pù chīh-tao t'ā-mên k'ĕn-pu-k'ĕn kéi wo huàn hsièn-ch'ién. |
| 12.(B) 我想他們肯罷. 並且，你要是在那裏存錢，一定沒有問題. | Wó hsiăng t'ā - mên k'ĕn pa. Pìng-ch'iĕh, nĭ yào-shih tsài nà-li ts'ún ch'ién, í - tìng méi-yŭ wèn - t'í. |

(At the Bank)

| | |
|---|---|
| 13.(C) 先生，我還想請教你一件事. 我要到別的地方去旅行. 路上帶的錢太多了不方便; 你看我應當怎麽樣辦? | Hsiēn-shêng, wŏ hái hsiáng ch'ĭng-chiào ni í - chièn shìh. Wŏ yào tào piéh-tê tì-fang ch'ù lŭ-hsíng. Lù shàng tài tê ch'ién t'ài tō lê pù fāng-pièn; nĭ k'àn wŏ yīng-tāng tsĕn-mo yàng pàn? |
| 14. 會計: 你旅行的時候，是中國旅行 | K'uài - chì: Ní lŭ - hsíng - tê shíh-hou, shìh Chūng-kuo Lŭ-hsíng |

| | |
|---|---|
| 社招待你嗎？要是他們招待你，他們可以給你想辦法，不要你帶很多的現錢。 | Shè chāo-tài ni ma? Yào-shih t'ā-mên chāo-tài ni, t'ā-mên k'ě-i kéi ni hsiǎng pàn-fǎ, pú yào nǐ tài hěn tō-tê hsièn-ch'ién. |
| 15.(C) 我不一定住在中國旅行社，也許住在青年會。 | Wǒ pù í-tìng chù tsài Chūng-kuo Lǚ-hsíng Shè, yéh-hsǔ chù tsài Ch'īng-nién-huì. |
| 16. 會計：不管你打算待在甚麼地方，我看你可以把所有的錢換成旅行支票。 | K'uài-chì: Pù-kuǎn ní tǎ-suan tāi(3) tsài shén-mo tì-fang, wǒ k'àn ní k'ě-i pǎ só-yǔ-tê ch'ién huàn ch'éng lǚ-hsíng chīh-p'iào. |
| 17.(C) 好，謝謝你；我要這樣辦。請你數一數這些錢，一共是五百元。 | Hǎo, hsièh-hsieh ni; wǒ yào chè-yàng pàn. Ch'íng ni shǔ-i-shu chè-hsieh ch'ién, í-kùng shìh wú-pǎi yüán. |
| 18. 會計：不錯，是五百元。這本旅行支票，請你在每張上簽名罷。 | K'uài-chì: Pú ts'ò, shìh wú-pǎi yüán. Chè-pěn lǚ-hsíng chīh-p'iào, ch'íng ni tsài měi chāng shàng ch'iēn-míng pa(4). |
| 19.(C) 請問，現在美金是甚麼行市？ | Ch'ǐng wèn, hsièn-tsài Měi-chīn shìh shén-mo háng-shih? |
| 20. 會計：一百塊中國錢換……　…… | K'uài-chì: Ì-pǎi k'uài Chūng-kuo ch'ién huàn ... ... ... (5) |

| | |
|---|---|
| 塊美國錢. | k'uài Mĕi-kuo ch'ién. |
| 21.(C) 五百塊中國錢合美金多少? | Wú-păi k'uài Chūng-kuo ch'ién hế Mĕi-chīn tō-shăo? |
| 22. 會計: 合美金……元. | K'uài-chì: Hế Mĕi-chīn ... ... yüán. |
| 23.(C) 甚麽方法寄錢最快? | Shến-mo fāng-fă chì ch'ién tsuì k'uài? |
| 24. 會計:電匯最快. 你現在要寄錢到美國去嗎? | K'uài-chì: Tièn-huì tsuì k'uài. Nĭ hsièn-tsài yào chì ch'ién tào Mĕi-kuo ch'ù ma? |
| 25.(C) 不, 我現在沒有錢寄到美國去; 我是給我的朋友打聽的. 打攪你得很. 謝謝. | Pū, wŏ hsièn - tsài méi - yŭ ch'ién chì tào Mĕi-kuo ch'ù; wŏ shìh kéi wŏ-tê p'ếng-yu tă-t'īng tê. Tá-chiáo ni tê hến(6), hsièh-hsieh. |

NOTES:

(1) "Yéh-hsŭ" and "huò-chế", in the sense of "perhaps", can be used interchangeably. The former is more colloquial and is more commonly used in north China, while the latter is more literary and more often used in the south.

(2) See special note on word order, at end of this lesson.

(3) The Distinction between "Chù" 住 and "Tāi" 待

Both "chù" and "tāi" have the sense "to stay". The former is more formal or literary, the latter is colloquial.

(4) It would be incorrect to say "Ch'íng ni ch'iēn-míng tsài mĕi chāng shàng" - "Please sign your name on each page", instead of "Ch'íng ni tsài mĕi chāng shàng ch'iēn-míng"; because "tsài mĕi chāng shàng" is a modifier, an adverbial phrase of place modifying "ch'iēn-míng".

(5) Since the exchange rate frequently changes, this place is left blank, to be filled in by the student so that the sentence will be correct and up-to-date.

(6) This is a Szechwan expression meaning, literally, "Disturb you to the extreme". It has become popular in Kuo-yü. Many people prefer to say "hǎo-tê hěn" instead of "hěn hǎo".

3. Translation

1.(A) I am not familiar with this place; do you know which bank is good? Please recommend one to me.

2.(B) My money is deposited at the Ta-lu Bank. I know the manager there. If you would like to deposit money there, I can go with you to see him.

3.(A) I have more than five hundred dollars [which I] want to deposit in a bank. Do you think it would be good to deposit it in the Ta-lu Bank?

4.(B) After you deposit it, will you often want to draw money?

5.(A) No, I shall not often want to draw money. I plan to deposit the sum of money [for] two years.

6.(B) Since you are thinking of depositing it [for] two years, perhaps it would be well to deposit it in the Chiao-t'ung Bank.

7.(A) Why?

8.(B) Because the interest they give is a little higher, [and they are] also very reliable.

9.(A) I have another matter [on which] I want to ask your advice (or, to ask you to advise me).

10.(B) Don't be formal; what is it?

11.(A) Besides this amount of money, I have a draft [and] two checks. I wonder whether they will be willing to cash them for me.

12.(B) I think they will be willing. Moreover, if you deposit money there, [there should] certainly be no question [about it].

13.(C) Sir, I still want you to advise me on a matter. I want to go traveling to some other places. Carrying too much money on the way is not convenient. What do you think I should do?

14.Cashier: When you travel, will the China Tourist Bureau serve you? If they serve you, they will think of some method [so that] you will not have to take too much cash with you.

15.(C) I am not certain about staying at the China Tourist Bureau; perhaps I shall stay at the Y.M.C.A.

16.Cashier: No matter where you plan to stay, I think it would be all right to change all the money into traveler's checks.

17.(C) Fine, thank you. I shall do it that way. Please count this money, altogether five hundred dollars.

18.Cashier: Right, it is five hundred dollars. In this book of traveler's checks, please sign your name on each one.

19.(C) May I ask, what is the rate of exchange for gold dollars now?

20.Cashier: A hundred dollars Chinese money changes [for] ... ... gold dollars.

21.(C) How much would five hundred dollars Chinese money amount to in gold dollars?

22.Cashier: It would amount to ... ... gold dollars.

23.(C) What is the fastest way of sending money?

24.Cashier: It is fastest to send it by wire. Do you want to send money to America now?

25.(C) No, I have no money now to send to America; I am making inquiries for a friend. [I] have disturbed you too much, thank you.

4. Exercises

a. "Fill-in" sentences:

| | |
|---|---|
| 1. Ch'íng ni tsài ... ... ... shàng ch'iēn-míng. | Please sign (this check / letter / book etc.). |
| 2. Wǒ yào mǎi ì-pěn ... ... ... ... | I want to buy a (copy of ... ... ... / book of traveler's checks etc.). |
| 3. Wǒ yào ts'ún ... ... | I want to deposit (a book / money / things etc.). |
| 4. Ch'íng ni kéi wo ... ... | Please (do something for me) / (give me ... ...). |
| 5. Ch'ǐng wěn, hsièn-tsài ... shìh shěn-mo háng-shih? | May I ask, what is the rate of exchange now for ... ? |
| 6. Ch'ú lê ... ... ǐ-wài, hái yǔ ... ... ? | Besides ... ... , is there still ... ... ? |
| 7. Wó yéh-hsǔ ... ... , yéh-hsǔ pù ... ... | Perhaps I shall ... ... , perhaps not. |
| 8. Wǒ pù kuán nǐ ... ... , nǐ í-tìng ... ... | I don't care whether you ... , you must ... ... |

b. Translate into English:

1. 這個問題我要請你指教.

2. 也許他不肯給我換支票.

3. 他既然認識你,他就可以給你打聽了.

4. 旅行的時候,最方便是用旅行支票、
5. 並且,支票帶得太多很危險、
6. 我所有的錢都存在大陸銀行、
7. 那個銀行很可靠,我也跟那兒的會計很熟、
8. 我剛到這個地方來,所看見的人,都是生人,一個熟人也沒有、
9. 我要把這二十塊錢的票子換成五塊的,一塊的,跟一毛的、
10. 我在銀行的存款不多了、

c. Translate into Chinese:

1. I want to send this money immediately.
2. What is the rate of exchange for gold dollars today?
3. Please send him one thousand Chinese dollars by wire.
4. One thousand Chinese dollars amounts to ... ... dollars gold.
5. I will not draw money from the bank within (translate: ǐ-nèi) these three years.
6. Besides this amount of money, I have a draft for two hundred dollars.
7. I often have to use checks.
8. It is inconvenient to have too many people living in one room.
9. Which is the most reliable bank? Please make inquiries for me.
10. Which is the fastest way to send money? Please advise [me].

## CONVERSATIONAL CHINESE

### On Word Order and Sentence Structure

Students who have reached this point have become familiar with most of the grammatical elements used in Chinese. One of the points which are likely to cause confusion is the word order of a Chinese sentence, especially as the same idea may be expressed in different ways by various speakers. This is because Chinese, like English, is a highly flexible language, and at the same time very idiomatic. Sometimes a sentence which is grammatically correct sounds strange to a native Chinese because it is not idiomatic. Detailed and reliable rules to govern the word order of sentences have not been discovered for the Chinese language as for German or French. The best practice for students is to listen constantly to the speech of idiomatic speakers of Chinese and to read idiomatic Chinese texts, until at last they can feel that one expression is awkward or strange to their ears and another sounds harmonious or correct. On the other hand, no student can expect to learn to speak correctly without some understanding of the grammatical structure of the language. A study of sentence analysis will clear up many obscurities and help to prevent inaccuracies in translation.

To explain Chinese grammar entirely by the use of the same grammatical terms that are used to explain European languages is a dangerous practice, for the grammatical elements of one language are not necessarily the same as the corresponding elements of another language. Chinese and English grammatical elements do not always correspond. But it is also not very good to create many new terms which may sometimes be confusing. For this reason, as far as possible, the well-known terms are used here. In order to help the student acquire a sense of the proper construction of a Chinese sentence, its various elements will be discussed in turn.

The simplest Chinese sentence consists of two parts: subject and predicate. A more complicated sentence may have four or five parts: subject, verb, direct object, indirect object, complement, besides the adjectives and adverbs which may modify these parts.

A. Subject

The subject of a Chinese sentence is that part which precedes the predicate. It includes common and proper nouns, personal, relative, interrogative, and demonstrative pronouns, numerals, and infinitives. In Chinese, when proper and common nouns relate to the same subject, the proper noun always precedes, as in "Chāng hsiēn-shêng", "Pěi-chīng Lǘ-kuǎn", never follows as in English "Mr. Jones", "Hotel Peking".

B. Verb

The essential part of the predicate is the verb. There are simple and compound, transitive and intransitive verbs. In general, the position of a simple or compound transitive verb in a sentence is the same in Chinese as in English.

| Subject | Verb | Object | | |
|---|---|---|---|---|
| "T'ā | chiào | wo" | - | "He calls me". |
| 他 | 叫 | 我 | | |

"Wǒ má-fan ni" - "I trouble you".
我 麻煩 你
"Wǒ tá-chiáo ni" - "I disturb you".
我 打擾 你

Some Chinese transitive verbs are formed into compounds which are used like intransitive verbs, by suffixing a noun which is the usual object of the verb. Such compounds are "nièn-shū" 念書 - "to read-books, to study"; "ch'īh-fàn" 吃飯 - "to eat-rice, to eat, to dine"; "tsò-shìh" 作事 - "to do-business, to work".

When such a compound is used intransitively, the adverb of place stands between the subject and the verb; it should never follow the verb. Examples:

| Subject | Adverb of place | Verb | |
|---|---|---|---|
| "Wǒ | tsài hsüéh-hsiào | nièn-shū" | - "I study at school". |
| 我 | 在學校 | 念書 | |
| "Wǒ | tsài fàn-t'īng | ch'īh-fàn" | - "I eat in the dining room". |
| 我 | 在飯廳 | 吃飯 | |
| "Wǒ | tsài wài-mien | tsò-shìh" | - "I work outside". |
| 我 | 在外面 | 作事 | |

Beginning students should guard against using such incorrect expressions as "Wǒ nièn-shū Chūng-wén tsài - - Tà-hsüéh" or "Wǒ ch'īh-fàn tsài fàn-t'īng".

In a sentence where no subject is expressed, or where the logical subject stands in the position of an object or complement, the adverbs of time or place, or both, precede the verb.

| Adverb of time | Adverb of place | Verb | | |
|---|---|---|---|---|
| "Tsó-t'ien | | hsià-yǔ | lê" | - "Yesterday [it] rained", or "Yesterday rain fell". |
| 昨天 | | 下雨 | 了 | |
| | "Tūng-pien | ch'ū | t'ài-yang lê" | - "In the east the sun came out". |
| | 東邊 | 出 | 太陽了 | |
| "Chīn-nien | É-kuo | hsià | tà hsüěh" | - "This year, [in] Russia, there is heavy snow". |
| 今年 | 俄國 | 下 | 大雪 | |

A compound consisting of a main verb and a co-verb, such as "chìn-lai" 進來 or "ch'ū-ch'ü" 出去, may be used alone like a single intransitive verb (see Lesson 15, note 3), or an adverb of place or an object may be inserted between the two parts. Examples:

"Chìn tào chè-li lai" 進到這裏來 - "Come in to this place".

"Ch'ū tào nà-li ch'ü" 出到那裏去 - "Go out there".

"Hsièn-tsài wǒ chì ch'ǐ-lai lê"現在我記起來了 - "I remember now".

"Ná ch'ū ì-pěn shū lai" 拿出一本書來 - "Take out a book".

C. Direct Object

As has already been indicated, the normal position of a direct object is after the verb, but there are exceptions.

a. When "pǎ"把 is used before the direct object, the object precedes the verb. Examples:

"Wó pǎ chō-tzǔ ná tsǒu lê" 我把桌子拿走了 - "I took the table away".

"Wó pǎ chè-pěn shū k'àn wán lê"我把這本書看完了 - "I read this book through".

b. When the object is followed by "yěh" 也 or "tōu"都 in the sense of "even" or with intensifying force, it precedes the verb.

"Wǒ shuí yěh pú jèn-shih" 我誰也不認識- "I do not know anyone at all".

"T'ā shén-mo shìh tōu pú tsò"他什麽事都不做 - "He does no work whatever".

"Wǒ hsièn-tsài í-kê ch'ién yěh méi-yǔ" 我現在一個錢也沒有- "I do not have even one penny now".

In these three sentences the direct objects are "shuí", "[shén-mo] shìh", and "[í-kê] ch'ién".

c. For the sake of emphasis, the object may sometimes precede the subject and verb. For example:

| Object | Subject | Verb | |
|---|---|---|---|
| "T'ā-tê huà<br>他的話 | wǒ<br>我 | t'īng pù tǔng"<br>聽不懂 | - "His speech I hear [but] do not understand". |
| "Nà-kê tzù<br>那個字 | wǒ<br>我 | k'àn pù ch'īng-ch'u"<br>看不清楚 | - "That character I can not see clearly". |

D. Indirect Object

The position of the indirect object and its relation with the direct object and with the verb are as follows:

a. The indirect object usually follows the verb and precedes the direct object.

| Subject | Verb | Indirect object | Direct object | | |
|---|---|---|---|---|---|
| "Chè-kê jén<br>這個人 | kěi<br>給 | hái-tzǔ<br>孩子 | t'áng<br>糖 | ch'īh"<br>吃 | - "This man gives the child candy to eat". |

"Wǒ chièh kěi t'a ch'ién" - "I lend him money".
我 借 給 他 錢

b. When "pǎ" 把 is used and the direct object precedes the verb, the indirect object follows the verb.

| Subject | Direct object | Verb | Indirect object | Complement | |
|---|---|---|---|---|---|
| "Chè-kê jén | pǎ t'áng | kěi | hái-tzǔ | ch'īh" | - "This man gives the child candy to eat". |
| 這個人 | 把糖 | 給 | 孩子 | 吃 | |
| "Wó | pǎ ch'ién | chièh kěi | t'a | yùng" | - "I lend him money to use". |
| 我 | 把錢 | 借給 | 他 | 用 | |

c. When the indirect object is preceded by a word meaning "for" or "in behalf of", it is placed before the verb.

| Subject | Indirect object | Verb | Direct object | |
|---|---|---|---|---|
| "Wó mǔ-ch'in | kéi wǒ tì-ti | tsò | hsiéh" | - "My mother makes shoes for my younger brother". |
| 我母親 | 給我弟弟 | 做 | 鞋 | |
| "Wó | kěi t'a | hsiěh | hsìn" | - "I write a letter for him". |
| 我 | 給他 | 寫 | 信 | |

Another way of expressing the same idea is to have the indirect object follow the direct object, but in this case "kěi" 給 in the sense of "to" must be inserted between them.

| Subject | Verb | Direct object | | Indirect object | |
|---|---|---|---|---|---|
| "Wó | kěi | ì-tǒ huā | kěi | Wáng hsiáo-chieh" | - "I give a flower to Miss Wang". |
| 我 | 給 | 一朶花 | 給 | 王小姐 | |
| "Wǒ | sùng | ì-p'íng chiú | kěi | Chāng hsiēn-shêng" | - "I send a bottle of wine to Mr. Chang". |
| 我 | 送 | 一瓶酒 | 給 | 張先生 | |

This Chinese expression corresponds exactly to the English "I give a flower to Miss Wang", but it is less usual and less idiomatic than the examples in paragraph (a) above.

NOTE: See also Lesson 17, pp. 118-119, on the uses of "kěi".

E. Complement

The complement usually follows the object.

| Subject | Verb | Object | Complement | |
|---|---|---|---|---|
| "Wó | ch'ǐng | t'a | tsò chiào-yüán" | - "I invite him to be a teacher". |
| 我 | 請 | 他 | 做教員 | |
| "Wǒ | k'àn | t'a | hěn měi" | - "I consider her (literally, see her [as]) very beautiful". |
| 我 | 看 | 他 | 很美 | |

F. Adjectives

Adjectives include single words, phrases, and relative clauses. Although modifiers are not an integral part of the sentence, their position must be discussed.

In Chinese as in English, adjectives are used both attributively (in which case they precede the noun modified) and predicatively. When used predicatively, the Chinese adjective needs no copula ("shìh" 是), but follows the noun directly. For example: "kāo shù" 高樹 - "tall tree", "shù kāo" - "[the] tree is tall"; "hsiǎo shān" 小山 - "small hill", "shān hsiǎo" 山小 - "[the] hill is small"; "t'iēn ch'áng" 天長 - "the day is long"; "Chè-kê mén k'uān, nà-kê mén chǎi" 這個門寬,那個門窄 - "This door is wide, that door is narrow". The word "shìh" is used as a copula only for special emphasis, as in "Shù shìh kāo" 樹是高 - "The tree is [really] tall".

Adjectives of indefinite quantity, such as those meaning much, little, many, few, enough, too much ("t'ài tō" 太多), are habitually used predicatively* in Chinese. Thus it is idiomatic to say "Chè-kê fáng-tzŭ-tê jén t'ài tō" 這個房子的人太多 - "The men in this room are too many", rather than "Chè-kê fáng-tzŭ yǔ t'ài tō-tê jén" 這個房子有太多的人 - "There are too many people in this room".

An adjectival phrase consisting of two or more words followed by the particle "tê" 的 usually precedes the noun it modifies. For example:

| Adjective | Noun | | |
|---|---|---|---|
| "Tǐng-hòu-tê | chǐh" | - | "very thick paper". |
| 頂厚的 | 紙 | | |
| "Sān-ch'ǐh-kāo-tê | shù" | - | "three-foot-high tree". |
| 三尺高的 | 樹 | | |

If the adjectival expression includes a verb, it is a relative clause, which, again, precedes the noun it modifies, although in English translation it usually follows. For example:

---

*"Hěn tō" 很多 - "much, many, very much, very many", and "hěn shǎo" 很少 - "little, few, very little, very few", may either precede or follow the noun they modify. Thus for "There are many people", one may say "Yú hěn tō-tê jén" or "Jén hěn tō". But it is not idiomatic to say "Yǔ t'ài tō-tê jén" for "There are too many people"; one should say "Jén t'ài tō lê".

| Subject | | Predicate | |
|---|---|---|---|
| Relative clause | Noun | | |
| "Wó sŏ-nièn-tê 我所念的 | Chūng-kuo tzù 中國字 | tōu wàng lê" 都忘了 | - "The Chinese characters which I studied have all been forgotten". |
| "Chièh-nǐ-ch'ién-tê 借你錢的 | nà-kê jén 那個人 | tsŏu lê" 走了 | - "That man who borrowed your money has gone away". |

NOTE that, in translating Chinese into English, one should first determine which word is the main substantive and which are modifiers, or which part of the sentence is principal clause and which relative clause, if any, and should translate the main substantive or the principal clause first. This hint will be found useful in translating either pai-hua or classical Chinese.

G. Adverbs

Adverbs include indicators of time, of place, and of manner; they include both words and phrases which tell when, where, and how, and also interrogative expressions such as "tsài ná-li?" 在那裏 - "where?", "tsěn-mo yàng?" 怎麼樣 - "how?", as well as some others.

Many Chinese adverbs precede the word they modify. The following words, when used adverbially, are among these: "tǐng" 頂, "hěn" 很, "tsuì" 最, "tō" 多, "tà" 大, "lǎo" 老, "kòu" 夠, "shíh-fēn" 十分. There are many others.

Some adverbs and adverbial phrases follow the adjectives they modify, as in the expressions "hǎo chí lê" 好極了 or "hǎo-tê hěn" 好的很 - "very good", "nán-k'àn chí lê" 難看極了 - "very ugly". Many other such expressions will be met with further along in these lessons.

Some adverbs and adverbial phrases follow the verb they modify, as in English "She sings beautifully".

| Subject | Verb | Adverb | |
|---|---|---|---|
| "Wŏ 我 | t'īng 聽 | ts'ò lê" 错了 | - "I heard wrongly" or "I misunderstood you". |
| "Wŏ 我 | tá 答 | tuì lê" 對了 | - "I answered correctly". |
| "T'ā 他 | nièn-shū 念書 | hěn k'uài" 很快 | - "He reads very fast". |
| "T'ā 他 | shuō-huà 說話 | t'ài màn" 太慢 | - "He speaks too slowly". |

For emphasis, the last two sentences can be idiomatically expressed as follows:

"T'ā nièn-shū nièn-tê hěn k'uài" 他念書念的很快 - literally, "He reads books reading to the degree of being very fast".

"T'ā shuō-huà shuō-tê t'ài màn" 他說話說的太慢 - literally, "He speaks speaking so as to be too slow".

When an adverb or adverbial phrase denotes a specific point or period of time, it precedes the verb.

"Wǒ míng-t'ien yào ch'ǜ" 我明天要去 - "I will go tomorrow".

"Chè sān nién tāng-chūng wǒ méi chièn kuò í-kê Chūng-kuo jén" 這三年當中我沒見過一個中國人 - "During these three years I have not seen a Chinese".

"Ts'úng ch'ǜ-nien shíh-í-yüèh tào chīn-nien èrh-yüèh, chè-kê tì-fang ch'áng hsià-hsüěh" 從去年十一月到今年二月，這個地方常下雪 - "From November of last year until February of this year, [it] snowed frequently in this place".

When an adverb indicates length of time, or stresses duration, it follows the verb.

"Wǒ tsài nà-li tāi lê sān t'iēn" 我在那裏待了三天 - "I stayed there three days".

"Wǒ tsài Chūng-kuo chù lê wǔ nién" 我在中國住了五年 - "I lived in China five years".

Adverbs of time precede adverbs of place. Examples:

| Subject | Adverb of time | Adverb of place | Verb |
|---|---|---|---|
| "Nǐ | chīn-t'ien | tsài chè-êrh | ch'īh-fàn"-"You eat here today". |
| 你 | 今天 | 在這兒 | 吃飯 |
| "Wǒ | tsó-t'ien | tsài hsüéh-hsiào | nièn-shū"-"I studied at school yesterday". |
| 我 | 昨天 | 在學校 | 念書 |

Adverbs of time or place precede the subject if the element of time or place is stressed in the sentence, but if the subject is stressed these adverbs follow it. Examples:

Emphasis on time: "Míng-t'ien Wáng hsiēn-shêng yào lái" 明天王先生要來 - "Tomorrow Mr. Wang will come".

Emphasis on subject: "Wáng hsiēn-shêng míng-t'ien yào lái" 王先生明天要來 - "Mr. Wang will come tomorrow".

Emphasis on place: "Tsài Měi-kuo wǒ nièn kuò sān nién shū" 在美國我念過三年書 - "In America, I studied for three years".

Emphasis on subject: "Wǒ tsài měi-kuo nièn kuò sān nién shū" 我在美國念過三年書 - "I studied in America for three years".

Adverbs of manner usually precede the verb they modify, as in "màn-mān-tê tsǒu" 慢慢的走 - "walk slowly". The positions of other adverbs in Chinese sentences is much the same as in English, therefore it is not necessary to go into further detailed discussion. See also Lesson 8, note 13, Lesson 9, notes 11 and 12, and Lesson 21, note 2.

## Summary

This brief survey of word order and sentence structure may be summarized as follows:

1. The subject usually precedes the predicate.
2. A proper noun precedes a common noun.
3. Adjective phrases and relative clauses precede the noun they modify.
4. Many adjectives and adverbs precede the word they modify.
5. Some adjectives and adverbs may follow the word they modify.
6. Names of larger divisions of time and place precede names of smaller divisions (Lesson 9, note 12).
7. Adverbial expressions denoting a specific point or period of time precede the verb; adverbial expressions stressing duration follow the verb.
8. Adverbs of time precede adverbs of place.

The following are common patterns of word-order in Chinese sentences:

1. Subject - predicate.
2. Subject - verb - object.
3. Object - subject - verb.
4. Subject - verb - object - complement.
5. Subject - adverb of time - verb.
6. Adverb of time - subject - verb.
7. Subject - adverb of place - verb.
8. Adverb of place - subject - verb.
9. Subject - adverb of time - adverb of place - verb.
10. Adverb of time - adverb of place - verb - object (in this sentence pattern no subject is expressed).
11. Subject - verb - indirect object - direct object.
12. Subject - verb - direct object - kěi - indirect object.
13. Subject - indirect object - verb - direct object.
14. Subject - pǎ - direct object - verb.
15. Subject - pǎ - direct object - verb - indirect object - complement.

This list of sentence patterns might be greatly extended. We have tried to keep the rules as brief as possible in order to avoid confusing the student. It is hoped that the student will master these simple grammatical hints and practise them so thoroughly that eventually he will be able to speak and write correct Chinese without hesitation.

### Exercise

Correct the following sentences, with special attention to idiomatic word order.

1. 我來昨天
2. 我怕旅行危險一點兒.
3. 我在住旅館 St. Louis.
4. 我有錢在上海銀行存.
5. 我走路在大街上.
6. 我跟你可以到學校走一塊兒嗎?
7. 我要買我的姐姐給有的中國東西.
8. 我不曉得多少是來回票從 Chicago 到 New York.
9. 中國人我所認識的是都回國了.
10. 請你簽字在每張上.

## Lesson 35 In a General Store

1. Vocabulary

| | | |
|---|---|---|
| 貨 | huò | Goods, cargo [seldom used alone]. |
| 物 | wù | Thing, animal, goods [seldom used alone]. |
| 貨物 | huò-wù | Goods. |
| 百貨店 | păi-huò-tièn | Store dealing in miscellaneous goods, "five and ten", small department store, general store [í-kê păi-huò-tièn]. |
| 百貨公司 | păi-huò kūng-ssū | Department store [í-kê păi-huò kūng-ssū]. |
| 品 | p'ĭn | Article, goods. Grade. [Seldom used alone.] |
| 日用品 | jìh-yùng-p'ĭn | Article of daily use [í-chièn jìh-yùng-p'ĭn]. |
| 衣 | ī | Clothing, coat [í-chièn ī]. |
| 襯 | ch'èn | Inner garment, underclothing [seldom used alone]. |
| 衫 | shān | Shirt, robe [seldom used alone]. |
| 襯衫 | ch'èn-shān | Shirt [í-chièn ch'èn-shān]. |
| 內衣 | nèi-ī | Undershirt [í-chièn nèi-ī]. |
| 穿 | ch'uān | To bore through. To put on (as clothing), to wear. |
| 戴 | tài (1) | To put on, to wear (as hat, glasses, gloves). |
| 賤 | chièn | Cheap, mean, poor. |
| 儉 | chiĕn (or chièn) | Economical, frugal. |
| 省 | shĕng | To save. Frugal. Province. |
| 儉省 | chién-shĕng | Economical, frugal. |
| 刀片 | tāo-p'ièn | Razor blade [í-kê tāo-p'ièn]. |
| 造 | tsào | To make, to build. |
| 打 | tă | To do (see also p.77). Dozen (in this sense the character is a transliteration of the first syllable of "dozen"). |
| 價 | chià | Price, value. |
| 打價 | tă-chià | To make a bargain, to reduce. |
| 受 | shòu | To receive, to accept, to bear, to suffer. An auxiliary forming a passive. |
| 騙 | p'ièn | To cheat, to swindle. |

| | | |
|---|---|---|
| 伺 | tz'ǔ | To spy, to wait upon. |
| 伺候 | tz'ǔ-hou | To wait upon, to serve. |
| 巾 | chīn | Napkin, kerchief, towel. |
| 毛巾 | máo-chīn | Towel [ì-t'iáo máo-chīn]. |
| 襪子 | wà-tzŭ | Stockings, socks [ì-shuāng wà-tzŭ]. |
| 手巾 | shǒu-chīn | Handkerchief [í-k'uài shǒu-chīn]. |
| 副 | fù | Deputy, vice--. A second, a duplicate. A numerative of pairs, etc. |
| 手套 | shǒu-t'ào | Gloves [í-fù shǒu-t'ào]. |
| 毛衣 | máo-ī | Woolen sweater [í-chièn máo-ī]. |
| 全 | ch'üán | The whole, entire, all, complete. |
| 胰子 | í-tzŭ | Soap [ì-k'uài í-tzŭ]. |
| 盒 | hế | Small box [í-kê hế-tzŭ]. A numerative of things contained in small boxes. |
| 牙 | yá | Tooth [í-kê yá]. |
| 膏 | kāo | Ointment, cream, plaster [seldom used alone]. |
| 牙膏 | yá-kāo | Tooth paste [ì-hế yá-kāo]. |
| 牙粉 | yá-fěn | Tooth powder [ì-pāo yá-fěn]. |
| 頂 | tǐng | Top, extreme. A numerative of hats, sedan chairs, etc. See also pp. 232, 281. |
| 帽子 | mào-tzŭ | Hat, cap [ì-tǐng or í-kê mào-tzŭ]. |
| 壞 | huài | Bad, spoiled, ruined, useless. |
| 句 | chǜ | A sentence. |
| 雖 | suī | Supposing. Though, even if. |
| 雖然 | suī-ján | Although, nevertheless. |
| 照 | chào | To look after, to reflect. According to. A pass. |
| 顧 | kù | To care for, to look after, to consider. |
| 照顧 | chào-kù | To pay attention to, to buy of, to patronize. |

2. Conversation

| | |
|---|---|
| 1.(A) 我想去百貨店買一點兒日用品，你要同我去嗎? | Wó hsiǎng ch'ü pǎi-huò-tièn mǎi ì - tiěn - êrh jìh-yùng-p'ǐn, nǐ yào t'úng wǒ ch'ü ma? |
| 2.(B) 好，我去。我要買幾件襯衫。我所有的內衣都穿破了。 | Hǎo, wǒ ch'ü. Wǒ yào mái chǐ-chièn ch'èn-shān. Wǒ só-yǔ - tê nèi - ī tōu ch'uān-p'ò lê. |
| 3.(A) 我知道中山路有一個很好的百貨店。那裏差不多甚麼都有。我們就去那裏買東西罷。 | Wǒ chīh-tao Chūng-shān Lù yǔ í - kê hěn hǎo - tê pǎi-huò-tièn. Nà - li ch'à - pu - tō shén - mo tōu yǔ. Wǒ - mên chiù ch'ü nà - li mǎi tūng-hsi pa. |
| 4.(B) 好罷。我們就去。 | Hǎo pa. Wǒ - mên chiù ch'ü. |
| 5.(A) 請問，你們這裏有保險刀跟刀片嗎? | Ch'ǐng wèn, nǐ - mên chè - li yǔ páo-hsiěn tāo(2) kěn tāo-p'ièn ma? |
| 6.(C) 我們有兩種保險刀；你要那一種? | Wǒ-mên yǔ liáng chǔng páo-hsiěn tāo; nǐ yào nǎ - i chǔng? |
| 7.(A) 請你把兩種都拿給我看一看。 | Ch'íng ni pá liáng chǔng tōu ná kéi wo k'àn - i - k'an. |
| 8.(C) 這種是英國貨，價錢貴一點兒。那種是美國造的，價錢賤一點兒。 | Chè chǔng shìh Yīng-kuo huò, chià-ch'ien kuèi ì - tiěn-êrh. Nà chǔng shìh Měi-kuo tsào-tê(3), chià-ch'ien chièn ì - tiěn - êrh. |
| 9.(A) 我看我還是儉省 | Wǒ k'àn wǒ hái-shìh chién-shěng |

| | |
|---|---|
| 一點兒罷．我要這一種便宜的．請你也給我半打刀片．多少錢? | ì - tiĕn - êrh pa. Wŏ yào chè-i chŭng p'ién - i - tê. Ch'íng ni yéh kéi wo pàn - tă tāo - p'ièn. Tō - shǎo ch'ién? |
| 10.(C) 兩塊九毛五． | Liăng-k'uài chiŭ-máo wŭ. |
| 11.(A) 兩塊五毛錢可以嗎? | Liăng-k'uài wŭ-máo ch'ién k'ĕ-i ma? |
| 12.(C) 先生，少了不賣．我們這裏不打價;說一句就是一句． | Hsiēn-shêng, shăo lê pú mài. Wŏ - mên chè - li pù tă - chià; shuō í chù chiù - shih í chù. |
| 13.(A) 好極了．我喜歡在這裏買東西．雖然貴一點，不會受騙． | Hăo chí lê. Wó hsĭ - huan tsài chè -li măi tūng-hsi. Suī-ján kuèi ì - tiĕn, pú huì(4) shòu p'ièn. |
| 14.(C) 是的．先生，你還要買甚麼? | Shìh - tê. Hsiēn -shêng, nĭ hái yào măi shén - mo? |
| 15.(A) 我還要買很多的東西;可是先請你伺候我的朋友罷，因爲他站了很久了．叫你受等，對不起． | Wŏ hái yào mái hĕn tō - tê tūng-hsi; k'ĕ-shih hsiēn ch'íng ni tz'ù - hou wŏ - tê p'éng - yu pa, yīn-wèi t'ā chàn lê hĕn chiŭ lê. (To B) Chiào ni shòu-tĕng(5), tuì pu ch'ĭ. |
| 16.(C) 先生，你要買甚麼? | Hsiēn-shêng, nĭ yào măi shén-mo? |
| 17.(B) 我要買一條毛巾， | Wŏ yào măi ì-t'iáo máo-chīn, |

三雙襪子，半打手巾；你們有沒有？

sān-shuāng wà-tzŭ, pàn-tá shǒu-chīn; nǐ - mên yǔ - mei - yu?

18.(C) 我們有，請你等一會兒，我就拿出來。

Wǒ - mên yǔ, ch'íng ní těng ì - huǐ - êrh, wǒ chiù ná ch'u-lai.

19.(B) 我還要買一副皮手套，一件毛衣，一頂帽子。

Wǒ hái yào mǎi í - fù p'í shǒu - t'ào, í - chièn máo - ī, ì - tǐng mào - tzŭ.

20.(C) 你要試一試嗎？

Nǐ yào shìh - i - shih ma?

21.(B) 不行，帽子戴不上，手套也戴不上。這件毛衣恐怕也不行，大小不合。

Pù hsíng, mào - tzŭ tài pú shàng, shǒu-t'ào yěh tài pú shàng. Chè-chièn máo - ī k'ǔng-p'à yěh pù hsíng, tà - hsiǎo pù hế.

22.(C) 先生，對不起，我們這裏的手套，毛衣，帽子，給你都太小了，因爲你太高太大了。

Hsiēn - shêng, tuì pu ch'ǐ, wǒ - mên chè - li tê shóu - t'ào, máo - ī, mào - tzŭ, kéi ni tōu t'ài hsiǎo lê, yīn - wèi nǐ t'ài kāo t'ài tà lê.

23.(A) 沒有法子，我們到別的百貨公司去找罷。

Méi - yǔ fá - tzŭ, wǒ - mên tào piéh-tê pǎi-huò kūng-ssū ch'ù chǎo pa.

24.(C) 先生們要買的東西都全了嗎？

Hsiēn-shêng-mên yào mǎi tê tūng-hsi tōu ch'üán lê ma?

25.(A) 我還要買些日用

Wǒ hái yào mǎi hsiēh jìh-yùng-

| | |
|---|---|
| 品：牙膏，牙刷，胰子，玻璃杯．請你給我最好的，不要壞的． | p'ǐn: yá - kāo, yá - shuā, í - tzǔ, pō - li pēi. Ch'íng ni kéi wo tsuì - hǎo - tê, pú yào huài - tê. |
| 26.(C) 先生，我們的貨物都是頂好的．牙膏賣完了．你要牙粉嗎? | Hsiēn-shêng, wǒ - mên-tê huò-wù tōu shìh tíng - hǎo - tê. Yá-kāo mài wán lê. Nǐ yào yá-fěn ma? |
| 27.(A) 好，我要牙粉．還有比這個更好的沒有? | Hǎo, wǒ yào yá - fěn. Hái yú pǐ chè - kê kèng - hǎo - tê méi-yǔ? |
| 28.(C) 沒有了．這是最好的． | Méi - yǔ lê. Chè shìh tsuì-hǎo - tê. |
| 29.(B) 一共多少錢? | Í - kùng tō - shǎo ch'ién? |
| 30.(C) 讓我算一算．一共兩塊七毛錢． | Jàng wo suàn - i suàn. Í - kùng liǎng-k'uài ch'ī-máo-ch'ién. |
| 31.(B) 這是三塊錢． | Chè shìh sān-k'uài-ch'ién. |
| 32.(C) 我找給你三毛． | Wó chǎo kéi ni sān-máo. |
| 33.(A) 請你給我包作兩包罷． | Ch'íng ni kéi wo pāo tsò liǎng pāo pa. |
| 34.(C) 先生，請你以後多多的照顧．再見． | Hsiēn-shêng, ch'íng ni ǐ - hòu tō - tō - tê chào - kù. Tsài chièn. |

NOTES:

(1) "Ch'uān" and "tài" are easily confused. Aside from the careful definitions which are given here, attention should be called

to the general distinction that "tài" is used in speaking of things which are worn on the head or on the hands, and "ch'uān" in speaking of articles which are worn elsewhere, such as coats, trousers, socks, shoes.

(2) "Páo-hsiěn tāo", literally "insured knife", is a term used in the neighborhood of Peking to mean a safety razor.

(3) See discussion of passive voice, at end of this lesson.

(4) Note that "huì", in the sense of "to be able, will, shall, may", is frequently used as a future auxiliary for a verb whose action may be conceived as a probable consequence of conditions. Cf. Lesson 18, note 7. Examples:

> "Wǒ huì hsiěh" 我會寫 - "I know how to write", or "I can write".
>
> "Wǒ huì kào-su t'a" 我會告訴他 - "I shall (or, I may) tell him".
>
> "Nǐ pú chiào t'a, t'ā yěh huì lái-tê" 你不叫他，他也會來的 - "[If] you do not call him, he is very likely [nevertheless] to come".

(5) "Shòu-těng" is a courteous phrase used to one who has been kept waiting. Literally, it means "to endure waiting".

2. Translation

1.(A) I intend to go to a general store to buy some articles of daily use. Do you want to go with me?

2.(B) All right, I'll go. I want to buy a few shirts. All the underwear I have is all worn out.

3.(A) I know there is a very good general store on Chung Shan Road. They have almost everything there. Shall we just go there to buy things?

4.(B) All right. Let's go right away.

5.(A) May I ask, do you have safety razors and blades here?

6.(C) We have two kinds of safety razors. What kind do you want?

7.(A) Please bring both kinds for me to see.

8.(C) This kind is made in England (English goods); the price is a little higher. That kind is made in America; the price is a little cheaper.

9:(A) I think I shall still be a little economical; I want this cheaper kind. Please give me half a dozen blades too. How much (money) [is it]?

10.(C) Two dollars and ninety-five cents.

11.(A) Will two dollars and fifty cents be all right?

12.(C) Sir, it is not sold for less. We do not bargain here; when we say something it means exactly that (literally, say one sentence, is exactly one sentence).

13.(A) Very good. I like to shop here. Although it's a little more expensive, [one] will not be cheated.

14.(C) That's right, sir. Do you want to buy anything more?

15.(A) I still want to buy many things, but first please wait on my friend, because he has been standing for a very long time. - I have kept you waiting, I'm sorry.

16.(C) Sir, what do you want to buy?

17.(B) I want to buy a towel, three pairs of socks, half a dozen handkerchiefs; do you have them?

18.(C) We have; please wait a moment, I'll bring them out.

19.(B) I still want to buy a pair of leather gloves, a sweater, [and] a hat.

20.(C) Would you like to try them on?

21.(B) It won't do. [I] can't put on the hat, [I] can't put on the gloves either. I'm afraid this sweater also won't do; the size doesn't fit.

22.(C) Sir, I'm sorry, the gloves, sweaters, and hats which we have here are all too small for you, because you are too tall and too big.

23.(A) There's no [other] way; let's go to another department store to look.

24.(C) Gentlemen, have you finished all the shopping you want to do?

25.(A) I still want to buy some articles of daily use: tooth paste, toothbrush, soap, a glass tumbler. Please give me the best; [I] don't want [anything] bad.

26.(C) Sir, our goods are all of the highest quality. The tooth paste is sold out. Do you want tooth powder?

27.(A) All right, I'll [take] tooth powder. Is there anything that is still better than this?

28.(C) There is not. This is the best.

29.(B) How much money is it altogether?

30.(C) Let me calculate. Altogether, two dollars and seventy cents.

31.(B) This is three dollars.

32.(C) I return to you thirty cents in change.

33.(A) Please wrap [the things] in two packages for me.

34.(C) Sir, please patronize us more and more after this. Goodby.

4. Exercises

a. "Fill-in" sentences

| | |
|---|---|
| 1. Wǒ chè- ... ... p'ò lê. | This ... ... of mine is worn out. |
| 2. Wǒ yào pǎ chè-chāng ...-k'uài-ch'ién-tê p'iào-tzǔ huàn ch'éng ... ... | I want to change this (number) ... - dollar banknote into (fives (singles (dimes etc.). |

| | |
|---|---|
| 3. Hsièn-tsài mǎi ... ... hěn pù júng-i. | Now it is very difficult to buy ... .. |
| 4. Tūng-t'ien yào ch'uān ... ... | In winter [one] needs to wear ... |
| 5. Wǒ ch'áng mái Měi-kuo ... | I often buy American ... |
| 6. Chè-kê kūng-ssū-tê huò-wù hěn ... ... | The goods of this store are very ... ... |
| 7. Chīn-nien Shèng-tàn-chiéh, wǒ yào kěi t'a chì ... ... | This Christmas, I want to send him ... ... |
| 8. Wǒ yào mǎi ì tǎ ... ... | I want to buy a dozen ... ... |
| 9. T'ā suī-ján ... ... , k'ě-shih ... ... | Although he ... ... , yet ... ... |

b. Translate into English:

1. 不客氣的舖子沒有人常去照顧.
2. 這個百貨店的東西不壞,價錢也很便宜.
3. 我有一次在那裏買了一頂帽子跟一件襯衫.
4. 這一條毛巾破了.你看,這兒有一個窟窿.
5. 這個公司有美國造的毛衣.
6. 這雙鞋的大小不合,你買回去也沒有用.
7. 請你給我買一雙襪子,一副手套.

8. 我的保險刀現在不能用,因為沒有刀片、

9. 我們買的東西,一共多少錢?

10. 我不會算賬、我應當找給你多少?

c. Translate into Chinese:

1. I often buy things at the general store on Chung-shan Road.
2. Today I put on a new hat and a pair of new shoes.
3. All the things that I want,I can get at the small general store.
4. These articles of daily use should be bought first.
5. Last week I bought a cheap shirt - I was cheated.
6. Although I do not have much (tō-shǎo) money, I like to buy good things.
7. I must save some money and mustn't spend too much.
8. These English goods will be still more expensive after a few weeks.
9. I wanted to buy a good toothbrush, but I was unable to find [one]. (Use cháo.)
10. There is no help for it; you must do it yourself.

## On the Passive Voice

Passive constructions, which have been briefly referred to in previous notes, will be discussed here more in detail. There are two common sentence patterns of passive construction.

a. Subject - shìh - actor - verb - tê.

"Chè-chǔng shìh Měi-kuo tsào tê"這種是美國造的 - "This kind was made in America".

"Chè-shuāng hsiéh shìh wó mǎi tê"這雙鞋是我買的 - "This pair of shoes was bought by me".

b. Subject - indicator of passive voice - actor - verb - lê.

"Chè-chù huà pèi wǒ shuō kuò lê" 這句話被我說過了 - "This sentence has been said by me".

In these patterns we can see that the subject is placed first, the verb last, and the indicator of the passive voice in the middle. The order of the sentence is different from that in English.

There are several indicators of the passive voice:

a. "Shòu" 受 - "to receive, to suffer".

"Pú huì shòu p'ièn" 不會受騙 - "will not suffer cheating", i.e., will not be cheated.

b. "Pèi" 被 - "to suffer, to be an object of", is the most commonly used of this group of verbs. Examples:

"Pèi ná" 被拿 - "to be seized".

"Wǒ pèi t'ā p'ièn lê" 我被他騙了 - "I was cheated by him".

c. "Chiào" 叫 - "to call, to cause", is used passively in the sense of "to be called", and also serves as an auxiliary in passive constructions. Examples:

"T'ā chiào Lǐ Sān" 他叫李三 - "He is called Li San".

"T'ā chiào jén tǎ lê" 他叫人打了 - "He was beaten by somebody".

d. "Jàng" 讓 - "to yield, to allow". Example:

"Chè-pěn shū jàng t'ā mǎi lê" 這本書讓他買了 - "This book was bought by him".

e. "Kěi" 給 - "to give". Example:

"Wǒ-tê shū kěi t'ā tiū lê" 我的書給他丟了 - "My book was lost by him".

Examples of sentences which contain passive constructions:

1. 他的東西叫人拿走了.
T'ā-tê tūng-hsi chiào jén ná tsǒu lê.

2. 他的家叫火燒了.
T'ā-tê chiā chiào huǒ shāo lê.

3. 你別讓他騙了.
Nǐ piéh jàng t'ā p'ièn lê.

4. 這個東西讓他拿去了.
Chè-kê tūng-hsi jàng t'ā ná-ch'ü lê.

5. 你被他打了.
Nǐ pèi t'ā tǎ lê.

6. 他被我請了.
T'ā pèi wó ch'ǐng lê.

7. 今天有人請客;我是被請的一個.
Chīn-t'ien yǔ jén ch'ǐng k'è; wǒ shìh pèi-ch'ǐng-tê í-kè.

8. 我要念的書,被人拿走了.
Wǒ yào nièn-tê shū, pèi jén ná tsǒu lê.

9. 那塊點心被小孩子吃了.
Nà k'uài tiěn-hsīn pèi hsiǎo hái-tzǔ ch'īh lê.

10. 那個字是我寫的.
Nà-kê tzǔ shìh wó hsiěh-tê.

11. 這個鐘是英國造的.
Chè-kê chūng shìh Yīng-kuo tsào-tê.

12. 這個電報是什麼時候打的?
Chè-kê tièn-pào shìh shén-mo shíh-hou tǎ-tê?

## Lesson 36 Special Expressions and Review

### 1. Useful Phrases and Word Combinations

[The following material is supplied partly to help students acquire a large working vocabulary, and partly to suggest varied subjects for classroom conversation. Each student in turn may be required to make a sentence using one of the suggested phrases, or may be asked a question using these expressions.

The material in this section is intended to help students to be prepared for unexpected questions, and to answer readily on various subjects. In the beginning, it does not matter if the sentences are short or incomplete.]

| | | | |
|---|---|---|---|
| 1. | 洗一個澡 | hsǐ í-kê tsǎo | To take a bath. |
| 2. | 洗手 | hsí shǒu | To wash the hands. |
| 3. | 點燈 | tiěn těng | To light a lamp. |
| 4. | 開燈 | k'āi těng | To turn on a light. |
| 5. | 關燈 | kuān těng | To turn out the light. |

| | | |
|---|---|---|
| 6. 取下來 | ch'ǚ-hsia-lai | To take down. |
| 7. 取出來 | ch'ǚ-ch'u-lai | To take out, to select. |
| 8. 算了罷 | suàn lê pa | That will do; to have had enough. |
| 9. 算不了甚麼 | suàn pu liǎo shến-mo | Of no special account; it's a mere nothing. |
| 10. 不上算 | pú shàng suàn | Does not pay. |
| 11. 這還合算 | chề hái hế suàn | This is still worth while, is still economical. |
| 12. 很不合算 | hến pù hế suàn | Very uneconomical, very unwise. |
| 13. 算錯了 | suàn ts'ò lê | To reckon wrongly. |
| 14. 支局 | chīh-chű | Branch office. |
| 15. 支出 | chīh-ch'ū | Expenditure. To disburse. |
| 16. 辦不到 | pàn pu tào | Unable to accomplish; impracticable. |
| 17. 辦不了 | pàn pu liǎo | Cannot be managed; unable to handle. |
| 18. 他很會辦事 | T'ā hến huì pàn-shìh | He is very capable in managing affairs. |
| 19. 成語 | ch'ếng-yǚ | Set phrase, idiom. |
| 20. 現成的 | hsièn-ch'ếng-tê | Ready-made. |
| 21. 底下人 | tǐ-hsia-jên | The man below; a servant, follower. |
| 22. 底片 | tǐ-p'ièn | Photographic negative. |
| 23. 難題 | nán t'í | Difficult problem. |
| 24. 囘答 | huí-tá | Reply, answer. |
| 25. 報告 | pào-kào | To report. A report. |
| 26. 報館 | pào kuǎn | Newspaper office. |
| 27. 管事的 | kuǎn-shìh-tê | Housekeeper, manager. |
| 28. 我不管 | wǒ pù kuǎn | I don't care; it's none of my business. |
| 29. 管錢的 | kuǎn-ch'ién-tê | Cashier. |
| 30. 管不住 | kuǎn pu chù | Unable to control. |
| 31. 你管你的罷 | Nǐ kuán nǐ-tê pa | You mind your own business. |
| 32. 管理得很好 | kuán-lǐ tê hến hǎo | Well managed. |

33. 沒有人管理 Méi-yǔ jén kuán-lǐ No one takes care [of it].
34. 挖苦人 wā-k'u jén To ridicule people.
35. 不要挖苦我 Pú yào wā-k'u wo Don't ridicule me; don't be sarcastic.
36. 破壞 p'ò-huài To destroy, to spoil. Demolition.
37. 大家 tà-chiā Together, all together.
38. 我們大家一塊兒去 Wǒ-mên tà-chiā í-k'uài-êrh ch'ù Let's all go together.
39. 床鋪 ch'uáng p'ū Bed and bedding.
40. 鋪床 p'ū ch'uáng To make a bed.
41. 滿意 mǎn-ì Satisfactory, satisfied.
42. 歡送會 huān-sùng huì Farewell party.
43. 接車 chiēh ch'ē To meet [someone] at the railway station.
44. 送車 sùng ch'ē To say goodby at the railway station.
45. 送她回去 sùng t'a huí-ch'ü Escort her home.
46. 你有甚麼意見? Ní yǔ shén-mo ì-chien? What idea do you have? What is your idea?
47. 我沒有甚麼意見 Wǒ méi-yǔ shén-mo ì-chien I have no idea.
48. 意見不合 ì-chien pù hé Of different opinions.
49. 鬧意見 nào ì-chien To be at odds, to wrangle over conflicting opinions.
50. 太鬧了 t'ài nào lê Too noisy.
51. 還剩多少? Hái shèng tō-shǎo? How much is left?
52. 剩一半 shèng í-pàn Half is left.
53. 剩不了多少 shèng pù liǎo tō-shǎo Not much is left.
54. 天亮了 T'iēn liàng le It is dawn.
55. 天還沒亮 T'iēn hái méi liàng It is not yet dawn.
56. 預先 yù-hsiēn Beforehand.
57. 請你預先告訴我 Ch'íng ni yù-hsiēn kào-su wo Please tell me beforehand.
58. 安全 ān-ch'üán Safe, in security.
59. 安心 ān hsīn To compose the mind.
60. 掛念 kuà-nièn To be anxious, to think of, to worry.

| | | |
|---|---|---|
| 61. 請你安心, 不要掛念我 | Ch'íng nǐ ān-hsīn, pú yào kuà-nièn wo | Please feel at ease, don't worry about me. |
| 62. 安排 | ān-p'ai | To arrange, to set in order. |
| 63. 甚麼事情都安排好了 | Shén-mo shìh-ch'ing tōu ān-p'ai hǎo lê | Everything has been set in good order. |
| 64. 不要信他所說的話 | Pú yào hsìn t'ā sǒ-shuō-tê huà | Don't believe what he says. |

2. Story

[The following narrative will be found useful not only for vocabulary review but also as reading practice. Or, a portion of it may be read aloud to the class to be translated at once, in order to train their aural comprehension.]

NOTE: This story introduces one new character: "tǎo" 島 - "island", which occurs in "Ch'īng-tǎo" 青島 (postal system "Tsingtao"), the name of a port on the coast of Shantung.

王大春要到北平清華大學(1)去念書. 他是上海人. 從小就一直在上海, 還沒有甚麼機會到別的地方旅行. 他聽說北平的學校很好, 並且有很多有名的地方, 所以這次他能去北平是他最快樂的一件事.

在青島他有幾個好朋友, 所以他預備在那兒停幾天, 玩一玩, 看一看朋友.

那時候正是夏天. 坐火車很熱, 所以他想先坐船到青島. 從上海到青島的船雖然不少, 可是夏天坐船旅行的人很多. 他給船公司打了幾次電話才定好了一間二等艙房.

大春的船是禮拜五上午八點鐘開的. 那天他起來

的很早. 六點半吃了早飯; 他的母親跟妹妹已經把他的行李都預備好了. 大春一共有四件行李, 兩個箱子, 兩個皮包. 七點鐘他們雇了一輛汽車, 全家開到碼頭去.

那天, 上船的旅客很多. 等他找着了他的艙房, 已經是開船的時候. 他看着船慢慢的離開碼頭, 過了幾分鐘, 他就看不見他的母親跟妹妹了.

那兩天天氣很好, 風平浪靜, 在船上很舒服. 下午大春坐在船面上看報的時候, 有一個外國人走過來問他:『先生到那兒去?』

大春說:『我到北平去, 可是先要到青島停幾天. 先生貴姓? 現在去那兒?』

外國人說:『敝姓 Johnson; 我的中國姓是張. 我也要到北平去.』

大春:『張先生, 貴國是那國? 你的中國話說的眞好.』

張先生:『過奬, 過奬. 敝國是美國. 我在美國學過一年中國話, 所以我現在還能說一點兒. 你貴姓? 你到北平去作甚麼?』

大春:『敝姓王. 我去念書.』

張先生:『你要進那一個學校?』

大春:『清華大學. 張先生去過北平嗎?』

張先生:『我去年去過北平一次. 上次我是坐飛機去的. 幾個鐘點就到了. 我也去清華玩過. 那個學校很大, 地方也很美. 你有機會在那個學校念書, 真太好了.』

他們說到這裏, 聽見飯廳裏打鐘. 他們知道已經是吃晚飯的時候, 就一塊兒進去吃飯.

大春每天都跟張先生在一塊兒玩. 他們慢慢的成了很好的朋友. 張先生告訴了他很多美國的故事也常常幫他練習英文. 所以時候很容易的就過去了.

禮拜日晚上十點鐘, 船到了青島. 從遠的地方看岸上的燈, 特別的好看. 大春在離開上海的前一天, 已經寫了一封航空信給他的朋友, 張廣識, 請他來接船. 所以他剛下船就看見了廣識.

廣識:『大春! 一路上(2)都好嗎?』

大春:『這次旅行海上一點風浪都沒有, 所以很舒服. 你近來好嗎? 我們三年沒有見面了; 你還是跟從前一樣.』

廣識:『我很好, 謝謝. 我已經給你在大陸旅館定好了一間房. 那家旅館是青島最大的一個, 房間舒服, 交通方便, 價錢也不太貴. 我希望你喜歡那個地方. 現在我們就雇一輛汽車一直去罷, 好不好?』

大春:『好罷. 這太麻煩你了, 多謝. 我的脚夫就在前面, 讓他把我的行李拿到汽車上去罷.』

大春在青島三天; 廣識帶着他到各地方去玩. 他玩的很開心. 第四天大春想他應當快點兒去北平了. 就對廣識說:『廣識, 我想我應當走了. 明天早上九點三十五分鐘有一班特別快車到北平. 要是我錯過這班快車, 就要等到星期日.』

廣識:『後天沒有車去北平嗎?』

大春:『後天只有慢車. 我不喜歡坐慢車, 因爲太慢了.』

廣識:『我很希望你在這裏能再多玩幾天. 旣然你一定要走, 我也沒有法子. 還有好些地方你沒有去過. 你下次來的時候, 我再帶你去罷.』

星期四的早上廣識雇了一輛汽車跟大春到火車站去. 大春坐的是二等睡車, 所以他一點不麻煩的就上了火車. 火車還有十分鐘才開. 大春對廣識說:『請回罷. 不要等車開了. 謝謝你. 我到了北平一定立刻給你寫信.』

廣識說:『好. 希望你常給我寫信. 再見.』

NOTES:

(1) "Ch'īng-huá", usually spelled "Tsing Hua" in English, is the name of a famous university in Peiping.

(2) "Í-lù" means "on the way, throughout the whole journey".

3. Translation

Wang Ta-ch'un intended to go to Tsing Hua University, in Peiping, to study. He is a native of Shanghai. Since childhood straight [through his life], he had been in Shanghai, and had not yet had a chance to travel to other places. He had heard it said that the schools in Peiping are very good, and besides that there are many famous places [there]. Therefore, this time when he could go to Peiping was one of his most delightful events.

In Tsingtao he had several good friends. Therefore he planned to stay there a few days, to amuse himself for a while, and to visit his friends.

At that time it was just summertime. To travel by train is very hot, so he thought he would go first by boat to Tsingtao. Although the boats from Shanghai to Tsingtao are not few, yet in summer people who travel by boat are very many. He had to telephone to the steamship company several times before he could reserve a second-class cabin.

Ta-ch'un's boat sailed Friday at eight in the morning. That day he got up very early. At half past six he ate breakfast; his mother and his younger sister had already packed his baggage. Ta-ch'un had four pieces of baggage altogether, two trunks and two suitcases. At seven o'clock they hired a taxi, [and] the whole family drove to the wharf.

On that day, there were many travelers on board ship. By the time he had found his cabin, it was already sailing time. He saw the ship slowly leave the wharf, and after a few minutes he (then) could not see his mother and sister.

The weather was delightful on those two days. The wind blew gently and the waves were calm. It was very comfortable on board. In the afternoon, as Ta-ch'un was reading a newspaper on the top deck, there was a foreigner who came over and asked him, "Where are you going, sir?"

Ta-ch'un replied, "I am going to Peiping, but I shall stop off at Tsingtao for a few days. What is your name, sir? Where are you going now?"

The foreigner said, "My (humble) name is Johnson. My Chinese surname is Chang. I am going to Peiping too."

Ta-ch'un: "Mr. Chang, what is your nationality? Your Chinese is very well spoken."

Mr. Chang: "You are too complimentary. I am an American. I studied Chinese in America for a year; so I can now speak a little. What is your name? What are you going to do in Peiping?"

Ta-ch'un: "My name is Wang. I am going to study."

Mr. Chang: "What school do you intend to enter?"

Ta-ch'un: "Tsing Hua University. Mr. Chang, have you been in Peiping?"

Mr. Chang: "I went to Peiping once last year. Last time I went by airplane. In only a few hours we had arrived. I also visited Tsing Hua. That school is very large, the place also is very beautiful. It is really wonderful that you have the opportunity to study at that university."

As their conversation reached this point, they heard the bell being struck in the dining hall. They knew it was already supper time, and they went in together to eat.

Every day, Ta-ch'un amused himself together with Mr. Chang. Gradually they became very good friends. Mr. Chang told him many American stories, and frequently helped him to practice English. So the time passed very easily.

On Sunday evening at ten o'clock the ship arrived at Tsingtao. From a distance it was especially beautiful to see the lights along the shore. A day before he left Shanghai, Ta-ch'un had written an air mail letter to his friend Chang Kuang-shih, asking him to come to meet the ship. So as soon as he got off the ship, he immediately saw Kuang-shih.

Kuang-shih: "Ta-ch'un! Were you well on the whole journey?"

Ta-ch'un: "During this trip, the sea was very calm (literally, no wind and waves at all). So it was very comfortable. How are you these days? We haven't seen [each other's] faces for three years; you still look the same as before."

Kuang-shih: "I am very well, thank you. I have already reserved a room for you in the Continental Hotel. That hotel is one of the biggest in Tsingtao. The rooms are comfortable, transportation is convenient, [and] the price also is not too high. I hope you will like that place. Now let's hire a taxi right away and drive there directly, is that all right?"

Ta-ch'un: "All right. This troubles you too much, many thanks. My porter is just ahead, let him take my baggage to the car."

Ta-ch'un was in Tsingtao three days; Kuang-shih took him to visit various places. He enjoyed himself very happily. On the fourth day Ta-ch'un thought that he should hurry a little to go to Peiping. He then said to Kuang-shih, "Kuang-shih, I think I ought to leave. Tomorrow morning at nine-thirty-five there is an express train to Peiping. If I miss this train, I'll have to wait till Sunday."

Kuang-shih: "Is there no train to Peiping the day after tomorrow?"

Ta-ch'un: "The day after tomorrow there is only a slow train. I don't like to take a slow train because it's too slow."

Kuang-shih: "I wish very much that you could enjoy yourself here a few days longer. Since you really have to go, I can't help it either. There are still many places to which you haven't gone. Next time you come, I'll take you [sight-seeing] again."

Thursday morning Kuang-shih hired a taxi and accompanied Ta-ch'un to the railway station. Ta-ch'un took a second-class sleeper, so he had no trouble at all when he boarded the train. There were still ten minutes before the train started. Ta-ch'un said to Kuang-shih: "Please go back. You don't have to wait until the train leaves. Thank you. When I arrive in Peiping, I'll certainly write you a letter at once."

Kuang-shih said: "All right, I hope that you will write to me often. Goodby!"

## Lesson 37 Review (continued)

王大春坐的火車早上七點鐘到了北平的東車站.他下了車叫一個脚夫把他的行李拿下火車.他把兩件小的行李隨身帶,兩件大的行李交給運輸公司,讓運輸公司那天下午拿到清華大學.

他在車站門口看見了他的老朋友,李國英.李國英一看見他就說:『老王,(1)我今天早上很早就起來了.天還沒有亮,我就坐洋車到車站接你.等了兩個鐘頭你才來.』

大春:『小李,(2)對不起.我坐的火車從天津慢了半點鐘,所以晚了.』

國英:『現在已經差不多八點了.我們趕快坐電車回我家吃早飯罷.家母昨天晚上告訴我,他今天早上給你預備了鷄粥.他知道你很喜歡吃鷄粥.』

大春:『太麻煩你了.多謝,多謝.』

國英:『我們是老朋友了;别客氣了.你今天可以住在我家裏,明天早上我們坐洋車到青年會,從青年會我們可以坐公共汽車到清華大學去.』

大春跟國英到家的時候,國英的母親已經等了他們很久.大春先跟國英的母親說了幾句,後來大家就去飯廳吃早飯.大春喝了不少的粥,吃了兩片麵包.

吃過了飯，國英就帶大春到各地方去看看．大春，因爲在火車上沒有睡好，所以那天晚上他回來的很早．九點多就睡了．

第二天早上，國英差一刻八點起來．看見大春一個人在客廳裏看報．他就問大春：『今天的消息怎麽樣?』

大春：『沒有甚麽新的新聞.』

國英：『現在先別說國家大事了．讓我們去吃早飯罷．吃了早飯，我們還要趕青年會九點一刻的公共汽車去清華呢.』

他們九點五分到了青年會．他們每個人用四毛五分錢買了一張車票，上了公共汽車．那時候車裏已經有很多的人．那些人都是清華大學的學生跟教員．有不少的人跟國英點頭說話．

清華大學離北平不很遠；公共汽車走了半點鐘就到了．他們一下車就看見了大春的幾個熟朋友．大家見了面都很快樂．那天晚上大春就住在學校裏了．他告訴國英說：『國英，我想這兩天以內我不回北平去了．明天你回到北平以後，請你告訴李太太說我謝謝他．我去北平的時候，一定去你家給他老人家請安.』(3)

NOTES:

(1) "Lǎo" prefixed to the surname is a familiar manner of address to old friends and servants.

(2) "Hsiǎo" prefixed to the surname is a familiar manner of address to an intimate friend who is younger than the speaker.

(3) "Lǎo-jén-chia" is a polite expression used in referring to elderly persons or parents. Here "chia" is a suffix and loses its tone.

Translation

The train which Wang Ta-ch'un took arrived at the East Station, Peiping, at seven o'clock in the morning. He got off the train and called a porter to take his baggage out of the train. He carried the two small pieces of baggage with him, and handed the two large pieces over to the transportation company, letting the transportation company take [them] to Tsing Hua University that afternoon.

At the entrance of the station, he saw his old friend, Li Kuo-ying. On seeing him, Li Kuo-ying then said: "Lao Wang, I got up very early this morning. When it had not yet dawned (literally, the sky not yet bright), I was already taking a ricksha to the station to meet you. [I] had waited two hours before you came."

Ta-ch'un: "Hsiao Li, I'm sorry. The train which I took was half an hour late leaving Tientsin. So [I am] late."

Kuo-ying: "Now it is nearly eight o'clock. Let's hurry to take a street car and return to my house to eat breakfast. Last night my mother told me that she would prepare chicken congee this morning for you. She knows that you like very much to eat chicken congee."

Ta-ch'un: "[I] trouble you too much, many thanks."

Kuo-ying: "We are old friends; don't be formal. Today you can stay at my house, tomorrow morning we shall ride in a ricksha to the Y.M.C.A., from the Y.M.C.A. we can take a bus to Tsing Hua University."

When Ta-ch'un and Kuo-ying arrived at [Kuo-ying's] home, Kuo-ying's mother had already been waiting for them a long time. Ta-ch'un first spoke a few words (literally, sentences) with Kuo-ying's mother, and then they all went together into the dining room to eat breakfast. Ta-ch'un drank not a little congee and ate two pieces of bread. After eating, Kuo-ying then took Ta-ch'un sight-seeing to various places. Ta-ch'un, because he had not slept well on the train, therefore returned very early that evening. After nine o'clock, he immediately went to sleep.

The next morning, Kuo-ying got up at a quarter to eight o'clock. He saw Ta-ch'un alone in the sitting room reading a newspaper. He then asked Ta-ch'un: "What kind of news is it today (literally, Today's news is what kind)?"

Ta-ch'un: "There is no new news."

Kuo-ying: "Now, we'd better not first talk about the great affairs of the nation. Let's go and eat our breakfast. After eating breakfast, we still have to catch the nine-fifteen bus at the Y.M.C.A. to go to Tsing Hua."

They arrived at the Y.M.C.A. at five minutes after nine. They each spent forty-five cents to buy a bus ticket, and got into the bus. At that time there were already very many people in the bus. Those people were all students and teachers of Tsing Hua University. There were not a few people who nodded to Kuo-ying and spoke to him.

Tsing Hua University is not very far from Peiping. The bus was going for half an hour, and then they arrived. As soon as they got down from the bus, they immediately saw several of Ta-ch'un's intimate friends. They were all very happy to see each other. That evening Ta-ch'un stayed at the school. He told Kuo-ying: "Kuo-ying, I think during these two days (literally, within these two days) I shall not go back to Peiping. Tomorrow, after you go back to Peiping, please tell Mrs. Li I thank her. When I go to Peiping, I shall certainly go to your house to pay my respects to your honored mother."

CONVERSATIONAL CHINESE

# PART VII IN VARIOUS SITUATIONS

## Lesson 38 In a Barber Shop

1. Vocabulary

| | | |
|---|---|---|
| 髮 | fǎ (1) | Hair of the head [seldom used alone]. |
| 頭髮 | t'óu-fa | Hair of the head [ì-kēn 根 t'óu-fa]. |
| 理髮 | lí-fǎ | To dress the hair. |
| 理髮館 | lí-fá-kuǎn | Hair-dressing shop, barber shop [í-kê or ì-chiā lí-fá-kuǎn]. |
| 師 | shīh | Teacher, expert. A division in the Chinese army. |
| 理髮師 | lí-fǎ-shīh | Hair-dressing expert, i.e., barber [í-kê lí-fǎ-shīh]. |
| 匠 | chiàng | Workman, mechanic [seldom used alone]. |
| 理髮匠 | lí-fǎ-chiàng (2) | Barber [í-kê lí-fǎ-chiàng]. |
| 又 | yù (3) | Again, also, furthermore. |
| 藝 | ì | Art, skill, technique [seldom used alone]. |
| 手藝 | shǒu-i | Skill in hand work, handicraft. |
| 脫 | t'ō | To take off. |
| 畫 | huà | Picture [ì-chāng huà]. To paint, to draw. |
| 畫報 | huà-pào | A pictorial magazine [ì-pěn huà-pào]. |
| 段 | tuàn | Section, part, paragraph, passage. |
| 大衣 | tà-ī | Overcoat [í-chièn tà-ī]. |
| 留 | liú | To keep, to detain, to leave behind. |
| 關係 | kuān-hsi | Relation, consequence. |
| 沒有關係 | méi-yǔ kuān-hsi | It is of no consequence, it doesn't matter. |
| 剪 | chiěn | To cut, as with scissors or shears. |
| 馬 | mǎ | Horse [ì-p'ī 匹 mǎ]. |
| 馬路 | mǎ-lù | Road, avenue [ì-t'iáo mǎ-lù]. |
| 由 | yú | From. To permit. |
| 刮 | kuā | To shave off, to scrape. |
| 臉 | liěn | Face (sometimes used in the sense of "reputation"). |

| | | |
|---|---|---|
| 刮臉 | kuā-liĕn | To shave. |
| 鬍子 | hú-tzŭ | Beard [ì-k'ŏu 口 hú-tzŭ]. |
| 另 | lìng | Separate. Another. Besides. |
| 另外 | lìng-wài | Over and above, extra. Besides. |
| 加 | chiā | To add to, to affix. |
| 梳 | shū | To comb. A comb [ì-pă shū]. |
| 舊 | chiù (4) | Old, worn out. Formerly. |
| 洗頭 | hsĭ-t'óu | To wash the head, to shampoo. |
| 淨 | chìng | Clean, pure. |
| 乾淨 | kān-ching | Clean. |
| 頭油 | t'óu-yú | Brilliantine. |
| 頭水 | t'óu-shuĭ | Hair lotion, hair tonic. |
| 本來 | pĕn-lái | Original. Originally, usually. |
| 暖 | nuăn | Warm. |
| 和 | hé | Agreeable. And, with (see p. 150). To mix. |
| 暖和 | nuăn-hê | Warm. |
| 費 | fèi | Fee. To spend. |
| 小費 | hsiăo-fèi | A tip (money). |
| 但 | tàn | But, only. |
| 不但 | pú tàn | Not only. |
| 疼 | t'éng | Sore, painful. To love. |
| 脣 | ch'ún | Lips [seldom used alone]. |
| 膚 | fū | Skin. Superficial. |
| 皮膚 | p'í-fu | Skin. |
| 零錢 | líng-ch'ién | Small change. |
| 聽 | t'ìng | To receive, to comply with. See also p. 89. |

2. Conversation

1.(A) 我今天下午想去理髮. 你的頭髮也 — Wŏ chīn-t'ien hsià-wú hsiăng ch'ù lí - fă. Nĭ - tê t'óu - fa yéh

| | |
|---|---|
| 很長了. 你高興跟我一塊兒去嗎? | hěn ch'áng lê. Nǐ kāo-hsìng kěn wǒ í-k'uài-êrh ch'ǜ ma? |
| 2.(B) 好罷. 我想去刮鬍子. 今天早上我找不着新的刀片, 舊的又不夠快, 所以我沒有刮. 你平常去那一家理髮館? | Hǎo pa. Wó hsiǎng ch'ǜ kuā hú-tzǔ. Chīn-t'ien tsǎo-shang wó chǎo pù cháo hsīn-tê tāo-p'ièn, chiù-tê yù pú kòu k'uài, só-í wǒ méi-yǔ kuā. Nǐ p'íng-ch'áng ch'ǜ nǎ-i-chiā lí-fá-kuǎn? |
| 3.(A) 我平常去華美理髮館. 那裏幾個理髮匠的手藝不但很好, 並且價錢也便宜. | Wǒ p'íng-ch'áng ch'ǜ Huá-měi Lí-fá-kuǎn. Nà-li chǐ-kê lí-fǎ-chiàng-tê shǒu-i pú tàn hěn hǎo, pìng-ch'iěh chià-ch'ien yěh p'ién-i. |
| 4.(B) 那家理髮館是不是在對面那條馬路? 要不要給小費? | Nà-chiā lí-fá-kuǎn shìh-pu-shih tsài tuì-mien nà-t'iáo mǎ-lù? Yào-pu-yao kéi hsiǎo-fèi? |
| 5.(A) 給不給由你, 沒關係. | Kěi-pu-kei yú nǐ, méi kuān-hsi. |
| 在理髮館 | (Tsài lí-fá-kuǎn) |
| 6.(A) 座滿了. 我們坐在那邊的椅子上看畫報罷. | Tsò mǎn lê. Wǒ-mên tsò tsài nà-pien-tê ǐ-tzǔ shàng k'àn huà-pào pa. |
| 7.(B) 這些都是舊畫報, 我都看過了. 這個 | Chè-hsieh tōu shìh chiù huà-pào, wǒ tōu k'àn kuò lê. Chè-kê |

| | |
|---|---|
| 房子很暖和，你覺 | fáng-tzŭ hĕn nuăn-hê, nĭ chüéh- |
| 得嗎？我得把大衣 | tê ma? Wó téi pă tà - ī |
| 脫下來. | t'ō - hsia - lai. |
| 8.(C, 理髮師) 先生, | (Lí - fá - shīh) Hsiēn - shêng, |
| 這邊有一個空位. | chè - pien yŭ í - kê k'ūng wèi. |
| 那一位先生先理？ | Nă - i - wèi hsiēn-shêng hsiēn lĭ? |
| 9.(B, to A) 你先理罷. 我 | Nĭ hsiēn lĭ pa. Wŏ |
| 不過來刮鬍子. 我 | pú - kuò lái kuā hú - tzŭ. Wŏ |
| 還沒看完這段新聞 | hái méi k'àn wán(5) chè tuàn hsīn-wĕn |
| 呢. | ni. |
| 10.(C) 先生要留長一點, | Hsiēn-shêng yào liú ch'áng ì-tiĕn, |
| 還是翦短一點？ | hái-shìh chién tuăn ì - tiĕn? |
| 11.(A) 請你翦短一點罷. | Ch'íng ni chién tuăn ì-tiĕn pa. |
| 我的頭髮長得很快. | Wŏ-tê t'óu-fa chăng tê hĕn k'uài. |
| 12.(C) 先生要翦甚麼樣 | Hsiēn-shêng yào chiĕn shĕn-mo yàng- |
| 子？ | tzŭ? |
| 13.(A) 就照以前的樣子 | Chiù chào ĭ-ch'ién-tê yàng-tzŭ |
| 翦罷. 不過後面我 | chiĕn pa. Pú - kuò hòu-mien wŏ |
| 要翦高一點. | yào chiĕn kāo ì-tiĕn. |
| 14.(C) 請你看上面的頭 | Ch'íng ni k'àn shàng-mien-tê t'óu- |
| 髮怎麼樣？ | fa tsĕn - mo - yàng? |
| 15.(A) 上面的長頭髮要 | Shàng-mien-tê ch'áng t'óu-fa yào |
| 翦短一點. | chién tuăn ì-tiĕn. |
| 16.(C) 我拿鏡子給你照 | Wŏ ná chìng-tzŭ kéi ni chào- |

| | |
|---|---|
| 一照．你看怎麼樣? | i-chao. Nǐ k'àn tsěn-mo yàng? |
| 17.(A) 很好．你的手藝眞不錯． | Hěn hǎo. Nǐ-tê shǒu-i chěn pú ts'ò. |
| 18.(C) 過奬，過奬．先生要刮臉嗎? | Kuò-chiǎng, kuò-chiǎng. Hsiēn-shêng yào kuā-liěn ma? |
| 19.(A) 我今天早上已經刮過一次了，再刮一次也不要緊，因爲我常常一天刮兩次．刮臉要另外加錢嗎? | Wǒ chīn-t'ien tsǎo-shang ǐ-ching kuā kuò í tz'ǔ lê, tsài kuā í tz'ǔ yěh pú yào-chǐn, yīn-wèi wǒ ch'áng-ch'áng ì t'iēn kuā liǎng tz'ǔ. Kuā-liěn yào lìng-wài chiā ch'ién ma? |
| 20.(C) 不用另外加錢．可是洗頭要加兩毛錢．先生要洗頭嗎? | Pú yùng lìng-wài chiā ch'ién. K'ě-shih hsǐ-t'óu yào chiā liǎng-máo-ch'ién. Hsiēn-shêng yào hsǐ-t'óu ma? |
| 21.(A) 好罷．請你給我洗乾淨一點． | Hǎo pa. Ch'íng ni kéi wo hsǐ kān-ching ì-tiěn. |
| 22.(C) 這水涼嗎? | Chè shuǐ liáng ma? |
| 23.(A) 不涼，正好．請你手輕一點． | Pù liáng, chèng hǎo. Ch'íng ni shǒu ch'īng ì-tiěn. |
| 24.(C) 先生要用頭油，還是用頭水? | Hsiēn-shêng yào yùng t'óu-yú, hái-shìh yùng t'óu-shuǐ? |
| 25.(A) 都用一點罷．我的頭髮本來是往後梳的，不是兩邊分 | Tōu yùng ì-tiěn pa. Wǒ-tê t'óu-fa pěn-lái shìh wàng hòu shū tê, pú shìh liǎng piēn fěn |

| | |
|---|---|
| 的. | tê. |
| 26.(C) 對不起. 我忘了. 我再拿鏡子來給你照一照. 你看行嗎? | Tùi pu ch'ǐ. Wǒ wàng lê. Wǒ tsài ná chìng-tzǔ lai kéi ni chào-i-chao. Nǐ k'àn hsíng ma? |
| 27.(A) 好極了. 一共多少錢? | Hǎo chí lê. Í-kùng tō-shǎo ch'ién? |
| 28.(C) 一共六毛錢. | Í-kùng liù-máo-ch'ién. |
| 29.(A) 這是七毛五. 不用找了. | Chè shìh ch'ī-máo-wǔ. Pú yùng chǎo lê. |
| 30.(C) 謝謝. 那位先生請坐罷. | Hsièh-hsieh. Nà-wèi hsiēn-shêng ch'ǐng tsò pa. |
| 31.(B) 我只要刮鬍子. | Wó chǐh yào kuā hú-tzǔ. |
| 32.(C) 就是, 先生. | Chiù-shih, hsiēn-shêng. |
| 33.(B) 怎麽這樣疼啊? 嘴脣上的皮膚刮破了罷? | Tsěn-mo chè-yàng t'ěng a? Tsuǐ-ch'ún-shàng-tê p'í-fu kuā-p'ò lê pa? |
| 34.(C) 沒有, 沒有. | Méi-yǔ, méi-yǔ. |
| 35.(B) 好罷. 這是一塊錢, 請你找我一些零錢罷. | Hǎo pa. Chè shìh í-k'uài-ch'ién, ch'íng ni cháo wo ì-hsiēh líng-ch'ién pa. |
| 36.(C) 我找你七毛五. 謝謝. | Wǒ cháo ni ch'ī-máo-wǔ. Hsièh-hsieh. |
| 37.(B) 謝謝. | Hsièh-hsieh. |

PART V...

NOTES:

(1) Hair on the human head is call... and the hair of animals, is called "...

(2) "Lí-fǎ-shīh" is a polite term for ... "lí-fǎ-chiàng" means an old-fashioned ba...

(3) The Distinction between "Yù" and "Tsài...

"Yù" has the following meanings: (a) "fur... dy, "T'ā pú hùi tsò, yù pú t'ìng huà" 他不會作... can't do it and still does not take advice"; "T... tǔng Fà-wén" 他懂德文,又懂法文 - "He knows ... knows French"; (b) "both ... and ...": "yù è yù k... 渴 - "both hungry and thirsty"; "yù lěng yù hsià-yǔ" ... 下雨 - "both cold and raining"; (c) "again" (usually ... to an action or situation which is already past): "Wǒ yù hsie... lê" 我又寫錯了 - "I have written it wrong again"; "Wǒ yù ch... k'àn t'a" 我又去看他 - "I went to see him again".

"Tsài" 再 in the sense of "again" differs from "yù" in that "tsài" usually is used when the action or situation referred to is in the future. The following examples show this use of "tsài": "tsài chièn" or "tsài hùi" 再見,再會 - "goodby (see you again)"; "Míng-t'ien tsài shuō pa" 明天再說吧 - "Let's speak of this again tomorrow". In such sentences as these, "yù" cannot take the place of "tsài". (See also the special note at end of Lesson 21.)

(4) The Distinction between "Chiù" and "Lǎo" 老

"Lǎo" in the sense of "old" is applied to living creatures (including plants), and to age as an abstraction; "chiù" is used of inanimate objects. For instance: "lǎo jén" 老人 - "old man", "lǎo shù" 老樹 - "old tree"; "chiù hsiéh" 舊鞋 - "old shoes", "chiù ch'ē" 舊車 - "old car".

(5) "Wán", "to finish, to end", denotes that the action expressed by the preceding verb has been finished or has come to an end. Here "k'àn wán" may be considered as a compound verb and may be translated "finished reading". Similar expressions are: "tsò wán" - "finished doing", "ch'īh wán" - "finished eating".

3. Translation

1.(A) I want to have a haircut this afternoon (literally, I want to go to dress hair this afternoon). Your hair also is very long. Would you like to go with me?

2.(B) All right. I want to go to shave ([my] beard). This morning

...w blade, and the old one wasn't sharp ... shave. Which barber shop do you usually

... the Hua-mei Barber Shop, where not only the ...al barbers is very good, but also the prices ...e.

...he barber shop on the opposite avenue? Is it nec-... tip?

...r not, as you please; it doesn't matter.

... the barber shop)

...The seats are all occupied. Let's sit in the chairs over there and read the pictorial magazines.

...(B) These are all old pictorial magazines, I've looked over all of them. This room is very warm, do you feel it? I must take off my overcoat.

8.(C, the barber) Sir, there is a vacant seat over here. Which gentleman will have [his hair] dressed first?

9.(B, to A) You [be attended to] first. I came only to be shaved. I still haven't finished reading this passage of the news.

10.(C) Do you want to keep [your hair] longer or cut [it] shorter, sir?

11.(A) Please cut it shorter. My hair grows very fast.

12.(C) What style do you prefer, sir? (Literally, You want to cut what style?)

13.(A) Cut it according to my previous style. But I want the back cut higher.

14.(C) Please look, how about the hair on top?

15.(A) The long hair on top must be cut shorter.

16.(C) I'll get a mirror and let you look at it (literally, to re-flect for you). What do you think?

17.(A) Very good. You are very skillful (literally, Your hand-skill really not bad).

18.(C) You over-praise me. Do you want a shave, sir?

19.(A) I've already shaved once this morning. It doesn't matter whether I shave again, because I usually shave twice a day. Is there any extra charge for shaving? (Literally, does shaving need to add extra money?)

20.(C) No extra charge. But there is an extra charge of twenty cents for shampoo (literally, head-washing needs to add two dimes). Do you want your head washed, sir?

21.(A) All right. Please wash it cleaner for me.

22.(C) Is this water cool?

23.(A) Not cool, just right. Please rub gently (literally, please your hands be lighter).

24.(C) Do you want brilliantine or hair lotion, sir?

25.(A) Use both a little. My hair is usually combed back, not parted (literally, divided into two sides).

26.(C) I'm sorry, I forgot. I'll bring the mirror again for you to take a look. Do you think it will do?

27.(A) Very good. How much altogether?

28.(C) Altogether, sixty cents.

29.(A) Here is seventy-five cents. Never mind the change.

30.(C) Thank you. That gentleman, please be seated.

31.(B) I only want a shave.

32.(C) Yes, sir.

33.(B) Why is it so sore? Is the skin of my lips scratched?

34.(C) No, no.

35.(B) All right. This is one dollar, please give me some small change.

36.(C) I give you seventy-five cents. Thank you.

37.(B) Thank you.

4. Exercises

a. "Fill-in" sentences

| | |
|---|---|
| 1. Wǒ-tê ... ... hěn ch'áng. | My ... is very long. |
| 2. ... tsò-wei tōu ... lê. | ... seats are all ... |
| 3. T'ā-tê ... ... pù hǎo. | His ... ... is not good. |
| 4. Chè-kê lí-fǎ-shīh-tê ... ... hến hǎo, pú-kuò yǔ ì-tiěn-êrh ... ... | This barber's ... ... is very good, but he is too ... ... |
| 5. Nǐ yào k'àn ... ... ma? | Do you want to see ... ... ? |
| 6. Wó tsǎo-shang méi-yǔ ... ... | This morning I did not ... ... |
| 7. Ch'íng ni ná ... ... kéi wo. | Please bring me [the] ... ... |

b. Translate into English:

1. 你拿甚麽來梳頭?

2. 這裏的理髮師的手藝很好.

3. 他先看完畫報才做事.

4. 理髮館離這裏不遠.

5. 天氣好不好，對我沒有關係。

6. 天氣暖和的時候，我最喜歡旅行。

7. 由(or,從)這兒往南走，就是那家理髮館。

8. 請你找(給)我一點零錢。

9. 他不但會開汽車，並且會開飛機。

10. 這件事由他去做吧。

c. Translate into Chinese:

1. I want to read this section of the news.

2. My beard is too long.

3. How much do you have to pay for a haircut in China?

4. Do you want to use a mirror?

5. When I entered the barber shop, the barber asked me to sit down.

6. If his skill is good, I will give him more tips.

7. Usually I part my hair on the left side, not on the right side.

8. What hair lotion do you use?

9. The price at that place is high, but those barbers are skillful.

10. When you finish [getting a] haircut, please wait for me here.

## Lesson 39 In a Theater

1. Vocabulary

| | | |
|---|---|---|
| 城 | ch'éng | City [í-tsò ch'éng]. |
| 影 | yǐng | Shadow, reflection [seldom used alone]. |
| 電影 | tièn-yǐng | Moving pictures (literally, electric shadows) [í-kê tièn-yǐng]. |

| | | |
|---|---|---|
| 院 | yüàn | Hall, courtyard [í-kê yüàn-tzŭ]. |
| 電影院 | tièn-yǐng-yüàn | Moving picture theater [í-kê or ì-chiā tièn-yǐng-yüàn]. |
| 彩 | ts'ăi | Color. Lucky. Prize (as in a lottery). |
| 五彩片子 | wú-ts'ăi p'ièn-tzŭ | Colored moving picture [ì-chāng wú-ts'ăi p'ièn-tzŭ]. |
| 如 | jú | If, like, as. Equal to, as to, according to. |
| 不如 | pù jú | Had better. Not so good as. |
| 術 | shù | Art, trick [seldom used alone]. |
| 藝術 | ì-shù | Art. |
| 演 | yĕn | To perform, to practise. |
| 表 | piăo | To show, to manifest. See also p. 61. |
| 表演 | piáo-yĕn | To perform, to demonstrate. Performance. |
| 廣告 | kuăng-kào | Advertisement [í-kê kuăng-kào]. |
| 但是 | tàn-shih | But. |
| 商 | shāng | Commerce. Commercial. To discuss. |
| 商量 | shāng-liang | To discuss, to consult, to deliberate upon. |
| 究 | chiù | To examine into, to investigate. After all, eventually. [Seldom used alone.] |
| 竟 | chìng | To finish. After all, finally, actually, nevertheless. [Seldom used alone.] |
| 究竟 | chiù-chìng | After all, really. |
| 反 | făn | To turn over, to turn back. Opposite, contrary. But, yet. To rebel. |
| 反對 | făn-tuì | To oppose, to object to. |
| 贊 | tsàn | To assist. |
| 贊成 | tsàn-ch'éng | To agree, to support. (Literally, to help accomplish.) |
| 哭 | k'ū | To cry, to weep. |
| 笑 | hsiào | To laugh. |
| 總 | tsŭng | To sum up, to bring together. All. Always. |
| 總要 | tsŭng-yào | Must, to have to. Anyway. |
| 決 | chüéh | To decide, to cut off. |
| 決定 | chüéh-tìng | To decide. |

| | | |
|---|---|---|
| 分開 | fĕn-k'ai | To divide widely, to separate. |
| 廂 | hsiāng | Side room. |
| 包廂 | pāo-hsiāng | A box in a theater [í-kê pāo-hsiāng]. |
| 願 | yüàn | To be willing, to desire, to wish. |
| 願意 | yüàn-i | To be willing. |
| 劇 | chǜ | A play [seldom used alone]. |
| 劇情 | chǜ-ch'íng | The plot of a play. |
| 簡 | chiĕn | Simple, easy [seldom used alone]. |
| 簡單 | chiĕn-tan | Simple. |
| 主 | chŭ | Master, host. Main. |
| 主角 | chú-chiăo | The most important person, the principal character in a play [í-kê chú-chiăo]. |
| 明星 | míng-hsīng (1) | Bright star, a "star" actor or actress [í-kê míng-hsīng]. |
| 高明 | kāo-míng | Lofty and intelligent, excellent (of high attainments). |
| 實 | shíh | Real, true, sincere. |
| 實在 | shíh-tsài | Really. |

2. Story

| | |
|---|---|
| 今天是星期六, | Chīn-t'ien shìh hsīng-ch'í-liù, |
| 我們下午沒有課. | wŏ - mên hsià - wŭ méi - yŭ k'è. |
| 吃完了午飯, 我們 | Ch'īh wán lê wŭ - fàn, wŏ - mên |
| 從學校出來, 進城 | ts'úng hsüéh-hsiào ch'ū-lai, chìn ch'éng |
| 去看電影. 小李說, | ch'ü k'àn tièn-yĭng. Hsiăo Lĭ shuō, |
| 他要看戲, 可是老 | t'ā yào k'àn hsì, k'ĕ-shih Lăo |
| 張跟別的三位都想, | Chāng kĕn piéh-tê sān-wèi tōu hsiăng, |
| 看戲太貴了, 不如 | k'àn hsì t'ài kuèi lê, pù jú |
| 看電影好. | k'àn tièn-yíng hăo. |
| 城裏的電影院有 | Ch'éng-lĭ-tê tièn-yĭng-yüàn yú |

| | |
|---|---|
| 五家；今天演的全是新片子．我們商量究竟要上那一個戲院．老張說：『隨便那一個都行．只要是我沒有看過的，我就不反對．』 | wǔ chiā; chīn-t'ien yĕn-tê ch'üán shìh hsīn p'ièn-tzŭ(2). Wŏ-mên shāng-liang chiù-chìng yào shàng nă-i-kê hsì-yüàn. Lăo Chāng shuō: "Suí-pièn nă-i-kê tōu hsíng. Chĭh yào-shih wŏ méi-yŭ k'àn kuò tê, wŏ chiù pù făn-tuì." |
| 我說：『那麼，我們先看報紙上電影的廣告罷．我們去平安電影院，好不好？那兒今天的片子是 Ingrid Bergman 演的 'For Whom the Bell Tolls'．那個片子很有名．』大家都贊成． | Wŏ shuō: "Nà-mo, wŏ-mên hsiēn k'àn pào-chĭh shàng tièn-yĭng-tê kuăng-kào pa. Wŏ-mên ch'ù P'íng-ān Tièn-yĭng-yüàn, hăo-pu-hao? Nà-êrh chīn-t'ien-tê p'ièn-tzŭ shìh Ingrid Bergman yĕn-tê 'For Whom the Bell Tolls'. Nà-kê p'ièn-tzŭ hĕn yŭ-míng." Tà-chiā tōu tsàn-ch'éng. |
| 小李問我：『除了 Ingrid Bergman 以外，你還喜歡那一個電影明星？』 | Hsiáo Lĭ wèn wo: "Ch'ú lê Ingrid Bergman ĭ-wài, nĭ hái hsĭ-huan nă-i-kê tièn-yĭng míng-hsīng?" |
| 我說：『我也喜歡 Bette Davis. 但是我不想跟我的女朋友去看她的片子．看 | Wŏ shuō: "Wó yéh hsĭ-huan Bette Davis. Tàn-shih wŏ pù hsiăng kĕn wŏ-tê nŭ p'éng-yu ch'ù k'àn t'ā-tê p'ièn-tzŭ. K'àn |

| | |
|---|---|
| 完她的片子以後，她老愛哭.』 | wán t'ā - tê p'ièn - tzǔ ǐ - hòu, t'ā lǎo ài k'ū." |
| 我說完，大家都笑了. 小李說:『還是你今天跟我去看電影好. 今天沒有人坐在你旁邊哭.』這句話說的老張也大笑起來了. | Wǒ shuō wán, tà - chiā tōu hsiào lê. Hsiáo Lǐ shuō: "Hái-shìh nǐ chīn-t'ien kěn wǒ ch'ǜ k'àn tièn-yíng hǎo. Chīn-t'ien méi-yǔ jén tsò tsài nǐ p'áng-piēn k'ū." Chè-chǜ huà shuō-tê Lǎo Chāng yěh tà hsiào ch'ǐ-lai lê. |
| 我說:『別笑了. 我們現在也應當走了. 平安電影院的票不容易買. 星期六下午電影院裏的人多的不得了. 要是不早去，恐怕我們要在門口等上一兩個鐘頭.』 | Wǒ shuō: "Piéh hsiào lê. Wǒ-mên hsièn-tsài yěh yīng-tāng tsǒu lê. P'íng - ān Tièn - yǐng - yüàn-tê p'iào pù júng-i mǎi. Hsīng-ch'í-liù hsià-wǔ tièn-yǐng-yüàn lǐ tê jén tō-tê pù té liǎo(3). Yào-shih pù tsǎo ch'ǜ, k'ǔng-p'à wǒ-mên yào tsài mén-k'óu těng shàng ì-liǎng - kê chūng-t'óu." |
| 我們就坐電車到電影院. 很多人站在賣票的地方. 我們等了半點鐘，就進去了. | Wǒ-mên chiù tsò tièn-ch'ē tào tièn-yǐng-yüàn. Hěn tō jén chàn tsài mǎi-p'iào-tê tì-fang. Wǒ-mên těng lê pàn-tiěn-chūng, chiù chìn-ch'ü lê. |
| 老張問:『你們喜 | Lǎo Chāng wèn: "Nǐ - mên hsǐ- |

歡坐在樓上，還是喜歡坐在樓下?』

小李說:『我想坐樓上包廂.』

我說:『不行罷. 我們買的是樓下的電影票，不能坐樓上. 樓上電影票的價錢不會是六毛五分錢的.』

小李說:『你錯了. 我們的票是甚麼地方都可以坐的.』

說了半天，大家不能决定坐在樓上還是坐在樓下.

老張說:『這麼樣罷. 願意坐樓上的就坐樓上，願意坐樓下的就坐樓下. 我們人太多了，總要分開坐. 現在樓上跟樓下都不會有六個座位在一塊兒

huan tsò tsài lóu-shàng, hái-shìh hsǐ-huan tsò tsài lóu-hsià?"

Hsiáo Lǐ shuō: "Wó hsiǎng tsò lóu-shàng pāo-hsiāng."

Wǒ shuō: "Pù hsíng pa. Wǒ-mên mǎi-tê shìh lóu-hsià-tê tièn-yǐng p'iào, pù nếng tsò lóu-shàng. Lóu-shàng tièn-yǐng p'iào-tê chià-ch'ien pú huì shìh liù-máo wǔ-fēn-ch'ién-tê."

Hsiáo Lǐ shuō: "Nǐ ts'ò lê. Wǒ-mên-tê p'iào shìh shến-mo tì-fang tōu k'ě-i tsò tê."

Shuō lê pàn t'iēn(4), tà-chiā pù nếng chüéh-tìng tsò tsài lóu-shàng, hái-shìh tsò tsài lóu-hsià.

Lǎo Chāng shuō: "Chè-mo yàng pa. Yüàn-i tsò lóu-shàng tê chiù tsò lóu-shàng, yüàn-i tsò lóu-hsià tê chiù tsò lóu-hsià. Wǒ-mên jến t'ài tō lê, tsǔng-yào fēn-k'ai tsò. Hsièn-tsài lóu-shàng kēn lóu-hsià tōu pú huì yǔ liù-kê tsò-wei tsài í-k'uài-êrh

的.』

tê."

我說:『要是分開了，我們看完了電影以後，大家怎麼樣會面?』

Wǒ shuō: "Yào-shih fěn-k'ai lê, wǒ-mên k'àn wán lê tièn-yíng ǐ-hòu, tà-chiā tsěn-mo yàng huì mièn?"

小李說:『我們在樓梯旁邊等罷. 那裏也有椅子坐.』

Hsiáo Lǐ shuō: "Wǒ-mên tsài lóu-t'ī p'áng-piēn těng pa. Nà-li yéh yú ǐ-tzǔ tsò."

說完了以後，老張跟小李兩個人上樓去坐包廂去了. 我們在樓下前排找着了四個空座，坐下.

Shuō wán lê ǐ-hòu, Lǎo Chāng kěn Hsiáo Lí liǎng-kê jén shàng lóu ch'ü tsò pāo-hsiāng ch'ǜ lê. Wǒ-mên tsài lóu-hsià ch'ién p'ái chǎo cháo lê ssǜ-kê k'ūng tsò, tsò-hsia.

這張片子很長. 看完了，大家出來已經是六點鐘了.

Chè-chāng p'ièn-tzǔ hěn ch'áng. K'àn wán lê, tà-chiā ch'ū-lai ǐ-ching shìh liù-tiěn-chūng lê.

小李說:『你說這個五彩片子怎麼樣?』

Hsiáo Lǐ shuō: "Nǐ shuō chè-kê wú-ts'ǎi p'ièn-tzǔ tsěn-mo yàng?"

我回答說:『還好. 劇情雖然簡單，不過女主角做得很好. 她的表演藝術實在

Wǒ huí-tá shuō: "Hái hǎo. Chǜ-ch'íng suī-ján chiěn-tan, pú-kuò nǚ chú-chiǎo tsò tê hén hǎo. T'ā-tê piáo-yěn í-shù shíh-tsài

高明.我真喜歡她.」 kāo-míng. Wŏ chēn hsĭ-huan t'a."

NOTES:

(1) "Míng-hsīng" is usually used as an abbreviation of "tièn-yĭng míng-hsīng", and is applied to "star" moving picture actors and actresses. "Chú-chiăo" is applied to principal characters in plays, political movements, and triangle love affairs.

(2) The original meaning of "p'ièn-tzŭ", "a card", has been extended to "picture". Here it is an abbreviation of "tièn-yĭng p'ièn-tzŭ", "moving picture".

(3) "Pù tế liăo", literally "cannot end", means "distressing, terrible, awful", and is used in the same way as such English colloquialisms as "terribly crowded", "awfully nice".

(4) "Pàn t'iēn", "half a day", is an exaggerated expression often used in Peiping to denote a long time.

3. Translation

Today is Saturday; we have no lessons in the afternoon. [When we had] finished eating lunch, we came out of the school and entered the city to see a moving picture. Hsiao Li said he wanted to see a play, but Lao Chang and the other three all thought [that] seeing a play would be too expensive, [and that] we had better see a moving picture.

There are five moving-picture theaters in the city; what were performed today were all new pictures. We discussed which theater [we] really wanted to go to. Lao Chang said: "Any one will do. Only those which I haven't seen (i.e., so long as it's one I haven't seen), I'll not object."

I said: "In that case, let's first look up the moving picture advertisements in the newspaper. [If] we go to the P'ing-an Theater, will that be all right? The picture there today is 'For Whom the Bell Tolls', played by Ingrid Bergman. That picture is very famous." Everyone agreed.

Hsiao Li asked me: "Besides Ingrid Bergman, what other moving-picture stars do you like?"

I said: "I also like Bette Davis. But I don't like to go with my girl friend to see her pictures. After seeing her pictures, she always likes to cry."

After I said that, everybody laughed. Hsiao Li said: "You had better go with me today to see the moving picture. Today no one will sit by your side [and] cry." This sentence was spoken so as to make Lao Chang also laugh heartily.

I said: "Don't laugh. We should go now. Tickets at the P'ing-an Theater are not easy to buy. On Saturday afternoon it's terribly crowded at the moving-picture theaters. If we don't go early, [I'm] afraid we'll have to wait at the entrance one or two hours."

We then took a street car [and] arrived at the theater. Many people stood at the box-office. After waiting half an hour, we then went in.

Lao Chang asked: "Would you like to sit upstairs, or would you like to sit downstairs?"

Hsiao Li said: "I want to sit in a box upstairs."

I said: "[Do you think] that will do? What we have bought are downstairs tickets, [we] can't sit upstairs. The cost of upstairs tickets would not be sixty-five cents."

Hsiao Li said: "You are mistaken. Our tickets are such that we can sit anywhere."

After talking for a long while, [we] all could not decide [whether we] should sit upstairs or downstairs.

Lao Chang said: "Let's [do] this way. Those who want to sit upstairs will sit upstairs; those who want to sit downstairs will sit downstairs. We are too many people; we have to sit separately. Now, there won't be six vacant seats in one row upstairs or downstairs."

I said: "If [we] are separated, how shall we meet after we have seen the picture?"

Hsiao Li said: "Let's wait by the side of the stairs. There are chairs to sit on there, too."

After saying this, both Lao Chang and Hsiao Li went upstairs to sit in a box. We found four vacant seats in the front row downstairs, [and] sat down.

This picture was very long. After seeing it, [when] everybody came out, it was already six o'clock.

Hsiao Li asked: "What do you think of this colored picture?"

I replied: "Fairly good. Although the plot was simple, yet the female principal character acted very well. Her art of expression is truly excellent. I really like her."

4. Exercises

a. "Fill-in" sentences

| | |
|---|---|
| 1. Chīn-t'ien ... ... mǎi ... ... p'iào. | It is ... ... to buy ... ... tickets today. |
| 2. Ní těng lê ... ... ... ? | ... ... have you been waiting? |
| 3. Wó těng lê ... ... ... | I have been waiting ... ... ... |
| 4. Wǒ-mên tsò tsài chề-li ... ... tsò tsài nà-li? | Shall we sit here ... there? |
| 5. Nǐ tsò tsài ǐ-tzŭ-tê ... ... tếng nǐ-tê ... ... | You sit by the ... of the chair to wait for your ... ... |
| 6. Wǒ-mên tsài ... ... chǎo cháo lê ... ... | We have found in the ... ... ... ... |

7. Wǒ-mên ... ... ... huì mièn? ... shall we meet?

b. Translate into English:

1. 我剛從電影院出來、
2. 你說這個五彩片子怎麼樣?
3. 樓上包廂的票價貴不貴?
4. 等了半天他還沒來、
5. 大家不能决定到那裏去看電影、
6. 我們都贊成在樓下坐、
7. 今天演的都是新片子、
8. 男主角演得不錯、
9. 這位老朋友老愛喝酒、
10. 人是舊的好、衣是新的好、

c. Translate into Chinese:

1. After supper we went to the theater.
2. I desire to go to see the picture.
3. My girl friend does not like to sit upstairs.
4. Who went there, besides Mr. Wang?
5. We'd better take a street car to the school.
6. It is too expensive to see a play.
7. We must decide which place we really want to go to.
8. If you wait at the entrance, he won't be able to see you.
9. The moving-picture theater is always very crowded on Sunday.
10. I want to discuss with you whether it is better to see a moving picture or to see a play.

## On the Expression "Ch'ǐ-lai" 起來

The expression "ch'ǐ-lai" means "to arise, to get up", as in "tsǎo-shang ch'ǐ-lai" 早上起來 - "to get up in the morning". Its use as a co-verb meaning "up, to start" has been discussed in Lesson 23, note 6. Now that we have a larger vocabulary, its uses may be more fully illustrated.

(1) It means "up", both literally and figuratively, as in English "get up" and "take up the subject".

"Chàn ch'ǐ-lai" 站起來 - "to stand up".

"Kuà ch'ǐ-lai" 掛起來 - "to hang up".

"Hsiáng ch'ǐ-lai" 想起來 - "to think of, to recollect".

(2) It indicates the beginning of an action or state.

"K'ū ch'ǐ-lai" 哭起來 - "to start to cry".

"Hsiào ch'ǐ-lai" 笑起來 - "to start to laugh".

NOTE: When "ch'ǐ" and "lai" are separated by the object of the main verb, the expression means "to begin, to start".

"T'án ch'ǐ huà lai" 談起話來 - "to begin to talk".

"Hsià ch'í yǔ lai" 下起雨來 - "It began to rain".

(3) When "ch'ǐ-lai" as a co-verb is preceded by a negative word, such as "pū" 不, it indicates temporary inability to perform the action of the main verb. In this use, "lai" is sometimes omitted without changing the meaning.

"Hsiǎng pu ch'ǐ-lai" 想不起來 - "cannot recall".

"Ná pu ch'ǐ-lai" 拿不起來 - "cannot take, impossible to raise".

## Lesson 40 In a Bookstore

1. Vocabulary

| | | |
|---|---|---|
| 開學 | k'āi hsüéh | Opening school. School opens. |
| 自來水筆 | tzǔ-lái-shuí-pǐ | Fountain pen (literally, self-coming-liquid pen) [ì-chīh tzǔ-lái-shuí-pǐ]. |
| 碎 | sùi | Broken. Fragments. |
| 零碎 | líng-sùi | Miscellaneous, fragmentary. |
| 擠 | chǐ | Crowded, To crowd, to press against. |
| 輪 | lún | A turn, a change (as of a scheduled order), a wheel. |

| | | |
|---|---|---|
| 挑 | t'iāo | To choose, to pick out. To carry on the shoulders. |
| 漂 | p'iào | Smart, bright, fresh. |
| 漂亮 | p'iào-liang | Pretty, smart, bright. |
| 至少 | chìh-shǎo | At least. |
| 夥 | huǒ | Numerous [lit.]. Partner. |
| 夥計 | huǒ-chi | Shop assistant. Partner, comrade. [í-kê huǒ-chi.] |
| 尖 | chiēn | Sharp. Point. |
| 筆尖 | pǐ-chiēn | Nib or point of a pen [í-kê pǐ-chiēn]. |
| 吸墨紙 | hsī-mò-chǐh | Blotting paper [ì-chāng hsī-mò-chǐh]. |
| 色 | sè | Color, sort. Beauty, lust. |
| 黃金色 | huáng-chīn-sè | Yellow gold color. |
| 筆套 | pi-t'ào | Cap of a pen [í-kê pǐ-t'ào]. |
| 鉛 | ch'iēn | Lead [the metal]. |
| 鉛筆 | ch'iēn-pǐ | Lead pencil, pencil [ì-chīh ch'iēn-pǐ]. |
| 簿 | pù | Notebook, account book. |
| 練習簿 | lièn-hsi-pù | Exercise book [ì-pěn lièn-hsi-pù]. |
| 日記簿 | jìh-chì-pù | Diary, log book [ì-pěn jìh-chì-pù]. |
| 櫃 | kuèi | Shop-counter, cupboard, chest. |
| 櫃台 | kuèi-t'ái | A counter in a shop [í-kê kuèi-t'ái]. |
| 橡 | hsiàng | Oak tree, rubber tree [seldom used alone]. |
| 橡皮 | hsiàng-p'í | Rubber, eraser [í-k'uài hsiàng-p'í]. |
| 起先 | ch'ǐ-hsiēn | At first. |
| 世 | shìh | World, generation. |
| 界 | chièh | Boundary, world, circle. |
| 世界 | shìh-chieh | World [í-kê shìh-chieh]. |
| 歷 | lì | To pass through, to experience [lit.]. A calendar. |
| 史 | shǐh | History [lit.]. |
| 歷史 | lì-shǐh | History. |
| 地理 | tì-lǐ | Geography. |

| | | |
|---|---|---|
| 雜 | tsá | Confused, miscellaneous, mixed. |
| 雜誌 | tsá-chìh | Magazine [ì-pěn tsá-chìh]. |
| 圖 | t'ú | Diagram, chart. To scheme. |
| 地圖 | tì-t'ú | Map [í-fù or ì-chāng tì-t'ú]. Atlas [ì-pěn tì-t'ú]. |
| 生意 | shēng-i | Business. |
| 科 | k'ē | Course of study, department, clinic. |
| 科學 | k'ē-hsüéh | Science. Scientific. |

2. Conversation

| | |
|---|---|
| 1.(A) 你上那兒去，小李? | Nǐ shàng nǎ-êrh ch'ǜ, Hsiáo Lǐ? |
| 2.(B) 今天開學，我想上書鋪去買點兒東西. | Chīn-t'ien k'āi hsüéh, wó hsiǎng shàng shū-p'ù ch'ǜ mái tiěn-êrh tūng-hsi. |
| 3.(A) 好，我跟你一塊兒去. 我想買一枝自來水筆和一本日記簿. | Hǎo, wǒ kěn nǐ í-k'uài-êrh ch'ü. Wó hsiáng mǎi ì-chīh tzǜ-lái-shuí-pǐ hé ì-pěn jìh-chì-pù. |
| 4.(B) 我要買的零碎東西很多. 我們一塊兒走罷. | Wǒ yào mǎi tê líng-suì tūng-hsi hěn tō. Wǒ-mên í-k'uài-êrh tsǒu pa. |

(In the bookstore)

| | |
|---|---|
| 5.(A) 你看，人這樣擠. 那些夥計都忙不過來了. 不知道要等多久才輪到我們買哪. | Nǐ k'àn, jén chè-yàng chǐ. Nà-hsieh huǒ-chi tōu máng-pu-kuò-lái(l) lê. Pù chīh-tao yào těng tō chiǔ ts'ái lún tào wǒ-mên mǎi na. |

| | |
|---|---|
| 6.(C) 先生要買甚麼? | Hsiēn-shêng yào mǎi shén-mo? |
| 7.(A) 我要買一枝自來水筆. 你有那幾種可以給我挑的? | Wǒ yào mǎi ì-chīh tzǔ-lái-shuí-pǐ. Ní yǔ ná chí chǔng k'ě-i kéi wo t'iāo tê? |
| 8.(C) 我們這裏有三種. Parker筆最好, 不過這種筆, 價錢也不一樣. 要是先生要好的, 最好買五十一號的. | Wǒ-mên chè-li yǔ sān chǔng. Parker pǐ tsuì hǎo, pú-kuò chè chúng pǐ, chià-ch'ien yěh pù í-yàng. Yào-shih hsiēn-shêng yào hǎo-tê, tsuì hǎo mǎi wǔ-shíh-í hào tê. |
| 9.(A) 請你拿給我看看. | Ch'íng ni ná kéi wo k'àn-k'àn. |
| 10.(C) 先生, 你看, 這枝筆多漂亮! 筆尖跟普通的不一樣. 寫在紙上, 墨水立刻就乾了, 用不着吸墨紙. 黃金色的筆套, 你看多美啊! | Hsiēn-shêng, nǐ k'àn, chè-chīh pǐ tō p'iào-liang! Pǐ-chiēn kēn p'ǔ-t'ūng-tê pù í-yàng. Hsiěh tsài chǐh shàng, mò-shuǐ lì-k'è chiù kān lê, yùng pù cháo hsī-mò-chǐh. Huáng-chīn-sè-tê pǐ-t'ào, nǐ k'àn tō měi a! |
| 11.(A) 多少錢一枝? | Tō-shǎo ch'ién ì-chīh? |
| 12.(C) 不過十五塊美國錢. | Pú-kuò shíh-wǔ k'uài Měi-kuo ch'ién. |
| 13.(A) 那太貴了. 有别的便宜一點兒的沒有? | Nà t'ài kuèi lê. Yǔ piéh-tê p'ièn-i ì-tiěn-êrh tê méi-yǔ? |

14.(C) 有. 這枝十塊錢, 也不錯.

Yǔ. Chè-chīh shíh-k'uài-ch'ién, yěh pú ts'ò.

15.(A) 好, 我就買這枝. 還有, 請你給我一本日記簿, 一枝五分錢的鉛筆, 一塊五分錢的橡皮, 兩個一分錢一個的筆尖, 五個一毛錢一本的練習簿.

Hǎo, wǒ chiù mǎi chè-chīh. Hái-yǔ, ch'íng ni kéi wo ì-pěn jìh-chì-pù, ì-chīh wǔ-fēn-ch'ién-tê ch'iēn-pǐ, í-k'uài wǔ-fēn-ch'ién-tê hsiàng-p'í, liǎng-kê ì-fēn-ch'ién í-kè tê pǐ-chiēn, wǔ-kê ì-máo-ch'ién ì-pěn tê lièn-hsi-pù.

16.(B) 老王, 請你等我一會兒, 我到對面的櫃台買幾本課本.

Lǎo Wáng, ch'íng ni těng wo ì-huǐ-êrh, wǒ tào tuì-mièn-tê kuèi-t'ái mái chí-pěn k'è-pěn.

17.(D) 請問, 先生要買甚麽?

Ch'ǐng wèn, hsiēn-shêng yào mǎi shén-mo?

18.(B) 我要買一本中文會話的書.

Wǒ yào mǎi ì-pěn Chūng-wén huì-huà-tê shū.

19.(D) 這裏有一本. 不知道合不合用.

Chè-li yǔ ì-pěn. Pù chīh-tao hé-pu-hê yùng.

20.(B) 還好. 我要買一本; 多少錢?

Hái hǎo. Wǒ yào mǎi ì-pěn; tō-shǎo ch'ién?

21.(D) 兩塊半錢. 先生, 你還要別的東西不要?

Liǎng-k'uài-pàn-ch'ién. Hsiēn-shêng, nǐ hái yào piéh-tê tūng-hsi pu yào?

| | |
|---|---|
| 22.(B) 我也想買中國歷史和中國地理的課本. | Wó yěh hsiáng mǎi Chūng-kuo lì-shǐh hé Chūng-kuo tì-lǐ-tê k'è-pěn. |
| 23.(D) 中國歷史還有一本在這裏, 可是中國地理的課本已經賣完了. | Chūng-kuo lì-shǐh hái yǔ ì-pěn tsài chè-li, k'ě-shih Chūng-kuo tì-lǐ-tê k'è-pěn ǐ-ching mài wán lê. |
| 24.(B) 那麼請你給我那本歷史罷. 一共多少錢? | Nà-mo ch'íng ni kéi wo nà-pěn lì-shǐh pa. í-kùng tō-shǎo ch'ién? |
| 25.(D) 兩本書一共是四塊五毛五. 你還要別的東西嗎? | Liáng-pěn shū í-kùng shìh ssǔ-k'uài wǔ-máo-wǔ. Nǐ hái yào piéh-tê tūng-hsi ma? |
| 26.(B) 我要買一張世界地圖. | Wǒ yào mǎi ì-chāng shìh-chieh tì-t'ú. |
| 27.(D) 對不起, 已經賣完了. | Tuì pu ch'ǐ, ǐ-ching mài wán lê. |
| 28.(B) 那麼請你把書包起來罷. 我還要買航空信封, 航空信紙, 和郵票. | Nà-mo ch'íng ni pǎ shū pāo ch'ǐ-lai pa. Wǒ hái yào mǎi háng-k'ūng hsìn-fěng, háng-k'ūng hsìn-chǐh, hé yú-p'iào. |
| 29.(D) 請你到旁邊那個櫃台去買罷. | Ch'íng ni tào p'áng-piēn nà-kê kuèi-t'ái ch'ù mǎi pa. |
| 30.(A) 小李, 你買完了 | Hsiáo Lǐ, ní mǎi wán lê |

| | |
|---|---|
| 沒有? 你不是說要買鉛筆, 日記簿, 和練習簿嗎? 我都給你買了. | méi - yǔ? Nǐ pú shìh shuō yào mǎi ch'iēn - pǐ, jìh - chì - pù, hé lièn-hsi-pù ma? Wǒ tōu kéi ni mǎi lê. |
| 31.(B) 謝謝你, 我忘了. 想不到人這樣擠, 我們還可以這樣快的就把東西買好了. | Hsièh-hsieh ni, wǒ wàng lê. Hsiǎng pú tào jén chè-yàng chǐ, wǒ-mên hái k'ě-i chè-yàng k'uài-tê chiù pǎ tūng-hsi mái hǎo lê. |
| 32.(A) 我起先以爲至少要等半個鐘頭才輪到我們買這些零碎東西. 那裏知道這樣快. 這裏的生意眞好. 剛才我想買本六月份的科學雜誌, 也賣完了. | Wó ch'ǐ-hsiēn ǐ-wéi chíh-shǎo yào těng pàn-kè chūng-t'óu ts'ái lún tào wǒ-mên mǎi chè-hsieh líng-suì tūng-hsi. Ná - li chīh-tao chè-yàng k'uài. Chè - li - tê shēng-i chēn hǎo. Kāng-ts'ái wó hsiǎng mái pěn liù-yüèh fèn tê K'ě-hsüéh Tsá-chìh, yěh mài wán lê. |
| 33.(B) 我們到別家書鋪去罷. | Wǒ-mên tào piéh chiā shū-p'ù ch'ù pa. |

NOTE:

(1) "Máng-pu-kuò-lái", literally "busy not able to pass through", is an idiom meaning having more on hand than one can accomplish, or having no time to spare. It is very difficult to translate this phrase literally, but an approximate translation is "very busy" or "too busy".

3. Translation

1.(A) Where are you going, Hsiao Li?
2.(B) Today school opens; I intend to go to a bookstore to buy some things.

3.(A) Good, I'll go with you. I intend to buy a fountain pen and a diary.

4.(B) The miscellaneous things that I want to buy are very many. Let's go together.

5.(A) Look, the people are so crowded. Those salesmen are all extremely busy. [I] don't know how long [we] shall have to wait before it will be our turn to buy.

6.(C) What do you want to buy, sir?

7.(A) I want to buy a fountain pen. How many kinds can you give me to choose from?

8.(C) We have here three kinds. The Parker pen is the best, but for pens of this kind the prices are not the same. If you, sir, want a good one, [it would be] best to buy a number fifty-one.

9.(A) Please bring it for me to look at.

10.(C) Look, sir, how pretty this pen is! [Its] nib is different from ordinary ones. [When you] write on paper, the ink dries immediately; it is not necessary to use blotting paper. The golden-yellow cap, see how beautiful!

11.(A) How much for one?

12.(C) Only fifteen dollars American money.

13.(A) That's too expensive. Do you have others a little cheaper?

14.(C) Yes. This ten-dollar one also is not bad.

15.(A) Good, then I'll buy this one. Besides, please give me a diary, a five-cent lead pencil, a five-cent rubber eraser, two one-cent(-each) pen-points, [and] five ten-cent(-each) exercise books.

16.(B) Lao Wang, please wait for me a moment; I'm going to the opposite counter to buy several (volumes of) textbooks.

17.(D) May I ask, what do you want to buy, sir?

18.(B) I want to buy a book on Chinese conversation.

19.(D) There is one book here. [I] don't know whether it suits your needs or not.

20.(B) Fairly well. I want to buy a copy; how much?

21.(D) Two dollars and a half. Sir, do you still want anything else?

22.(B) I also intend to buy textbooks on Chinese history and Chinese geography.

23.(D) There is still one copy of a Chinese history here, but the textbooks on Chinese geography are already sold out.

24.(B) Well, then, please give me that history book. How much altogether?

25.(D) The two books altogether are four dollars and fifty-five cents. Do you still want anything else?

26.(B) I want to buy a world map.

27.(D) Sorry, already sold out.

28.(B) Then please wrap up the books. I also want to buy air mail envelopes, air mail letter paper, and stamps.

29.(D) Please go to that neighboring counter to buy [those].

30.(A) Hsiao Li, have you finished buying? Didn't you say you wanted to buy lead pencils, a diary, and exercise books? I've bought them all for you.

31.(B) Thank you, I forgot. [I] didn't expect that when it was so crowded we still would be able to buy things so quickly.

32.(A) I thought at first that we would have to wait at least half an hour before it would be our turn to buy these miscellaneous things. [I] didn't know it would be so quick. The business here is good. I've just thought of buying the June issue of the Scientific Journal; it was sold out too.

33.(B) Let's go to another bookstore.

4. Exercises

a. "Fill-in" sentences

| | |
|---|---|
| 1. Wó hsiáng mǎi ... ... | I intend to buy ... ... |
| 2. Ní mǎi lê hěn tō ... ... tūng-hsi. | You have bought very many ... ... things. |
| 3. Chè-chīh pǐ ... ... ... ? | ... ... [does] this pen [cost]? |
| 4. Chià-ch'ien ... -pu- ... ? | Is the price ... or not? |
| 5. Chì ì-fěng ... ... hsìn tào ... yào tō-shǎo yú-p'iào? | How much postage is needed to send a(n) ... ... letter to ... ? |
| 6. Chè-hsieh shū tōu shìh ... ... k'è-pěn. | These books are all ... ... textbooks. |
| 7. Ch'íng ni ... ... wo nà-... ... shū. | Please ... ... me those ... ... books. |

b. Translate into English:

1. 我現在忙不過來.

2. 甚麽時候才輪到我?

3. 我看這朶花至少要賣五毛錢.

4. 那個書鋪裏的東西很貴.

5. 我們下個禮拜才開學.
6. 要是你跟他出去,他的母親就不高興了.
7. 雖然小李買的東西很貴,可是很好.
8. 他說中國話說得很快,並且他說的是標準國語.
9. 我可以在這裏坐一會兒嗎?
10. 你買的地圖合用不合用?

c. Translate into Chinese:

1. The diaries are all sold out.
2. It is so crowded here; let's go home.
3. The fountain pen is really pretty.
4. At first, I didn't know the price was so high.
5. I want to choose several lead pencils.
6. Do you know how long it will be before it's our turn to buy those books?
7. If this geography book does not suit your purpose, you had better not buy it.
8. The book which I bought is a history textbook.
9. You go to that counter and you'll be able to get magazines and newspapers.
10. Please give me ten three-cent stamps, sir.

## On Numeratives

Many of the numeratives (see Lesson 3, note 7) used in Chinese have been introduced, attached to nouns, in the vocabularies of the preceding lessons. For purposes of review and general reference, the uses of numeratives are summed up here. A numerative is inserted between (1) a numeral and a noun; (2) a demonstrative adjective and a noun; (3) the interrogative "nǎ" 那 and a noun; (4) the interrogative "chǐ" 幾 and a noun. Examples:

"Ssǔ-pěn shū" 四本書 - "four books".
"Chè-kê hsiǎo hái" 這個小孩 - "this little child".
"Nà-chāng chō-tzǔ" 那張桌子 - "that table".
"Nǎ-i-kê jén?" 那一個人? - "Who? What person?"
"Nǎ-i-pěn shū?" 那一本書? - "Which book?"
"Chǐ-chīh pǐ?" 幾枝筆? - "How many pens?"

### A List of the Common Numeratives

| | | |
|---|---|---|
| 張 | chāng | "To extend", used for sheets of paper, pictures, maps, tables, etc. |
| 家 | chiā | "A house, a family", for stores, banks, barber shops, etc. |
| 架 | chià | "A frame", for airplanes, clocks, etc. |
| 間 | chiēn | "A division", for shops, rooms, houses. |
| 件 | chièn | "An article", for articles of clothing, and for affairs. |
| 枝 | chīh | "A twig", for long cylindrical objects, such as pencils or cigarettes. |
| 隻 | chīh | "Single", for animals, for ships, and for one of things usually found in pairs, such as shoes, stockings, feet, eyes. |
| 種 | chǔng | "Kind, sort", for a number of nouns, including papers, soldiers, things. |
| 句 | chǜ | "A sentence", for phrases and sentences. |
| 份 | fèn | "A portion", for copies of periodicals. |
| 封 | fēng | "To seal", for letters. |
| 幅 | fú | "A border, a hem", for pictures, maps, etc. |
| 副 | fù | "A set", for things in pairs or sets, such as spectacles, gloves, shoe-laces, scrolls. |
| 下 | hsià | "A time", for strokes or beats. |
| 回 | huí | "An occasion", for times or turns. |
| 個 | kè | "An individual", a general numerative used for persons and things. |
| 棵 | k'ē | For trees. |

顆 k'ē "A small round thing", for pearls, beads, etc.

根 kēn "A length", for long things, such as sticks, bamboos, poles, ropes, strings.

塊 k'uài "A lump", for dollars, and for pieces of meat, land, etc.

管 kuǎn "A tube", for tubular things, such as pens, flutes, tubes of tooth paste.

粒 lì "A grain", for grains, beads, etc.

輛 liàng "A cart", for vehicles.

面 mièn "A surface", for mirrors, drums, etc.

把 pǎ "To grasp", for things with handles, such as knives, and for chairs.

排 p'ái "A row", for things or persons in rows.

本 pěn "A volume", for books.

筆 pǐ "A pen", for amounts of money, items of account.

匹 p'ī "A mate", for horses and mules.

片 p'ièn "A slice, a flake", for slices of meat or bread.

雙 shuāng "A pair", for things in pairs, such as chopsticks, shoes, socks.

套 t'ào "A wrapper", for sets, as of books, cups, clothing.

條 t'iáo "A length", for animals, fish, pairs of trousers, roads, streets, and some other long objects.

頂 tǐng "Top", for hats and sedan chairs.

朵 tǒ "A cluster, a head", for flowers and clouds.

層 ts'éng "A layer", for storeys of buildings, divisions of a topic, etc.

座 tsò "A seat", for temples, mountains, cities.

對 tùi "A pair", for things in pairs.

頓 tùn "A meal", for meals.

位 wèi "A seat", a respectful numerative for persons.

NOTE: The Distinction between "Shuāng" 雙 and "Tùi" 對

The character 雙 originally represented two birds standing together on a hand. It means "a pair, two, both, double, even". It usually refers to things which are customarily used in pairs and not singly, such as hands, eyes, shoes, socks, chopsticks. "Shuāng-shêng-tzǔ" 雙生子 means "twins".

The original meanings of "tùi" are "to be opposite to, to reply; a pair". It refers to things which face each other or stand together, such as a pair of pillars, stone lions, or flower vases, husband and wife, twins, or a pair of chairs. "Tuì" is also used in the sense of "a pair" in speaking of two persons who are in some way peculiar.

Various words denoting length, weight, capacity, etc., are used in the same way as numeratives. Examples:

"Ì-ch'ĭh pù" 一尺布 - "a foot of cloth".

"Liáng-mŭ tì" 兩畝地 - "two 'mu' of land".

"Í-pàng t'áng" 一磅糖 - "a pound of sugar".

"Ì-pēi ch'á" 一杯茶 - "a cup of tea".

NOTE: Omission of Numeratives

Numeratives may be ommitted under the following conditions:

(1) When persons or things are referred to in a general way without specification:

"T'ā mǎi shū" 他買書 - "He buys books".

"Wǒ k'àn p'éng-yu" 我看朋友 - "I visit friends".

(2) When an interrogative sentence is formed with "tō-shǎo" or with "shén-mo":

"Ní yǔ tō-shǎo ch'ién?" 你有多少錢? - "How much money have you?"

"Ní yǔ shén-mo shū?" 你有甚麼書? - "What books do you have?"

(3) "Nién" 年 and "t'iēn" 天 do not need a numerative; people say simply "liǎng nién, sān nién; liǎng t'iēn, sān t'iēn".

## Lesson 41 In a Hospital

1. Vocabulary

| | | |
|---|---|---|
| 痛 | t'ùng (1) | Painful, sore. |
| 發燒 | fā-shāo | To have fever. |
| 體 | t'ĭ | Body [seldom used alone]. |
| 體溫表 | t'ĭ-wēn-piǎo(2) | A clinical thermometer [í-kê t'ĭ-wēn-piǎo]. |
| 度 | tù | A measure, a limit. An astronomical, thermometrical, or geographical degree. To pass. |
| 熱度 | jê tù | Degree of fever. |

| | | |
|---|---|---|
| 病 | pìng | Sick. |
| 馬上 | mǎ-shàng (3) | At once, without delay. |
| 護 | hù | To protect [seldom used alone]. |
| 看護 | k'ān-hù | Nurse [í-kê k'ān-hù]. |
| 胃 | wèi | Stomach. |
| 胃口 | wèi-k'ou | Appetite. |
| 呼 | hū | To breathe out, to call. |
| 呼吸 | hū-hsi | To exhale and inhale. |
| 累 | lèi | Tired. To trouble. |
| 化 | huà | To change, to transform, to digest, to melt. |
| 消化 | hsiāo-huà | To digest. Digestion. |
| 部 | pù | Part, department, class. A set of books. |
| 深 | shēn | Deep. |
| 針 | chēn | Needle, pin [ì-k'ē 顆 or í-kê chēn]. |
| 打針 | tǎ-chēn | To inject. Injection. |
| 驗 | yèn | To examine. |
| 血 | hsüèh | Blood. |
| 血管 | hsüèh-kuǎn | Blood vessel [í-kê hsüèh-kuǎn]. |
| 醫 | ī | To heal [seldom used alone]. |
| 醫生 | ī-shêng | Medical doctor [í-kê ī-shêng]. |
| 大夫 | tài-fu (4) | Medical doctor [í-kê tài-fu]. |
| 醫院 | ī-yüàn | Hospital [í-kê ī-yüàn]. |
| 內科醫生 | nèi-k'ē ī-shêng | Physician [í-kê nèi-k'ē ī-shêng]. |
| 外科醫生 | wài-k'ē ī-shêng | Surgeon [í-kê wài-k'ē ī-shêng]. |
| 趁 | ch'èn | To go, to follow, to avail oneself of. |
| 耳 | ěrh | Ear [seldom used alone]. |
| 耳朵 | ěrh-to | Lobe of the ear, ear [ì-chīh or í-kê ěrh-to; í-tuì ěrh-to]. |
| 似 | ssù | Like. As if. |
| 張開 | chāng k'āi | To open wide. |

| | | |
|---|---|---|
| 喉 | hóu | Throat, gullet. Guttural. [Seldom used alone.] |
| 嚨 | lúng | Throat [seldom used alone]. |
| 喉嚨 | hóu-lúng | Throat. |
| 胸 | hsiūng | Breast [seldom used alone]. |
| 胸口 | hsiūng-k'ǒu | Chest. |
| 難受 | nán-shòu | Hard to bear, uneasy. |
| 舌頭 | shé-t'ou | Tongue [í-kê shé-t'ou]. |
| 肺 | fèi | Lungs. |
| 方子 | fāng-tzŭ | A doctor's prescription [í-kê fāng-tzŭ]. |
| 開方子 | k'āi fāng-tzŭ | To write a prescription. |
| 藥 | yào | Herbs, medicine. |
| 害 | hài | To injure, to suffer from. |
| 利害 | lì-hai | Serious, severe, dangerous. |
| | lì-hài | Advantage and disadvantage. |

2. Conversation

1.(A) 十點鐘了，你怎麼還不起來? — Shíh-tiĕn-chūng lê, ní tsĕn-mo hái pù ch'ǐ-lai?

2.(B) 我不大舒服，有一點兒頭痛. 剛才我拿前天買的體溫表，試了體溫，熱度是一百度. — Wǒ pú tà shū-fu, yǔ ì-tiĕn-êrh t'óu-t'ùng. Kāng-ts'ái wǒ ná ch'ién-t'ien-mǎi-tê t'ǐ-wĕn-piăo, shìh lê t'ǐ wĕn, jè tù shìh ì-păi tù.

3.(A) 你前天買體溫表，今天發燒，你好像預先知道要生病似的. 我看你還是去 — Nǐ ch'ién-t'ien mǎi t'ǐ-wĕn-piăo, chīn-t'ien fā-shāo, ní hǎo-hsiàng yǜ-hsiēn chīh-tao yào shĕng pìng shìh tê(5). Wǒ k'àn nǐ hái-shìh(6) ch'ǜ

| | |
|---|---|
| 醫院見見大夫罷. | ī-yüàn chièn-chien tài-fu pa. |
| 4.(B) 好的. 請你打一個電話叫一輛汽車來. 我馬上穿衣服. | Hǎo - tê. Ch'ǐng ni tǎ í - kê tiěn-huà chiào í-liàng ch'ì-ch'ē lai. Wó mǎ-shàng ch'uān ī-fu. |

(At the hospital)

| | |
|---|---|
| 5.(B) 現在可以掛號嗎? | Hsièn-tsài k'ě-i kuà-hào ma? |
| 6.(C) 可以. 你要看外科醫生, 還是看內科醫生? | K'ě - i. Nǐ yào k'àn wài - k'ē ī-shêng, hái-shìh k'àn nèi-k'ē ī-shêng? |
| 7.(B) 我想我要見一見內科醫生. | Wó hsiáng wǒ yào chièn-i-chien nèi-k'ē ī-shêng. |
| 8.(D) 李先生, 請坐. 醫生一會兒就來. 我現在先給你試試體溫表. | Lǐ hsiēn-shêng, ch'ǐng tsò. Ī -shêng ì-huǐ-êrh chiù lai. Wǒ hsièn-tsài hsiēn kéi ni shìh-shih t'ǐ-wēn-piǎo. |
| 9.(E) 李先生, 你覺得怎麼樣? | Lǐ hsiēn-shêng, nǐ chüéh-tê tsěn-mo yàng? |
| 10.(B) 我的頭有一點疼, 並且累得很. 我昨天被一位朋友請去吃飯. 我吃了很多的醬油雞, 燒鴨, 豆腐, 糖醋排骨, 和零零碎碎的東西; | Wǒ-tê t'óu yǔ ì - tiěn t'ěng, pìng-ch'iěh lèi-tê hěn. Wǒ tsó-t'ien pèi í-wèi p'ěng-yu ch'ǐng ch'ù ch'īh-fàn. Wǒ ch'īh lê hěn tō-tê chiāng - yú - chī, shāo - yā, tòu - fu, t'áng - ts'ù p'ái - kǔ, hé líng-ling sùi-sui-tê tūng-hsi; |

| | |
|---|---|
| 喝酒也喝得太多了. | hē chiú yěh hē-tê t'ài tō lê. |
| 所以生病了. | Só - ǐ shēng pìng lê. |
| 11.(E) 你以前病過嗎? | Ní ǐ - ch'ién pìng kuò ma? |
| 12.(B) 我從來沒有病過. | Wǒ ts'úng-lái(6) méi-yǔ pìng kuò. |
| 這是頭一次. | Chè shìh t'óu - i - tz'ǜ. |
| 13.(E) 趁這個機會休息 | Ch'èn chè-kê chī-hui hsiū-hsi |
| 幾天也很好. 讓我 | chǐ t'iēn yéh hěn hǎo. Jàng wo |
| 來看看你的眼睛, | lái k'àn-k'an nǐ - tê yěn-ching, |
| 你的耳朵跟舌頭. | nǐ - tê ěrh - to kěn shé - t'ou. |
| 請你張開嘴. 你的 | Ch'íng ni chāng-k'āi tsuǐ. Nǐ-tê |
| 喉嚨疼嗎? 你覺得 | hóu-lung t'éng ma? Nǐ chüéh-tê |
| 難受嗎? 你的牙不 | nán - shòu ma? Nǐ - tê yá pù |
| 很好; 你應當去見 | hěn hǎo; nǐ yīng-tāng ch'ǜ chièn- |
| 見牙科醫生. 現在 | chien yá-k'ē ī-shêng. Hsièn-tsài |
| 讓我來聽聽你的肺 | jàng wo lái t'īng-t'ing nǐ-tê fèi- |
| 部. 請你深深的呼 | pù. Ch'íng ni shēn-shên-tê hū- |
| 吸一下. 請再來一 | hsi í hsià. Ch'ǐng tsài lái í |
| 次. 好, 沒有甚麼. | tz'ǜ. Hǎo, méi - yǔ shén - mo. |
| 14.(B) 我還覺得胃有一 | Wǒ hái chüéh - tê wèi yǔ ì - |
| 點疼. 我沒有胃口 | tiěn t'éng. Wǒ méi-yǔ wèi-k'ou |
| 吃東西. | ch'īh tūng-hsi. |
| 15.(E) 不要緊. 我叫看 | Pú yào-chǐn. Wǒ chiào k'ān- |
| 護拿藥給你吃. | hù ná yào kéi ni ch'īh. |
| 16.(B) 大夫, 你看我在 | Tài - fu, nǐ k'àn wǒ tsài |

| | | |
|---|---|---|
| | 醫院要住幾天? 要不要打針? | Ī - yüàn yào chù chǐ t'iēn? Yào-pu - yao tǎ - chēn? |
| 17.(E) | 都不要. 吃了藥, 好好的休息幾天, 就沒有事了. 等一會兒, 看護要取一點血去檢驗. | Tōu pú yào. Ch'īh lê yào, hǎo - hāo - tê hsiū-hsi chǐ t'iēn, chiù méi-yǔ shìh lê. Těng ì - huǐ - êrh, k'ān - hù yào ch'ǔ ì-tiěn hsüèh ch'ù chiěn-yèn. |
| 18.(B) | 要驗血嗎? 我怕痛. | Yào yèn hsüèh ma? Wǒ p'à t'ùng. |
| 19.(E) | 一點兒不痛, 不要緊. | Ì - tiěn - êrh pú t'ùng, pú yào - chǐn. |
| 20.(A) | 老李, 大夫來過了, 他說了些甚麽? | Láo Lǐ, tài - fu lái kuò lê, t'ā shuō lê hsiēh shén-mo? |
| 21.(B) | 他沒說甚麽, 只檢查了一下眼睛, 耳朵, 牙, 舌頭, 喉嚨, 胸口. 剛才看護從我的血管裏取一點血去驗. 我看是昨天我吃得太多了, 消化不好. | T'ā méi shuō shén - mo, chíh chiěn-ch'á lê í hsià yěn-ching, ěrh - to, yá, shé - t'ou, hóu-lung, hsiūng-k'ǒu. Kāng-ts'ái k'ān-hù ts'úng wǒ-tê hsüèh-kuán lǐ ch'ǔ ì-tiěn hsüèh ch'ù yèn. Wǒ k'àn shìh tsó-t'ien wǒ ch'īh-tê t'ài tō lê, hsiāo-hua pù hǎo. |
| 22.(A) | 大夫給你開了方子嗎? | Tài-fu kéi ni k'āi lê fāng-tzǔ ma? |
| 23.(B) | 他給我開了一個 | T'ā kéi wo k'āi lê í - kê |

| | |
|---|---|
| 方子. | fāng-tzŭ. |
| 24.(A) 你每天要吃幾次藥? | Ní mĕi t'iēn yào ch'īh chĭ tz'ŭ yào? |
| 25.(B) 我每天要吃三次藥. 都在飯後吃. | Wó mĕi t'iēn yào ch'īh sān tz'ŭ yào, tōu tsài fàn hòu ch'īh. |
| 26.(A) 這個藥好吃不好吃? | Chè-kê yào hăo-ch'īh pu hăo-ch'īh? |
| 27.(B) 這個藥實在不好吃, 苦極了. | Chè-kê yào shíh-tsài pù hăo-ch'īh, k'ŭ chí lê. |
| 28.(A) 大夫說你的病利害不利害? | Tài-fu shuō nĭ-tê pìng lì-hai pu lì-hai? |
| 29.(B) 他說不利害, 休息幾天就好了. | T'ā shuō pú lì-hai, hsiū-hsi chĭ t'iēn chiù hăo lê. |
| 30.(A) 那麼, 你好好的休息. 我明天三點鐘帶一點水果來看你. | Nà-mo, ní hăo-hāo-tê hsiū-hsi. Wŏ míng-t'ien sān-tiĕn-chūng tài ì-tiĕn shuí-kuŏ lái k'àn ni. |
| 31.(B) 不敢當, 太打攪你了. | Pù kăn tāng, t'ài tá-chiáo ni lê. |
| 32.(A) 不客氣. 明天見. | Pú k'ê-ch'i. Míng-t'ien chièn. |

NOTES:

(1) "T'ùng" and "t'éng" 疼, in the sense of "pain" or "sore", can be used interchangeably.

(2) The Chinese expression for an ordinary thermometer is "hán-shú piăo" 寒暑表 - "cold and heat indicator".

(3) "Mǎ-shàng", literally "on horseback", thus ready to go, means "quickly, with all speed, at once": "Mǎ-shàng chiù lái" - "I'll come at once". Although this is a southern rather than a Pekingese expression, it is too common to be omitted from this course in practical conversation.

(4) "Tài-fu", originally a title for a high official, and then given to a physician holding high rank, has become a common colloquial term for any physician. It is used especially in northern China, while "Ī-shêng" is the more common term in southern China.

(5) "Hǎo-hsiàng" means "very much like, as if, seems". The word 似, when used in conjunction with "hǎo-hsiàng" and followed immediately by the particle "tê", loses its tone and is pronounced "shih". The phrase "hǎo-hsiàng ... shih-tê" means "as if". This sentence may be translated "You seemed to know beforehand that you were going to be sick."

(6) The Distinction between "Hái-shìh" and "Pù jú" 不如

"Hái-shih" here conveys the sense of "had better", and may be replaced by "pù jú". However, these two phrases are not always interchangeable and sometimes are different in meaning.

"Pù jú", besides "had better", may mean "not equal to, not as ... as ... ". For example: "Wǒ k'àn-shū pù jú t'ā k'uài" 我看書不如他快 - "I do not read as fast as he does".

"Hái-shìh", besides "had better", has the following meanings: (a) "(either ...) or"; (b) "still", to indicate that an action or a state of affairs remains the same: "Wǒ huí-lai tê shíh-hou, t'ā hái-shìh tsài nà-li nièn-shū" 我回來的時候，他還是在那裏念書 - "When I came back, he was still there studying"; (c) in the expression of a judgment or preference, "hái-shìh" implies the superlative or the comparative degree of the adjective concerned: "Wǒ k'àn hái-shìh chê̌-pě̌n shū hǎo" 我看還是這本書好 - "I think, after all, this book is the best".

(7) "Ts'úng-lái", literally "from coming", means "heretofore, from the beginning, at any time". "Ts'úng-lái méi-yǔ" means "has (have) never been".

3. Translation

1.(A) It's ten o'clock now; why haven't you go up yet?

2.(B) I feel a bit indisposed (literally, not quite comfortable); I have a little headache. Just now I took the fever thermometer which I bought day before yesterday, to take my temperature. The temperature (literally, degree of heat) was one hundred degrees.

3.(A) You bought the thermometer the day before yesterday, [and] then you get fever today! You seemed to know beforehand that you were going to be sick. I think you'd better go to the hospital and see a doctor.

4.(B) All right. Please make a telephone call and get a taxi to come. I'll put on [my] clothes at once.

5.(B) May I register now?

6.(C) Yes, you may. Do you want to see a surgeon or a physician?

7.(B) I think I want to see a physician.

8.(D) Please be seated, Mr. Li. The doctor will come soon. Now I'll first have you try the thermometer.

9.(E) How do you feel, Mr. Li?

10.(B) I have a little headache (literally, my head has a little pain), and moreover I'm very tired. Yesterday I was invited by a friend to dinner. I ate very much soy-sauce chicken, roast duck, bean curd, sweet and sour spare-ribs, and other miscellaneous things; I also drank too much wine. So I became sick.

11.(E) Have you ever been sick before?

12.(B) I have never been sick before. This is the first time.

13.(E) It would be very well to take this opportunity to rest a few days. Let me see your eyes - your ears and tongue. Please open your mouth wide. Is your throat sore? Do you feel distressed? Your teeth are not very good, you ought to go to see a dentist. Now let me listen to your lungs. Please take a deep breath. Once more, please. Fine, there is nothing [wrong].

14.(B) I also feel that there is a little pain in my stomach. I have no appetite to eat [any]thing.

15.(E) It's not important. I'll tell the nurse to get some medicine for you to take.

16.(B) Doctor, do you think I'll have to stay in the hospital several days? Will I have to have an injection (or not)?

17.(E) None of that is necessary. Take the medicine, rest well for a few days, then it will be nothing. Wait a moment, the nurse will take a little blood for examination.

18.(B) Do you have to examine my blood? I'm afraid of pain.

19.(E) No pain at all; it doesn't matter.

20.(A) Lao Li, the doctor has come; what did he say?

21.(B) He didn't say anything, he only examined my eyes, ears, teeth, tongue, throat, and chest. Just now the nurse took a little blood from my vessels for examination. I think I ate too much yesterday, and my digestion isn't good.

22.(A) Did the doctor write a prescription for you?

23.(B) He wrote a prescription for me.

24.(A) How many times a day do you have to take the medicine?

25.(B) I have to take it three times a day, every [time it] is to be taken after meals.

26.(A) Is this medicine pleasant to take?

27.(B) This medicine is really unpleasant to take, very bitter.

28.(A) Did the doctor say whether your illness is serious?

29.(B) He said it was not serious; after a few days' rest [I] shall be all right.

30.(A) Well then, you rest well. Tomorrow at three o'clock I'll bring some fresh fruit and come to see you.

31.(B) I dare not accept such a favor; I've troubled you too much.

32.(A) Don't mention it. See you tomorrow.

4. Exercises

a. "Fill-in" sentences

| | |
|---|---|
| 1. Wǒ tsài ... ... yào chù ... ... ? | (How many days) do I have to stay in (the hospital)? |
| 2. Wǒ ná ... ... ... lai shìh wǒ-tê ... ... | I take a (clinical thermometer)to try my (temperature). |
| 3. Ch'íng ni chiào ... ... ch'ì-ch'ē ... | Please call (a) taxi (to come). |
| 4. Wǒ ... t'ùng. | I have ... ache. |
| 5. Wǒ-tê ... ... t'ùng-tê hěn. | My ... ... is very sore. |
| 6. Wǒ yào ch'ù k'àn ... ... ī-shêng. | I want to go see a ... ... doctor. |
| 7. Chīn-t'ien wǒ ... ... | Today I ... ... |
| 8. Nǐ ... ... chǐ t'iēn, chiù ... lê. | You (rest) a few days, and then [you'll] (recover). |

b. Translate into English:

1. 我到醫院去掛號。
2. 你要等一會兒，醫生還沒有來。
3. 我要看的是外科醫生，不是內科醫生。
4. 這個地方沒有好牙科大夫。

5. 因為你吃得太多,所以你的消化不好.

6. 以後吃東西,不要吃得太多.

7. 不要緊,我拿藥給你吃.

8. 你好好的休息休息,過了幾天,你就好了.

9. 我喉嚨有一點兒痛.

10. 我心裏難過的時候,抽很多的煙;好過的時候,我也抽很多的煙.

c. Translate into Chinese:

1. He didn't say anything.
2. I don't feel well today.
3. Do you go to see a doctor when you are sick?
4. Besides examining my eyes, he also examined my ears.
5. I had a headache when I was invited to dinner.
6. Yesterday I was given an injection by the doctor, who told me to take a rest.
7. I don't want to take the medicine, because it is too bitter.
8. Please wait a moment; the nurse will come to take your temperature.
9. What did the doctor say when he came to see you?
10. I told him that I had no appetite.

## PART VII, LESSON 41

### On Chinese Verbs

### A Review and Summary

The Chinese verb is very simple, because there is no inflection, but moods and tenses are indicated by the addition of auxiliary verbs and particles. All Chinese verbs are regular. For the purpose of review, the important points concerning verbs are summarized as follows:

Indicative mood

The present tense, as in "wǒ shuō" 我說 - "I speak", "t'ā shuō" 他說 - "he speaks", is very simple.

The past or perfect tense is indicated by "lê" 了 or "tê" 的 following the verb, or following the object if any. Thus:

"Wǒ shuō lê" 我說了 - "I said" or "I have spoken".

"Wǒ kào-su t'a lê" 我告訴他了 - "I told him", "I have told him".

The past or perfect tense is not so definite in Chinese as in French or German. But if it is desired to be more definite as to past time, such emphatic expressions as "ǐ-ching" 已經 - "already", "tsáo-ǐ" 早已 - "long ago", "kuò" 過 - "over", and "wán" 完 - "finished" are used. Examples:

"Wó ǐ-ching shuō lê" 我已經說了 - "I have already spoken".

"T'ā tsáo-í tsǒu lê" 他早已走了 - "He has gone long ago".

"Wǒ ch'īh kuò lê" 我吃過了 - "I have eaten".

"Wǒ k'àn wán lê" 我看完了 - "I have finished reading".

To express the past perfect tense, it is necessary to have comparison with another past tense, as in:

"Wǒ k'àn wán nà-pěn shū ǐ-hòu, wǒ ch'ù k'àn tién-yǐng lê" 我看完那本書以後,我去看電影了 - "After I had finished reading that book, I went to see a show".

The future tense is indicated by the auxiliary verbs "yào" 要, "chiù" 就, or "hùi" 會, as in:

"T'ā yào lái" 他要來 - "He will come".

"T'ā chiù lái" 他就來 - "He will come immediately".

"T'iēn hùi hsià-yǔ" 天會下雨 - "It is likely to rain".

If the future is already indicated in the sentence by an adverb of time, it is not necessary to use an auxiliary verb. For example:

"T'ā míng-t'ien lái" 他明天來 - "He will come tomorrow".

The progressive and imperfect tenses, and the present participle, are indicated by "cho" 着, "chěng ... cho" 正...着, or "chèng ... tsài" 正 ... 在, as in:

"Wǒ tsò-cho" 我坐着 - "I am sitting".

"T'ā lái-tê shíh-hou, wǒ chèng nièn-cho shū" 他來的時侯,我正念着書 - "When he came, I was just reading".

Imperative mood

The imperative mood is indicated by "pa" 吧, as in:

"Ch'ù pa" 去吧 - "Go" or "Let's go".

"Nǐ nièn-shū pa" 你念書吧 - "(You) study".

A strong prohibition is indicated by "piéh" 别 or "pú yào" 不要, without "pa". Examples:

"Nǐ pú yào shuō" 你不要説 - "Don't talk".

"Nǐ piéh shuō" 你别説 - "Don't talk".

NOTE: "Piéh", which may be considered to be a contraction of "pú yào", is more common in northern China, "pú yào" in the south.

Subjunctive mood

The subjunctive mood is indicated by the use of "k'ě-i" 可以 - "may, might", "huò-chě" 或者 or "huò" - "perhaps", "yéh-hsǔ" 也許 or "hsǔ" - "perhaps", "yào-shih" 要是 - "if", "k'ǔng-p'à" 恐怕 - "[I] am afraid", and similar expressions. Examples:

"Wǒ míng-nien k'ě-i huí kuó" 我明年可以回國 - "I may return to [my own] country next year".

"Wǒ huò-chě ch'ù, huò-chě pú ch'ù, pù í-tìng" 我或者去,或者不去,不一定 - "I may go, I may not, [I am] uncertain", "Whether I go or not is uncertain".

"Míng-t'ien yéh-hsǔ hsià-hsüěh" 明天也許下雪 - "Perhaps it will snow tomorrow".

"Yào-shih wó yǔ ch'ién, wǒ í-tìng yào mái hěn tō-tê shū" - 要是我有錢,我一定要買很多的書 - "If I had money, I certainly would buy many books".

Passive voice

The passive voice is indicated by "pèi" 被, "chiào" 叫, "shòu" 受, "jàng" 讓, and "kěi" 給, as has been explained in the special note at the end of Lesson 35, and also by "ái" 挨, "to suffer", which is idiomatically used in the expression "ái tǎ" 挨打 - "to suffer beating, to be beaten".

Co-verbs

The use of co-verbs has been explained in Lesson 15, note 3 and footnote. They usually express the manner or direction of the action of the main verb. Some of the words commonly used as co-verbs are "ch'ū" 出, "chìn" 進, "ch'ǐ-lai" 起來, "kuò" 過, "húi" 回, and "shàng" 上. The following common expressions are formed with co-verbs:

"Ch'ū-ch'ü" 出去 - "to go out", "tsǒu-ch'u-ch'ü" 走出去 - "to walk out".

"Ch'ū-lai" 出來 - "to come out", "tsǒu-ch'u-lai" 走出來 - "to walk out".

"Chìn-lai" 進來 - "to come in" (towards the speaker).

"Chìn-ch'ü" 進去 - "to go in" (away from the speaker).

"Kuò-lai" 過來 - "to come over".

"Kuò-ch'ü" 過去 - "to go over".

"Ná húi-lai" 拿回來 - "to bring back" (toward the speaker).

"Ná húi-ch'ü" 拿回去 - "to take back" (away from the speaker).

## Lesson 42 Review

1. Useful Phrases and Word Combinations

| | | | |
|---|---|---|---|
| 1. | 戴帽 | tài mào | To put on a hat. |
| 2. | 脫帽 | t'ō mào | To take off the hat. |
| 3. | 穿鞋 | ch'uān hsiéh | To put on shoes. |
| 4. | 脫鞋 | t'ō hsiéh | To take off shoes. |
| 5. | 木匠 | mù-chiàng | Carpenter. |
| 6. | 畫畫 | huà huà | To paint a picture, to paint. |
| 7. | 畫家 | huà-chiā | Painter (of pictures), artist. |
| 8. | 有關係沒有? | Yǔ kuān-hsi méi-yǔ? | Does it matter? |
| 9. | 我跟她沒有甚麼關係. | Wǒ kēn t'ā méi-yǔ shén-mo kuān-hsi | I have no relation with her. |
| 10. | 冬大衣 | tūng tà-ī | Winter overcoat. |
| 11. | 秋大衣 | ch'iū tà-ī | Autumn overcoat. |
| 12. | 留一個條 | liú í-kê t'iáo | To leave a slip [of paper], to leave a word. |

13. 留客 liú k'ề To keep a guest.

14. 有一定的標準 yǔ í-tìng-tê piāo-chǔn There is a certain standard.

15. 旅費 lǚ-fèi Traveling expenses.

16. 用費太大 yùng fèi t'ài tà Too much expenditure.

17. 藝術家 ì-shù-chiā Artist.

18. 演說 yěn-shuō To make a speech.

19. 演說家 yěn-shuō-chiā Orator.

20. 可笑得很 k'ě-hsiào-tê hěn Very ridiculous.

21. 那太笑話了. nà t'ài hsiào-huà lê That is too much a joke, that is too ridiculous.

22. 請你講一個笑話. Ch'íng ni chiǎng í-kê hsiào-huà Please tell a joke.

23. 我天天起的很早. Wǒ t'iēn-t'iēn ch'ǐ-tê hěn tsǎo I get up every day very early.

24. 天天都是這麼樣. T'iēn-t'iēn tōu shìh chè-mo yàng It's like this every day.

25. 天氣暖和 T'iēn-ch'i nuǎn-hê The weather is warm.

26. 溫煖 wēn-nuǎn Warm.

27. 和氣 hé-ch'i Affable, agreeable, friendly.

28. 明天開學 Míng-t'ien k'āi hsüéh School opens tomorrow.

29. 後天開課 Hòu-t'ien k'āi k'è Day after tomorrow class work begins.

30. 買了好些零零碎碎的東西. Mǎi lê hǎo-hsiēh líng-líng-sùi-sui-tê tūng-hsi Bought a good many miscellaneous things.

31. 零碎事太多了 Líng-sùi shìh t'ài tō lê Too much miscellaneous work.

32. 輪班作事 lún-pān tsò-shìh To work by turns.

33. 挑好的 t'iāo hǎo-tê To choose the good one.

34. 她的聲音尖極了. T'ā-tê shēng-yin chiēn chí lê Her voice is very sharp.

35. 我的鉛筆不尖了. Wǒ-tê ch'iēn-pǐ pù chiēn lê My pencil is not sharp.

36. 他是世界上有名的科學家. T'ā shìh shìh-chieh shàng yǔ-míng-tê k'ē-hsüéh-chiā He is a world-famous scientist.

37. 美國史 Měi-kuo shǐh American history.

38. 中國地理 Chūng-kuo tì-lǐ Chinese geography.

39. 我病了. Wǒ pìng lê I am sick, I have been sick.

40. 我有病. Wó yǔ pìng I am sick.

| | | |
|---|---|---|
| 41. 病好了 | pìng hǎo lê | Convalescent, cured. |
| 42. 毛病 | máo-ping | Flaw, defect. |
| 43. 他有甚麼病? | T'ā yǔ shěn-mo pìng? | What trouble has he? |
| 44. 他病得利害嗎? | T'ā pìng tê lì-hai ma? | Is he seriously ill? |
| 45. 有利無害 | Yǔ lì wú hài | There is advantage, no disadvantage. |
| 46. 眼科 | yěn-k'ê̄ | Eye clinic. |
| 47. 耳鼻喉科 | ěrh-pí-hóu-k'ê̄ | Ear, nose, and throat clinic. |
| 48. 他害怕. | T'ā hài-p'à | He is afraid. |
| 49. 他怕他有肺病. | T'ā p'à t'ā yǔ fèi pìng | He is afraid he has pumonary tuberculosis. |
| 50. 他怕打針. | T'ā p'à tǎ chēn | He is afraid of taking an injection. |
| 51. 不要怕難. | Pú yào p'à nán | Don't be afraid of difficulties. |
| 52. 禮物 | lǐ-wù | Gift, present. |
| 53. 新發明 | hsīn fā-míng | New invention, new discovery. |
| 54. 點名 | tiěn-míng | To call the roll (literally, to dot the names). |
| 55. 點一點 | tiěn-i-tien | To check one by one. |
| 56. 你想怎麼辦好呢? | Nǐ hsiáng tsěn-mo pàn hǎo ni? | What, in your opinion, is it best to do? |
| 57. 怎麼辦呢? | Tsěn-mo pàn ni? | What shall I do? |
| 58. 他很正經. | T'ā hěn chèng-ching | He is very serious, he is very dignified. |

2. Interpreting Practice - A Lazy Teacher

[Interpreting practice supplied with previous lessons has been chiefly from Chinese to English. In order to give the students training in making short speeches or relating anecdotes in Chinese, a story in English is offered here. The instructor may wish to read this story paragraph by paragraph, and have the students translate each paragraph promptly into Chinese, making complete sentences and keeping the language as clear and correct as possible.]

Once upon a time (ts'úng-ch'ién) there was a lazy (pú-yùng-kūng-tê) teacher. He frequently went to class without having prepared the lesson. When he reached the classroom, he asked the students, saying: "Have you prepared the lesson?" The students replied: "We have not prepared." This teacher, much displeased, said: "Before you came to class, you did not prepare your lesson well. You only want me to explain it to you; what use is that? Could you understand? The class is dismissed!"

So the students all left class.

The second time he went to class, this teacher again had not prepared the lesson, and he went to class. After he had called the roll, he stopped a moment, then asked the students: "Have you prepared today's lesson well?" The students in a loud voice answered: "We all have prepared the lesson well!" This teacher said: "If you have all prepared the lesson, then it is not necessary for me to lecture. Well, let's dismiss class!"

The third time, when it was the moment for him to go to class, that teacher still had not prepared the lesson. When he arrived at class, he again asked the students: "Have you prepared today's lesson well?" Half of the students said: "We have prepared it well." The other half-class said: "We have not prepared." The students thought, today this teacher could not fail to explain the lesson.

This teacher thought a moment, and thought out a very good method. He very gravely said: "Those people in the half of the class who have prepared the lesson, tell that half who have not prepared. There is no need for me to lecture to you. Dismiss class, dismiss class!"

3. Reading Practice

我剛從學校囘來，就聽見妹妹在樓上叫，『哥哥，你有好些禮物擱在桌子上．明天是你的生日，你不會忘了罷？你想我要給你甚麼東西？』弟弟站在樓梯旁邊，他問我：『哥哥，你明天生日，是你的好日子，應當請客了．至少也得請我們看電影．』後來母親就說：『你們別淨跟哥哥鬧了．國英，我看你應當去理髮了．明天你跟他們去玩，六點囘來吃飯．我預備了好些菜，請了幾位客人來吃晚飯．』

妹妹跟着就說：『哥哥，你一會兒去理髮，你告訴理髮師翦短一點兒．你的頭髮實在太長了，有點兒像藝術家的樣子．我明天要請一位朋友來．她長得很漂亮．我想介紹給你．不過你要請我去看電影才成，那麽，我可以請她一塊兒去.』

我說:『好，我一定請你的朋友去. 她跟你同班嗎?』

『不，她跟我不同班.』

妹妹這樣說，我就明白了. 她很高興的指給我看:『這是我給你的禮物，那是弟弟給你的. 媽媽給你的禮物，還沒有拿出來哪.』

第二天早上，母親一看見我就說:『國英，你今天長一歲了. 我高興極了. 我給你買了一套新衣服，一打手巾，同四雙襪子.』

妹妹接着說:『哥哥，你別忘了我給你的日記簿. 你說好看嗎? 我昨天在書鋪裏，人擠得不得了. 找了半天才找着了賣日記簿的櫃台，又等了半天夥計才過來問我買甚麽.』

我也看見弟弟買的一打鉛筆. 我說:『謝謝你們. 你們給我這樣好的禮物，我請你們看電影. 妹妹，你的朋友不是要來嗎?』

我還沒有說完，那位朋友就從門口進來了. 誰知道她是一位很可愛的小孩兒! 妹妹對着我笑. 我也笑起來了.

我一共買了四張票. 有兩張是小孩半價票. 弟弟跟那位小朋友看得很快樂. 可是從電影院出來，小弟弟就說不舒服. 我趕快叫一輛汽車囘家.

王大夫請來了. 他試試他的體溫, 聽聽他的胸口, 看看他的舌頭和喉嚨. 他說:『不要緊. 他吃了藥就好了.』

那一天晚上, 大家都不快樂. 可是第二天弟弟就好了.

Translation

I had just come back from school when I heard [my] younger sister call from upstairs: "Elder brother, you have a number of presents [which have been] put on the table. Tomorrow is your birthday, you won't forget that, will you? What do you think I will give you?" [My] younger brother stood beside the stairs; he asked me: "Elder brother, tomorrow is your birthday, [it] is your lucky day, you should invite guests. At least you must invite us to see a moving picture." After that, mother (then) said: "You children, don't only make fun of your elder brother. Kuo-ying, I think you ought to get a haircut. Tomorrow you will go out to amuse yourself with them, [and] come back to dinner at six o'clock. I've prepared a number of dishes [and] have invited several guests to come to dinner."

Younger sister, following up, immediately said: "Elder brother, after a while when you go out to get a haircut, tell the barber to cut it a little shorter. Your hair is really too long; you look a little like an artist. Tomorrow I want to invite a friend to come. She is growing very pretty. I would like to introduce [her] to you. But you must invite me to a show, then it will be all right. Then I can invite her too (to go together)."

I said: "Fine, I shall certainly invite your friend to go. Is she in the same class with you?"

"No, she and I are not in the same class."

[When] younger sister spoke in this way, then I understood. She very happily pointed out [the presents] for me to look: "This is the present I give you, that is what younger brother gives you. Mama's gift to you has not yet been brought out.

The next morning, mother as soon as she saw me (then) said: "Kuo-ying, today you are one year older. I am very happy. I've bought for you a new suit of clothes, a dozen handkerchiefs, and four pairs of socks."

Younger sister, continuing, said: "Elder brother, you mustn't forget the diary I bought for you. Do you think (literally, say) it's pretty? Yesterday I was in the bookstore; it was awfully crowded. [I] had searched for a long time before I found the counter where diaries are sold, [and I] again had waited a long time before a salesman came over and asked what I wanted to buy."

I also saw the dozen lead pencils younger brother had bought. I said: "Thank you. You give me such fine presents, I will invite you to see a moving picture. Younger sister, doesn't your friend want to come?"

I still hadn't finished speaking, when that friend came in at the door. Who would know that she was a very lovable little child! Younger sister, facing me, laughed. I also began to laugh.

I bought four tickets altogether, two of which were children's half-price tickets. Younger brother and that little friend enjoyed looking very much (literally, saw in such a way that they were very happy), but [when we] came out of the moving picture theater, little brother then said that he didn't feel well. I hurried to call a taxi to return home.

Dr. Wang came [at our] request. He tested his (body) temperature, listened to his chest, looked at his tongue and throat. He said: "It's not important. [After] taking medicine, he will be well."

That night, everybody was not happy. However, the next day little brother was all right.

CONVERSATIONAL CHINESE

## PART VIII CONVERSATIONS WITH VARIOUS PEOPLE

### Lesson 43 With a Friend at the New Year

1. Vocabulary

| | | |
|---|---|---|
| 恭 | kūng | Respectful, reverent. |
| 恭喜 | kūng-hsǐ | To congratulate. Congratulations. |
| 祝 | chù | To pray, to bless. |
| 熱鬧 | jè-nao | Excited and clamorous, crowded and noisy, gay. Clamor. |
| 放 | fàng | To let go, to set free, to lay down, to put. |
| 仗 | chàng | To rely upon, to fight. |
| 炮仗 | p'ào-chàng | Firecracker. |
| 聲音 | shēng-yin | Voice, noise. |
| 睡覺 | shuì-chiào | To sleep. |
| 示 | shìh | To notify, to show. |
| 表示 | piǎo-shìh | To show. Indication. |
| 思 | ssū | To think. |
| 意思 | ì-ssū | Meaning, idea [ì-tiěn 點 ì-ssū]. Interest. |
| 戚 | ch'ī | Related to. To pity. [Seldom used alone.] |
| 親戚 | ch'īn-ch'i | Relative [í-kê ch'īn-ch'i]. |
| 玩意兒 | wán-ì-êrh | Toy [í-kê wán-ì-êrh]. |
| 糕 | kāo | Cake, pastry. |
| 蛋 | tàn (1) | Egg [seldom used alone]. |
| 雞蛋糕 | chī-tàn-kāo | Sponge cake [í-k'uài chī-tàn-kāo]. |
| 年糕 | nién-kāo | Cake made of glutinous rice, for the New Year celebration. |
| 花生 | huā-shēng | Peanut [ì-k'ē huā-shēng]. |
| 瓜子 | kuā-tzǔ | Melon seed [ì-k'ē kuā-tzǔ]. |
| 趣 | ch'ù | Interesting, amusing. |
| 祖 | tsǔ | Ancestor [seldom used alone]. |
| 祖先 | tsǔ-hsiēn | Ancestor. |
| 燭 | chú | Candle, torch [ì-chīh chú]. |

| | | |
|---|---|---|
| 神 | shén | God, spirit, divinity, deity. |
| 活 | huó or huò | To live. Alive, active. |
| 入 | jù | To enter. |
| 西洋 | Hsī-yáng | Europe, the West. |
| 舞 | wǔ | To brandish, to posture. |
| 跳舞 | t'iào-wǔ | Dancing. To dance. |
| 玩龍燈 | wán-lúng-tēng (2) | "To play dragon lantern", to perform the dragon dance or dragon parade. |
| 獅 | shīh | Lion [í-kê shīh-tzŭ]. |
| 舞獅 | wǔ-shīh | Lion-dance. |
| 擺 | pǎi | To move to and fro. To arrange. |
| 動 | tùng | To move. |
| 迎 | yíng | To welcome, to go to meet. |
| 拉 | lā | To draw, to pull, to drag. |
| 倒 | tǎo | To fall over, to topple. |
| | tào | To pour out. On the contrary, and yet, still. |
| 鼓 | kǔ | Drum [í-kê kǔ]. |
| 切 | ch'iēh | To cut, to carve. |
| | ch'ièh | In earnest, important. |
| 一切 | í-ch'ièh | All. Every. |

2. Conversation

| | |
|---|---|
| 1.(A) 恭喜，恭喜，李先生．今天我來給你拜年． | Kūng - hsǐ, kūng - hsǐ, Lǐ hsiēn-shêng. Chīn-t'ien wǒ lái kéi ni pài-nién. |
| 2.(B) 不敢當，王先生．我祝你今年萬事如意． | Pù kǎn tāng, Wáng hsiēn-shêng. Wǒ chù ni chīn-nien wàn-shìh jú-ì(3). |
| 3.(A) 謝謝．這是你第一次在中國過新年， | Hsièh-hsieh. Chè shìh nǐ tì-í tz'ù tsài Chūng-kuo kuò hsīn-nién, |

你喜歡到外邊去玩玩嗎?

ní hsǐ-huan tào wài-pien ch'ǜ wán-wan ma?

4.(B) 好極了. 中國人過新年眞是熱鬧; 昨天晚上不停的放炮仗. 聲音大極了. 我一晚沒有睡好.

Hǎo chí lê. Chūng-kuo jến kuò hsīn-nién chễn shìh jề-nao; tsó-t'ien wǎn-shang pù-t'íng-tê fàng p'ào-chàng. Shễng-yin tà chí lê. Wǒ ì wǎn méi-yǔ shuì hǎo.

5.(A) 我們過新年實在是熱鬧. 昨天晚上有很多的人沒有睡覺. 他們坐着談話, 叫作『守*歲』. 有的人還把門開着. 到深夜不關, 表示『迎春』或『迎接新年』的意思.

Wǒ-mên kuò hsīn-nién shíh-tsài shìh jề-nao. Tsó-t'ien wǎn-shang yú hễn tō-tê jến méi-yǔ shuì-chiào. T'ā-mên tsò-cho t'án-huà, chiào tsò "shǒu suì". Yǔ-tê jến hái pǎ mến k'āi-cho, tào shến yèh pù kuān, piǎo-shìh "yíng-ch'ūn(4)" huò "yíng-chiēh hsīn-nién" tê ì-ssǔ.

6.(B) 王先生, 你看, 從那邊走過來的那些小孩跟大人, 他們的衣服好看不好看?

Wáng hsiēn-shêng, nǐ k'àn, ts'úng nà-pien tsǒu-kuò-lai-tê nà-hsieh hsiǎo hái kễn tà jến, t'ā-mên-tê ī-fu hǎo-k'àn pu hǎo-k'àn?

7.(A) 很好看. 過年的時候, 他們多半穿新衣服, 到親戚朋

Hễn hǎo-k'àn. Kuò-nién-tê shíh-hou, t'ā-mên tō-pàn ch'uān hsīn ī-fu, tào ch'īn-ch'i p'ếng-



*For shǒu, see p. 384

| | |
|---|---|
| 友的家裏去拜年. | yu-tê chiā-li ch'ǜ pài-nién. |
| 8.(B) 小孩們好像覺得很高興, 是不是? | Hsiǎo hái-mên hǎo-hsiàng chüéh-tê hěn kāo-hsìng, shìh-pu-shih? |
| 9.(A) 他們很高興, 因爲他們的父母跟一切年長的人都給他們『紅包』. | T'ā-mên hěn kāo-hsìng, yīn-wèi t'ā-mên-tê fù-mǔ kěn í-ch'ièh nién-chǎng-tê jén tōu kěi t'ā-mên "húng-pāo". |
| 10.(B) 甚麼叫『紅包』? | Shén-mo chiào "húng-pāo"? |
| 11.(A) 這是用紅紙包的錢. 拜年的時候, 年長的人給他們拿來買炮仗, 或者買別的玩意兒. | Chè shìh yùng húng chǐh pāo tê ch'ién. Pài-nién-tê shíh-hou, nién-chǎng-tê jén kěi t'ā-mên ná-lai mǎi p'ào-chàng, huò-ché mǎi piéh-tê wán-ì-êrh. |
| 12.(B) 我聽說你們過新年的時候, 預備各樣好吃的東西, 是不是? | Wǒ t'īng-shuō nǐ-mên kuò-hsīn-nién-tê shíh-hou, yù-pei kè yàng hǎo-ch'īh-tê tūng-hsi, shìh-pu-shih? |
| 13.(A) 是的, 每一家預備了雞, 肉, 魚, 跟各樣的糖果, 年糕, 雞蛋糕, 花生, 瓜子, 和別的點心給親戚朋友吃. | Shìh-tê, měi-ì chiā yù-pei lê chī, jòu, yú, kěn kè-yàng-tê t'áng-kuǒ, nién-kāo, chī-tàn-kāo, huā-shěng, kuā-tzǔ, hé piéh-tê tiěn-hsīn kěi ch'īn-ch'i p'éng-yu ch'īh. |
| 14.(B) 那有意思極了. | Nà yǔ ì-ssǔ chí lê. |

| | |
|---|---|
| 15.(A) 還有，這些好吃的東西，也拿來拜祖先. | Hái-yǔ, chè-hsieh hǎo-ch'īh-tê tūng - hsi, yěh ná - lai pài tsǔ - hsiēn. |
| 16.(B) 怎麼樣拜呢? | Tsěn-mo yàng pài ni? |
| 17.(A) 每家點上很好看的燈，香，跟燭，神台上擱着筷子，碗，酒杯，跟好吃的東西. 每一個人對着祖先牌子拜幾拜. 意思是：一方面給祖先拜年，一方面請祖先吃新年飯. 好像他們還是活着的樣子. | Měi chiā tiěn-shang hěn hǎo-k'àn-tê těng, hsiāng, kěn chú, shén-t'ái shàng kē-cho k'uài-tzǔ, wǎn, chiǔ pēi, kěn hǎo-ch'īh-tê tūng-hsi. Měi - í - kè jén tùi-cho tsǔ-hsiēn p'ái-tzǔ pài chǐ pài. Ì - ssǔ shìh: ì fāng - mièn kéi tsǔ-hsiēn pài-nién, ì fāng-mièn ch'íng tsǔ-hsiēn ch'īh hsīn-nién fàn. Hǎo-hsiàng t'ā-mên hái shìh huó-cho tê yàng-tzǔ. |
| 18.(B) 聽說還有跳舞，是不是? | T'īng - shuō hái - yǔ t'iào - wǔ, shìh-pu-shih? |
| 19.(A) 不是西洋的跳舞. 那是玩龍燈或者舞獅. | Pú shìh Hsī-yáng-tê t'iào-wǔ. Nà shìh wán-lúng-těng huò-ché wǔ-shīh. |
| 20.(B) 怎麼樣玩呢? | Tsěn-mo yàng wán ni? |
| 21.(A) 龍燈是一條用布作的，很長的龍，分作十幾段，每一 | Lúng-těng shìh ì-t'iáo yùng pù tsò tê, hěn ch'áng - tê lúng, fēn tsò shíh-chǐ tuàn; měi-í- |

個人管一段，各段接起來以後，那條長龍就可以在空中左右的擺動了．這一班舞龍燈的人預先練習好了，所以舞起來的時候，很好看．要是在晚上，龍燈裏面點燭，那更有趣了．

kê jén kuǎn í tuàn. Kè tuàn chiēh ch'ǐ-lai ǐ-hòu, nà-t'iáo ch'áng lúng chiù k'ě-i tsài k'ūng-chūng tsǒ yù tê pǎi-tùng lê. Chè-ì pān wǔ-lúng-tēng tê jén yù-hsiēn lièn-hsi hǎo lê, só-ǐ wú ch'ǐ-lai tê shíh-hou, hěn hǎo-k'àn. Yào-shih tsài wǎn-shàng, lúng-tēng lǐ-mien tiěn chú, nà kèng yǔ-ch'ù lê.

22.(B) 舞獅是怎麼樣的？

Wǔ-shīh shìh tsěn-mo yàng tê?

23.(A) 舞獅也差不多跟舞龍燈一樣．不過沒有燈，也沒有那麼多人．

Wǔ-shīh yěh ch'à-pu-tō kēn wǔ-lúng-tēng í-yàng. Pú-kuò méi-yǔ tēng, yěh méi-yǔ nà-mo tō jén.

24.(B) 爲甚麼沒有那麼多人？

Wèi shén-mo méi-yǔ nà-mo tō jén?

25.(A) 普通舞獅頭要一兩個人．獅身只是一塊很長的布，一個人拉着．他們舞起來的時候，一會兒站起，一會兒倒過來，很好看．

P'ǔ-t'ūng wǔ shīh-t'óu yào ì-liǎng-kê jén. Shīh-shēn chǐh shìh í-k'uài hěn ch'áng-tê pù, í-kê jén lā-cho. T'ā-mên wú ch'ǐ-lai tê shíh-hou, ì-huǐ-êrh chàn ch'ǐ, ì-huǐ-êrh tǎo-kuò lai, hěn hǎo-k'àn.

| | |
|---|---|
| 26.(B) 我希望，我有一天能夠加入去玩．王先生，我怎麽聽見打鼓跟放炮仗的聲音? | Wǒ hsī - wàng, wó yǔ i t'iēn nếng-kòu chiā-jù ch'ǜ wán. Wáng hsiēn-shêng, wó tsěn-mo t'īng-chien tá kǔ kěn fàng p'ào-chàng tê shěng-yin? |
| 27.(A) 那就是練習舞獅或者舞龍的音樂． | Nà chiù-shih lièn-hsi wǔ-shīh huò - chế wǔ - lúng - tê yīn-yüèh. |
| 28.(B) 我們去看看，好嗎? | Wǒ - mên ch'ǜ k'àn - k'an, hǎo ma? |
| 29.(A) 好的，不過我想請你到我的一位親戚家裏去．在那裏你可以看見一點兒我們過新年的樣子． | Hǎo - tê, pú - kuò wó hsiǎng ch'íng ni tào wǒ-tê í-wèi ch'īn-ch'i chiā-li ch'ü. Tsài nà-li ní k'ě - i k'àn-chien ì-tiěn-êrh wǒ-mên kuò-hsīn-nién-tê yàng-tzǔ. |
| 30.(B) 很好．我們就去罷． | Hến hǎo. Wǒ - mên chiù ch'ǜ pa. |

NOTES:

(1) A synonym for "chī-tzǔ-êrh" 雞子兒 - "hen's egg" is "chī-tàn-êrh".

(2) The term "wán-lúng-tēng", usually loosely translated "dragon-dance", may include the lion-dance. The "dance" is performed during the first fifteen days of the New Year. At night, the dragon's head and tail are portrayed by huge paper lanterns, with other lanterns representing the body. Each lantern is carried in procession by a boy or young man, to music and firecrackers. During the day, a different performance is given with a dragon made of cloth.

(3) "Wàn-shìh jú-ì", "[may] everything [be] in accordance with [your] desire", is an expression of greeting used at the New Year and on other festive occasions.

(4) The Chinese New Year usually comes in February. After a fortnight's carnival, exchanging visits, banqueting, enjoying the "dragon-dance", etc., farmers begin their spring work.

3. Translation

1.(A) Congratulations, Mr. Li. Today I come to extend to you [my] New Year greetings.

2.(B) You honor me, Mr. Wang. I pray that this year everything (literally, ten thousand things) may be in accordance with your desires.

3.(A) Thank you. This is the first time you spend the New Year in China; would you like to go sight-seeing?

4.(B) Very much indeed. The Chinese are really very much excited [about] passing the New Year; last night [they] incessantly set off firecrackers. The noise was extremely loud. I didn't sleep well all night.

5.(A) Our passing the New Year is really exciting. Last night there were very many people who didn't sleep. They were sitting up talking; [this] is called "watching the old year out". Some people even open their doors and do not close them in the deep night, to show [their] intention to "welcome the spring" or "welcome the New Year".

6.(B) Mr. Wang, look, those children and grown people coming from that direction, are their clothes not good-looking?

7.(A) Very good-looking. At the time of passing the New Year, most of them put on new clothing and go to the homes of their relatives and friends to offer New Year congratulations.

8.(B) The children seem to be in high spirits, don't they?

9.(A) They are in very high spirits, because their parents and all the older people give them "red packages".

10.(B) What is a "red package"?

11.(A) This is money wrapped up in red paper. At the time of offering New Year congratulations, the older people give [these] to them to buy firecrackers and other playthings.

12.(B) I have heard that when you people pass the New Year, you prepare every sort of good things to eat; is that true?

13.(A) Yes, every family prepares chicken, pork, fish, and every sort of preserved fruits, New Year rice cakes, sponge cakes, peanuts, melon seeds, and other delicacies for relatives and friends to eat.

14.(B) That is very interesting.

15.(A) Furthermore, these good things to eat are also used in worshiping the ancestors.

16.(B) How do they worship?

17.(A) Every family lights very beautiful lanterns, incense, and candles, putting on the altar chopsticks, bowls, wine-cups, and good things to eat. Everyone bows several times to the tablets of the ancestors. The meaning is: on the one hand, to offer New Year's congratulations to the ancestors; on the other hand, to invite the ancestors to the New Year's dinner. It is as if they were still living.

18.(B) I've heard there is dancing too. Is that true?

19.(A) It's not Western dancing. That is dragon-lantern playing or lion-dancing.

20.(B) How is that played?

21.(A) A dragon lantern is a very long dragon made of cloth, divided into ten or more sections; each man manages one section. After each section is connected [with the next], that long dragon can be moved in the air to left and right. This group of dragon-lantern dancers rehearses well beforehand, so that when [they] dance it is very beautiful. If it is at night, candles are lighted inside the dragon-lantern; that is more interesting.

22.(B) What is the lion-dance like?

23.(A) The lion-dance is somewhat like the dragon-lantern dance. But there is no lantern, and also it doesn't take so many men.

24.(B) Why doesn't it take so many men?

25.(A) Ordinarily one or two men are needed to dance with the lion-head. The lion-body is only a long sheet of cloth, pulled by one man. When they dance, at one moment they stand up, and at another moment they topple over; [it is] very beautiful.

26.(B) I hope that some day I can participate in such entertainment. Mr. Wang, why do I hear the noise of beating drums and of setting off firecrackers?

27.(A) That is the music for rehearsing the lion-dance or the dragon-lantern dance.

28.(B) Shall we go and look?

29.(A) All right, but I thought of inviting you to go to the home of a relative of mine. There you can see a little of our way of spending the New Year.

30.(B) Very good. Let's go, then.

4. Exercises

a. Answer the following questions in Chinese:

[Beginning at this point, the "fill-in" sentences are replaced by questions which are designed to provide more material for classroom conversation.]

1. 你每年都回家過新年嗎？

2. 你給人家拜年的時候，普通說的第一句話，是甚麼？

3. 在這一課裏，那一個是第一次在中

國過新年的?

4. 過新年的時候,是不是每一個鋪子都關門?

5. 在美國有沒有人舞獅?

6. 要是你星期六不回家,你到那兒去玩?

7. 在中國,龍燈是怎麽樣玩的?

8. 甚麽叫作守歲?

9. 甚麽叫作紅包?

10. 過聖誕節的時候,你們作些甚麽事?

b. Translate into English:

1. 西洋人過聖誕節的時候很熱鬧嗎?

2. 在這裏我們不放炮仗,因為聲音太大了.

3. 明天我要去打一個電報,給我的朋友賀新年.

4. 過年的時候,你夜裏睡覺嗎?

5. 你一會兒弄這樣,一會兒弄那樣,我看你是作不好的.

6. 他一面作事,一面念書,兩方面都

弄不好.

7. 我在這裏沒有親戚，只有一個朋友.

8. 晚上吃過飯，我們到跳舞場去跳舞.

9. 請你把桌子上的書，擺在書架子[*1]上.

10. 天黑了，我們快一點兒點燈吧.

c. Translate into Chinese:

1. We respect our ancestors, but we don't have to worship them.
2. Some people like clamorous life,[*2] some like quiet life.
3. What is the meaning of this word? I can't understand it.
4. Every night I take a street car to my relative's home.
5. When we opened a meeting last Sunday, the room was very crowded.
6. At the meeting we had tea, peanuts, melon seeds, and sponge cake.
7. But we did not put milk and sugar in our tea.
8. I was told that this is the Chinese way of drinking tea.
9. It is very interesting to play with the children when they play with their toys.
10. We light two red candles and put them on the table.

## Lesson 44 With a Chinese Student

1. Vocabulary

| | | |
|---|---|---|
| 認得 | jèn-té | To know, to recognize. |
| 好在 | hǎo-tsài | Fortunately. It is a good thing that ... |
| 府 | fǔ | Residence, prefecture, palace [seldom used alone]. |
| 政府 | chèng-fǔ | Government [í-kê chèng-fǔ]. |
| 制 | chìh | Regulation, law. To restrict, to govern, to make. |



*1 bookshelf.

*2 shēng-huo, see p. 385.

| | | |
|---|---|---|
| 制度 | chìh-tu | System, regulation [ì-chǔng or í-kê chìh-tu]. |
| 畢 | pì | To end, to finish. |
| 業 | yèh | Profession, trade, estate [seldom used alone]. |
| 畢業 | pì-yèh | To graduate. Graduation. |
| 年限 | nién-hsièn | Limit of years. |
| 大概 | tà-kài | Probably, generally speaking. A general summary. |
| 比方 | pǐ-fang | For instance (literally, "compare [with others in the same] category"). |
| 相 | hsiāng | Mutual. |
| | hsiàng | Photograph. State minister. |
| 相信 | hsiāng-hsìn | To believe. |
| 注 | chù | To fix the eyes or mind on. To flow out. |
| 注重 | chù-chung | To emphasize. |
| 裝 | chuāng | To dress, to load, to pack. To feign, to pretend. Dress. |
| 服裝 | fú-chuāng | Dress [ì-chǔng fú-chuāng]. |
| 初 | ch'ū | At first. To begin. Beginning. |
| 級 | chí | Class, rank. |
| 算學 | suàn-hsüéh | Mathematics, arithmetic. |
| 物理 | wù-lǐ | Physics. |
| 化學 | huà-hsüéh | Chemistry. |
| 生物學 | shēng-wù-hsüéh | Biology. |
| 軍 | chūn | Army. Military. |
| 軍裝 | chūn-chuāng | Military uniform, armor [í-t'ào chūn-chuāng]. |
| 訓 | hsùn | Training, teaching. To instruct. |
| 訓練 | hsùn-lien | To train. Training. |
| 軍事訓練 | chūn-shìh hsùn-lien | Military training. |
| 圖畫 | t'ú-huà | Picture, drawing [ì-chāng or ì-fú t'ú-huà]. |
| 免 | miěn | To avoid, to remit, to forgive. |
| 免費 | miěn-fèi | Free of fees, free of expense. |
| 私 | ssū | Private. |

| | | |
|---|---|---|
| 私立 | ssū-lì | Privately established. |
| 活動 | huó-tùng | Activity. Active, movable. |
| 運動 | yǜn-tùng | Sports, movement. To exercise, to move. |
| 球 | ch'iú | Ball [í-kê ch'iú]. |
| 籃 | lán | Basket. |
| 網 | wǎng | Net, web. |
| 足 | tsú | Foot. Enough. |
| 足球 | tsú-ch'iú | Football [í-kê tsú-ch'iú]. |
| 排球 | p'ái-ch'iú | Volley-ball [í-kê p'ái-ch'iú]. |
| 籃球 | lán-ch'iú | Basketball [í-kê lán-ch'iú]. |
| 網球 | wǎng-ch'iú | Tennis. Tennis ball [í-kê wǎng-ch'iú]. |
| 式 | shìh | Pattern, shape, fashion [seldom used alone]. |
| 育 | yǜ | To rear, to nurture [seldom used alone]. |
| 體育館 | t'ǐ-yǜ-kuǎn | Gymnasium [í-kê t'ǐ-yǜ-kuǎn]. |
| 猜 | ts'āi | To guess. |
| 玩笑 | wán-hsiào | To make fun, to joke. |
| 學費 | hsüéh-fèi | Tuition. |
| 圖書館 | t'ú-shū-kuǎn | Library [í-kê t'ú-shū-kuǎn]. |
| 柳樹 | liǔ-shù | Willow tree [í-kê liǔ-shù]. |
| 划 | huá | To row. A rowboat. To scratch (as a match). |
| 河 | hé | River [ì-t'iáo hé]. |

2. Conversation

| | |
|---|---|
| 1.(A) 我來晚了罷，張先生。 | Wǒ lái wǎn lê pa, Chāng hsiēn-shêng. |
| 2.(B) 不晚，來的正好。我恐怕你不認得路，所以我站在學校門口等你。 | Pù wǎn, lái - tê chèng hǎo. Wó k'ǔng-p'à nì pú jèn-té lù, só-í wǒ chàn tsài hsüéh-hsiào mén-k'óu těng nì. |

| | |
|---|---|
| 3.(A) 我是不認得路。好在我說的話那個車夫明白，他把我拉到這裏來了。 | Wǒ shìh pú jèn-tế lù. Hǎo-tsài wǒ shuō-tê huà nà-kê ch'ễ-fu míng-pai, t'ā pá wo lā tào chề-li lái lê. |
| 4.(B) 我們進去罷，李先生。 | Wǒ-mên chìn-ch'ü pa, Lǐ hsiēn-shêng. |
| 5.(A) 這裏的學生多嗎？ | Chề-li-tê hsüéh-shêng tō ma? |
| 6.(B) 不很多，大學部不過三百人，中學部有五百人。現在十二點，同學剛下課。 | Pù hěn tō, tà-hsüéh pù pú kuò sān-pǎi jén, chūng-hsüéh pù yǔ wú-pǎi jén. Hsièn-tsài shíh-èrh tiěn, t'ūng-hsüéh(1) kāng hsià k'è. |
| 7.(A) 你們都穿這樣的服裝嗎？ | Nǐ-mên tōu ch'uān chề-yàng-tê fú-chuāng ma? |
| 8.(B) 是的。這樣的服裝很普通。不只學生穿，在政府作事的人也穿。因爲從前孫中山先生常常穿這樣的衣服，所以叫作中山裝。 | Shìh-tê. Chề-yàng-tê fú-chuāng hến p'ǔ-t'ūng. Pù chǐh hsüéh-shêng ch'uān, tsài chềng-fu tsò-shìh-tê jén yěh(2) ch'uān. Yīn-wèi ts'úng-ch'ién Sūn Chūng-shān hsiēn-shêng ch'áng-ch'áng ch'uān chề-yàng-tê ī-fu, só-ǐ chiào tsò Chūng-shān chuāng. |
| 9.(A) 貴國的學校制度，大概跟敝國的一樣罷。 | Kuèi-kuó-tê hsüéh-hsiào chìh-tu, tà-kài kến pì-kuó-tê í-yàng pa. |

| | |
|---|---|
| 10.(B) 差不多．但是從畢業的年限說，我們的制度跟你們的新制一樣．那就是小學六年，初級中學三年，高級中學三年，大學四年． | Ch'à-pu-tō. Tàn-shih ts'úng pì-yèh-tê nién-hsièn shuō, wǒ-mên-tê chìh-tu kēn nǐ-mên-tê hsīn chìh í-yàng. Nà chiù-shih hsiǎo-hsüéh liù nién, ch'ū-chí chūng-hsüéh sān nién, kāo-chí chūng-hsüéh sān nién, tà-hsüéh ssù nién. |
| 11.(A) 有甚麼不同的地方? | Yǔ shén-mo pù-t'úng-tê tì-fang? |
| 12.(B) 有的；比方說罷，小學跟中學的畢業考試，是由中國的地方政府來管的．中學每星期的功課很多，大概有三十五個鐘頭．普通中學是預備學生進大學的．要是預備教書，或作別的事，就得要進別的中等學校了． | Yǔ-tê; pǐ-fang shuō pa, hsiǎo-hsüéh kēn chūng-hsüéh tê pì-yèh k'ǎo-shìh, shìh yú Chūng-kuo-tê tì-fang chèng-fǔ lái kuǎn tê. Chūng-hsüéh měi hsīng-ch'í-tê kūng-k'è hěn tō, tà-kài yǔ sān-shíh-wǔ-kê chūng-t'óu. P'ǔ-t'ūng chūng-hsüéh shìh yù-pei hsüéh-shêng chìn tà-hsüéh tê. Yào-shih yù-pei chiào-shū, huò tsò piéh-tê shìh, chiù těi(3) yào chìn piéh-tê chūng-těng hsüéh-hsiào lê. |
| 13.(A) 那麼，你們中學的功課，是不是跟我們的一樣? | Nà-mo, nǐ-mên chūng-hsüéh-tê kūng-k'è, shìh-pu-shih kēn wǒ-mên-tê í-yàng? |

14.(B) 我相信，是一樣的．我們有歷史，地理，算學，物理，化學，生物學，圖畫，音樂等等．我們很注重科學．

Wǒ hsiāng-hsìn, shìh í-yàng-tê. Wǒ-mên yǔ lì-shǐh, tì-lǐ, suàn-hsüéh, wù-lǐ, huà-hsüéh, shēng-wù-hsüéh, t'ú-huà, yīn-yüèh těng-těng. Wǒ-mên hěn chù-chung k'ē-hsüéh.

15.(A) 剛才我看見有些學生穿軍裝；你們這裏也有軍事訓練嗎？

Kāng-ts'ái wǒ k'àn-chien yǔ-hsiēh hsüéh-shêng ch'uān chūn-chuāng; nǐ-mên chè-li yéh yǔ chūn-shìh hsùn-lien ma?

16.(B) 有的．每一星期學生都有幾點鐘的訓練．

Yǔ-tê, měi-ì hsīng-ch'í hsüéh-shêng tōu yǔ chí tiěn-chūng-tê hsùn-lien.

17.(A) 你們的小學跟中學是不是免費的？

Nǐ-mên-tê hsiǎo-hsüéh kěn chūng-hsüéh shìh-pu-shih miěn-fèi tê?

18.(B) 公立的．免費；私立的收費．有的私立學校，學費收得很貴．

Kūng-lì-tê, miěn-fèi; ssū-lì-tê shōu fèi. Yǔ-tê ssū-lì hsüéh-hsiào, hsüéh-fèi shōu-tê hěn kuèi.

19.(A) 學生除了上課以外，還有甚麼別的活動？

Hsüéh-shêng ch'ú lê shàng-k'è ǐ-wài, hái-yǔ shén-mo piéh-tê huó-tùng?

20.(B) 有的；這就是課外活動．比方說罷，

Yǔ-tê; chè chiù-shih k'è-wài huó-tùng. Pǐ-fang shuō pa,

| | |
|---|---|
| 他們有各種運動. 足球, 排球, 籃球, 網球, 都是最普通的. | t'ā-mên yǔ kè chǔng yùn-tùng. Tsú-ch'iú, p'ái-ch'iú, lán-ch'iú, wǎng-ch'iú, tōu shìh tsuì p'ǔ-t'ūng-tê. |
| 21.(A) 你們的足球是美國式的嗎? | Nǐ-mên-tê tsú-ch'iú shìh Měi-kuo shìh-tê ma? |
| 22.(B) 不是; 我們的足球是英國式的. | Pú shìh; wǒ-mên-tê tsú-ch'iú shìh Yīng-kuo shìh-tê. |
| 23.(A) 前面那一座房子是不是體育館? | Ch'ién-mien nà-í-tsò fáng-tzǔ shìh-pu-shih t'ǐ-yù-kuǎn? |
| 24.(B) 是的, 你猜中了. 我們進去看看罷. | Shìh-tê, nǐ ts'āi chùng(4) lê. Wǒ-mên chìn-ch'ü k'àn-k'an pa. |
| 25.(A) 你們這兒的籃球場很好. 我眞想, 現在就打球. | Nǐ-mên chè-êrh-tê lán-ch'iú-ch'ǎng hěn hǎo. Wǒ chēn hsiǎng, hsièn-tsài chiù tǎ ch'iú. |
| 26.(B) 好! 我們到裏面去換衣服罷. 我們這兒有毛巾, 胰子. 打完了球, 可以去洗一個澡. | Hǎo! Wǒ-mên tào lǐ-mien ch'ü huàn ī-fu pa. Wǒ-mên chè-êrh yǔ máo-chīn, í-tzǔ. Tǎ wán lê ch'iú, k'ě-i ch'ü hsǐ í-kê tsǎo. |
| 27.(A) 我是開玩笑的, 不是眞的要去打. 請你帶我去看看你們的圖書館罷. | Wǒ shìh k'āi wán-hsiào tê, pú shìh chēn-tê yào ch'ü tǎ. Ch'ǐng ni tài wo ch'ü k'àn-k'an nǐ-mên-tê t'ú-shū-kuǎn pa. |

| | |
|---|---|
| 28.(B) 好．我們圖書館的書很多．外國書當中，英文書最多．法文，德文，跟日文的書也有． | Hǎo. Wǒ-mên t'ú-shū-kuǎn-tê shū hěn tō. Wài-kuó shū tāng-chūng, Yīng-wén shū tsuì tō. Fà-wén, Té-wén, kēn Jìh-wén-tê shū yéh yǔ. |
| 29.(A) 貴校的校園很大，風景也很美． | Kuèi hsiào-tê hsiào-yüán hěn tà, fēng-chǐng yéh hěn měi. |
| 30.(B) 我們這兒倒是有山有水．那邊是一條小河，兩岸的柳樹，實在好看． | Wǒ-mên chè-êrh tào(5) shìh yǔ shān yú shuǐ. Nà-pien shìh ì-t'iáo hsiǎo hé, liǎng àn-tê liǔ-shù, shíh-tsài hǎo-k'àn. |
| 31.(A) 河裏可以划船嗎？ | Hé lí k'ě-i huá ch'uán ma? |
| 32.(B) 可以．我們現在去划船正好，因爲同學都去吃飯了，人不會擠． | K'ě-i. Wǒ-mên hsièn-tsài ch'ù huá ch'uán chèng hǎo, yīn-wèi t'úng-hsüéh tōu ch'ù ch'īh-fàn lê, jén pú huì chǐ. |
| 33.(A) 河水清綠得眞可愛．你看柳葉在風裏擺來擺去，水裏的倒影多美啊！ | Hé shuǐ ch'īng lǜ tê chēn k'ě-ài. Nǐ k'àn liǔ yèh tsài fēng lí pǎi lái pǎi ch'ù, shuí-lǐ-tê táo-yǐng tō měi a! |
| 34.(B) 在這兒過夏天倒不錯．李先生，讓我來划罷．我們划到對岸去．那裏有 | Tsài chè-êrh kuò hsià-t'ien tào pú ts'ò. Lǐ hsiēn-shêng, jàng wo lái huá pa. Wǒ-mên huá tào tuì àn ch'ü. Nà-li yǔ |

| | |
|---|---|
| 一家飯館，我們可 | ì - chiā fàn - kuǎn, wǒ-mên k'ě- |
| 以在那兒吃午飯. | i tsài nà - êrh ch'īh wǔ - fàn. |
| 35.(A) 好. 划船累了的 | Hǎo. Huá ch'uán lèi lê tê |
| 時候，吃飯更覺得 | shíh-hou, ch'īh-fàn kèng chüéh-tê |
| 有味兒. | yǔ wèi - êrh. |

NOTES:

(1) "T'úng-hsüéh", "schoolmates", is now frequently used by teachers as a polite term of address to their students.

(2) "Pù chǐh ... yěh ... " means "not only ... but also ... ". Another example of its use: "Chīn-t'ien pù chǐh hsià-hsüěh, yěh hsià-yǔ" 今天不只下雪.也下雨 - "Today it is not only snowing, but also raining".

(3) See note on the use of 得, at end of this lesson.

(4) When pronounced "chùng" (fourth tone), 中 means "to hit the mark, to gain an end".

(5) "Tào" here means "however, though, after all, still". Other examples: "Chè tào pú ts'ò" 這倒不錯 - "This is not bad, though"; "Nà tào pú yào-chǐn" 那倒不要緊 - "That doesn't matter, however"; "T'ā shuō hǎo, nǐ tào shuō pù hǎo" 他說好.你倒說不好 - "He says it is good, you however say it is not good"; "Nà tào hǎo" 那倒好 - "That is still good".

3. Translation

1.(A) I am afraid I have come late, Mr. Chang.

2.(B) Not late, [you] come just right. I was afraid you wouldn't know the way, and so I stood at the school entrance to wait for you.

3.(A) I really didn't know the way. Fortunately, that ricksha puller understood my speech, and he brought (literally, pulled) me here.

4.(B) Let's go in, Mr. Li.

5.(A) Are there many students here?

6.(B) Not very many; in the college division there are only three hundred people, in the high school (literally, middle school) division there are five hundred people. [It is] now twelve o'clock, the schoolmates are just leaving class.

7.(A) Do you all wear this sort of dress?

8.(B) Yes. This sort of dress is very common. Not only students wear [it], but also the people who work in the government wear [it]. Because formerly Mr. Sun Chung-shan often wore this sort of dress, so [it is] called the Chung-shan dress.

9.(A) The school system of your honorable country is probably the same as that of our humble country?

10.(B) Almost. Speaking merely of the requirement of years for graduation, [one may say] our system and your new system are the same. That is, six years for primary school, three years for junior high school, three years for senior high school, four years for college.

11.(A) Are there any differences (literally, different places)?

12.(B) There are some; for instance, the graduation examinations for the primary and high schools are managed by the Chinese local government. In high school the lessons every week are very many; generally there are thirty-five hours. Ordinary high schools prepare students to enter college. If [one] prepares to teach, or to do other work, then he must enter other secondary schools.

13.(A) Well then, are your high school subjects the same as ours?

14.(B) I believe they are the same. We have history, geography, mathematics, physics, chemistry, biology, drawing, music, and so forth. We emphasize science very much.

15.(A) Just now I saw some students wearing military uniforms; do you have military training here?

16.(B) Yes, every week all the students have several hours of military training.

17.(A) Are your primary schools and high schools free of fees?

18.(B) [If they are] publicly established, [they are] free, [if] privately established, [they] collect fees. Some private schools charge very high tuition (literally, collect tuition so as to be very expensive).

19.(A) Besides attending classes, what other activities do the students (still) have?

20.(B) There are some; these are extra-curricular activities. For instance, they have every kind of sport. Football, volleyball, basketball, tennis are the commonest.

21.(A) Is your football American style?

22.(B) No, our football is English style.

23.(A) Is that building ahead a gymnasium?

24.(B) Yes, you've guessed right. Let's go in [and] look.

25.(A) Your basketball court here is very good. I really want to play (literally, strike ball) right now.

26.(B) Fine! Let's go inside to change our clothes. We have towels and soap here. After playing, we can go to take a bath.

27.(A) I was joking; I don't really want to play. Please (you) take me to see your library.

28.(B) All right. The books in our library are very many. Among foreign books, English books are most numerous. There are also French, German, and Japanese books.

29.(A) The school garden of your honorable school is very large, and the landscape is very beautiful.

30.(B) We have hills and streams here, after all. Over there is a small river; the willow trees on its two banks are really beautiful.

31.(A) Can boats be rowed on the river?

32.(B) Yes. It will be just right for us to go rowing now, because the schoolmates all go to eat and it won't be crowded.

33.(A) The water of the river is so green that it is really lovely. See, the willow leaves sway to and fro in the wind; how beautiful the inverted image is in the water!

34.(B) It is not bad, after all, to pass the summer here. Mr. Li, let me row. We'll row to the opposite bank. On that side there is a restaurant; we can eat [our] noon meal there.

35.(A) Good. When [we are] tired from rowing, [we'll] appreciate the flavor more in eating.

4. Exercises

a. Answer the following in Chinese:

1. 你每天到那裏去運動？
2. 你甚麼時候在中學畢業？
3. 你在小學要念幾年？八年還是六年？
4. 你在中學的時候，每星期上幾堂課？
5. 你最喜歡念那一國的文字？
6. 你們學校的風景，是不是很好看？
7. 你在美國看見中國式的房子嗎？
8. 你上小學和中學的時候，要交學費嗎？

9. 你愛打籃球，還是打足球.
10. 你還喜歡打別的球嗎？
11. 你們這一班有多少同學？

b. Translate into English:

1. 我沒有受過甚麼特別訓練？
2. 河裏的風浪太大，我們不能去划船.
3. 我的哥哥在醫院，我得去看他.
4. 火車走得快，可是飛機飛得更快.
5. 我猜他星期日一定來，因為上個星期他給我寫信，說過一兩天，他就要到這兒來.
6. 我不請他，他倒來了.
7. 公立的學校是不是比私立的學校好？
8. 美國的政府跟英國的不一樣，跟中國的也不同.
9. 天氣好的時候，我坐在河邊畫畫.
10. 各科的畢業年限不一樣，有的四年，有的六年，有的八年.

c. Translate into Chinese:

1. He sits in the reception room and jokes with the guests.
2. In summer we frequently row a boat, and also play tennis.
3. Among the subjects I am now studying, I like physics and chemistry best.
4. Here we play English football, we do not play American football.
5. In autumn when the leaves fall, we feel a bit chilly.
6. People often say that Chinese food tastes good.
7. When you are hungry, you feel that the food is delicious.
8. I can't play volley-ball; I must go to study at the library.
9. Do you think that the Japanese language is easy to learn?
10. It is difficult, though. But if you work hard, you will not feel it too difficult.

### On the Use of "TÉ" ("TĚI") 得

The different meanings of the character 得 when it is pronounced "těi" and when it is pronounced "té" call for special discussion.

(1) "Tê" is used after a verb to indicate the possibility or potentiality of the action; in this use it has the same meaning as "néng" 能. For example:

"T'ā-tê pìng hǎo lê, ch'īh-tê tūng-hsi lê" 他的病好了，吃得東西了 - "He has recovered from illness; [he] can eat now".

"Nà-kê tì-fang, ch'ù-tê ch'ù pu té?" 那個地方，去得去不得，- "That place, can one go there or not?"

"K'àn-tê chièn; k'àn pu chièn" 看得見，看不見 - "can see; cannot see".

"Nǐ chì-tê ma? Wǒ chì-tê. Wǒ pu chì té." 你記得嗎？我記得，我不記得。- "Can you remember it? I remember. I cannot recall."

"Wǒ pú jèn-té. Wǒ jèn pu té." 我不認得。我認不得 - "I cannot recognize it." (Note: the difference between these two sentences is that the former means simply "I cannot (or, do not) recognize it"; the latter means "I try to recognize it but do not succeed".)

(2) "Tê" is used to indicate the manner of an action or a state, in which case it usually has the function of "so, so as to, so that".

"T'ā shuō-tê tà-chiā tōu hsiào lê" 他說得大家都笑了 - "He spoke so that everyone laughed".

"Ch'ūn-t'ien-tê shù-yèh lǜ-tê k'ě-ài" 春天的樹葉綠得可愛 - "Spring-time's tree-leaves green lovely", i.e., "In spring the leaves are so green as to be lovely".

"Pìng-tê lì-hai" 病得利害 - "extremely sick".

"Wó tsǒu-tê lèi chí lê" 我走得累極了 - "I walked so [much] that I am very tired".

NOTE that in this use 得 may be replaced by 的. See Lesson 13, note 7.

(3) "Tê" following a verb may form a passive participle, and in this use may be followed by an adverb.

"Nà-fēng hsìn hsiěh-tê pù hǎo" 那封信寫的不好 - "That letter is not well written".

"Chè-chièn shìh-ch'ing pàn-tê hǎo" 這件事情辦得好 - "This matter is well handled".

(4) "Té" is used in combination with "lê" 了 (or "liǎo" for emphasis), to indicate the possibility of the completion of an action. See also note at end of Lesson 23, page 171.

"Chè-chièn shìh nǐ pàn-tê liǎo, wó k'ě pàn pu liǎo" 這件事你辦得了，我可辦不了 - "This affair you can handle; I cannot handle it".

"Wǒ shòu pu liǎo, nǐ shòu-tê liǎo ma?" 我受不了，你受得了嗎? - "I cannot bear it, can you bear it?"

"Tsò-té lê" 作得了 - "It is done, it is ready".

(5) "Těi" means "must, ought, to have to, to be compelled to".

"Ní těi ch'ǜ shàng k'è" 你得去上課 - "You must go to class".

"Wó těi tsò-kūng" 我得作工 - "I have to work".

"Ní téi hsiǎo-hsīn" 你得小心 - "You must be careful".

(6) "Těi" is used in the following combinations for euphony and emphasis:

"Míng-t'ien tsúng-těi té" 明天總得得 - "Tomorrow at all events it must be ready".

"Méi-yŭ piéh-tê fá-tzŭ, chíh-tĕi ch'ü chù ī-yüàn" 沒有別的法子，只得去住醫院 - "There is no other way, but to go and stay in the hospital".

"Ní ch'ǐng k'è, wŏ pì*-tĕi ch'ü" 你請客、我必得去 - "[If] you invite guests, I certainly must go".

## Lesson 45 With a Chinese Worker

1. Vocabulary

| | | |
|---|---|---|
| 機關 | chī-kuān (1) | Organ, administrative organization, public office [í-kê chī-kuān]. |
| 廠 | ch'ăng | Workshop, yard, shed [seldom used alone]. |
| 工廠 | kūng-ch'ăng | Factory [í-kê kūng-ch'ăng]. |
| 附 | fù | To attach, to follow. |
| 附近 | fù-chìn | Near, neighboring. |
| 鄉 | hsiāng | Country, village. Rustic. |
| 鄉下 | hsiāng-hsia | Country. |
| 工人 | kūng-jén | Workman [í-kê kūng-jén]. |
| 資 | tzū | Property, funds. To help. [Seldom used alone.] |
| 資本 | tzū-pĕn | Capital. |
| 資本家 | tzū-pĕn-chiā | Capitalist [í-kê tzū-pĕn-chiā]. |
| 工會 | kūng-huì | Labor union [í-kê kūng-huì]. |
| 工業 | kūng-yèh | Industry. |
| 工作 | kūng-tsò | Work. |
| 工錢 | kūng-ch'ien | Wages. |
| 辦理 | pàn-lǐ | To manage. |
| 伸 | shēn | To extend, to straighten, to stretch. |
| 守 | shŏu | To guard, to keep, to observe. |
| 祕 | mì | Secret, private, occult. |
| 祕密 | mì-mi | Secret. |
| 部分 | pù-fên | Part, section, fraction. |

---

* 必 pì - must; certainly, necessary.

| | | |
|---|---|---|
| 小時 | hsiǎo-shíh(2) | Hour. |
| 設 | shè | To establish, to set up. If. |
| 嚴 | yén | Stern, strict. Father. |
| 形 | hsíng | Form. |
| 情形 | ch'íng-hsing | Condition. |
| 還 | huán | To return, to repay. See also p. 121. |
| 增 | tsēng | To increase. |
| 增加 | tsēng-chiā | To increase. |
| 生活 | shēng-huo | Life, a living. |
| 生活費用 | shēng-huo fèi-yùng | Cost of living. |
| 過活 | kuò-huó | To live on, to live, to make a living. |
| 死 | ssǔ | To die. Death. |
| 傷 | shāng | To wound, to injure, to be hurt. |
| 罷工 | pà-kūng | To go on strike. |
| 低 | tī | Low. |
| 解 | chiěh | To loosen, to explain. |
| 和解 | hé-chiěh | To conciliate. |
| 勞 | láo | Labor, trouble. To trouble, to toil. |
| 勞工 | láo-kūng | Labor. |
| 勢 | shìh | Power, influence [seldom used alone]. |
| 力 | lì | Strength. |
| 勢力 | shìh-li | Power, influence [ì-chǔng shìh-li]. |
| 結 | chiēh<br>chiéh | To produce.<br>To make a contract, to conclude. A knot. |
| 結果 | chiēh-kuǒ | Result. |
| 良 | liáng | Good. |
| 改 | kǎi | To change, to amend, to correct. |
| 改良 | kǎi-liáng | To reform, to improve. |
| 出頭 | ch'ū-t'óu | To take the lead, to come to the front. |
| 發生 | fā-shēng | To happen, to arise, to produce. |

| | | |
|---|---|---|
| 教育 | chiào-yǜ | Education. |
| 左右 | tsǒ-yù | About. Neighborhood. |

2. Conversation

| | |
|---|---|
| 1.(A) 李先生，想不到我一出門就看見你．你上那兒去? | Lǐ hsiēn-shêng, hsiǎng pu tào wǒ ì ch'ū mén chiù k'àn-chien ni. Nǐ shàng nǎ-êrh ch'ü? |
| 2.(B) 我想上公園去．今天禮拜天，各機關關門．剛才到公立圖書館去還書，誰知道也不開門．今天你不用作工罷，高先生． | Wó hsiǎng shàng kūng-yüán ch'ü. Chīn-t'ien lǐ-pài-t'iēn, kè chī-kuān kuān mén. Kāng-ts'ái tào kūng-lì t'ú-shū-kuǎn ch'ǜ huán shū, shuí chīh-tao yěh pù k'āi mén. Chīn-t'ien nǐ pú yùng tsò-kūng pa, Kāo hsiēn-shêng. |
| 3.(A) 今天休息．我跟你一塊兒到公園去，好不好? | Chīn-t'ien hsiū-hsi. Wǒ kēn nǐ í-k'uài-êrh tào kūng-yüán ch'ǜ, hǎo - pu - hao? |
| 4.(B) 好的．高先生，你在那兒作事? | Hǎo - tê. Kāo hsiēn - shêng, nǐ tsài nǎ-êrh tsò-shìh? |
| 5.(A) 我在附近鄉下一個化學工廠作工． | Wǒ tsài fù-chìn hsiāng-hsia í-kê huà-hsüéh kūng-ch'ǎng tsò-kūng. |
| 6.(B) 你們的工廠很大嗎? 有多少工人? | Nǐ-mên-tê kūng-ch'áng hěn tà ma? Yǔ tō - shǎo kūng - jén? |
| 7.(A) 我們的工廠很小；只有一百多工人． | Wǒ-mên-tê kūng-ch'ǎng hén hsiǎo; chíh yǔ ì - pǎi tō kūng - jén. |

資本也不夠，常常要跟資本家借錢.

Tzŭ-pĕn yĕh pú kòu, ch'áng-ch'áng yào kĕn tzŭ-pĕn-chiā chièh ch'ién.

8.(B) 中國有大工廠嗎?

Chūng-kuo yŭ tà kūng-ch'ăng ma?

9.(A) 有，可是不很多. 中國有些大工廠，說是有重要的發明，可是嚴守秘密，不讓外面的人知道.

Yŭ, k'ĕ - shih pù hĕn tō. Chūng-kuo yŭ-hsieh tà kūng-ch'ăng, shuō shìh yŭ chùng-yào-tê fā-míng, k'ĕ - shih yén shŏu mì - mi, pú jàng wài-mien-tê jén chīh - tao.

10.(B) 這些大工廠是私人開辦的嗎?

Chè-hsieh tà kūng-ch'ăng shìh ssū jén k'āi pàn tê ma?

11.(A) 不，多半是我們政府開辦的. 也有一部分重工業，是政府跟商人合辦的.

Pū, tō - pàn shìh wŏ - mên chèng - fŭ k'āi pàn tê. Yéh yŭ í pù - fên chùng kūng - yèh, shìh chèng-fŭ kĕn shāng-jén hé pàn-tê.

12.(B) 你現在每天要作幾小時工作?

Nĭ hsièn-tsài mĕi t'iēn yào tsò chí hsiăo-shíh kūng-tsò?

13.(A) 八小時. 在我們的工廠裏，一天二十四小時都作工. 因爲我們分作三班，每班八小時.

Pā hsiăo-shíh. Tsài wŏ-mên-tê kūng-ch'áng lĭ, ì t'iēn èrh-shíh-ssù hsiăo-shíh tōu tsò-kūng. Yīn-wèi wŏ-mên fĕn tsò sān pān, mĕi pān pā hsiăo-shíh.

14.(B) 你們每禮拜的工錢，大概有多少? 對不起，我這樣的

Nĭ - mên méi lĭ - pài - tê kūng-ch'ien tà - kài yŭ tō - shăo? Tùi pu ch'ĭ, wŏ chè - yàng - tê

問你，我不過想知道一點兒中國的情形.

wèn ni, wǒ pú-kuò hsiǎng chīh-tao ì-tiěn-êrh Chūng-kuo-tê ch'íng-hsing.

15.(A) 不要緊. 我們這裏不是照禮拜算的，是按月或者按日算的. 普通的工人，要是手藝不好的，大概一塊錢一天. 手藝好的可以得到兩塊或兩塊五毛錢一天.

Pú yào - chǐn. Wǒ - mên chè-li pú shìh chào lǐ-pài suàn-tê, shìh àn yüèh huò-chě àn jìh suàn-tê. P'ǔ - t'ūng - tê kūng - jén, yào - shih shǒu - i pù hǎo - tê, tà- kài í - k'uài-ch'ién ì t'iēn. Shǒu - i hǎo - tê k'ě - i té tào liǎng-k'uài huò liǎng-k'uài wǔ-máo ch'ién ì t'iēn.

16.(B) 你們的工錢這樣低，生活費用這樣高，怎麼能過活呢?

Nǐ-mên-tê kūng-ch'ien chè-yàng tī, shēng-huo fèi-yùng chè - yàng kāo, tsěn-mo néng kuò - huó ni?

17.(A) 是不容易過活. 可是近來我們的工錢增加了，因爲一方面有手藝的工人好像減少，一方面現在工廠開得很多，所以作工的機會也很多.

Shìh pù júng - i kuò - huó. K'ě-shih chìn-lái wǒ-mên-tê kūng-ch'ien tsēng-chiā lê, yīn-wèi ì fāng - mièn yú-shǒu-i-tê kūng - jén hǎo-hsiàng chién-shǎo, ì fāng-mièn hsièn-tsài kūng-ch'ǎng k'āi-tê hěn tō, só - ǐ tsò-kūng-tê chī - hui yéh hěn tō.

18.(B) 你們會不會罷工?

Nǐ - mên huì - pu - hui pà - kūng?

19.(A) 有的時候我們會罷工. 但是政府總出來和解. 你得知道中國勞工的勢力沒有美國的那樣大.

Yǔ - tê shíh - hou wǒ - mên huì pà-kūng. Tàn-shih chèng-fú tsǔng ch'ū-lai hé-chiěh. Ní těi chīh-tao Chūng-kuo láo-kūng-tê shìh-li méi - yú Měi-kuo-tê nà-yàng tà.

20.(B) 是嗎? 那是資本家有勢力了.

Shìh ma? Nà shìh tzū - pěn-chiā yǔ shìh-li lê.

21.(A) 這倒不見得, 因爲和解的結果, 總是我們工人得到一點兒便宜. 不是減少一點兒工作時間, 就是增加一點兒工錢.

Chè tào pú chièn - tê, yīn-wèi hé-chiěh-tê chiēh-kuǒ, tsǔng shìh wǒ-mên kūng-jén té - tào ì-tiěn-êrh p'ién-i. Pù shìh chién-shǎo ì-tiěn-êrh kūng-tsò shíh-chiēn, chiù-shih tsēng-chiā ì-tiěn-êrh kūng-ch'ien.

22.(B) 你們工人要是受傷了, 生病了, 或是爲工作死了, 怎麼辦呢?

Ni-mên kūng-jén yào-shih shòu shāng lê, shēng pìng lê, huò-shih wèi kūng-tsò ssǔ lê, tsěn-mo pàn ni?

23.(A) 沒有法子. 可是在新式的工廠裏, 有醫生看病. 工人用不着出錢. 要是爲工作死了, 工廠另外把錢給他的家

Méi - yǔ fá - tzū. K'ě - shih tsài hsīn-shìh-tê kūng-ch'áng lǐ, yǔ ī-shêng k'àn pìng. Kūng-jén yùng pu cháo ch'ū ch'ién. Yào-shih wèi kūng-tsò ssǔ lê, kūng-ch'ǎng lìng-wài pǎ ch'ién kěi t'ā-tê chiā-

| | |
|---|---|
| 人. | jến. |
| 24.(B) 這倒不錯. | Chề tào pú ts'ò. |
| 25.(A) 有些大工場還有房子給工人住，收費很便宜. | Yǔ-hsieh tà kūng-ch'ăng hái yǔ fáng-tzū kĕi kūng-jến chù, shōu fèi hĕn p'ién-i. |
| 26.(B) 那麼，你們對現在的工廠生活一定很滿意了. | Nà - mo, nǐ - mên tùi hsièn-tsài-tê kūng-ch'ăng shĕng-huo í-tìng hến măn - ì lê. |
| 27.(A) 不. 還有好些地方要改良的. 好在我們有工會. 有甚麽事情發生，工會就可以出頭辦理. | Pū. Hái yú hăo - hsiēh tì-fang yào kăi-liáng-tê. Hăo-tsài wŏ - mên yǔ kūng-hùi. Yǔ shến-mo shìh-ch'ing fā-shĕng, kūng-hùi chiù k'ĕ-i ch'ū-t'óu pàn-lǐ. |
| 28.(B) 你剛才不是說你們的勞工勢力不大嗎? | Nǐ kāng-ts'ái pú shìh shuō nǐ-mên-tê láo - kūng shìh - li pú tà ma? |
| 29.(A) 雖然不大，不過可以慢慢的伸長. | Suī - ján pú tà, pú - kuò k'ĕ - i màn-mān-tê shĕn chăng. |
| 30.(B) 你的工廠有小孩兒作工嗎? | Nǐ-tê kūng-ch'ăng yú hsiăo hái-êrh tsò-kūng ma? |
| 31.(A) 有. 他們多半在十五歲左右. 十五歲以下作工的很少. | Yŭ. T'ā - mên tō - pàn tsài shíh - wŭ sùi tsŏ - yù. Shíh - wŭ sùi ǐ-hsià tsò-kūng-tê hến shăo. |
| 32.(B) 你們的工人都受 | Nǐ-mên-tê kūng-jến tōu shòu |

| | |
|---|---|
| 過很多的教育嗎? | kuò hěn tō - tê chiào-yù ma? |
| 33.(A) 不一定. 有的受過很多的教育, 有的很少. | Pù í - tìng. Yǔ - tê shòu kuò hěn tō - tê chiào - yù, yǔ-tê hěn shǎo. |
| 34.(B) 我們快到公園了罷? | Wǒ-mên k'uài tào kūng-yüán lê pa? |
| 35.(A) 快到了. 拐彎就是. | K'uài tào lê. Kuǎi wān chiù-shih. |

NOTES:

(1) "Chī-kuān", "administrative organization, public office", is commonly used in such combinations as "hsüéh-hsiao 學校 chī-kuān" - "school organization", "chiào-yù 教育 chī-kuān" - "educational organization", "chūn-shìh 軍事 chī-kuān" - "military organization", "yǜn-shū 運輸 chī-kuān"- "transportation organization".

(2) "Hsiǎo-shíh" means literally "small hour", and is used to distinguish the modern hour, which is one twenty-fourth of a day, from the old Chinese division of time, which was one twelfth of a day. "Hsiǎo-shíh" and "chūng-t'óu" can be used interchangeably, but the former is used without any numerative ("ì hsiǎo-shíh", "liáng hsiǎo-shíh"), while the latter does take a numerative (see Lesson 28, note 1).

3. Translation

1.(A) Mr. Li, [I] didn't expect to see you the moment I came out. Where are you going?

2.(B) I think of going to the park. Today is Sunday; every office is closed. Just now [I] went to the public library to return a book; who [would have] known that it also was not open! Today you probably don't have to work, Mr. Kao.

3.(A) Today [I] rest. Shall I go with you to the park?

4.(B) Good! Mr. Kao, where do you work?

5.(A) I work at a chemical factory in the country near [here].

6.(B) Is your factory very big? How many workers are there?

7.(A) Our factory is very small; there are only [a few] more than a hundred workers. The capital also is insufficient; we constantly have to borrow money from the capitalists.

8.(B) Are there large factories in China?

9.(A) There are, but not very many. Some large factories of China are said to have made important inventions, but they are strictly kept secret; outside people are not allowed to know.

10.(B) Are these large factories put into operation by private individuals?

11.(A) No, most of them are put into operation by cur government. There is also a part of the heavy industry [which] is jointly managed by the government and by merchants.

12.(B) At present, how many hours a day do you have to work?

13.(A) Eight hours. In our factory, work goes on twenty-four hours a day. Because we are divided into three groups, each group [works] eight hours.

14.(B) About how much are your wages each week? Please excuse me for asking you in this way; I only wish to know a little about conditions in China.

15.(A) It doesn't matter. We don't calculate by weeks here, we calculate by months or days. Ordinary workers, if not skilled (literally, skill not good), [receive] about one dollar a day. Skilled [workers] may get two dollars or two dollars and fifty cents a day.

16.(B) Your wages so low and the cost of living so high, how can you live?

17.(A) It isn't easy to live. But recently our wages are increasing, because on the one hand skilled workers seem to be growing fewer, and on the other hand, at present, there are very many factories opened, therefore opportunities for work are also very many.

18.(B) Do you know how to go on strike?

19.(A) Sometimes we can strike. But the government always comes out to reconcile [the two sides]. You must know that the power of Chinese labor is not so great as that of American [labor].

20.(B) Is that so? Then it is the capitalists who are powerful.

21.(A) That is not the case, though, because the result of the reconciliation is always that we workers get a little advantage. If it is not that working hours are reduced a little, then it is that wages are increased a little.

22.(B) If you workers receive an injury, become sick, or die because of work, what is to be done?

23.(A) Nothing can be done (literally, there is no method). But in the new factories, there are doctors to look after the sick. Workers don't have to pay money. If [one] dies from work, the factory will, in addition, pay money to his family.

24.(B) After all, this is not bad.

25.(A) Some large factories also have houses for workers to live in; the fees charged are very reasonable.

26.(B) In that case, you must be very well satisfied with modern factory life.

27.(A) No. There are still many places which need to be reformed.

Fortunately, we have labor unions. [When] anything happens, the labor union takes the lead to manage it.

28.(B) Didn't you say, a moment ago, that the power of your labor is not great?

29.(A) Although not great, yet [it] can gradually increase (literally, can extend and grow).

30.(B) Are there children working in your factory.

31.(A) There are. Most of them are about fifteen years old. Under the age of fifteen, workers are very few.

32.(B) Have all your workers had much education?

33.(A) Not necessarily. Some have had much education, some very little.

34.(B) Won't we soon arrive at the park?

35.(A) [We'll] soon arrive. Turn the corner and there it is.

4. Exercises

a. Answer the following in Chinese:

1. 在美國一個手藝不好的工人,大概一小時,可以得多少錢?

2. 你贊成罷工嗎?

3. 美國東部的生活費用,是不是比西部的高?

4. 現在的工人每星期要作多少小時的工作?

5. 美國公用事業 (public utilities) 完全是私人辦理的嗎?

6. 你能够說出幾個交通工具的名字嗎?請說幾種.

7. 你相信政府可以管工會嗎?

8. 你現在受的訓練嚴不嚴？

9. 在中國工人的工錢是按(or 照)禮拜算的，還是按月算的？

10. 你喜歡鄉下的生活，還是喜歡大城市的生活？

b. Translate into English:

1. 我不能跟你去，我實在忙不過來。

2. 你能跟我到圖書館去借一本書，並且還這兩本書嗎？

3. 今年這個大學的學生增加了；可是那個大學的學生減少了。

4. 有的人辦事很嚴；有的人辦事很寬。

5. 昨天我很用功預備功課，今天考試的結果是我第一。

6. 他在這個城裏頭有很大的勢力，因為普通人都相信他。

7. 有甚麼事情發生，他總出頭辦理。

8. 因為工人罷工，所以有一部分的工業由政府來管。

9. 你能借我一點兒資本,讓我開一家小鋪子嗎?

10. 你要多少,我就給你好了.

c. Translate into Chinese:

1. I had completed my college education before I came here.
2. I lent him some money last month and he returned it today.
3. A part of the work was done by my father, and so the result was very good.
4. I want to improve the condition, but I have no power.
5. The cost of living in China was low, but now it is high.
6. I am busily working at a near-by school organization.
7. Now there is a shortage of all teachers and workers (translate: teachers and workers are all not enough).
8. Some articles of daily use are hard to get here, because this is a small city.
9. It is now about ten o'clock; my watch has stopped.
10. **The problem of labor is very important.**

## Lesson 46 With a Girl

1. Vocabulary

| | | |
|---|---|---|
| 浮 | fóu or fú | To float, to drift. |
| 浮水 | fù-shuǐ | To swim, to float. |
| 目 | mù | Eye, item, title [seldom used alone]. |
| 題目 | t'í-mu | Title, subject, examination question [í-kê t'í-mu]. |
| 腦 | nǎo | Brain [seldom used alone]. |
| 頭腦 | t'óu-nǎo | Brain, mind [í-kê t'óu-nǎo]. |

| | | |
|---|---|---|
| 社會 | shè-huì | Society [í-kê shè-huì]. |
| 服從 | fú-ts'úng | To obey, to comply, to submit. |
| 自由 | tzǔ-yú | Freedom. Free. |
| 地位 | tì-wei | Position, place. |
| 養 | yǎng | To support, to raise, to nourish. |
| 固 | kù | Firm, strong, obstinate. Certainly, naturally. |
| 頑固 | wán-ku | Stubborn, conservative. |
| 庭 | t'íng | Court, hall. |
| 家庭 | chiā-t'íng | Family, home [í-kê chiā-t'íng]. |
| 官 | kuān | Official. Officer [í-kê kuān]. |
| 職 | chíh | Official duty [seldom used alone]. |
| 職業 | chíh-yèh | Occupation, job [ì-chǔng chíh-yèh]. |
| 享 | hsiǎng | To enjoy, to receive. |
| 享受 | hsiǎng-shòu | To enjoy. |
| 主人 | chǔ-jén | Master, mistress, host, hostess. |
| 失 | shīh | To lose, to miss. |
| 失望 | shīh-wàng | Disappointed. |
| 憐 | lién | To pity, to have mercy. |
| 可憐 | k'ě-lién | Pitiable. To pity. |
| 施 | shīh | To bestow, to grant, to aid. |
| 施行 | shīh-hsíng | To put into operation, to give. |
| 當然 | tāng-ján | Of course, naturally. Ought. |
| 替 | t'ì | To substitute, to act for. |
| 分別 | fēn-pieh | Difference. To distinguish, to depart. |
| 樣式 | yàng-shìh | Fashion, pattern [í-kê yàng-shìh]. |
| 素 | sù | Simple, plain. Vegetable. |
| 鮮 | hsiēn | Fresh, new. |
| 鮮明 | hsiēn-míng | Bright, clear. |
| 顏 | yén | Color, face [seldom used alone]. |

| | | |
|---|---|---|
| 顏色 | yén-sê | Color [ì-chŭng yén-sê]. |
| 守舊 | shŏu-chiù | Conservative. |
| 扮 | pàn | To dress up, to disguise. |
| 打扮 | tă-pan | To dress up. Style of dress. |
| 行動 | hsíng-tùng | Action, deportment [ì-chŭng hsíng-tùng]. |
| 行爲 | hsíng-wei | Behavior [ì-chŭng hsíng-wei]. |
| 補 | pŭ | To repair, to mend. |
| 擦 | ts'ā | To rub, to brush. |
| 慣 | kuàn | Accustomed to. |
| 習慣 | hsí-kuàn | Habit [í-kê hsí-kuàn]. |
| 例 | lì | Usage, law, regulation. |
| 例外 | lì-wài | Exception [í-kê lì-wài]. |
| 越 | yüèh (1) | To exceed, to overstep, to pass over. |
| 注意 | chù-ì | To pay attention. Attention. |
| 勇 | yŭng | Brave [seldom used alone]. |
| 勇氣 | yŭng-ch'ì | Courage. |
| 較 | chiào | To compare. |
| 際 | chì | Juncture, boundary. Conditions. |
| 交際 | chiāo-chì | Social intercourse. |
| 態度 | t'ài-tu | Attitude, manner, demeanor. |
| 閒 | hsién | Leisure. Idle. |
| 安閒 | ān-hsién | Calm, quiet, peaceful. |
| 感 | kăn | To influence, to be affected, to feel. |
| 情感 | ch'íng-kăn | Feeling, sentiment. |
| 俗 | sú | Vulgar, common. |
| 風俗 | fēng-su | Custom, usage. |

2. Conversation

| | |
|---|---|
| 1.(A) 張小姐，你剛從學校回來嗎? | Chāng hsiáo-chieh, nĭ kāng ts'úng hsüéh-hsiào húi-lai ma? |

| | |
|---|---|
| 2.(B) 不，李先生，我去浮水；剛回來。你跟我哥哥一塊兒到青年會去了嗎？怎麽這樣晚才回來？ | Pū, Lǐ hsiēn-shêng, wǒ ch'ù fù - shuǐ; kāng huí - lai. Nǐ kěn wǒ kě - kê í - k'uài - êrh tào Ch'īng-nién-huì ch'ù lê ma? Tsěn-mo chè-yàng wǎn ts'ái huí-lai? |
| 3.(A) 是的．我們在青年會聽演說．題目是：『中國的女人』 那個人演說聲音很低，我差不多聽不見他的話． | Shìh-tê. Wǒ-mên tsài Ch'īng-nién-huì t'īng yěn-shuō. T'í-mu shìh: "Chūng - kuo - tê nǚ - jên." Nà-kê jén yěn-shuō shěng-yin hěn tī, wǒ ch'à - pu - tō t'īng pu chièn t'ā - tê huà. |
| 4.(B) 李先生，他講了些甚麽？ | Lǐ hsiēn-shêng, t'ā chiǎng lê hsiēh shén - mo? |
| 5.(A) 他大概是講男女平等的事情．不過他講的不好，我很失望． | T'ā tà-kài shìh chiǎng nán-nǚ p'íng-těng-tê shìh-ch'ing. Pú-kuò t'ā chiǎng - tê pù hǎo, wó hěn shīh - wàng. |
| 6.(B) 是嗎？說到男女平等，我覺得我們從前中國的女人是最可憐的．我們那時候除了服從以外，一點兒自由都沒有． | Shìh ma? Shuō - tào nán-nǚ p'íng-těng, wǒ chüéh-tê wǒ-mên ts'úng-ch'ién Chūng-kuo-tê nǚ-jên shìh tsuì k'ě - lién - tê. Wǒ - mên nà shíh-hou ch'ú lê fú-ts'úng ǐ-wài, ì-tiěn-êrh tzǔ-yú tōu méi-yǔ. |
| 7.(A) 這不見得罷，張 | Chè pú chièn - tê pa, Chāng |

| | |
|---|---|
| 小姐．中國女人在家庭裏不是很有地位的嗎？她們從前雖然不能在社會作事，不過他們在家裏教養孩子，不是同樣的爲社會作事嗎？ | hsiáo-chieh. Chūng-kuo nǚ-jên tsài chiā-t'íng lǐ pú shìh hěn yǔ-tì-wei-tê ma? T'ā-mên ts'úng-ch'ién suī-ján pù něng tsài shè-huì tsò-shìh, pú-kuò t'ā-mên tsài chiā-li chiāo yǎng hái-tzǔ, pú shìh t'úng-yàng-tê wèi shè-huì tsò-shìh ma? |
| (B) 你的頭腦有點兒頑固．女人在家庭裏那裏有地位？她們的一生*就是管家，別的事情都沒有她們的份兒．比方說罷，從前的女人可以到外邊去作事嗎？從前的女人可以跟男人一樣去上學嗎？從前的女人可以作官嗎？ | Nǐ-tê t'óu-nǎo yú tiěn-êrh wán-ku. Nǚ-jên tsài chiā-t'íng lí nǎ-li yǔ tì-wei? T'ā-mên-tê ì shěng chiù-shih kuān chiā, piéh-tê shìh-ch'ing tōu méi-yǔ t'ā-mên-tê fèn-êrh. Pǐ-fang shuō pa, ts'úng-ch'ién-tê nǚ-jên k'ě-i tào wài-pien ch'ǜ tsò-shìh ma? Ts'úng-ch'ién-tê nǚ-jên k'ě-i kěn nán-jên í-yàng ch'ǜ shàng hsüéh ma? Ts'úng-ch'ién-tê nǚ-jên k'ě-i tsò kuān ma? |
| 9.(A) 不過從前的女人不見得完全沒有自由．在家裏她們還是主人．男人雖然 | Pú-kuò ts'úng-ch'ién-tê nǚ-jên pú chièn-tê wán-ch'üán méi-yǔ tzù-yú. Tsài chiā-li t'ā-mên hái shìh chǔ-jên. Nán-jên suī-ján |

*I-shěng--all one's life.

在外邊作事，家裏的事情是由女人來管的．這一點你不能說不對罷．

tsài wài-pien tsò-shìh, chiā-li-tê shìh-ch'ing shìh yú nǚ-jên lái kuǎn tê. Chè - ì tiěn nǐ pù nếng shuō pú tùi pa.

10.(B) 你說得對．可是，李先生，你為甚麽替舊制度說話？你知道，要是現在還是施行舊制度，你就不能這樣舒服的坐在客廳裏跟我隨便說話了．

Nǐ shuō - tê tùi. K'ě - shih, Lǐ hsiēn-shêng, nǐ wèi shến-mo t'ì chiù chìh-tu shuō-huà? Nǐ chīh-tao, yào-shih hsièn-tsài hái shìh shīh-hsíng chiù chìh-tu, nǐ chiù pù nếng chè-yàng shū-fu-tê tsò tsài k'è-t'īng lǐ kěn wǒ suí-pièn shuō-huà lê.

11.(A) 你說要是施行舊制度，我不能跟你隨便說話嗎？

Nǐ shuō yào-shih shīh-hsíng chiù chìh - tu, wǒ pù nếng kěn nǐ suí-pièn shuō-huà ma?

12.(B) 當然了．一個年輕女人可以在客廳裏跟一個男人自由說話嗎？

Tāng - ján lê. Í - kê nién-ch'īng nǚ-jên k'ě-i tsài k'è-t'īng lǐ kěn í - kê nán - jên tzǔ - yú shuō-huà ma?

13.(A) 你這樣說，我明白了．那麽，你們現在是很自由了．

Nǐ chè - yàng shuō, wǒ míng-pai lê. Nà - mo, nǐ - mên hsièn-tsài shìh hěn tzǔ-yú lê.

14.(B) 男女的機會是平等了．女人可以作

Nán-nǚ-tê chī-hui shìh p'íng-těng lê. Nǚ - jên k'ě - i tsò

官，可以作各種的職業，可以享受男人同樣的教育．我們的社會地位，不像從前那樣可憐了．

kuān, k'ě-i tsò kè chǔng-tê chíh-yèh, k'ě-i hsiǎng-shòu nán-jên t'úng-yàng-tê chiào-yù. Wǒ-mên-tê shè-huì tì-wei, pú hsiàng ts'úng-ch'ién nà-yàng k'ě-lién lê.

15.(A) 照你看來，你們跟西洋女人有甚麼分別呢？

Chào nǐ k'àn lái, nǐ-mên kěn Hsī-yáng nǚ-jên yǔ shén-mo fēn-pieh ni?

16.(B) 不同的地方多哪！比方說穿衣服罷．我們的樣式跟西洋女人的不同．還有，在中國年老的女人穿的衣服總是素的，她們普通都不挑鮮明的顏色；她們實在太守舊了．我覺得是比不上西洋的女人．

Pù-t'úng-tê tì-fang tō na! Pǐ-fang shuō ch'uān ī-fu pa. Wǒ-mên-tê yàng-shìh kěn Hsī-yáng nǚ-jên-tê pù t'úng. Hái yǔ, tsài Chūng-kuo nién-lǎo-tê nǚ-jên ch'uān-tê ī-fu tsǔng shìh sù-tê, t'ā-mên p'ǔ-t'ūng tōu pù t'iāo hsiēn-míng-tê yén-sê; t'ā-mên shíh-tsài t'ài shǒu-chiù lê. Wǒ chüéh-tê shìh pǐ pu shàng Hsī-yáng-tê nǚ-jên.

17.(A) 你這樣說，我就明白爲甚麼你們年老的女人不打扮了．從前我總不明白中國年老的女人沒有

Nǐ chè-yàng shuō, wǒ chiù míng-pai wèi shén-mo nǐ-mên nién-lǎo-tê nǚ-jên pù tǎ-pan lê. Ts'úng-ch'ién wó tsǔng pù míng-pai Chūng-kuo nién-lǎo-tê nǚ-jên méi-yǔ-

| | |
|---|---|
| 牙的時候，爲甚麼 | yá - tê shíh - hou, wèi shěn - mo |
| 不去請牙科醫生補 | pú ch'ù ch'ǐng yá-k'ē ī-shêng pǔ |
| 牙．還有，她們的 | yá. Hái - yǔ, t'ā - mên - tê |
| 臉不擦粉，這又是 | liěn pù ts'ā fěn, chè yù shìh |
| 跟西洋的老太太們 | kěn Hsī-yáng-tê lǎo t'ài-t'ai-mên- |
| 的習慣不一樣． | tê hsí-kuàn pù í-yàng. |
| 18.(B) 不過年青的女人 | Pú-kuò nién-ch'īng - tê nǚ - jên |
| 是喜歡打扮的． | shìh hsǐ - huan tǎ - pan - tê. |
| 19.(A) 我覺得我們西洋 | Wǒ chüéh - tê wǒ-mên Hsī-yáng- |
| 的年青女人普通不 | tê nién-ch'īng nǚ-jên p'ǔ-t'ūng pù |
| 怎麼樣的愛打扮． | tsěn - mo - yàng - tê ài tǎ - pan. |
| 說話行動也比較隨 | Shuō-huà hsíng-tùng yéh pǐ-chiào suí- |
| 便．可是普通的中 | pièn. K'ě-shìh p'ǔ-t'ūng-tê Chūng- |
| 國年青女人好像愛 | kuo nién-ch'īng nǚ-jên hǎo-hsiàng ài |
| 打扮，說話行動也 | tǎ-pan, shuō-huà hsíng-tùng yéh |
| 好像有一點兒不自 | hǎo-hsiàng yǔ ì-tiěn-êrh pú tzù- |
| 由，對不對？ | yú, tùi - pu - tui? |
| 20.(B) 這當然也有例外． | Chè tāng-ján yéh yǔ lì - wài. |
| 不過西洋女人好像 | Pú-kuò Hsī-yáng nǚ-jên hǎo-hsiàng |
| 越老越喜歡打扮， | yüèh lǎo yüèh hsǐ-huan tǎ - pan, |
| 中國女人越老越不 | Chūng-kuo nǚ-jên yüèh lǎo yüèh pú |
| 注意打扮． | chù - ì tǎ - pan. |
| 21.(A) 西洋女人是有勇 | Hsī-yáng nǚ-jên shìh yú yǔng- |
| 氣．從前的中國女 | ch'ì. Ts'úng-ch'ién-tê Chūng-kuo nǚ- |

| | |
|---|---|
| 人有點兒『聽天由命』. 你說我這句話對嗎? | jên yú tiĕn-êrh "t'ìng-t'iēn-yú-mìng"(2). Nǐ shuō wǒ chè-chù huà tùi ma? |
| 22.(B) 你說得很對. | Nǐ shuō - tê hěn tùi. |
| 23.(A) 我又覺得中國的女人愛靜, 西洋女人愛動. | Wǒ yù chüéh - tê Chūng- kuo-tê nǚ - jên ài chìng, Hsī-yáng nǚ - jên ài tùng. |
| 24.(B) 這句話怎麼說? 中國女人不見得不愛動. 她們也喜歡運動, 也喜歡旅行. | Chè - chù huà tsěn - mo shuō? Chūng-kuo nǚ-jên pú chièn-tê pú ài tùng. T'ā-mên yéh hsǐ-huan yǜn-tùng, yéh hsǐ-huan lǚ-hsíng. |
| 25.(A) 我不是從這兩方面說. 比方說交際罷. 你們好像沒有西洋女人那麼樣喜歡說話; 你們的態度很安閒, 不大表示情感. | Wǒ pú shìh ts'úng chè liǎng fāng-mièn shuō. Pǐ-fang shuō chiāo-chì pa. Nǐ-mên hǎo- hsiàng méi - yǔ Hsī-yáng nǚ-jên nà-mo yàng hsǐ-huan shuō-huà; nǐ-mên - tê t'ài-tu hěn ān - hsién, pú tà piǎo-shìh ch'íng - kǎn. |
| 26.(B) 這個我倒不覺得. 我本人就喜歡說話. | Chè- kê wǒ tào pù chüéh - tê. Wó pěn-jén(3) chìu hsǐ-huan shuō-huà. |
| 27.(A) 這當然是例外了. | Chè tāng-ján shìh lì-wai lê. |
| 28.(B) 我以爲中西女人行爲習慣的不同, 完全是因爲社會風 | Wó ǐ - wéi Chūng Hsī nǚ - jên hsíng-wei hsí- kuàn tê pù t'úng, wán-ch'üán shìh yīn-wèi shè-hùi fěng- |

俗的不同. 你說對不對? su tê pù t'úng. Nǐ shuō tuì-pu - tui?

29.(A) 對的. 你哥哥出來了. Tuì tê. Nǐ kē - kê ch'ū-lai lê.

30.(C) 李先生, 請進來吃飯罷. 飯得了. 你們還要談甚麼問題? Lǐ hsiēn-shêng, ch'ǐng chìn-lai ch'īh - fàn pa. Fàn tế lê. Nǐ-mên hái yào t'án shến-mo wền-t'í?

31.(B) 我們不過隨便談談罷了. 沒有甚麼問題. 李先生, 你剛才是贊成舊制度的. 你得知道從前有的地方男客跟女客是不同桌吃飯的. Wǒ-mên pú - kuò suí-pièn t'án-t'an pa lê. Méi-yǔ shến - mo wền - t'í. Lǐ hsiēn - shêng, nǐ kāng-ts'ái shìh tsàn-ch'ếng chiù chìh- tu te. Ní tĕi chīh-tao ts'úng-ch'ién yǔ - tê tì - fang nán k'ề kền nǔ k'ề shìh pù t'úng chō ch'īh-fàn tê.

32.(A) 是嗎? 那我贊成新制度了. Shìh ma? Nà wǒ tsàn-ch'ếng hsīn chìh-tu lê.

NOTES:

(1) "Yüèh ... yüèh ... " - "the more ... the more ... " is an expression of comparison used in both written and spoken Chinese. For example: "Yüèh tō yüèh hǎo" - "The more the better"; "Yüèh tà yüèh kuèi" - "The larger the more expensive". NOTE: "Yǜ"愈 - "more, better" - may be used interchangeably with "yüèh" in these expressions. "Yǜ tō yǜ hǎo" is equally correct and means the same as "Yüèh tō yüèh hǎo"; "yǜ" is more literary, "yüèh" more colloquial.

(2) "T'ìng-t'iēn-yú-mìng", meaning "to obey Heaven and follow fate", is a common expression of a pessimistic but resigned attitude toward life. It expresses a kind of fatalism.

(3) "Pěn-jén" - "the person in question, oneself in person", used after the first person pronoun, means "myself" and serves to emphasize the pronoun. Its meaning is similar to that of "tzǔ-chǐ" 自己

3. Translation

1.(A) Miss Chang, have you just come back from school?

2.(B) No, Mr. Li, I went swimming and have just come back. Did you and my elder brother go together to the Y.M.C.A.? Why do you come back so late?

3.(A) Yes. We were in the Y.M.C.A. listening to a speech. The subject was: "Women in China". The speaker's voice was very low; I could hardly hear what he said.

4.(B) Mr. Li, what did he say?

5.(A) In general, he spoke of the matter of equality between men and women. But he did not speak well; I was very much disappointed.

6.(B) Indeed? Speaking of equality between men and women, I think that formerly our Chinese women were most pitiable. At that time we had not a bit of freedom except obedience.

7.(A) It doesn't seem to have been so, Miss Chang. Don't Chinese women have a very much respected position in the family? Although formerly they could not work in society, yet didn't they teach and nourish the children in the family - wasn't that also work for society?

8.(B) Your mind is a little conservative. How could women have position in the family? Their whole life was [devoted to] household management, in all other matters they had no share. For instance, could women formerly go outside [their homes] to work? Could women formerly go to school in the same way as men? Could women formerly be officials?

9.(A) But it doesn't seem that women formerly were wholly without freedom. In the family they were still mistresses. Though men worked outside, household affairs were managed by women. You can't say that this point is not true.

10.(B) What you say is true. But, Mr. Li, why do you speak for the old system? You know, if the old system were still practised at present, you couldn't be comfortably sitting in the parlor in this way, talking with me at your pleasure.

11.(A) Do you say that if the old system were practised, I couldn't talk with you at my pleasure?

12.(B) Of course. Could a young woman talk freely with a man in the parlor?

13.(A) When you speak in this way, I understand. In that case, you are now very free.

14.(B) The opportunities for men and women are equal. Women can be officials, can do every sort of work, can enjoy the same education as men. Our position in society is not pitiable as [it was] formerly.

15.(A) As you see [it], what difference is there between you [Chinese women] and Western women?

16.(B) The points of difference are many! Take for example the clothes [we] wear. Our fashions are different from those of Western women. Furthermore, in China the clothing worn by old women is always plain; ordinarily none of them (literally, all not) choose bright colors; they are really too conservative. I feel [that they] cannot be compared with Western women.

17.(A) [When] you speak in this way, then I understand why your old women do not dress up and powder. Formerly I never understood why Chinese old women, when they have no teeth, do not go to see a dentist to have their teeth restored. Furthermore, their faces are not powdered; this again is not the same as the habits of Western old ladies.

18.(B) But the young women like to dress up and powder.

19.(A) I feel that our Western young women ordinarily do not like so much to dress up and powder. Their speech and actions are also comparatively informal. But the ordinary Chinese young women seem to like to dress up, and their speech and actions also seem a little less independent. Is this true?

20.(B) Of course there are also exceptions to this. But it seems that the older the Western women are, the more they like to dress up. The older the Chinese women are, the less attention they pay to dress and make-up.

21.(A) Western women do have courage. Formerly Chinese women had a little more [of the spirit of] "obeying Heaven and following fate". Do you think what I say is true?

22.(B) What you say is true indeed.

23.(A) I also feel that Chinese women like to be quiet, [while] Western women like to be active.

24.(B) What do you mean by this saying? Chinese women do not seem to dislike activity. They also like sports and also like travel.

25.(A) I am not speaking of these two points. Take for instance social intercourse. You don't seem to like to talk as much as Western women do. Your attitude is very quiet, you seldom show your feelings.

26.(B) I don't feel this, though. I myself like to talk.

27.(A) This of course is an exception.

28.(B) I think that the differences in the behavior and habits of Chinese and Western women are entirely due to the differences in social customs. Do you think so?

29.(A) That's right. Your elder brother is coming out.

30.(C) Mr. Li, please come in and eat [with us]. Dinner is ready. Do you still want to talk of any problems?

31.(B) We are only chatting informally. There are no problems. Mr. Li, just now you approved the old system. You should know that formerly in some places men guests did not dine at the same table with women guests.

32.(A) Is that true? Then I approve the new system.

4. Exercises

a. Answer the following in Chinese:

1. 上一次考試,題目難不難?
2. 你晚上閒着的時候,你聽無線電廣播嗎?
3. 你最喜歡聽那一種廣播,音樂,笑話,故事,演說,或者新聞?
4. 你覺得老年人是不是比較守舊一點兒?
5. 你有甚麼不良的習慣?
6. 一個人越老越覺得怎麼樣?
7. 你買衣服的時候,你挑那一種顏色?
8. 你的家庭是新式的,還是舊式的?
9. 你覺得中國人跟外國人,有甚麼不同的地方?
10. 甚麼人最能享受現在世界上的很舒服的生活?

b. Translate into English:

1. 在大城裏頭,不容易養成早睡早起的習慣.

2. 我有了新的衣服,就不願意穿舊的衣服.
3. 方的跟圓的東西,他分别不出來嗎?
4. 他沒有職業,現在是閒着.
5. 你以為他拿的包裹很輕嗎?那個包裹重極了.
6. 他吃了飯不到一個鐘頭,就說餓了,我還飽哪.
7. 我的鞋跟襪子都破了,請你替我補一補吧?
8. 南方跟北方的風俗習慣不一樣.
9. 我的女兒打扮起來很漂亮,我的朋友們都說她很會交際.
10. 她跟朋友談話的時候,外表總是很安閒的.

c. Translate into Chinese:

1. This pencil is shorter than that one, but longer than that piece of chalk.
2. The more you practise writing, the better your writing will be.
3. I do not like a hot summer, nor do I like a cold winter.
4. Do you believe that all men are equal?

5. I went to the Y.M.C.A. to listen to a lecture.
6. When someone invites me to dinner, I dress up.
7. I am comfortably sitting in this room, preparing tomorrow's lesson.
8. This color is too bright, but that color is too dark.
9. You must have courage to perform difficult tasks.
10. I pity those who are unemployed.

## Lesson 47 Supplementary Lesson and Review

1. Vocabulary

(a) Expressions of Behavior and State of Health

| | | |
|---|---|---|
| 怒 | nù | Anger. Angry. |
| 生氣 | shēng-ch'ì | To be angry. |
| 罵 | mà | To scold. |
| 悲哀 | pēi-āi | Sad. |
| 討厭 | t'ǎo-yèn | Dislike. Disgusting. |
| 頑皮 | wán-p'í | Mischievous, naughty. |
| 健康 | chièn-k'āng | Health. |
| 強 | ch'iáng | Strong. |
| 強健 | ch'iáng-chièn | Strong. |
| 軟 | juǎn | Soft. |
| 弱 | jè | Weak. |
| 傷風 | shāng-fēng | To catch cold. |
| 咳嗽 | k'é-sou | To cough. |
| 大便 | tà-pièn | To go to stool. Evacuation [í-tz'ǔ tà-pièn]. |
| 小便 | hsiǎo-pièn | To urinate. Urine. [í-tz'ǔ hsiǎo-pièn]. |
| 偷 | t'ōu | To steal. |
| 捉 | chō | To arrest, to seize, to catch. |

| | | |
|---|---|---|
| 賊 | tsê̌ or tséi | Thief, robber [í-kê tsê̌]. |
| 罪 | tsùi | Crime, sin. |
| 罰 | fá | To punish. |
| 挨罰 | ái-fá | To receive punishment. |
| 受罰 | shòu-fá | To receive punishment. |

(b) Agriculture and Business

| | | |
|---|---|---|
| 出口 | ch'ū-k'ǒu | To export. Exit. |
| 米 | mǐ | Rice. |
| 麥 | mài | Wheat. |
| 棉花 | mién-hua | Cotton. |
| 運河 | yǜn-hê̌ | Canal. |
| 田 | t'ién | Field, land. |
| 農業 | núng-yèh | Agricultural industry, agriculture. |
| 茶館 | ch'á-kuǎn | Tea house, coffee shop [í-kê ch'á-kuǎn]. |
| 一向 | í-hsiàng | Heretofore, formerly. |
| 國際貿易 | kuó-chì mào-i | International Trade. |
| 公事房 | kūng-shìh-fáng | Office [í-kê kūng-shìh-fáng]. |
| 辦公室 | pàn-kūng-shìh | Office [í-kê pàn-kūng-shìh]. |
| 大廉價 | tà-lién-chià | Great sale. |
| 商品 | shāng-p'ǐn | Commodity. |
| 減價 | chiěn-chià | Reduced price. To cut down prices. |
| 折 | chê̌ | To break off. |
| 折扣 | chê̌-k'òu | Discount. |
| 九折 | chiǔ-chê̌ | Ten per cent discount. |
| 九扣 | chiǔ-k'òu | Ten per cent discount. |
| 公債票 | kūng-chài-p'iào | Government bonds. |
| 賠本 | p'éi-pěn | To lose on capital or prime cost of anything. |
| 賺錢 | chuàn-ch'ién | To make money. |

(c) Household Terms

| | | |
|---|---|---|
| 傢具 | chiā-chü | Furniture. |
| 爐子 | lú-tzŭ | Stove [í-kê lú-tzŭ]. |
| 汽爐子 | ch'ì-lú-tzŭ | Radiator. |
| 地板 | tì-păn | Floor [í-k'uài tì-păn]. |
| 地毯 | tì-t'ăn | Rug [í-k'uài or ì-chāng tì-t'ăn]. |
| 煙碟 | yēn-tiéh | Ash tray [í-kê yēn-tiéh]. |
| 澡盆 | tsăo-p'én | Bathtub [í-kê tsăo-p'én]. |
| 洗臉盆 | hsí-liĕn-p'én | Wash basin [í-kê hsí-liĕn-p'én]. |
| 自來水 | tzŭ-lái-shuĭ | Water supply, running water. |
| 牆 | ch'iáng | Wall. |
| 廚房 | ch'ú-fáng | Kitchen [ì-chiēn ch'ú-fáng]. |
| 食物 | shíh-wù | Food. |
| 夾 | chiā | To press, to squeeze, to pinch. |
| 夾肉麵包 | chiā-jòu mièn-pāo | Pork sandwich [í-fèn chiā-jòu mièn-pāo]. |
| 據 | chù | Evidence. According to. |

2. Narrative

| | |
|---|---|
| 今天公司裏的商品大廉價。我剛才去買了很多食物。我買了兩磅西紅柿，一斤半蝦，一對龍蝦，一塊薑，三磅桃，一包米。買這些東西，都有九扣。我又到五層樓的傢具部買一鋪床，一 | Chīn-t'ien kūng-ssū lĭ tê shāng-p'ĭn tà-lién-chià. Wŏ kāng-ts'ái ch'ù măi lê hĕn tō shíh-wù. Wó măi lê liăng pàng hsī-húng-shìh, ì chīn pàn hsiā, í-tuì lúng-hsiā, í-k'uài chiāng, sān pàng t'áo, ì pāo mĭ. Măi chè-hsieh tūng-hsi, tōu yú chiŭ-k'òu. Wŏ yù tào wŭ ts'éng-lóu-tê chiā-chü pù măi í-p'ù ch'uáng, ì- |

張地毯．一個澡盆，一個洗臉盆，一個爐子．這些東西都有折扣．賣傢具的說，他們賣這些東西都賠本了．我說，作生意的那裏會賠本，頂多賺錢賺少一點兒就是了．買完東西很餓．我就到附近的茶館吃了一份夾肉麵包，一杯冰激淩．吃了還是不飽，我又叫一份火腿麵包，兩塊烤麵包．

吃完以後，我回到公司去．買個煙碟，買了十斤棉花，三碼布．公司的人告訴我，這年頭兒農業品都很便宜；米，麥，棉花，西紅柿，甚麼的都有

chāng tì-t'ǎn, í-kê tsǎo-p'ến, í-kê hsí-liěn-p'ến, í-kê lú-tzǔ. Chề-hsieh tūng-hsi tōu yǔ chế-k'òu. Mài-chiā-chü-tê shuō, t'ā-mên mài chề-hsieh tūng-hsi tōu p'éi-pěn lê. Wǒ shuō, tsò-shẽng-i-tê ná-li huì p'éi-pěn, tǐng tō chuàn ch'ién chuàn shǎo ì-tiěn-êrh chiù-shih lê. Mǎi wán tūng-hsi hěn è, wǒ chiù tào fù-chìn-tê ch'á-kuǎn ch'īh lê í-fèn chiā-jòu mièn-pāo, ì-pēi pīng-chī-líng. Ch'īh lê hái shìh pù pǎo, wǒ yù chiào í-fèn huó-t'uǐ mièn-pāo, liǎng-k'uài k'ǎo-mièn pāo.

Ch'īh wán ǐ-hòu, wǒ huí tào kūng-ssū ch'ù, mǎi kè yēn-tiéh, mái lê shíh chīn mién-hua, sān mǎ pù. Kūng-ssū-tê jến kào-su wo, chề nién-t'óu-êrh núng-yèh p'ǐn tōu hěn p'ién-i; mǐ, mài, mién-hua, hsī-húng-shìh, shến-mo-tê tōu yǔ

| | |
|---|---|
| 一點兒出口了. 國 | ì - tiěn-êrh ch'ū-k'ǒu lê. Kuó- |
| 際貿易也不像從前 | chì mào-i yěh pú hsiàng ts'úng-ch'ién |
| 一落千丈*的樣子. | í - lò - ch'iēn - chàng - tê yàng-tzŭ. |
| 我回到家裏, 我 | Wǒ huí tào chiā - li, wó |
| 母親看見我買了那 | mŭ-ch'in k'àn-chien wó mǎi lê nà- |
| 麼多的東西, 她大 | mo tō - tê tūng - hsi, t'ā tà |
| 怒, 把我罵了一頓. | nù, pá wǒ mà lê í tùn. |
| 我倒頑皮, 還跟母 | Wǒ tào wán - p'í, hái kēn mŭ- |
| 親開玩笑. 她更生 | ch'in k'āi wán-hsiào. T'ā kèng shēng- |
| 氣了. 那時候, 我 | ch'ì lê. Nà shíh - hou, wó |
| 把食物都拿到廚房 | pǎ shíh-wù tōu ná tào ch'ú - fáng |
| 去. 家裏沒有自來 | ch'ü. Chiā-li méi-yŭ tzù-lái- |
| 水, 我就在井旁, | shuǐ, wǒ chiù tsài chǐng p'áng, |
| 打點兒井水洗臉. | tá tiěn-êrh chíng-shuǐ hsí liěn. |
| 一會兒我就去看 | Ì - huì-êrh wǒ chiù ch'ù k'àn |
| 一個朋友, 他家裏 | í - kê p'éng - yu, t'ā chiā - li |
| 有十畝田地. 我告 | yŭ shíh mŭ t'ién-tì. Wǒ kào- |
| 訴母親我要出去. | su mŭ - ch'in wǒ yào ch'ū - ch'ü. |
| 她很冷淡的, 不說 | T'ā hěn lěng - tàn - tê, pù shuō |
| 一句話, 好像討厭 | í-chù huà, hǎo-hsiàng t'ǎo-yèn |
| 我頑皮的樣子. | wǒ wán-p'í-tê yàng - tzŭ. |
| 到了朋友的家裏, | Tào lê p'éng - yu - tê chiā-li, |
| 我才知道一個同學 | wǒ ts'ái chīh-tao í-kê t'úng-hsüéh |
| 死了. 他的身體一 | ssŭ lê. T'ā - tê shēn - t'ǐ í- |



*chàng, a measure of ten Chinese feet.

| | |
|---|---|
| 向不健康，很軟弱， | hsiàng pú chièn-k'āng, hěn juǎn-jè, |
| 不像他哥哥那樣的 | pú hsiàng t'ā kē-kê nà-yàng-tê |
| 強健．他常常傷風， | ch'iáng-chièn. T'ā ch'áng-ch'áng shāng-fēng, |
| 咳嗽．到最後那幾 | k'ê-sou. Tào tsuì hòu nà chǐ |
| 天，大小便都要看 | t'iēn, tà-hsiǎo-pièn tōu yào k'ān- |
| 護幫忙．據醫生的 | hù pāng-máng. Chù ī-shêng-tê |
| 意見，他不能活下 | ì-chien, t'ā pù néng huó hsià |
| 去了．不久，他眞 | ch'ù lê. Pù chiǔ, t'ā chēn- |
| 的死了．聽了這個 | tê ssǔ lê. T'īng lê chè-kê |
| 消息，我很悲哀． | hsiāo-hsi, wó hěn pēi-āi. |
| 這樣年青的孩子， | Chè-yàng nién-ch'īng-tê hái-tzǔ, |
| 在學校從來沒有挨 | tsài hsüéh-hsiào ts'úng-lái méi-yǔ ái |
| 過罰，行爲最好． | kuò fá, hsíng-wei tsuì hǎo. |
| 有一次他捉住一個 | Yǔ í tz'ù t'ā chō-chù í-kê |
| 偷東西的賊，把賊 | t'ōu-tūng-hsi-tê tsé, pǎ tsé |
| 關在公事房裏面． | kuān tsài kūng-shìh-fáng lǐ-mien. |
| 一會兒那個賊就從 | Ì-huǐ-êrh nà-kê tsé chiù ts'úng |
| 窗戶跳出去了．現 | ch'uāng-hu t'iào ch'ū-ch'ù lê. Hsièn- |
| 在說起來，也覺得 | tsài shuō ch'ǐ-lai, yěh chüéh-tê |
| 有趣．可是他現在 | yǔ ch'ù. K'ě-shih t'ā hsièn-tsài |
| 已經死了．我們覺 | ǐ-ching ssǔ lê. Wǒ-mên chüéh- |
| 得很悲哀． | tê hěn pēi-āi. |

3. Translation

Today there is a great sale of commodities at the department store. I have just gone to buy much food. I bought two pounds of tomatoes, one and a half catties of shrimps, a pair of lobsters, a piece of ginger, three pounds of peaches, a package of rice. [I] bought all these things at a ten per cent discount. I also went to the furniture department on the fifth floor and bought a bed, a rug, a bathtub, a wash basin, a stove. All these things had discounts. The furniture seller said they were losing money in selling all these things. I said, how could the business man lose money, at most he would only make less money. [After] buying things, being very hungry, I went to a neighboring tea house [and] ate a sandwich and a cup of ice cream. After eating, I still was not satisfied, and again ordered a ham sandwich and two slices of toast.

After eating, I went back to the department store [and] bought an ash-tray, ten catties of cotton, [and] three yards of cloth. The department store man told me that at present all agricultural products are very cheap; rice, wheat, cotton, tomatoes, and so forth all have a little [surplus for] export. International trade is not, as formerly, much depressed (literally, dropping ten thousand feet in one fall).

[When] I returned home, and my mother saw that I had bought so many things, she was very angry and scolded me. I was naughty, though, I still made fun of my mother. She was even more angry. At that time I took the food to the kitchen. At home there is no running water, [and so] I drew some well water to wash my face beside the well.

A little later I went to see a friend; at his home there are ten mu of fields. I told mother I was going out. She was very indifferent; [she] didn't say a word, seeming to dislike my naughtiness.

When I arrived at [my] friend's house I learned for the first time that a schoolmate had died. His body had always been unhealthy, very weak, not strong like his brother. He constantly caught cold and coughed. In the last few days, for both evacuating and urinating he had to have the help of a nurse. According to the opinion of the doctor, he couldn't live any longer. Before long, he really died. Hearing this news, I was very sad. This boy was so young; in school he had never been punished, [his] conduct was excellent. Once he caught a thief stealing things; he shut the thief in the office. After a moment that thief escaped out of a window. Now, speaking of this, [we] feel that it is very interesting. But now he is already dead. We feel very sad.

4. Reading Practice

從前有一位教員,他常常不預備功課,就去上課了.到了課堂裏,他問學生說,『你們預備功課了沒有?』學生回答說:『我們沒有預備.』這位教員很不高興的說:『你們上課以前不好好的預備功課.只要我跟你們講,有甚麼用? 你們聽得懂嗎? 下課罷!』

所以學生都下課了.

第二次上課的時候,這位先生又沒有預備功課, 就到班上去了. 他點過名以後, 停了一會兒, 就問學生說: 『你們今天的功課預備好了沒有?』 學生大聲的回答說: 『我們都預備好了!』

這位教員說: 『要是你們都預備好了, 就用不着我講了. 那麼, 下課罷.』

第三次上班的時候, 那位教員還是沒有預備功課. 到了班上, 他又問學生說: 『你們今天的功課預備好了嗎?』 有一半學生說, 『我們預備好了.』 另外一半說, 『我們沒有預備好.』 學生們想, 『今天這位教員, 不能不講書了.』

這位教員想了一想, 想出了一個很好的法子. 他很正經的說, 『你們這一半把功課預備好了的人, 告訴那一半沒有預備好的. 不用我講了. 下課, 下課!』

Compare the above story with your own Chinese translation of the English story in Lesson 42.

# GENERAL INDEX

GENERAL INDEX